1–2 KINGS

ABINGDON OLD TESTAMENT COMMENTARIES

1–2 KINGS

GINA HENS-PIAZZA

Abingdon Press
Nashville

ABINGDON OLD TESTAMENT COMMENTARIES
1–2 KINGS

Copyright © 2006 by Abingdon Press

This book is printed on acid-free paper.

Library of Congress Cataloging-in-Publication Data

Hens-Piazza, Gina, 1948-
    1-2 Kings / Gina Hens-Piazza.
        p. cm.—(Abingdon Old Testament commentaries)
    Includes bibliographical references.
    ISBN 0-687-49021-9 (binding: pbk., adhesive : alk. paper)
    1. Bible. O. T. Kings—Commentaries. I. Title. II. Title: First-Second Kings. III. Series.

BS1335.53.H46 2006
222'.507—dc22

                                                                    2006014086

06 07 08 09 10 11 12 13 14 15—10 9 8 7 6 5 4 3 2 1
MANUFACTURED IN THE UNITED STATES OF AMERICA

For my students,
with admiration and gratitude.

By wisdom a house is built,
and by understanding it is established;
by knowledge the rooms are filled
with all precious and pleasant riches.
(Prov 24:3-4)

CONTENTS

CONTENTS

CONTENTS

CONTENTS

CONTENTS

ACKNOWLEDGMENTS

For the past fourteen years it has been my pleasure to participate in the study of Scripture with numerous gifted students. Privileged to teach at the Jesuit School of Theology at Berkeley where students from over forty countries make up our small learning community, I am regularly instructed by the insights erupting when such a plurality of perspectives is unleashed in the interpretive enterprise. From the beginning to the end of this project, students' questions, discussions, and interpretations of the texts served as regular impetus for my own research and writing. For this I am deeply grateful. However, the debt to my students exceeds their encouragement during my work on this manuscript. Over the years, their passion for their studies, their deep spiritual commitment, and their infectious vitality and hope for the future regularly renewed and continue to renew my own commitment to my work.

Some of these talented students were the first to lay eyes on early versions of the project. Ann Naffziger and Kristin Simms worked through every chapter asking questions, raising objections, and offering critical comments. I owe a debt of gratitude to them for their thoughtful comments and steadfast efforts. My cherished colleagues at the Jesuit School and at the Graduate Theological Union have remained a steady support for the research and writing here. Colleagues regularly invited me to "think out loud" about these texts and to offer presentations for discussion. Some graciously volunteered to read and review drafts. In particular, Sandra Schneiders, John Endres, and Jean Francois Racine manifested tireless interest in the project and offered regular encouragement during the four years of writing. At critical intervals in the work my own institution provided support in the form of course reduction and financial resources for research assistance. When last-minute corrections had to be entered and computer problems arose, Rosie Chinea and Farrell Murphy provided invaluable assistance. I am deeply grateful for their work and especially for their good humor during those technical glitches.

Perhaps no one has been more helpful and patient than Carolyn Pressler, editor for this volume in the *Abingdon Old Testament Commentaries* series. I am immensely grateful for her numerous suggestions, painstaking editing, and enormous generosity of time and attention to the manuscript. Were I to reference her contributions, every page would bear her name. Whereas I take full responsibility for any error that may be present here, both she and Patrick Miller made crucial suggestions leading to a greatly improved final draft. Finally, my family remains my steady support in its enthusiasm for my work. Were it not for their encouragement and patience, over the years, this volume would not be possible.

INTRODUCTION

First and second Kings comprise the fifth and sixth books of the *Former Prophets*, the second division of the Hebrew Bible. In some early Jewish sources, 1 and 2 Kings were actually considered one book. Together with 1 and 2 Samuel they set forth a story of the Israelite monarchy from the time of Saul to the exile (960–586 B.C.E.).

Within the biblical canon, the interlacing historical, literary, and theological features of these books qualify 1 and 2 Kings as a unique and eclectic accomplishment. As they recount four centuries of monarchic rule in Israel, some of their compositional sources are undoubtedly historical. Still, they are not historical books per se. Subject of many literary overtures, the books of Kings boast a vast array of genres and forms. Some of the traditions, such as the stories comprising the Elijah-Elisha accounts (1 Kgs 17–2 Kgs 8), manifest remarkable literary integrity and poetic finesse. Yet even the category "literature" does not adequately capture the character of these works. Further, many have recognized the presence of an overarching theological viewpoint persisting across Kings. Most frequently noted is the consistent representation of God found throughout the various stories across the different literary landscapes. Still, this does not allow us to define these writings solely as theological works. It is evident that there are three elements—history, literary features, and theology—persistently present across these writings.

How then might we describe these tomes? Perhaps the books of Kings are best understood under that familiar rubric "salvation history." This implies that these writings, like the other books of the Bible, are testimonies composed over time to witness to a people's experience of God's involvement in the unfolding events of their lives. In the instance of Kings, these events constitute the era of monarchic rule. In making these faith professions, the traditions in Kings draw upon historical sources in order to fashion their theological assertions as artistic literature. Thus, defining 1 and 2 Kings by any one of these categories alone—history, literature, theology—shortchanges their character. Indeed, whereas each of the constitutive elements deserves consideration in the discussion that follows, it is only when they are taken together that we grasp the distinctiveness of the witness to faith in the books of Kings.

HISTORICAL CONSIDERATION OF THE BOOKS OF KINGS

At first glance, the title *1–2 Kings* encourages us to anticipate a book about history, a history of rulers and the activities of their reigns. The very notion of a king urges us to think of bygone eras when monarchs governed from palaces and when peasants lived under a royal ruling class rather than a republic or democracy. Hence, it is fair to come to books called Kings expecting an account of history.

But the books of Kings are part of a larger work, the Bible, whose purpose we associate less with human history governed by limitations of time and space than with an overarching panorama called "salvation history." *Story* rather than history is the operative genre here. Though these accounts narrate the past, the persons, places, events, and details have all been fashioned into tales that convey a particular message about God. What they tell about the past is always cast within the language of faith and is motivated by belief, rather than a historian's commitment to objectivity, factuality, or chronology.

Still, we can raise some historical questions, as we do of all stories, when we come to 1 and 2 Kings. Sources, authorship, as well as when these stories were composed, warrant inquiry. Besides being a part of the whole biblical canon, more specifically these books of Kings take up residence in a schema of works within the Bible known as the Deuteronomistic History. The Deuteronomistic History extends from Joshua through 2 Kings but also includes the framework of the book of Deuteronomy. Indeed, Deuteronomy 1–4, which stresses covenantal fidelity to Yahweh, has a formative role on the production of meaning throughout these books. The sacred traditions and theological ideas narrated in the book of Deuteronomy serve as the lens by which events across Joshua through 2 Kings are retold. The laws of Deuteronomy serve as the template by which kings and their deeds are constantly assessed. The person of Moses, so central to Deuteronomy, is frequently cited as authorization for the law and statutes to which the kings are subject (2 Kgs 18:6; 21:9). Hence, though we cannot name the actual author of these writings, the theological coherence that threads throughout the disparate traditions making up the books of Kings is often referred to as the work of the "Deuteronomist." We think of the Deuteronomist as an editor or a school of editors who fashioned together the bits and pieces of the records, traditions, and accounts stemming from the time of Israel's settlement in the land to the era of exile in light of Deuteronomic law and faith.

Exactly what these sources were is for the most part a matter of conjecture. The books of Kings themselves give some clues. They reference at least three definitive sources—the Book of the Acts of Solomon (1 Kgs 11:41); the Annals of the Kings of Judah (i.e., 1 Kgs 14:29; 15:7); and the Annals of the Kings of Israel (i.e., 1 Kgs 14:19; 15:31). Other formerly existing files are suggested by virtue of the kinds of material recorded in these books. Kings are characteristically introduced throughout the chapters by recounting their biographies (i.e., 1 Kgs 15:9-10; 16:8), implying existence of regal records. State archives likely preserved the districting orders and appointment of governors narrated in some of the Solomonic material (1 Kgs 4). Once existing files on foreign affairs, trade deals, and international treaties were likely drawn upon for some of the narratives of the divided monarchy. Architectural and archival records probably informed the narrative recounting the construction of the Solomonic palace and the temple (1 Kgs 5–7). That similar types of records from other ancient Near Eastern societies have been recovered increases the likelihood they existed in ancient Israel.

The date of composition of these books by the Deuteronomist cannot be precisely pinned down. The persistent theological integrity of these writings, connecting God's relationship to the people with their fidelity to the covenantal law, led Martin Noth to propose that a single individual composed the Deuteronomistic History during the exile (Noth, 9-12). With the understanding and wisdom of hindsight, this individual or group of individuals wove together stories and traditions in a way that witnessed to this theology.

Another widely held proposal grows out of a close reading of the traditions. Although there is a perceptible unity across these books, not all the theological representations completely cohere. Some parts of the tradition demonstrate a witness to God's unconditional covenant promises, while in other places the tradition argues that God's promises are conditioned upon fidelity to the law and statutes. Moreover, some of the accounts in 1 and 2 Samuel and 1 and 2 Kings appear to be in favor of the monarchy, whereas others bear evidence of a clear disdain for the establishment of kingship. These differences have led to the proposal that the book of Kings, along with the whole Deuteronomistic History, was the product of two editorial gestures (Cross, 224-28). One version likely grew out of the Josianic era (648–609 B.C.E.). Josiah, one of the later kings of Judah, is credited with addressing widespread apostasy by initiating a massive cultic reform. His efforts to centralize cult in Jerusalem, along with the composition of a promonarchic narrative, aimed to enkindle national spirit, reviving allegiance to the state. Such a setting would readily accommodate a theology assuring not only God's endorsement of kingship but also the Lord's unconditional fidelity toward the people no matter what failings they had succumbed to in the past. The scepter of divine justice and the accompanying punishment would still make room for the unconditional promise made to David (2 Sam 7).

In contrast, the experience of the end of the nation and exile in 587–586 B.C.E. would prompt a rewriting of this optimistic view of kingship and covenant. The destruction of Jerusalem coupled with the deportation of Judah's citizens to Babylon commenced the beginning of exile, one of the most formative periods in the biblical story. With the loss of land, king, and temple, it is easy to imagine the development of a second edition that would accommodate antimonarchic traditions and gravitate toward a more qualified understanding of divine blessings. In this version, the fate of the nation and the people's destiny itself depended upon fidelity to the Deuteronomic law. The experience of exile was evidence of the conditional nature of divine blessing. Hence, although the books of Kings cannot be read as history, the complexity of historical events echoes throughout these testimonies of a people's experience of God in their lives.

LITERARY CONSIDERATIONS AND THE BOOKS OF KINGS

The books of Kings set forth a rich storehouse of literary traditions. Though its stories twist and turn across the reigns of both northern and southern kings, an overarching ordering of the material is perceptible. Content, rather than form, suggests a three-part structure for these books. Picking up where the story of David left off in 2 Samuel, the first section (1 Kgs 1–11) opens with the ailing king on his deathbed. It records the succession and reign of Solomon, David's son, as the last king of the united kingdom. The second section (1 Kgs 12– 2 Kgs 17) narrates the tragic rupture of the nation into two states: Israel and Judah, and the subsequent accounts of each. Toward the close of this section, Israel and its capital Samaria fall prey to the imperialist campaign of Assyria. Finally, whereas the story of the nation of Judah continues in the third section (2 Kgs 18–25), it comes to a similar conclusion. Judah eventually succumbs to a foreign power. When Babylon destroys Judah and its capital Jerusalem, the period of exile begins. Hence, the books of Kings end with the end of the monarchy.

The three sections are comprised of large segments of tradition such as the Solomonic account (1 Kgs 1–11), or the lengthy tradition on Ahab's reign (1 Kgs 20–22), or the extended record describing Josiah's tenure (2 Kgs 22–23). These in turn give way to a vast catalog of literary forms that together craft the component units. Opening and closing formulas introducing each king, highly stylized speeches, prophetic oracles, and vows are among the many skillfully composed forms. A narrator's discourse weaves together these small segments of tradition to create the numerous accounts and stories composing these books. For example, the record of King Hezekiah's reign spans several chapters (2 Kgs 18–20). Making up this vast tradition are smaller units that create individual stories. The brief tale of Hezekiah's illness (2 Kgs 20: 1-11), for instance, employs a dialogue between the king and the prophet Isaiah, as well as an oracle and a prayer.

This world of stories, both large and small, displays three familiar literary stages in the development of the plot: exposition, crisis/problem, and resolution. For example, after an initial exposition that introduces Elijah's visit to the widow at Zarephath (1 Kgs 17:8-11), a problem is introduced (1 Kgs 17:12-15). The widow and her son are about to die of famine. Resolution, the last feature of plot, comes when Elijah declares the Lord's promise of sustenance to the woman, and she believes (1 Kgs 17:16). Food is provided for herself, her son, and the prophet. In conjunction with plot development, narrative tension can heighten and create suspense. Narrative speed can slow or be hurried depending upon what is important. Details can be abundant, commanding our attention, or they can be sketchy, urging us to read quickly. Some characters develop gradually across large sections of tradition, whereas others reside in the background, making only brief appearances. Finally, rhetorical devices such as word plays, repetitions, and parallels all work together with these other narrative features to compose the rich textures of these books. Attention to the literary dimensions of 1 and 2 Kings will be amply rewarded in our pursuit to understand these writings.

THE BOOKS OF KINGS AS A THEOLOGICAL WORK

Like any good literature, themes abound, linking together the various stories and infusing a unity to this vast work. The presence of enduring theological themes throughout Kings makes the influence of the Deuteronomist very palpable. The notion of God intimately involved in the reigns of the kings and in the lives of the people threads together a diverse collation of stories. Over the course of the two books, an understanding of God in the life of Israel expands and deepens as the Deuteronomist unveils the numerous dimensions of divine involvement.

Yahweh, who in the early traditions is understood first as a local deity and then as a national deity, is disclosed in Kings as Lord of a far more expansive domain. God is creator and Lord of the heavens and earth (2 Kgs 19:15). Even in Solomon's dedication of the temple, which occurs early in the tradition, God is recognized as the cosmological power responsible for all that hovers in existence (1 Kgs 8:9, 14-21, 27-30). In addition, this creator God oversees and controls the forces that other nations deify, the forces of nature themselves (2 Kgs 1:2-17; 4:8-37). Elijah the prophet was probably the most pronounced spokesperson for this theological disclosure. As his confrontation with the royal prophets demonstrated, Yahweh, not the Baals, was in charge of the natural elements upon which agriculture depends (1 Kgs 18:20-40). The Deuteronomists insist that Israel's God, the Lord, not other false gods, also rules history (1 Kgs 11:14, 23; 14:1-18; 2 Kgs 5:1-18; 10:32-33). The Lord controls the outcome of wars. In times of famine, God intervenes to feed the poor. The destiny of kings and the destiny of peasants all unfold according to God's design.

Yet this great all-powerful God who oversees the creation and the course of events in time and space is, in the Deuteronomist's theology, not a remote deity. Rather, across these stories, Yahweh is shown to be intimately caught up in the lives of the people. In dreams and visions, kings behold the Lord (1 Kgs 3:5-15; 9:2-9). Through mediators and the miraculous, God's presence is manifest (1 Kgs 18:41-46; 2 Kgs 19:1-37). Though dwelling in the temple, God is not confined. These stories witness God's responsiveness to the plight of the Shunnamite woman (2 Kgs 4:8-37). A food crisis among the brotherhood of prophets discloses divine involvement (2 Kgs 4:38-41). The Lord even intervenes in the life of a widow, restoring her son to life at the prophet's summoning (1 Kgs 17:17-24). This is a God who once promised to dwell among the people as blessing and continues to remain faithful to that commitment.

The Deuteronomist constantly calls attention to the first commandment, "I am the LORD your God . . . you shall have no other gods before me" (Exod 20:2-3). The oneness of God and the call to fidelity to God alone is what makes the rampant apostasy of kings so difficult. As it endures and continues to sway the whole people away from a covenantal understanding of the Lord, the apostasy becomes increasingly reprehensible. Most problematic of all, it flies in the face of the ultimate disclosure about God that is at the heart of Deuteronomy, beckoning recognition throughout Kings. "Hear, O Israel: The LORD is our God, the LORD alone" (Deut 6:4). This fundamental theological tenet stands in tension with the stories of the persistent turning away from the Lord and turning toward other deities. According to Kings, apostasy is the stumbling block that ultimately leads to the nation's demise and its experience of exile.

The numerous thematic theological threads interweaving these traditions attest to a maturing and deepening of the understanding of the covenantal God. Yet, this matter of God in relation to this covenant is the most complex and problematic disclosure of all across Kings. In other traditions in the Deuteronomistic History, God's promise of fidelity is unconditional (2 Sam 7). Despite human infidelity and failure, the Lord's steadfast presence and guarantee of a future knows no condition. Grounded in the covenant promised to David, God's preservation of the king, his offspring, and the nation would be steadfast even if at times they needed to be chastened. However, throughout Kings, the theology of covenant embedded in Deuteronomy echoes most resoundingly (1 Kgs 9:4-7). Moses called the people to a conditional covenant with God, one that unfolds concretely in blessing or curse depending upon the people's responsiveness or turning away from the Lord.

As mentioned earlier, whether these two understandings of the covenantal God are the result of one or more editorial efforts remains a point of debate. However, a theological solution might also be rallied in the face of this complexity. The conditional understanding of covenant ties itself to the traditions centered upon Moses. These were more likely the sacred stories told and retold by the people of the northern nation Israel. The unconditional understanding of covenant links directly to the line of David that governed the southern nation of Judah. The juxtaposition of both traditions within these writings not only serves to preserve the religious experience and heritage of both communities of the divided monarchy; in the books of Kings, it also explains the nation's failure in the land while at the same time enkindling a hope for the unending existence of a different kind of kingdom in the age to come.

COMMENTARY: 1 Kings

1 KINGS 1

As 1 Kings opens, it offers a glimpse of the essential humanity at play amid monarchic machinations. The reign of David is over. His weakened, old, passive condition, described in the opening verses of chapter 1, warrants a replacement. A dramatic power struggle erupts between Solomon and Adonijah in response to the implicit question, Who will ascend the throne of David? Just as interpreters struggle over the role of this story, the characters wrestle in response to this underlying question. The account that unfolds details how Solomon comes to the throne. Attention shifts away from the ailing David and spotlights the rise of the young king. An era that contrasts with the weak, pathetic close of the Davidic time is about to begin. The story of Solomon's inauguration and the public assent it receives raises expectations.

Literary Analysis

Chapter 1 narrates a complex story framed by its own literary borders. In the opening of the story (1:1-10), the disabled, frail condition of King David prompts Adonijah's plot to seize power and ascend the throne. In the conclusion (1:41-53), the inauguration of Solomon as king necessitates Adonijah's surrender of these ambitions as well as his plea for clemency. Tension is introduced early in the narrative when Adonijah holds a feast to commence the beginning of his rise to power. Toward the end of the story, that same feast occasions the demise of his agenda and renders him powerless (1:41-49).

Across the development of plot and its resolution, four speeches (vv. 11-14; 15-21; 22-27; 28-35) work to overturn Adonijah's plan. First, the prophet Nathan invites Bathsheba, Solomon's mother, to consider the life-threatening consequences for herself if Adonijah becomes king (1:11-14). He enlists her assistance to reverse the young man's plan. Second, Bathsheba, as instructed by Nathan, goes to David and informs him of Adonijah's scheming (1:15-21). Additionally, she challenges the ailing king to make good on a vow he made regarding Solomon's ascent to the throne. Third, Nathan joins Bathsheba before David and further coaxes the failing monarch (1:22-27). Finally, David proclaims Solomon as his successor and gives instructions for the inauguration (1:28-30, 32-37), to which Benaiah, commander of David's army, affirmatively responds.

Characteristic of Hebrew narrative, what the king orders is described as being immediately carried out. Solomon's inauguration fulfills David's orders and accomplishes what the four speeches aimed to procure. Narrative report records the details of the story's climax (1:38-40). Solomon is placed upon a mule and brought to Gihon. Zadok the priest takes a horn of oil from the tent and anoints Solomon king. As the ram's horn is blown, the people raise their voices in assent: "Long live King Solomon!" Narrative elaboration confirms the public assent. The people go up after him, play joyful music, and rejoice loudly. The narrative record of these events concludes on a celebratory note, and "the earth quaked" at their noise (1:40). The image conjures notions that even the earth participates in the great jubilation over the rise of a monarch. This occasion of the rise of a new star encourages such comprehensive rejoicing. However, the image of the earth "quaking" could also suggest a splitting or severing of the land and thus foreshadow something else. The following exegetical exposition will consider whether this image narrates the earth's rejoicing or serves as a threatening portent (vv. 41-53).

Exegetical Analysis

An Ailing King (1:1-4)

Chapter 1 opens in the private quarters of King David's bedroom. Directly, we are offered a brief but nevertheless unqualified assessment of the languishing monarch's condition. David is old and cold. No amount of blankets can warm him. This lackluster description is not only about David. The decline of the once powerful king creates a political crisis. The absence of a monarch at the helm creates a power vacuum. That David's own servants take steps to revive his vitality suggests the gravity of a waning ruler. With wishful fantasies of a bygone era, his servants enlist a young, beautiful virgin to rekindle his virility and to warm him. Abishag, a Shunammite from a small village in the northern tribal territory of Issachar, is brought to the king's chamber "to lie in [his] bosom" and to attend to him (1:2). The description echoes the earlier portrait of Bathsheba, who was also described as the one to "lie in his bosom" (2 Sam 12:3). Like Bathsheba, Abishag is described as beautiful. Images of the past when David was powerful, virile, and woefully unrestrained subtly resonate across the narrative and strain to quell the desperation of those responsible for his care. Perhaps the king's servants hoped contact with Abishag would heal him. That she was from Shunem, where Elisha the prophet would later restore a child to life by contact with the child's dead body, encouraged such expectations (2 Kgs 4:32-37). Or perhaps the plan to bring beautiful Abishag to the bedside of the frail king aims to revitalize him. Instead, the gesture not only fails, but further underscores the disabled condition of this monarch. Though the virgin Abishag sleeps with the king, David "did not know her sexually" (1:4). Such physical impotency in private affairs does not bode well for David's competence in the public sphere. The loss of virility and vitality signals a political crisis. Who will be David's heir? Who will ascend the throne?

A Great Feast (1:5-10)

Adonijah, the eldest of David's remaining sons born at Hebron and thus the likely heir, responds. Taking the initiative, Adonijah prepares for his own enthronement. As he gathers horsemen, chariots, and soldiers to go ahead of him, his forthright, carefully planned activity contrasts sharply with the unresponsive and sickly state of the king. Adonijah's expression of intent is clear, "I will be king" (1:5). The description of his handsome appearance and the indulgences of his father (1:6) remind us of another of David's sons, Absalom. Before he led a revolt to become king, Absalom also held a feast and gathered a regiment of soldiers. Although such parallels encourage us to think of Adonijah's sacrifice and feast as an occasion for self-coronation, he was more likely rallying his supporters and currying favor among his constituencies. The names of the invited guests suggest an assembly of familiar court officials we know from the past. Joab and Abiathar, early associates of David with an allegiance to the political climate before the unification of the northern tribes, join and support Adonijah. Indeed, his guest list includes "all the royal officials of Judah" (1:9), those who likely still identify with the self-governing tribal stronghold of the south before David established a capital at Jerusalem. The names of those not invited argue strongly for the partisan nature of Adonijah's activities. Benaiah, Zadok, and Nathan are not among the guests. It is more than coincidence that these government officials (who entered the David story after the move from Hebron to Jerusalem) are among the uninvited. This banquet at En-rogel and the divisions it suggests must be understood in light of the Judah-Israel tensions already present in 2 Sam 20. Those who long for the "good old days" rally around Adonijah in opposition to those committed to the unified nation and the future it holds.

Though he is mentioned last, Solomon, the son born to David in Jerusalem, numbers most poignantly among Adonijah's uninvited guests. That Solomon is introduced as "his brother" and not "the son of Bathsheba" highlights the significance of this omission and the familial nature of the latent divisions. Such oppositions can have consequences beyond familial confines. As we shall see in the chapters to come, the tensions between brothers, left unresolved, produce a deadly schism.

Four Speeches (1:11-37)

The scene now shifts from En-rogel to the royal court. Four speeches work to reverse Adonijah's plan. First, Nathan, the court prophet of David, speaks to Bathsheba (vv. 11-14). At the opening of his address, he inquires whether Bathsheba knows that

Adonijah has become king. He then tells her what she must do to reverse this situation. At the close of his address, he urges Bathsheba to confront David with this same question. Whether Nathan, the one responsible for conveying God's will to the king, acts in good faith remains uncertain. On two accounts, he gives Bathsheba instructions that raise suspicions as to his motives. Though Adonijah has not actually declared himself king, Nathan reports this as a fact. "Have you not heard that Adonijah son of Haggith has become king . . . ?" (1:12). Next, Nathan urges Bathsheba to remind David of an oath the king allegedly swore that would put Solomon on the throne. However, nowhere in 2 Samuel do we find such an oath on the part of David. On both scores we might wonder about Nathan's construction of the truth.

Moreover, the script Nathan provides for Bathsheba pairs David and Solomon as king and king-to-be in one rhetorical question over and against Adonijah as king in another. "Go in at once to King David, and say to him, 'Did you not, *my lord the king,* swear to your servant, saying: Your son *Solomon shall succeed me as king,* and he shall sit on my throne? Why then is Adonijah king?'" (1:13). Nathan's strategy seems troubling. If he can make David angry at his eldest son, he may be able to motivate even the ailing king to act. But to manipulate David, the prophet must first manipulate Bathsheba. Hence, he supplies the motive that will prompt her to cooperate. In his speech, Nathan introduces Adonijah as "the son of Haggith," reminding Bathsheba that the powerful role of queen mother is up for grabs. He goes further to ensure her cooperation reminding her that the stakes are nothing less than her life and the life of her son Solomon. Although we don't know Nathan's motive, he clearly takes advantage of both David's condition and Bathsheba's vulnerability. That Solomon becomes king as a result of Nathan's scheming raises questions about the legitimacy of the whole succession process. Moreover, the prophet's efforts to cultivate opposition in order to carry out his plan raise additional questions about Solomon's kingship.

Bathsheba delivers before David the second speech in this chapter (vv. 15-21). She carries out Nathan's order and goes to the king's bedchamber. The status of the king confined to his royal quarters is again rehearsed. The ruler is old and ill. Abishag attends the ailing monarch at his bedside. However, now the description serves to justify Bathsheba's speech. Replaced by the youthful Abishag, the security of Bathsheba's royal position is as precarious as the king's health. Mother of Solomon, she has urgent grounds on which to make her case. Invited to speak, she reviews for David what we already know but what David does not. According to her, Adonijah has become king. Indeed, we know he is at least planning to do so. David's lack of knowledge regarding these important public matters coincides with his lack of knowledge in the private sphere of sexual relations. As Bathsheba recites the allegations that Nathan has fed her, her embellishments reveal her vested interest. David's failure to act not only jeopardizes his reputation but also threatens her safety and that of Solomon in the royal court. Additionally, when Bathsheba reminds David of his oath, she adds, "You swore . . . by the LORD your God" (1:17). The use of God language reminds the king of his responsibility and thus his culpability before God if he remains indecisive. Earlier in his story, David's military leader, Joab, had sent the wise woman of Tekoa to trick the king into ruling in favor of his son Absalom (2 Sam 14:1-20). Now Nathan commissions another woman, Bathsheba, to prompt David's ruling on behalf of another son, Solomon.

The third speech commences when Nathan follows Bathsheba into the king's chamber and reinforces her story (vv. 22-27). Here, the Hebrew is more telling. Nathan did not merely "confirm her account" as he promised (v. 14); he "supplemented" her words. Though Nathan's construction of events is angled differently, it pursues the same outcome. In contrast to Bathsheba's observation of David's lack of knowledge of Adonijah's ascent, Nathan's opening inquiry questions whether David himself has instigated Adonijah's behavior and acted in favor of this son. Nathan follows this with a report of the gathering underway at En-rogel. His rendition portrays what may have been a campaign dinner as a royal coronation feast. Though Nathan numbered among the uninvited, he reports firsthand that Adonijah's guests eat, drink, and proclaim, "Long live King Adonijah!" (1:25).

Knowing full well that David did not instigate Adonijah's elevation, the prophet rhetorically crafts his speech to affect David both professionally and personally. On the one hand, the report of Adonijah's alleged acclamation as king is intended to incite anger on the part of a sickly but nevertheless still reigning monarch. On the other hand, it may also evoke a painful memory about David's other son Absalom's rebellious pursuit of the throne (2 Sam 15). Hence, alongside Bathsheba's account that highlights the conflict between brothers, Nathan's construal of the events enkindles hostility between father and son. Together, both speeches succeed in inciting David to act.

David delivers the fourth speech (1:28-37). Two parts structure his address. First, he summons Bathsheba. Though she apparently left the chambers when David conferred with his chief advisor Nathan, it is noteworthy that David now summons her and reveals his plan. The king indicates his personal resolve to make good on his word to her, as well as to address the constitutional crisis at hand. He recites the oath that she had recalled for him but with changes. Whereas Bathsheba recounted David swearing by "the LORD your God," David now swears by "the LORD, the God of Israel" (1:30). It is no surprise that the king's theology is subject to and crafted by his political priorities; for him, Yahweh is a national deity. The officials he summons in the second part of the address confirm these political commitments. He calls Nathan, his prophet; Zadok, his priest; and Benaiah, son of Jehoiada, commander of his military forces. Over and against Adonijah's cadre of Judahite officials, these men represent the rival establishment of the unified nation Israel.

With forthright decisiveness befitting a powerful monarch, David issues a series of orders that collectively will accomplish both the succession of Solomon as king and the fall of Adonijah. David commands them, "Take with you the servants of your lord" (1:33a), and mount Solomon on David's own mule. This will be a sure public sign of the king's own confirmation of the events. Next, they are to bring Solomon down to the spring Gihon (1:33b). Curiously, this site is close to En-rogel where Adonijah's feast is underway. Then Zadok and Nathan are commanded to anoint Solomon as king over Israel. Next, they are to "blow the trumpet [shofar]," the familiar means by which royal announcements are made to the people of the surrounding region. The sound of the shofar will surely be heard in En-rogel, less than a half mile outside the city limits. The sounding of the shofar is to be followed by the proclamation, "Long live King Solomon!" (1:34). After these inaugural gestures at Gihon, David's royal officials are ordered, "You shall go up following him" (1:35), with Solomon in the lead, another indication of this anointed one's ascent to kingship. Finally, David's list of commands culminates with a last edict: Solomon is to "enter and sit on my throne; he shall be king in my place" (1:35).

With this series of monarchic mandates, we reach the climax of the story; a dramatic turn of events has been brought about by a dramatic change in the king. As if awakened from a febrile slumber, the passive, unresponsive king now becomes active and decisive. Whether out of loyalty to Bathsheba, fidelity to an oath, or a determination to save both his honor and the work of his hands, that is, a unified Israel, David swings into action one last time. In response, Benaiah, David's army commander, makes public supplication that the Lord ordain the King's commands (vv. 36-37). His prayer confirms that the military will back the implementation of David's order.

Solomon Becomes King (1:38-40)

The narrative format now assumes the familiar command-fulfillment pattern. Swiftly, with the speed and efficiency befitting the obedience of a loyal subject, the narrative reports that all David commanded is carried out. Although the account summary does not correspond in order or in exact detail to the list of David's issuances (1:33-35), there is the overarching impression of fulfillment. Everything that the king ordered is in the process of being accomplished. Additional details add greater specificity and reality to the events. The "Cherethites" and the "Pelethites" are mentioned among those assembled to acknowledge the new ruler. Though the identity of these parties is uncertain, they were probably mercenaries of some sort. With no clear alliance to either of the Judahite or Israelite parties, these men might be counted on for their unflinching fidelity to the king. Given the partisan polarities threaded across this account, their enlistment is politically expedient. Additionally, when Zadok carries out the command to anoint Solomon, the narrative indicates he does so with oil from "the tent." This likely refers to the "tent of meeting" or "tent of the LORD," the symbol of divine presence dwelling among the people (2 Sam 7:2, 6; 1 Kgs 2:28). Thus, the designation of Solomon as king continues the tradition in which both Saul (1 Sam 10:1) and David (1 Sam 16:1, 13) were anointed.

Finally, with the sounding of the shofar and the acclamation of "all the people," David's oath finds fulfillment. However, as readers, we know that not "all the people" were present for this royal event. Besides the impracticality of assembling "all the people" with less than a day's notice for the coronation of a new king, we also know that many of the Judahite people were still gathered at Adonijah's dinner party. News of Solomon's coronation will send shock waves throughout the festivities at En-rogel and will prompt disbelieving guests to depart prematurely.

The End of One Celebration (1:41-50)

The noise coming from Gihon interrupts Adonijah's feasting at En-rogel. Jonathan, son of Abiathar, bursts forth on the scene just as the guests finish eating. With his announcement of Solomon's enthronement, not only is the meal over, but so also is Adonijah's bid for the throne. First, Jonathan summarizes what we already know. Solomon was anointed per David's order. Zadok, Nathan, and Benaiah, along with the Cherithites and Pelethites, mounted Solomon on David's own mule and proceeded to anoint him. The noise Adonijah and his guests heard was the city in an uproar. Solomon now sits on the throne. The sounding of the shofar signaled the beginning of one celebration and the conclusion of another.

Next, Jonathan adds to his account details and events about which we do not know. King David's servants have gathered around his bed to congratulate him. David in turn bows down upon his bed and acknowledges their greetings and the new king.

There is something disquietingly reminiscent about Jonathan's role as informant of these events. In 2 Sam 15:17, Jonathan departed from En-rogel to tell David that his rebellious son Absalom had ascended the throne. Now Jonathan travels to En-rogel to alert another ambitious son, Adonijah, that David's appointee, Solomon, has ascended the throne. In both instances, Jonathan is the herald of trouble for the kingship erupting from family discord.

Jonathan's return here, along with his alarming announcement, halts the celebration. Realizing that they had been at the wrong party, Adonijah's guests "got up trembling and went their own ways" (1:49). Hence, in contrast to the people who assemble and voice their assent to Solomon, Adonijah's guests scatter and move away from the would-be king. For his part, Adonijah "fears" and seeks refuge in the only power that can save him. He goes to "[lay] hold of the horns of the altar" (1:51). These are, most likely, protrusions on the four corners of the altar. To hold them fast evidently ensured one of divine protection.

Strife between Brothers (1:51-53)

The story ends with several "firsts." When Solomon sends for Adonijah, it is the first time in the whole episode that the brothers encounter each other. Upon meeting, Adonijah requests a vow that will protect him from his powerful brother. "Let King Solomon swear to me first that he will not kill his servant with the sword" (1:51). Adonijah's recitation is not only a plea for clemency but an acknowledgment of his subject-servant status before the new king.

This is also the first time we hear Solomon speak as he responds to his brother's request. Though Adonijah asked for a vow, Solomon instead delivers the terms of his existence. "If he proves to be a worthy man, not one of his hairs shall fall to the ground; but if wickedness is found in him, he shall die" (1:52). The expression, "Not one of his hairs shall fall from his head" in reference to Adonijah is chilling. On another occasion when David used it to ensure his son Absalom's safety, it became instead a portent of his end (2 Sam 14:11). It was by the very hairs of his own head

(2 Sam 18:9) that Absalom met his death. In several ways then, this exchange between Solomon and Adonijah is worrisome. The resolution of the story's conflict has not ended the strife between brothers.

Theological and Ethical Analysis

The elevation of Solomon as king is at the expense of his brother Adonijah. As Solomon's fortune rises, Adonijah's destiny falls. The one brother who would be king must do obeisance before the new monarch. The other brother who merely accepts the regnal office handed him by his father makes his first act as king a gesture of sovereignty over his brother. In the end, Solomon defines the terms of Adonijah's existence. Hence, this story of how Solomon became king also can be described in other ways. It is a story of strife between brothers, a kind of tale all too common and even foundational to the biblical tradition. Cain and Abel, Jacob and Essau, Joseph and his brothers, Amon and Absalom—the list is as endless as the reverberations triggered by each instance of fraternal strife.

As the primeval history of Genesis has warned, when hostilities between brothers go unchecked they are capable of spawning and nurturing more troublesome divisions. In this story, the strife between brothers may have done just that. The growing enmity between Solomon and Adonijah is not an isolated conflict. When other characters enter the story they, too, become entangled and embroiled in this division. As allies of one brother, they automatically become enemies of others. Bathsheba, the mother of Solomon, is threatened by the potential good fortune of Haggith, the mother of Adonijah. Joab, Adonijah's would-be secretary of defense, is opposed by his replacement, Benaiah, Solomon's soon-to-be appointed lieutenant of military affairs. At the level of religious affairs, the priests Zadok and Abiathar are at odds with each other in their regnal alliances. Even the unnamed others in Adonijah's party, "all . . . the king's sons, and all the royal officials of Judah" (1:9), are set in opposition to those groups of persons assembled around Solomon, "the Cherethites and the Pelethites" (1:38) and "all the people" (1:40) as a result of this brotherly strife. Such oppositions divide and multiply like cancerous cells and infect whole families, clans, and nations. Hence, strife between two brothers is never just a fraternal matter; it carries with it consequences for the entire world.

In our story, as one brother rises at another brother's expense, not only do the people rejoice, play music, and give voice to their assent, but we also hear that the "the earth quaked" (1:40). Whereas the resulting fissure may be a sign of rejoicing in its immediate context, it may also foreshadow something less joyous on the horizon. In the stories to follow, this instance of fraternal strife shows its potential to cultivate a schism of national proportions, the likes of which unfold in the tragedy to come.

1 KINGS 2

Chapter 2 recounts David's final instructions to the new king before his death. His fatherly advice is followed by an account of the bloody demise of dissenters to Solomon's new regime. That the chronicler seemed satisfied to report the transition of kingship from David to Solomon in one sentence ("When David was old and full of days, he made his son Solomon king over Israel" [1 Chron 23:1]) makes the report of these murderous escapades here particularly curious. Are these stories intended merely to explain how Solomon came to consolidate his kingship after his father's death? Or is something more at work here, something that may turn out to be both hauntingly congruent with the past as well as disquietingly present in the era to follow?

Literary Analysis

Two literary sections structure the material in this second chapter (vv. 1-12, 13-46). First, verses 1-12 narrate David's final instructions to Solomon followed by the obituary recording David's death. Content divides the speech into two distinct parts. In the first half (vv. 1-4), David attends to religious matters. Solomon must observe the covenant. In the second half (vv. 5-9), David addresses more mundane concerns. He offers a father's advice on how to deal with political upstarts. At the end of his final address to his son Solomon, a notice records that David, the aging monarch, dies (vv. 10-11). The conclusion of this section (v. 12) describes Solomon's ascent as "firmly established."

The second division of this chapter (vv. 13-46) sets forth a narrative account of how Solomon acts upon his now deceased father's directives and consolidates his reign; he issues orders to secure his rule in four isolated episodes (vv. 13-25, 26-27, 28-34, 36-46). In the process, the material serves to narrate a secure and successful transition between the close of the reign of one king and the beginning of his son's royal tenure.

The narrative summaries (vv. 12, 46b) that conclude each part of this chapter make this overarching intention clear. The statement "So Solomon sat on the throne of his father David; and his kingdom was firmly established" (2:12) closes part one. Its echo, "So the kingdom was established in the hand of Solomon" (2:46b), concludes part two. But security and success of such hierarchical establishments are not without high costs. The characters that are expended so that the transition can be carried out specify the price tag for the maintenance of this monarchic monopoly.

Exegetical Analysis

David's Farewell Address (2:1-9)

Having reigned forty years, seven in Hebron and thirty-three years in Jerusalem, "David's time to die" (2:1) draws near. In the familiar format of a dying hero (cf. Gen 49; Josh 23; 1 Sam 12), David delivers a farewell speech and directs it to his son Solomon, the newly enthroned heir. Two sets of instructions structure his address. A litany of religious admonitions that echo the language of the Deuteronomic law code craft the first set of directives. Solomon's attention must be riveted upon every possible divine mandate. David beseeches him to walk in God's ways and to observe God's statutes, commandments, ordinances and testimonies (2:3). The comprehensive nature of David's urgings appears bent upon enlisting Solomon's uncompromising and unwavering attention to all that God demands. On the one hand, context would lead us to believe that David is not simply urging Solomon's conformity to legal codes. As if the hour of death has brought him face-to-face with himself and where he has failed, David urges Solomon to seek relationship with the divine. In this final hour of self-reconciliation, the dying king reminds his son that his way must be bound up with a kind of spiritual conveyance of his whole being to the Lord. Only then will he, along with his heirs, conform to God's invitation "to walk before me in faithfulness with all their heart and with all their soul" (2:4).

On the other hand, David's speech betrays that hunger for power and prestige still maintains its grip on this king. After expansively encouraging Solomon's fidelity to Yahweh, David reveals another motivation. He affixes the prospect of prosperity and the negative consequences for disobeying the covenant as incentives for Solomon's unflinching obedience. Solomon's success and the continuance of his line is premised upon the condition of his utmost obedience to covenant. Here lies an apparent stumbling block in David's address. The covenant promised to David in the oracle by Nathan was unconditional (2 Sam 7). Nathan gave God's word that the Davidic line would never end. Why then does David himself apparently qualify the very nature of the covenant in his dying speech?

Some settle this difficulty by suggesting that the "throne of Israel" (2:4) refers only to the northern tribal territory about which covenant is conditional. Given the focus in the previous chapter on the erupting tension between the constituencies of Judah and the northern territory, despite unification, such an explanation here is plausible. The covenant promise to David as king of Judah was unconditional. However, with the extension of that covenant to the new politically precarious reality, the united Israel, the covenant becomes conditional. It now must be attended to with an unflinching steadfastness. The conditioning of the still-valid promise of an unending line of descendants aims to garnish uncompromising obedience from Solomon and his successors. Fidelity becomes the theological measuring rod by which all the Davidic monarchs will be assessed in the drama unfolding across the books of Kings. Moreover, the Deuteronomistic belief that fulfillment of God's promises is contingent upon human fidelity discloses something else. God is more than a national deity who acts on Israel's behalf regardless of the people's loyalty. The God portrayed as caught up in the national affairs of kings and the nation-state may actually be attending to a larger sphere of human concerns.

In the second half of his speech, David turns his attention to more immediate and concrete matters. On the heels of the instructions concerning covenant, we might expect him to outline actual instances for this obedience. Instead, we hear a three-part series of injunctions about how to deal with particular individuals, that is, Joab, the sons of Barzillai, and Shimei. One is to be cared for; two are to be killed.

First, David directs his attention to Joab. He recounts Joab's slaying of Abner and Amasa as if they were personal affronts to the dying king. Earlier, 2 Samuel offered explanations for these killings that David does not mention here. Abner had killed Joab's brother in self-defense (2 Sam 3). Amasa had been appointed to take over Joab's job (2 Sam 20). Though Joab had protected David on many occasions, served as his military commander, and even assisted in healing family relations, Joab's faithful service is of no account now. David only gives reasons to justify his assassination. Both crimes committed were in times of peace. However, only now is the issue of bloodguilt of concern. The bloodguilt will be on David and his house if the deeds are not expiated by Joab's own blood. Still, the specificity of the reasons for punishment that David gives is less clear than his directives as to what Solomon must do. The instructions specify that Solomon should act wisely. In the chapters that follow, wisdom unfolds as a distinctive feature in the characterization of Solomon. Sketched in the biblical tradition meriting its name, "wisdom" can be understood as the capacity to know right from wrong, the ability to judge justly, and the knowledge to act for the well-being of others. Again and again in the biblical tradition, Solomon is reported to be wise. Whether or not he actually lives up to that reputation will be left to the reader's judgment. In this story, David instructs Solomon to act wisely and not "let his [Joab's] gray head go down to Sheol in peace" (2:6);

that is, not let him die a natural death of old age. Although the language may seem cryptic, the message is not. Joab is to die.

In the next injunction, David levels an order to deal loyally with the sons of Barzillai the Gileadite. The very positive tone here contrasts sharply with the harsh, merciless tone of the preceding order and that of the one to follow. Barzillai had hosted and provided for David generously when he was fleeing from Absalom (2 Sam 17:27-29). Later David had tried to return the favor by offering hospitality to Barzillai (2 Sam 19:31-40). Whether out of graciousness or political savvy, David urges Solomon to preserve this loyal mutuality by providing for the Gileadite sons.

In the third and final round of instructions, David makes no equivocation regarding Shimei's destiny. Whether this is the same Shimei that we hear about as one who sided with Solomon in 1:8 is uncertain. That it might be the same individual, however, is deeply disturbing. Not even those who ally with the king are safe. However, the reason David gives for Shimei's execution is even more unsettling. Indeed, Shimei, a member of the house of Saul, did curse David for his ill treatment and dethronement of Saul's family many years earlier (2 Sam 16:5-14). However, later when he met David again, Shimei apologized for his outburst. David in turn granted him pardon and swore that his life would be protected (2 Sam 19:16-23). That promise and pardon seem of little value now. Again, as if to hide intentions behind the cover of language, David urges Solomon to use wisdom in this matter. Employing the same image used for Joab ("You must bring his gray head down with blood to Sheol" [2:9]), David condemns Shimei to death. This last death sentence concludes David's speech and marks his final gesture in life.

Death of One King and Ascent of Another (2:10-12)

The Deuteronomistic formula that will characterize the obituaries of kings in subsequent stories announces the king's death. "Then David slept with his ancestors . . ." (2:10). The career of this formative character has come to an end. His life witnessed the extremes of faithful servanthood to Yahweh alongside passion for power, bloodthirsty battles, and bouts of immorality. His conclud-

ing speech bears witness to that complexity. Alongside his injunctions to be faithful to God's covenant in its every ordinance and
decree, David also delivers instructions for the assassinations of
those who would be threats to his household's political stability.
But this death notice of a king is no cause for despair. Immediately
on the heels of the characteristic obituary formula comes notice of
monarchic replacement. Solomon has already ascended the throne.
Quickly, as if determined to fulfill his father's dying wishes, Solomon
moves to consolidate his power and position. With four dramatic
gestures he begins his reign.

Death of Adonijah (2:13-25)

Solomon's initial deed unfolds as a result of two conversations
(vv. 13-18, 19-24). The first exchange transpires between
Bathsheba and Adonijah (vv. 13-18). Though still smarting from
his aborted quest for the throne and the kingship ("You know that
the kingdom was mine, and that all Israel expected me to reign"
[2:15]), Adonijah beseeches Bathsheba to make a request to
Solomon on his behalf. He asks that she seek from his brother
Solomon permission to take Abishag the Shunammite as his wife.
Whether Adonijah's request is innocent or another attempt to
make a move on the throne is unclear. He may have been merely
trying to reinstate himself as member of the house of David, or he
may have hoped to secure a position that would make his retrieval
of the throne justified.

Though the narrative resists offering an explanation, there is
something pathetic but believable about the sincerity of
Adonijah's request. He recognizes the turn of events that made
Solomon king. He acknowledges that Yahweh was behind it. In
addition, he even refers to his brother as "King Solomon."
Further, the narrator makes no suggestion of ill motives on
Adonijah's part. Bathsheba, who acted to secure the throne for
Solomon, apparently perceives no threat. She willingly carries his
request to the king.

Now a second conversation commences between Bathsheba and
Solomon (2:19-24). First, they exchange courtly courtesies. Next,
Solomon honors the queen mother by seating her on a throne to

his right. As if to regard her wishes and good insight as tantamount to his own, he promises to grant her request before she even makes it known. No element of suspicion has tainted the apparently straightforward course of the story. We have every reason to believe that Solomon will say yes to this uncomplicated request. But Bathsheba's intercession on behalf of Adonijah ignites an outburst of outrage by Solomon. With bitter sarcasm, he supplants his promise to Bathsheba with a deadly oath concerning Adonijah. Without explanation to the queen mother or to the reader, Solomon makes his brother's request for a wife into a safety hazard for the kingdom. Without evidence, Solomon judges his brother's motive as treasonous. Without a trial, he sentences him to death. Hence, Solomon's first judgment as king yields a death sentence for his brother. The new king's first exercise of "wisdom" produces the first casualty. David's plan to secure the throne by disposing of Joab receives wider fulfillment under Solomon. The assassination of Adonijah will prompt the expulsion of Abiathar on the way to the eventual demise of Joab. The entire rival party will be done away with as Solomon consolidates his reign.

Abiathar's Expulsion (2:26-27)

With no narrative indication of Abiathar's presence before the king, Solomon now speaks to this priest as if he is an accomplice of Adonijah's undesignated crime. In his second act as king, Solomon judges the priest as deserving of death, yet suspends the sentence. Perhaps more out of fear than out of respect for the religious official, Solomon spares his life. He cites Abiathar's service over the years to his father David as the reason for his leniency. Still, the king banishes him from Jerusalem and confines him to his home in Anathoth, a small town not far from the capital. In addition, Solomon strips Abiathar of his role as royal priest. Unlike Adonijah's story, Abiathar's tale of dismissal is brief with no real plot. At best, it serves the larger story. Solomon's purge of the ranks in establishing his house is thorough and unrelenting. Even the priest who had served his father warrants exclusion. However, an even more disconcerting rendition lurks in the ranks of the tradition of interpretation. Some would argue that

Abiathar's expulsion now fulfills the divine word spoken against the house of Eli at Shiloh (1 Sam 3:14). Abiathar's connection to the house of Eli is grounded in a few fleeting references. As foretold of the house of Eli, their service to the house of the Lord would be cut off. A theology where banishment as the definition of one's human destiny fulfills God's plan is deeply disturbing.

The Disposal of Joab (2:28-34)

The third act of Solomon as king unfolds in the course of two parallel scenes. Both are characterized by three parts: first, a report about Joab is narrated (2:28-29a), and second, Solomon issues a command (2:29b). Finally, Benaiah moves to carry out the king's order (2:30). A brief narrative description introduces each scene.

As the story opens, Joab has presumably received the news of Adonijah's execution and Abiathar's exile. He flees to the tent of the Lord and grasps the horns of the altar. Like Adonijah, he seeks protection in the only power that can save him. At the same time he assumes a position where he can still negotiate terms for his existence. A brief note in the narrative qualifies his culpability and argues in favor of his character. While recounting that Joab was party to Adonijah, it reminds us he was not supportive of Absalom. Hence, there are grounds on which Joab can negotiate. Though a supporter of Adonijah, Joab was a faithful servant to David in the time of Absalom's revolt. However, Joab's fidelity to David is of no account to his son. When news of Joab's refuge in the tent reaches Solomon, the king orders Benaiah to go and to destroy him. Benaiah must have had some misgivings about violating sanctuary decorum, because although he departs to fulfill Solomon's order, he does not carry it out.

In the second part of the tale, Solomon must reissue the order for Joab's execution. This time he puts the burden of guilt upon Joab. He commissions Benaiah, "Do as he has said, strike him down and bury him" (2:31). Despite his scruples, the commander has to murder Joab as he clings to the horns of the altar, symbols of God's protective strength. Hence, Benaiah must bypass his regard for religious protocol in order to show his allegiance to the king. For his part, Solomon reveals here where his fidelity and commitments lie. His speech of justification discloses his self-interest. Joab will die because of the bloodguilt that threatens the house of David. A selective recall of Joab's past recounts two misdeeds and ignores the numerous occasions of Joab's allegiance to David. It is easy to see that with the elimination of this army commander, the military threat of the Judahites as conjured by Adonijah are all but extinct. With an obedience befitting the soon-to-be-appointed court officer, Benaiah disgraces the sanctuary and finally disposes of Joab. In turn, he is duly rewarded for his unflinching ruthlessness. With Abiathar in exile and Joab deceased, Solomon commissions Benaiah as head of his army and names Zadok as royal priest to fill the newly vacated posts.

Shimei's Execution (2:36-46)

The fourth act of Solomon is narrated in three parts. A lengthy speech by Solomon in the context of an encounter between the king and Shimei govern and parallel parts one and three (2:36-38, 41-46). A narrative section describing Shimei's journey to Gath to retrieve two of his slaves (2:39-40) separates the beginning and concluding frames.

In part one, Solomon summons Shimei. Without explanation, he confines the man's life and activity to Jerusalem. Shimei's unquestioning consent suggests he understands what is behind the order, and that he recognizes Solomon's authority to level such a mandate. Shimei is from the house of Saul. That he cannot leave the capital and cross the Kidron Valley isolates him from his home in Bahurim, east of Jerusalem. Whatever was left of his Saulide constituencies would be strongest there. Both David's deathbed instruction and Solomon's order here indicate that the Saulide threat to the throne may not be over yet.

Solomon's prohibition is accompanied by a carefully worded death penalty. If Shimei violates the restriction, he bears responsibility for his own death. "Your blood shall be on your own head" (2:37). Shimei's response conveys the impression that he has every intention to comply. He refers to Solomon as "my lord" and to himself as "your servant" (2:38). Thus he acknowledges not only

Solomon's kingship but also the king's power to carry out this agreement.

An intervening narrative description informs us that Shimei complies with Solomon's restriction. However, when two of his slaves escape, Shimei saddles his donkey and sets out to retrieve them. The loss of slaves poses a significant economic threat to the well-being of an ancient household. Shimei must travel to Gath, southwest of Jerusalem—the opposite direction from Bahurim, his own hometown. Upon reclaiming the two men, he promptly returns to his home in Jerusalem. The narrative leaves no doubt that he was not on a political mission to overthrow the throne, escape Solomon's restrictions, or enkindle insurrectionist sentiments. His movement out and back into Jerusalem was motivated by and confined to his own domestic concerns and livelihood.

In the third and final scene (2:41-46), Solomon once again summons Shimei. Having heard that the man had left Jerusalem, the king charges him with violating his parole. In a manner similar to the judgments he has made thus far, Solomon gives no consideration to where Shimei traveled, to why he went out, or to the fact that he returned. Trial, evidence, and testimony play no role when Solomon makes judgments. Rather, it is as if this literal violation of the law is the occasion for which Solomon has been waiting. Before ordering Shimei's execution, the king justifies himself by recalling the evil Shimei had done against David. He concludes that in contrast to Shimei's status as cursed before the Lord, Solomon and his father's throne will be blessed and established forever. Once again, he summons Benaiah, the court's hatchet man, to do his bidding. Indeed, Solomon has followed his father's orders and then some. With this fourth and final gesture in the name of establishing his kingdom, this newly inaugurated king sends another man to his death.

Theological and Ethical Analysis

As this story closes, we are not only invited to ponder the nature of the transition of the kingship, but more essentially we are drawn to consider the nature of humanity at play here amid this campaign of carnage. First, David instructs his son to do away with two of his past associates. Then Solomon, on the advice of his father, extends the death sentence to include a third party, as well as the exile of a fourth. Such calculated public butchery warrants some justifying rationale. Remedying previous offenses and fidelity to present oaths are among the explanations Solomon marshals as acceptable justification. But Solomon, like his father, possesses a selective memory about the past. In the case of Joab, this protector, defender, and faithful military lieutenant of David's era is remembered here only for two slayings. And when it comes to oaths, Solomon invents and interprets them as it suits him. Though Solomon charged Shimei to remain in Jerusalem, or "your blood shall be on your own head" (2:37), the new king later cites an apparently unrecorded oath sworn before God as justification for the man's death.

Despite the dubious rationale for the discharge of death sentences, Solomon's deceptive rhetorical defense does not completely deceive. At every turn in these four episodes, suspicions abound surrounding the truth and legitimacy of his explanations. They are manifest in the narrative and they make themselves known in the hearts of readers. In Solomon's rendition, Adonijah's request for Abishag's hand in marriage became grounds for his execution. However, Bathsheba, who was very instrumental in the rise of Solomon and the eventual downfall of Adonijah, appears to honor and respect the man's petition. In another instance, though Joab did support Adonijah's bid for the throne, the narrative makes the distinction that he did not stand behind David's son Absalom, who conducted a military revolution against his father in his quest to be king. Though the reader is reminded of these grounds on which to spare Joab, Solomon takes no account of such information. In that same story, Benaiah's scruples when it comes to sanctuary decorum contrast with Solomon's order to kill Joab as he clings to the horns of the altar. In the final tale, though Shimei did violate the letter of Solomon's decree, he certainly did not transgress the spirit of that ordinance. Hence, his assassination was clearly on technical grounds.

In subtle but nevertheless critical ways, the narrative itself conjures plenty of suspicion and reserve as to Solomon's deeds and his self-justifying defense. At the same time, we as readers find ourselves in a difficult position when invited to buy the story line and to offer our assent to this kingship. Whether read with an ancient sensibility or from a position of contemporary sentiment, the instructions of the dying king and the subsequent murderous actions of his son can only leave us aghast and horrified. Moreover, the flimsy pretexts upon which these instances of bloodshed are premised trigger our suspicion if not our outrage. None of the explanations justifying the executions across this chapter can obscure the commonality that underlies them. With the deaths of Adonijah, Joab, and the exile of Abiathar, the threat of the party rivaling Solomon before his enthronement finally subsides. Additionally, any threat to the throne by what remains of the Saulide household might well be discouraged by the execution of Shimei. No matter what explanation he marshals, it is impossible to ignore that each in this series of merciless episodes contributes to the consolidation of Solomon's power and throne.

Though little in these tales invites our emulation, still there are lessons to be learned here. We cannot help but be struck by the perils of ambition, the dangers of abusive power, and the habituation to violence that make it easier and easier to repeat such deeds. What is more, deception, whether of oneself or of others, is an essential accomplice in all these activities. It underwrites Solomon's murderous bloodshed on grounds of rhetorical ruse. However, the real ruse here eclipses any historical explanations or political motivations on the part of Solomon.

The great deception of these chapters is theological in nature. As chapter 2 opens, the first of David's final instructions rivets Solomon's attention upon the demand for covenantal faith. Fidelity to every law, decree, precept, and ordinance must command the new viceroy's vision and chasten his every act. But David doesn't stop there. These observances cannot merely be codes of conduct or blueprints for action. Solomon and his descendants are invited to hand themselves over to God in this covenantal kinship. A spiritual metamorphosis was to take place by their reign so as, in David's recall of God's pact, they would "walk before [God] in faithfulness with all their heart and with all their soul" (2:4).

The murderous escapades that follow on the heels of David's spiritual counsel make a mockery of such strivings. Even more disturbing, allusions and direct references to God's favor and involvement are woven throughout this tale of bloodshed and intrigue. Across both David's and Solomon's self-justifying explanations are claims of religious roots and citations of divine endorsement. On four occasions, God's divine plan is actually coupled with Solomon's deeds (2:23-24, 27, 32, 44). Such theological validation of personal and political agendas should always give us pause. Throughout the narrative, Yahweh's name is called upon to justify murder, sanction oaths, underwrite political ideology, and rubber-stamp a new sovereign and his despotic tactics. Yet there is no instance of God speaking or even the slightest hint of divine revelation in these stories. There is only divine silence.

In his final instructions on covenant, David draws special attention to the laws, regulations, statutes, and ordinances. These precepts came to be understood as regulating two spheres of relations: the people's relation to God ("You shall have no other gods before me") and their relation to one another ("You shall not murder . . . steal . . . commit adultery"). The two realms are integrally related. Love of neighbor is founded upon and tied to love of God. Hence, Israel's theocracy is meant to gradually yield a communitarian people rather than the hierarchy of monarchy. Within this holy assembly founded upon love and care of one another, distinctions between first and last, powerful and powerless, servant and master, are to fade gradually. The reminder and rehearsal of this divine-human pact juxtaposed alongside the dying monarch's instructions and son's egregious enactment and extension of these death sentences serves to judge what has been and what will be.

1 KINGS 3

The Deuteronomistic theology is at work in this story crafting a sorely needed model for kingship. With an excess of religious language nowhere else present in the account of the Solomonic era, chapter 3 sketches the portrait of the "ideal" king. Like the blueprint for a divinely appointed ruler outlined in Deut 17:14-20, the king is portrayed as the Lord's servant. Shades of the bloodthirsty despot of chapter 2 have all but faded. The Deuteronomistic model of a humble and worthy king has replaced the crude opportunist of the previous stories. In addition, the leitmotifs of wisdom, honor, and prosperity will serve as signals navigating the legitimation story of Solomon's kingship in the chapters that follow (1 Kgs 4–11). As such, they function not only as guides to telling the story of Solomon, but they also establish grounds for the assessment of this king in chapter 11.

Literary Analysis

The uncomplicated format of chapter 3 makes its intended program unmistakably clear. A three-part introduction (3:1-3) focuses upon Solomon, the people, and a theological assessment of the king. It serves as a foreword to both the two-part narrative that follows and to the account of Solomon's kingdom in subsequent chapters. After this introductory unit, a two-part structure frames the narrative account (3:4-15, 16-28). In the opening of part one (3:4-5), Solomon offers sacrifices at Gibeon and encounters God in a dream there. Then, at the conclusion of the tale, the king awakens from the dream, goes to Jerusalem, and offers sacrifice at the ark of the covenant (3:15). The description of the sacrificial offerings frames the dialogue between Solomon and God that unfolds across this single narrative scene. God asks what Solomon needs. Solomon answers with a lengthy speech and a request. Finally, God's response endows the king with gifts constituting the climax of the tale.

In part two (3:16-28), a trial concerning maternal rights over a child puts Solomon and his wisdom to the test. Two women come before the king and request his judgment in a conflict over the life of a child. After the women present their cases, the king issues an order. Based upon the women's responses, the monarch levels a judgment. The narrative concludes by reporting Israel's acknowledgment of God's wisdom in the king. Recognition of Solomon's wisdom ties this story to the preceding narrative of God's gift of wisdom. Whether this wisdom derives exclusively from the divine

gift or is tinged and thus compromised by David's earlier definition of wise action will be taken up in the following discussion.

Exegetical Analysis

Introduction (3:1-3)

Having narrated how Solomon came to the throne in chapters
1–2, the story now turns attention to Solomon's actual reign
(1 Kgs 3–11). Chapter 3 opens with a brief introductory summary.
Like an archival file in the royal store of records, verse 1 recounts
that Solomon made an alliance with the pharaoh of Egypt and
married his daughter. That she resides in the city of David is
explained with reference to the unfinished construction of
Solomon's own house as well as of the house of the Lord. In verse
2, the notation suggests this unfinished construction as the reason
why the people are still worshiping in the high places. The reason-
ing carries over into verse 3 and explains why even Solomon, the
king himself, is sacrificing and burning incense in the high places.
Inserted within this report disclosing an alliance, a marriage, and
building projects is a pronouncement of Solomon's love of the
Lord and Solomon's faithful following of David's statutes.

On the surface, the introduction offers a fairly neutral forecast
of Solomon's reign at home and abroad. He will be active on the
domestic front with building projects that will eventually serve the
people. He will be involved as an international figure making
agreements with foreign nations and marrying women from other
lands. However, when read in conjunction with the account that
follows, these opening verses suggest something more. Though
this brief introduction signals Solomon's accomplishments, it may
also alert us to his troubles.

The assertion that "Solomon loved the LORD" is preceded by a
description of the people worshiping in the high places, and followed by a report of Solomon also worshiping in the high places.
In Old Testament times, high places were often associated with
apostasy. That Solomon's love for the Lord is encircled by references to high places may forecast just how fragile his love will be.
Moreover, alliance with Egypt may signal his international

prowess, but it may also echo the warning against covenantal infidelity in Deut 28:68, where Egypt becomes a place of chastisement. Further, the account reports first that Solomon's house was unfinished. A similar report on the status of the temple project follows. The order of reporting on the status of these building projects may suggest where Solomon's priorities lie. Whether Solomon's love of the Lord signals a genuine kinship between God and the monarch characteristic of a theocracy or only a token piety founded upon religious formalism remains to be seen.

Behold, a Dream (3:4-15)

As the story opens, Solomon goes to Gibeon and encounters God in a dream. Gibeon was the principal high place, seven miles northwest of Jerusalem, where Solomon "used to offer a thousand burnt offerings" (v. 4). The narrative gives no clue whether this display of sacrificial excess was a gesture of religious fervor or a typical show of royal extravagance on the part of the king. Hence, that God comes to Solomon in a dream here does not necessarily result from the abundance or character of his sacrifices.

In the ancient Near Eastern world and throughout the Scriptures, dreams and visions were a common means by which deities communicated with people (Gen 17:1-12; 18:1-33; 26:2-5; Exod 3:2-12; Judg 13:3-17; Matt 2:19-20). Often persons seeking divine counsel would sleep at a shrine or sanctuary in order to be available for such communications. At the same time, Deut 13 warns those who love the Lord to be wary of diviners of dreams, as they can lead to the worship of other gods.

Significantly, God initiates the encounter: "Ask what I should give you" (v. 5b). The request, cloaked as a command, is remarkably simple, straightforward, and open. It is as if God takes no account of the Solomon we have been introduced to up to this point. What is more, God not only fails to recall the halfhearted, conflicted, and sinful Solomon who shed blood to assure his royal position; it seems that God also refuses to exercise omniscience regarding whether this same sinful man will change his ways.

Whereas that may surprise those of us who overhear this nocturnal encounter, there is also comfort. This is a God who seeks out Solomon in accordance with what the king needs rather than in light of what he deserves.

Solomon hastens to answer God's inquiry. As a prelude to setting forth his request, Solomon outlines the unfathomable difference between God and himself. First, he rehearses the unbridled love and generosity that the Lord has shown toward David and himself. With repetitive use of the emphatic pronoun "You," Solomon credits God with steadfast love of David, with the gift of a son for David, and with the bestowal of the kingship to Solomon (vv. 6-7). Solomon's unqualified view of his father's fidelity and steadfastness, though myopic, is likely because of a son's bias.

Next, Solomon outlines his own unworthiness before God. He describes himself as "only a little child" (v. 7). Undoubtedly, Solomon is not talking about being too young, as his son Rehoboam was born before he ascended the throne. Rather, such references to youth were characteristic expressions on the part of those called to tasks much grander than they are able to accomplish. For example, Jeremiah protests his call to prophecy with this same claim (Jer 1:6). Indeed, such claims were not only expressions of resistance but also expressions of humility in the face of enormous responsibility. The phrase "go out or come in" (v. 7) is a military idiom—Solomon's request for wisdom to lead his people well in battle.

With twofold purposefulness, Solomon raises his petitionary prayer and asks the Lord for "an understanding mind" (v. 9). The Hebrew underlying this phrase literally translates as "hearing heart." In this ancient milieu, the heart was the means of knowing and willing. Solomon needs "an understanding mind" in order to "govern this [God's] great people." In addition, he needs "an understanding mind" in order to enable him to discern "good and evil." In keeping with the model detailed in Deut 17:14-20, he refers to himself as "your servant" before the Lord (v. 7). He appears concerned with governing the people and ensuring their welfare.

A narrative statement introduces God's response by noting the Lord's disposition. "It pleased the Lord that Solomon had asked this" (v. 10). This is the first time God has communicated with

Solomon. Though we have heard both David and Solomon make claims about God's word, will, and promise, the divine reply here offers a firsthand glimpse of what God desires. In the opening of the reply, God cites gifts that Solomon refrained from asking for—long life, riches, and the death of his enemies. In the second half of the address, God favors Solomon by granting these very gifts and more. Juxtaposed between that which Solomon did not request and God's bestowal of these is the bestowal of the gift asked for. It is interesting to note that God revises Solomon's request. "But [you] have asked for yourself understanding to discern what is right . . ." (v. 11). As if to narrow the monarch's gaze, God edits Solomon's request ("an understanding mind . . . to discern between good and evil" [v. 9]) and fixes upon what is right. Then God grants Solomon a discerning mind to be riveted upon the good. In addition, we witness the nature of God by the divine bestowal of gifts in excess of Solomon's request. God not only provides him with a "discerning heart," God also offers wisdom. "I give you a *wise* and discerning mind" (v. 12).

The biblical tradition portrays wisdom as a kind of divine presence. A king guided by wisdom manifests the indwelling of the Lord among the people. This wisdom is not the product of practice or rigorous self-discipline, nor can it be inherited; wisdom can only be received. Hence, as a gift, wisdom's potential to manifest God's presence depends upon its reception. Solomon has been granted wisdom with which to rule God's people. His use or nonuse of the gift will have consequence for the entire nation.

Following this bestowal, God also grants Solomon that which he did not ask for, accoutrements befitting a king. First, Solomon hears that riches and honor are his. An elaboration of these follows. "No other king shall compare with you" (v. 13). The superlative adulation honors Solomon above all other rulers. In concert with this unsurpassed promise, God grants Solomon a long life. Here God replaces the third gift Solomon might have requested, ("life of your enemies" [v. 11]), with the bestowal of a long life for Solomon. The wisdom offered by God is not only accompanied by prosperity and honor, but is also life-giving. Such a paradigm for kingship stands in direct contrast to the "wise" actions David urged his son to take in chapter 2. Violence and the death of enemies is here replaced by honor and promise of long life.

However, the offer of long life is premised upon a big "if." God conditions the prospect of length of days for this king upon Solomon's fidelity. God's recall of the statutes and commandments in which David walked reminds us of the covenantal agreement. The covenant with David (2 Sam 7:4-17) was unconditional; the Davidic line would never end. However, David's recall of the covenantal promise to Solomon (1 Kgs 2:3-4) conditioned that promise of an heir upon attentiveness to all the statutes, laws, and ordinances, and to walking faithfully before God with all one's heart and soul. Now God ties the covenantal observances of statutes and laws with the promise of long life for but one heir. Whether this is another revision of the covenantal promise or a detailing of one aspect of the larger agreement remains a question. Throughout Kings, the notion of a conditional covenantal agreement will continue to stand in tension with the unconditional promise of an unending Davidic line. Both narrative and reader are invited to ponder whether this is a breach of contract. Though the dilemma may seem to warrant legal probing, the answer may lie in the realm of theological inquiry. Despite the attempts here of the Deuteronomist, as well as that of scholars down through the centuries, to pin down God, how God attends to covenantal agreement may continue to eclipse the confines of our logic and our imaginations.

The narrative brings the tale to a close with a report that Solomon awoke from what had been a dream. Immediately Solomon offers sacrifice. This time, however, he returns to Jerusalem and stands before the ark of the covenant of the Lord where he sacrifices the burnt offerings. Though the events of his reign recorded in the upcoming chapters will determine whether or not Solomon uses the gift of wisdom, his return to Jerusalem might be his first wise act. This move away from local shrines where apostasy is bred to the central sanctuary in Jerusalem where Yahweh dwells suggests a move in the right direction. Now wise counsel must make itself manifest in his governance, programs, and judgments for his people. Whether Solomon only dreamed of receiving wisdom or whether the dream was an actual bestowal of God's gift waiting to be received will make itself known in the course of his reign.

When Solomon was granted the gift of a wise, discerning heart, God also bestowed upon him an unparalleled outcome resulting from the use of the gift. In a stunning chiastic parallel, God envisions that "no one like you has been before you and no one like you shall arise after you" (v. 12). However, it is not enough to be given such a present. Gifts given must also be received and put to use. Hence, an unthinkable consequence may result if Solomon fails to use wisdom in his governing role. Indeed, there would be no king like Solomon before him and after him; no king like him would arise!

Two Women before the King (3:16-28)

Two models of kingship have emerged in chapters 1–3:15, each with separate endorsements. In chapters 1–2, and in the introduction to chapter 3 (vv. 1-3), ties to family and allies crafted kingship. Kingship founded upon David's advice for wise decisions was secured accordingly by executions and an exile. Whereas this paradigm of royal office stressed fidelity to covenant, it also employed tactics in governance diametrically opposed to the laws governing the covenantal relation. Public recognition served as the endorsement and legitimation of kingship according to this model. Images of an alliance with Egypt, foreign wives, worship at the high places, and building projects punctuated with a love of the Lord round out the template.

By contrast, chapter 3:4-15 sets forth a second alternative model of kingship according to which the office of ruler emerges as a divinely sanctioned appointment. Kingship is motivated by service to the people. The accoutrements of the royal office are not entitlements of the new monarch, but unrequested gifts from God. Emphasis on fidelity to the covenant is stressed in concert with the bestowal of a wise, discerning heart for governance. The welfare of the people is at the heart of the king. Covenantal loyalty is coupled with a moral concern for discerning right from wrong in matters of judgment. Instead of viewing kingship as a force for constraining others, the king himself is put under the Lord's constraints. His very life depends upon his attention to God and the covenantal agreement.

There is no doubt that wisdom functions as the defining epistemology during the reign of Solomon. However, whereas both these paradigms urge wise action, the objective and means differ markedly. What David counsels Solomon under the aegis of "acting wisely" stands over and against the fruit God intends from a wise and discerning heart. The king will continually have to negotiate and choose between two kinds of wisdom in the realization of his plans. The story that unfolds in verses 16-28 will illustrate just that.

As the story opens, a brief narrative introduction situates the "two women who were prostitutes" (v. 16) before the king. These social designations—prostitutes and king—highlight their differences as well as the social distance between them. The designation "prostitute," though not a social judgment here, signifies someone who lacks kinship and legal status in the community. Without male protection in a patriarchal society, prostitutes were like widows. With no legal statutes protecting them or their children, they were among society's most vulnerable members. That these women, the quintessential poorest of the poor, have the first documented audience before the king is noteworthy. The portrait of kingship as caught up with and adjudicating on behalf of the lowest of citizens here parallels God's overarching concern for justice and its administration for all as expressed in Deut 16:18-20.

The image of servant king is further enhanced by the introductory description of the women. The "two women who were prostitutes *came* to the king and *stood before* him" (v. 16) parallels the description of Solomon at the conclusion of the preceding story. "He *came* to Jerusalem where he *stood before* the ark of the covenant of the LORD" (v. 15). Despite the difference between women prostitutes and king, the parallel language lobbies in favor of kinship. Expectations are high that the women will be the recipients of a judgment according to the gift the king received from God.

With three alternating speeches, the two women set forth their dispute. First, one woman offers a lengthy description of both the context and the crisis (vv. 17-21). The women, who live together in a house, each gave birth three days apart. There were no witnesses to the events. While the first woman slept at night, the other woman lay upon her own child and then took this woman's baby and replaced it with the dead infant. This alleged tragedy and thievery in the dark of night gives way to the first woman's detection of death and deception in the light of day. She concludes, "When I looked at him closely in the morning, clearly it was not the son I had borne" (v. 21). Because she claims to recount events that occurred while she slept, her testimony warrants the king's cross-examination.

The other woman now speaks. Though she speaks like a defendant, she does not defend herself. In contrast to the first woman's lengthy presentation, this woman merely denies and reverses the charges. "No, the living son is mine, and the dead son is yours" (v. 22). Her unexplicated accusation incites the third and final speech of this episode. The first woman levels a countercharge that produces a forensic deadlock before the king. "No, the dead son is yours, and the living son is mine" (v. 22b). The woman's repetition of the key words *living* and *dead* captures the heart of the dispute. This struggle and the need for judgment are a matter of life and death.

Immediately, a brief speech by the king addresses the dispute. After all, the protection and adjudication on behalf of the widow and the poor were the hallmarks of a virtuous king. In Deut 10:18, the protection of the poor was the prerogative of Israel's God. Psalm 82 extols Yahweh as the only true judge and protector of the weak. As mediator of God's judgment, the ideal king in Israel would attend to the needs of the poor. However, though the king addresses the plight of the women, what he does could raise questions about his fitness for the job ahead.

First, the king acts as a supreme court addressing the unsolvable problem. But his startling injunction, that a sword be brought to him, generates confusion and unsettling ambiguity. The sword was a symbol and tool of violence and punishment in Israel. Ehud slew Eglon, the king of Moab, with a sword (Judg 3:12-23). Nathan prophesied that the sword would never depart from David's house as a result of his sin against Uriah (2 Sam 12:10). At the same time, the sword often symbolized authority to execute justice. In the song of Moses, Yahweh, the Divine Judge, is portrayed with a sword in hand (Deut 32:41-42). Similarly, the sword is associated with authority in judgment throughout the prophetic texts. Hence, Solomon's summons for a sword conjures up an ambiguous meaning. The image, which connotes authority to judge as well as potential to do violence, reminds us of the two paradigms of kingship weighing upon this king.

A report that the sword was brought before the king (v. 24) is followed by another order by the king. "Divide the living boy in two; then give half to the one and half to the other" (v. 25). His repetition in language—"half to the one"; "half to the other"— conveys a certain level of impartiality expected of a judicial officer.

What follows offers us a brief reprieve from the flood of direct speech that has carried the story thus far. We are told, "The woman whose son was alive [spoke] to the king—because compassion for her son burned within her" (v. 26). In Hebrew, *compassion* is the plural form of the root word for *womb*. In keeping with the maternal motif, the compassion welling up in the woman traces its stirrings to her womb. The rousing of these sentiments overrides her claim on a life and causes her to speak. She offers to relinquish the child. Hence she proposes a different sacrifice that contrasts with Solomon's proposed sacrifice of her child. She is willing to relinquish the child in order to save him. But before Solomon has occasion to respond, her compassionate, self-sacrificing offer incites a vindictive retort from the other woman. She, like the king, dispassionately calls for the child to be divided in two.

The contrasting responses of the women reveal their true social identities; one is fit for motherhood, and the other is not. It appears that Solomon's ruse to determine the real mother's identity worked. Although the king's scheme facilitates the judicial assessment, the women judge themselves. The true mother's response nullifies the king's order. The king seizes upon the evidence and quickly amends his order. Duplicating the words of the self-sacrificing woman, "Give [her] the living boy; do not kill him" (vv. 26b-27), the king issues a new decision. At this juncture in the story Solomon's decision is recognized as wise. The true mother's willingness to surrender her son prompts a public evaluation of Solomon's decision.

The story concludes with Israel's recognition of Solomon's wisdom. "All Israel heard of the judgment that the king had rendered; and they stood in awe of the king, because they perceived that the wisdom of God was in him, to execute justice" (v. 28). The progression of speech in this story makes Israel's perception of God's wisdom in the king contingent upon the compassion and action of one of the king's subjects. The community's recognition of the king's wise decision grows out of the woman's bold decision here. Indeed, the outcome yields a just and wise settlement. But when the narrative reports on Israel's response to the king's deeds and decisions, it clouds with ambiguity the window through which we glimpse their response. "And they stood in awe of the king" (v. 28). The Hebrew verb enlisted here is *yare,* which means literally "to be afraid." It is used in some places to connote awe and respect, as well as to narrate fear and trembling. Hence the story closes somewhat inconclusively as far as Israel is concerned. We must decide whether this first appropriation of Solomon's gift conjures awe or evokes fear on the part of those he would govern in the years to come.

Theological and Ethical Analysis

Given its location on the heels of the dream at Gibeon, it is easy to read this tale of the two mothers before Solomon as proof of his reception of God's gift. The paradigm of kingship that was sketched in 3:4-15, as bent upon the welfare of the people, appears to reign over this story. The two women not only have access to the king, but as representatives of the least in a society, their audience with him suggests just how available this new king is. He who will later oversee massive building projects, conduct international trade, and even play host to the queen of Sheba, is also available for service to the poorest of the poor among his people. The meeting between sovereign lord and his nameless subjects conjures images of a king who is truly servant. Moreover, the priority and preponderance of speech afforded the women in this encounter suggests a king who attentively listens to the concerns of his people.

It is only when the king issues his order that fateful echoes of the other paradigm of kingship sketched in chapters 1–3:3 reverberate. To be sure, traditional interpretation unquestionably assumes that Solomon had no intention of carrying out the order to slice the child in half. But the death-defying order, though only a trick, confounds and ruptures the continuity with the preceding image of the king at Gibeon who is a servant of the Lord. Even as a staged strategy, the order for death over a matter concerning life is all too reminiscent of David's deathbed counsel and Solomon's subsequent massacring maneuvers in the preceding chapter.

Some would argue that the end justifies the means here. After all, Solomon's order for death was never carried out and it did result in a just resolution. The real mother was identified. Still, we must ponder whether any proposal to do violence is defensible even if it can harvest some good. Solomon's judicial strategy constitutes a dangerous move on behalf of justice. At best, it manifests itself as a cruel trick that blackmails motherhood. At worst, it appears to gamble human life and put God's wisdom on trial.

With our purview of history we may be more reticent than "all Israel" to unresistantly claim that "wisdom" has prevailed here. Are threats to do horrific violence justifiable even if they end up producing acceptable results? Hindsight has shown us how embargoes aimed at curtailing human rights violations often cultivate more suffering and further enmity. Wars fought for the sake of a just peace have too often been at the expense of massive human suffering and loss of innocent lives. Winnowing of justice through the exercise of wisdom is a complex, long-term, and human-centered enterprise. It is not set on rapid-fire results and does not often attract quick public recognition or assent. Seasoned by the lessons of history, we are left with haunting questions as this story closes. Was it Solomon's wisdom to divide the child in two that enabled the recognition of one woman as the mother, thus prompting Israel's awe and respect? Or was it a compassionate mother's unthinkable surrender of her own child that made Solomon's decision appear wise and thus evoke Israel's fear and trembling?

1 KINGS 4

In step with the spirit of the previous tale, chapter 4 illustrates that God has bestowed upon Solomon the gifts promised at Gibeon. Though we have heard little about his tenure as a ruler or as an international force, chapter 4 reports that the divine promise of prosperity and world fame has been fulfilled. It even reports that God continued to grant Solomon "very great wisdom, discernment, and breadth of understanding" (v. 29), and that Solomon "was wiser than anyone else" (v. 31). All that God promised Solomon in the dream epiphany at Gibeon has been realized. Whether Solomon has made good use of these divine outpourings remains to be seen.

Literary Analysis

Whereas chapter 3:16-28 sketched a king with an opportunity to use wisdom in judgment, chapter 4 offers a glimpse of Solomon with the potential to administrate wisely. However, the form of what follows contrasts sharply with the suspenseful plotline of the story of the two mothers before a king. In the absence of all drama, chapter 4 reports with lists, names, and numbers the status of Solomon as administrator of Israel and as sovereign throughout the world. As if drawn from official archives, the rolls and tallies give the impression of a well-documented, long-established, and successful administration.

Both the process of transmission as well as the various sources that have been employed to craft this account of rosters and records contributes to a series of textual and historical problems. First, the traditional chapter and verse numbering in English translations does not correspond with those in the Hebrew text. Here we will follow the NRSV. Second, believing that the text digresses from its earliest format, some translators rearrange some of the verses to correspond with what they think is the "original" order of this material. Again, we will continue to read with the NRSV. Indeed, there are signs of a text that has been disrupted over the years. There are gaps and incongruities in the naming of Solomon's officials in verses 8-19. In some cases, only the father's name of one of the king's appointees appears, and in other instances, the name is missing altogether. Despite these difficulties, a discernible format structures the material across this chapter. Many have noted that the report on internal administrative matters (vv. 1-20) and the report on external international involvements (vv. 21-25) divide the bulk of the chapter into two main blocks. Each part is introduced with a statement about Solomon as king (vv. 1, 21), and concludes with a summary about how Israel and Judah are faring under his reign (vv. 20, 25). Having twice reported on the well-being of the people, verses 26-28 offer a brief addendum about horses and chariots as further signs of the abiding prosperity in his kingdom. Finally, the concluding verses celebrate Solomon's renown (vv. 29-34). The portrait of the king here is utterly positive. Both Israel and Judah, as well as the whole world, benefit from his giftedness.

Exegetical Analysis

Internal Administrative Matters (4:1-20)

Under Solomon, the people of Israel have become a nation-state. An introductory statement (v. 1) stressing the scope of Solomon's kingship "over all Israel" warrants the subsequent description of an elaborate government to tend to the whole people. Across two collections of tallies and records that follow, the narrative creates an impression of a well-organized, complex governing structure. In part one of the description, a list enumerates the offices of central government and the officeholders (vv. 2-6). Following, a second list records the districts into which Solomon has divided the kingdom, with the names of the officers appointed over each district listed (vv. 7-19). This report on the internal organization of government concludes with an assessment of how Judah and Israel are faring as a result. They are prospering.

In the list enumerating the government offices, we hear the names of those making up the Solomonic cabinet (vv. 1-6). Azariah, son of Zadok, serves in a highly influential capacity as chief priest (v. 2). Benaiah continues in his appointment as commanding officer of the army (v. 4). The two sons of Nathan, Azariah and Zabud, are in charge of the district officers who watch over the provisioning and act as the personal advisor to the king, respectively (v. 5). Jehoshaphat, whom we know from King David's reign (2 Sam 8:16), serves as recorder (v. 3). Surprisingly, Abiathar is also named here (v. 4). Whether this record stems from an earlier text or the priest was actually brought back from exile is unknown. It may be that the record includes Abiathar here so that history would give the impression that the wrong done to him has been corrected. Inclusion of his name along with these other familiar names also suggests continuity with the past, particularly with David's reign.

In addition to David's appointees, new names number among the list. Elihoreph and Ahijah (v. 3) are secretaries to the new administration, along with Ahishar (v. 6) who has charge of the palace. These signify that Solomon's government, though a continuation of David's empire, will include new faces as it charts its own course and direction. Finally, the list concludes with the name of Adoniram (v. 6). His charge, the administration of forced labor, ends this litany on an ambivalent note. Although the name is new, the practice is not. In this instance, a break with policies of David that also employed forced labor (2 Sam 20:24), would have been a wise judgment. Its continuation under Solomon will ultimately indict his reign (1 Kgs 12:18).

The second list (vv. 7-19) describes the divisions of Solomon's kingdom. Each of the twelve districts (v. 7) is responsible for supplying provisions one month of the year for the king and his household. The appointment of twelve officials over all Israel (v. 7) anticipates continuity with the twelve tribal divisions recorded in Josh 13–22. However, many of the districts include names that are unfamiliar and do not conform to the former tribal designations or locations. Whereas five tribes identified in verses 7-19 do resonate with the past, the overall impression is that a new order has begun.

Even the division into twelve districts is no longer tied to the number of tribes of earlier traditions. The twelve districts are all in northern territory. Mention of Judah in verse 19 in the conclusion of the listing would make the count thirteen. Since each region was to provide for the king and his household one month of the year, twelve districts would ensure royal provisions for one full annual cycle. Though the rationale behind the divisions is unclear, the seasons and the available crops may have been the determining factors.

That Judah resides outside the list of provisioning regions as in the previous record (vv. 2-6) ends this tally on a dubious note. Indeed, there is no mention of Judah being districted, nor is there any indication that Judah was subject to the obligation of providing provisions for the royal court. Were the prospects of peace and well-being a more costly commodity for the people of the north than they were for the inhabitants of the south? Would the continuation of the forced labor policy (v. 6) for those who could not fulfill their taxation requirement be more of a threat to the inhabitants of Israel than to the people of Judah? When verse 20 summarizes that Solomon's administration brought about a positive outcome for both Israel and Judah, we can only wonder if he did so equitably.

International Influence (4:21-25)

In the second block of material (vv. 21-28), attention turns to records and reports that register Solomon's international influence. The narrative account sketches the extent of his kingdom, his impact upon the world, the daily provisions required to support such an establishment, and the consequent domestic tranquility for his people.

The expanse of Solomon's kingdom mirrored and even exceeded that of his father David. The report claims that his realm extended from the Euphrates River in the east to Philistia in the west. More specifically, verse 24 demarcates Tiphsah, which is east of Aleppo in Assyria, as the eastern limit. Gaza, which is the southernmost part of the western Mediterranean border in Philistia, marks the western extreme. In addition, the narrative paints the impression that Solomon not only ruled a vast dominion, but that he actually ruled over and received tribute from all the kingdoms surrounding Judah and Israel. Whereas the historical accuracy of these descriptions is quite likely exaggerated, the report succeeds in testifying that God fulfilled the divine promise made at Gibeon. Solomon is honored, and greatest among kings.

The grand size of the empire warrants a sizable ruling body. The litany of daily provisions (vv. 22-23) testifies to the needs of an expansive royal class. The description indicates that fine meats and dry goods were in plentiful supply. This grocery list of daily provisions (vv. 22-23) regularly provided by the twelve districts, suggests Solomon's family and the associated royal class were well cared for.

Such a taxation policy was not without its rewards, even for the people of the north. According to this idealized report, the inhabitants of the land lived in peace and security. "Judah and Israel lived in safety . . . all of them under their vines and fig trees" (v. 25). Living on the land safely accompanied with the implied plentiful harvest echoes the promises made to the ancestors (Gen 22:17-18; Lev 26:3; Deut 12:10). The intended image here is that the land was indeed "flowing with milk and honey" and the people were "safe from their enemies." Subtly, the narrative joins Solomon's story with the rich history of sacred traditions. God's promises both to Solomon and to the ancestors were being fulfilled.

Horses and Chariots (4:26-28)

In verses 26-28, we hear that Solomon has acquired an immense number of horses for his chariots. Though brief, this addendum contains two textual problems in verse 26 that must be addressed. The NRSV mistakenly translates that Solomon had twelve thousand "horsemen." The Hebrew reads twelve thousand "horses." Also, a scribe may have erred when entering "forty thousand stalls." More likely, it was to read "four thousand" stalls, which is consistent with the chronicler's account in 2 Chr 9:25. The information about the vast numbers of horses in the king's militia, as well as the food, stalls, and provisions made available for them, seems at first glance to contribute to the idealized portrait of the comprehensive well-being in the Solomonic era. This king's bounty extends even to the animals. However, here we read again a reference to the officers, those in charge of the twelve districts, who took turns providing for both Solomon and for "all who came to King Solomon's table." In addition to supplying provisions for these royal persons, the officers also must provide quotas of barley and straw for the king's animals.

This twofold responsibility doubles the burden on the people. The excess of daily provision—thirty cors of choice flour (approximately 187 bushels); sixty cors of meal (approximately 375 bushels); ten fat oxen; twenty pasture-fed cattle; and one hundred sheep, deer, gazelles, roebucks, and fatted fowl (vv. 22-23)—for the king and his house's upkeep was extreme. The additional requirement of food for twelve thousand horses places a preposterous burden upon each district. If the price tag for peace and prosperity continues to rise, so also could negative sentiments toward Solomon and his reign. The problem is aggravated when 1 Kings is read in light of Deut 17:16, which strictly forbids the king from accumulating "many horses for himself." In addition, it mandates against sending men to Egypt to acquire more horses, something Solomon will order in due time (1 Kgs 10:26-28). Hence, the appearances of peace and prosperity here may well portend peril in the future.

Solomon's Reputed Fame (4:29-31)

Like the preceding verses, the conclusion to chapter 4 is devoid of story. With a two-part summary, it makes claims about Solomon's wisdom (vv. 29-31) and offers evidence of that gift (vv. 32-34). At the end of each section, Solomon's international renown is rehearsed. In drumroll fashion, with an excess of exaltation and superlatives, this conclusion makes clear that all the preceding evidence of Solomon's administrative success and fame at home and abroad stems from his acquisition of wisdom.

In the first part (vv. 29-31), an exhaustive exposition details the claims about this wisdom. This wisdom includes excesses in both understanding and breadth of knowledge. Its scope matches the scope of Israel's population, as both are said to number the sands on the seashore. It credits Solomon with a wisdom that surpasses those most noted for this quality in the ancient Near Eastern world. His wisdom exceeds that of the people of the East in general and of Egypt in particular. More specifically, it outshines even certain individuals that the biblical tradition (1 Chr 2:6; 6:33) named for their wisdom. Hence, that this first part ends with the claim that Solomon's fame spread throughout all the surrounding nations is no surprise.

In the second part of this grand summation, we are offered evidence of Solomon's wisdom beyond that which we have encountered thus far in the archival lists and tallies. Besides his wise administrative capacities and decisions, Solomon manifests a breadth of knowledge that includes recitation of proverbs and songs. Moreover, this knowledge of plants, great and small, as well as of animals, birds, reptiles, and fish further demonstrates this brilliance. From knowledge for ordering and running of a nation to information about the least of its creatures, Solomon's wisdom exceeds all limits. Like the preceding section, the final catalogue of evidence leads to international recognition of Solomon. This time, international figures actually seek him out and visit him. The closing verse not only makes clear the reason for these records and lists of accomplishments but also serves as a segue to chapter 5, which opens with King Hiram of Tyre sending his representatives to Solomon.

Theological and Ethical Analysis

At first glance, the records and lists, coupled with the grand summation, would have us believe that Solomon is both a wise and successful administrator. His reign as king over "all Israel" has brought peace and well-being to the people. His stature among the nations has brought him international fame and renown.

Though we are offered a glimpse of a well-supplied and well-secured empire, and of a king with international status, we have no account of what Solomon himself did to accomplish all this. The lists of his high officials (vv. 2-6), of the twelve districts and their officials (vv. 7-20), and of the boundaries of his kingdom, along with the provisions needed to support it (vv. 21-28), offer no clear indication of the king's actions. In all of these records, Solomon is either subject of a passive verb (vv. 1, 21) or portrayed according to what he "has" or what others have done for him (vv. 7, 22, 26, 27). Hence, these records on the internal political well-being of the nation and international fame of the king are less expressions about "Solomon and all his wisdom," as tradition would have it, than a witness that promises made by God to Solomon have been fulfilled. At Gibeon, God promised honor and riches, a discerning mind to govern the people, international acclaim among sovereigns of the earth, and most of all, wisdom (1 Kgs 3:10-13). In this chapter, the records suggest that the divine promises of honor, riches, discernment, and international acclaim have been fulfilled. In addition, the opening verse of the grand summation (vv. 29-34) explicitly states that God has made good on the promises made at Gibeon. "God gave Solomon very great wisdom, discernment, and breadth of understanding as vast as the sand on the seashore" (v. 29).

But Solomon's dream at Gibeon was not only an epiphany punctuated with divine promises; a warrant was placed upon the new king and his rule. He was required to walk in God's ways, to observe divine statutes, and to attend to the covenantal laws (1 Kgs 3:14). At the time, Solomon indicated that attention to governing all the people was of far greater concern than his own glory and honor. Further, in the final format of the canon, Deut 17:14-20 stands as a measuring rod for assessing the faithfulness of a servant king. The well-being of all the people, a tenure of a just administration, and a fidelity to covenant must cloak the honorable king's rule.

Though the reports and lists of chapter 4 give evidence that God has kept the promises made to Solomon, these records do raise questions about where Solomon's own fidelities lie. Although they give no indication of his deeds, they carry evidence of his policies. That he continued the policy of enforced labor instituted under David raises concerns about his commitment to rule the people wisely. That he appears to have favored the inhabitants of Judah, even perhaps exempting them from the provisioning requirement, casts suspicion about his concern for the well-being of all the people. That he acquired an extensive number of horses and chariots creates narrative tension between the portrait of this king and the law in Deuteronomy. Though God has bestowed upon Solomon an abundance of the promised blessings and bequeathed the gift of wisdom, Solomon seems to have discounted the demands of covenantal fidelity and the obligation to rule justly placed upon him at Gibeon. Perhaps, in his mind, it *was* only a dream.

1 KINGS 5

Solomon has an ambition. He is determined to build a temple in Jerusalem, a dream that David had but was never able to fulfill (2 Sam 7). Capitalizing upon the good relations with Hiram of Phoenicia fostered by his father, Solomon successfully negotiates a deal with this king that secures building materials for the project. However, Solomon must have laborers to carry out the plan, and he cannot secure them from Phoenicia. The realization of Solomon's dream rests upon the conscription of workers from his own people. Hence, the weight of the king's ambitions will be borne upon the backs of his own subjects.

Literary Analysis

In contrast to the archival reporting of chapter 4, a brief story about diplomatic negotiations crafts the first twelve verses of chapter 5. The impersonal reporting of the royal administrative files is replaced by an abundance of first-person speech in the form of messages. These exchanges divide the tale into three parts. First Hiram, king of Tyre, sends his servants to Solomon (v. 1). This opening gesture serves as a transition both illustrating how "all the kings of the earth" regarded Solomon (4:34), and providing warrant for the story that follows. Next, Solomon responds to the Phoenician monarch with a proposal and a contract (vv. 2-6). An abundance of theological language scripts the political deal. Third, Hiram responds enthusiastically (v. 7). He revises the proposal and edits the contractual details (vv. 8-9). A narrative summary (vv. 10-12) reports confirmation of the agreement, as well as peace and a treaty between the kings of Israel and Tyre. The summary also makes clear once again that God is abundantly bestowing the gifts promised to Solomon at Gibeon—wisdom, peace, and honor among kings.

In the later portion of this chapter (vv. 13-18), the narrative resumes its earlier formal archival reporting. An agreement with Hiram is in place. Having secured materials for his project, Solomon now needs workers before temple construction can begin. Verses 13-18 detail the conscription process. Like the lists and records of chapter 4, an administrative miscellany (vv. 13-18) tallies the work groups, sets forth job descriptions, specifies numbers, indicates tenure of employment, and overviews the organization of the laborers.

Exegetical Analysis

Three Exchanges between Solomon and Hiram (5:1-9)

When the narrative opens, we are first told that King Hiram sends ambassadors to Israel's newly anointed monarch, King Solomon. Hiram is king of Tyre, a chief city of Lebanon situated on the Mediterranean coast. It was famous for its "cedars of Lebanon." Historical records of this period often refer to the "cedars of Lebanon" specifically in regard to their use in important building projects. Though Hiram's gesture follows naturally on the heels of the report of Solomon's international renown, it may not have been prompted solely by Solomon's reputation. The good diplomatic relations that this king had with David in earlier tales echo here. In one story, this friendship produced a house of cedar and stone for David and his family (2 Sam 5:11). The continuation of amicable diplomatic ties with David's heir crafts the impression of potential commercial benefits for Hiram.

Solomon, in turn, seizes the opportunity to do business with Hiram. He sends a message that capitalizes upon Hiram's initial diplomatic overture (vv. 2-6). However, unlike Hiram's gesture, Solomon's message is not just an act of cordial diplomacy. An ambitious building project prompts the accompanying business proposal backed by theological claims. Playing upon the good relations between his father and Hiram, Solomon recalls that David, consumed by warfare, was not able to build a temple for the Lord. Eventually, the Lord put his enemies "under the soles of his feet" (v. 3).

Whether to suggest continuity between David and himself or to highlight God's special favor of him, Solomon describes the current state of national well-being as the Lord's doing. He reports that now the Lord has provided him rest and freedom from misfortune and adversary. It is an ideal time to undertake this national venture. Again capitalizing on the positive relations of the past, Solomon asserts that undertaking this construction with Hiram's assistance would fulfill God's word to David.

With a prelude that suggests that Hiram would be participating in God's work, Solomon then submits his order for materials. He requests that Hiram supply cedars for the building project. In exchange, Solomon offers that his servants join Hiram's workers. He also promises to pay whatever wages the king of Tyre determines. Solomon concludes his message with praise for the Sidonians and thus, indirectly, for Hiram.

Hiram responds with his own expression of praise both for the Lord and for Solomon in all his wisdom. The expressions of mutual admiration probably reveal more about diplomatic courtesies or the posturing of potential business partners rather than any personal feelings between kings. In general, Hiram agrees to the proposal, although, in detail, he levels a counterproposal that bespeaks of his business savvy. He will provide trees, both cedar and cypress. Solomon will provide food, both wheat and oil. Hiram's men will cut the trees and transport them by sea to the place Solomon indicates. Solomon's workers will transport them by land to the place they will be used. The language of mutuality and equity characterize Hiram's proposal. As Hiram meets Solomon's need, Solomon will satisfy Hiram's needs.

A Deal Confirmed (5:10-12)

Amid all these business machinations, it is easy to lose sight of the narrative's overarching attestation. As Solomon enters into his first international treaty, the narrative reminds us again of the divine presence amid the plan. "The LORD gave Solomon wisdom, as promised him" (v. 12). Once again the Lord is making good on the promises made at Gibeon. However, the verdict is still out as to whether Solomon will actually make use of this gift.

It is important to note that the cost for the lumber, which Solomon agreed to, is high. Although the measurement of a cor remains uncertain, it may be as much as six and a half bushels. At twenty thousand cors, Solomon is obliging Israel to provide approximately one hundred thirty thousand bushels of wheat, along with about twenty cors of fine olive oil. Moreover, this was not just a one-time payment. The account relates, "Solomon gave this to Hiram year by year" (v. 11). We do not know how many years this contract continued, but we are certain of the burden this placed upon Israel. Such a commitment of resources and persons warranted a national commitment as well as an international treaty. The narrative summary of this deal documents only the international treaty and the continued peace between the two kings. The commitment of Israel to the plan along with "continued peace" between Solomon and his own people remains in question. Whether the people of Israel deemed the price of this peaceful agreement between kings too costly will be revealed in the upcoming chapters.

The Conscription of Laborers (5:13-18)

The sealed deal for building materials between kings has consequences for the citizens of Israel and Judah. Solomon now needs workers in order for the construction of the temple to begin. Indeed, building this architectural edifice requires two groups of workers. The first company, made up of thirty thousand workers, will join Hiram's men in Lebanon cutting and transporting the timber. Working in shifts, they will labor one month in Lebanon, and two months at home. The narrative does not specify travel time, but it is a safe guess that these individuals spent an additional month traveling to and from their workplaces. Because the text describes them as "the levy," a Hebrew word used in verse 13, referring to Canaanite laborers, we are uncertain whether this group included only Canaanites. Conscription into forced labor of those Canaanites still living in Israel is not out of the question. In the past, Israel had imposed such burdens upon the Canaanites remaining in the land (Josh 16:10; 17:13; Judg 1:28, 30, 33, 35). Whether this group involved only the Canaanites or actually refers to the people of Israel, it is a demanding imposition, costing these persons as much as four months of their year.

The second conscripted group enlists one hundred fifty thousand Israelites. Some eighty thousand of them would cut the stone. The other seventy thousand would transport the gigantic boulders to Jerusalem for the temple's foundation. The painstaking labor involved quarrying, dressing, and moving the costly limestone. Although nothing remains of Solomon's temple today, the great foundation rocks still in place from Herod's reconstruction give us some idea of the size of the stone required. Each of the great colossal boulders, carefully hewn and squared, weighs several tons.

Finally, the summary (v. 18) identifies not only laborers drawn from the people of Israel and from Hiram's company for the designated tasks; a third group, the Gebalites, skilled craft-workers, are also employed. The Gebalites reside on the coast north of Tyre, independent of Hiram's domain. Hence, we may assume that employment of these outside artisans had its own costly price tag beyond what Solomon had already agreed to pay Hiram.

Theological and Ethical Analysis

Solomon's grand plan to build a house for the name of the Lord appears to be in concert with God's plan. The king authorizes his request to Hiram by recalling God's word to David, "Your son, whom I will set on your throne in your place, shall build the house for my name" (v. 5). However, the plan envisioned in the story depends upon the conscription of forced labor. If, indeed, some of the enlisted laborers are Canaanites, then forced labor is likely to become slave labor. In that the liberation from the bondage of the

Egyptians is the centerpiece of Israel's story of salvation, the enslavement of another people is very problematic. Even if the labor forces involve only Israelites, problems are likely. The prospects of abuse, injury, inequities, and injustices are as numerous as Solomon's enlisted forces. For example, does the policy impose itself upon all Israelites, those from both Israel and Judah? Are some families exempt from service? On what basis are 3,300 supervisors chosen (v. 15)? Who is responsible for the family left behind if someone is injured or killed? The introduction of the policy of "forced labor" is extremely problematic and invites a whole host of problems for this king.

Moreover, we do not know on what terms Solomon conscripted these two groups. We know that Solomon offered to pay Hiram's workers whatever wages he set (v. 6). We are also told that Solomon agreed to supply Hiram an exorbitant amount of wheat and oil in exchange for materials and workers. It is likely he paid the Gebalites for their artistic work in wood and stone. However, we have no indication of what Solomon will pay his own two groups of workers, or even *if* they will be paid. Was this work viewed as civic duty? Or was it construed as religious privilege? Even if a spirit of volunteerism animated the forced-labor groups in the name of religious service, such impositions upon people's lives can become liabilities.

Throughout chapters 4 and 5, we are reminded how God provided rest, peace, wisdom, and honor to Solomon—all that was promised him at Gibeon. Solomon, for his part, asked for "an understanding mind" so as to be able to govern the people and discern right from wrong. The narrative assures that God has supplied all that was requested and more; and though that same narrative does not explicitly state whether Solomon used these gifts, it does give evidence that the king seems to have risked compromising the livelihood, well-being, and sustenance of the people.

1 KINGS 6 AND 7

The account of the construction and dedication of the temple in Jerusalem (6–9:10) comprises the centerpiece of the Solomonic tradition (1–11) and constitutes the hallmark of the Solomonic era. Chapters 6 and 7, the report of the construction, compose the first part of that account. Having secured the supplies and laborers for his ambitious project, Solomon now turns to the actual building, decorating, and furnishing of the temple. In addition, an even more extensive project undertaken by this king, namely, the construction of the palace complex, is also reported here.

Although no traces of Solomon's temple exist today, the report in chapters 6 and 7's inventory provides enough details about architectural features, measurements, and materials to have captured the imaginations of artists for centuries and encouraged various rough sketches of the achievement. Though the description of the project resists attempts to map with accuracy the design here, the account of the size and scope of the project are themselves intended to elicit a response. At first glance, they conjure awe at Solomon's building feat and win high praise for the king. Indeed, it is difficult to deny that the memory of Solomon's splendor as a builder must have instigated this report. However, a closer study of the reported details may disclose something more. Whereas the temple appears to be built in the name of the Lord and subsequently dedicated (8–9:10) in praise of Israel's God, Solomon is the one who is most often named here and ultimately the center of praise.

Literary Analysis

Though chapters 6 and 7 set forth an account reporting the construction of Solomon's temple, any expectation of a carefully organized, detailed record befitting such a grand accomplishment is quickly frustrated. The inventory-like description is fraught with problems. We find variant sequencing of materials used in the construction, duplications of decorative details, elusive architectural terms, and shifts in the ordering of descriptions and construction procedures. Whereas these and other textual problems plague attempts to grasp accurately the nature of the temple, they likely attest to a long and perhaps circuitous history in the development and composition of this tradition.

An introduction (6:1) announcing the beginning of the construction and a conclusion (7:51) heralding its completion frame and contain the untidiness within. Although an orderly blueprint of this building project eludes us, the account orders itself into three major sections (6:1-38; 7:1-12; and 7:13-51). Each section is demarcated by its own introduction—6:1, 7:1, and 7:13—with the introduction in 6:1 performing double duty for both the narrative as a whole and the report of the first section (6:1-38).

The first part (6:1-38) narrates the building of the temple structure. A description of the work on the exterior and interior of the holy edifice divides the report into two parts. The first section (1-10) provides a somewhat disorderly glimpse of the framework and design of the exterior construction. In verses 11-13, a divine revelation to Solomon intervenes and disrupts the exposition of the building blueprint. This brief interruption concludes as quickly as it begins. The second half of the report (14-38) turns to the interior of the building and offers details on its partitioning and composition.

Part two (7:1-12) is somewhat of a surprise. It abandons the recording of the temple construction and instead turns attention to the building of Solomon's palace complex. It focuses upon the external design and the building materials used. Momentarily shifting attention away from the project being built in the name of the Lord, it extends Solomon's splendor and finesse as a builder beyond the temple precincts.

The third and final part (7:13-51) of the account returns to the temple project and concentrates upon the interior finishings and furnishings of this holy place. The completion of the temple requires some interior decorating. The passage records the design and crafting of cultic objects, temple furnishings, decoration, and implements. The pool of precious and extravagant materials used in the construction thus far—stone, wood, and gold—is now extended to include bronze. Hiram of Tyre, whose skill working with bronze complements the work of Solomon's goldsmiths, crafts the last of the recorded accoutrements needed to ready the temple for completion.

In place of plot, character development, or narrative tension that would make for a good story across these chapters, the building of the temple is recounted in impartial reportlike fashion. This kind of writing is not unique to the Hebrew tradition; it has many parallels in other ancient Near Eastern inscriptions, which like the account in chapters 6 and 7 memorialize sovereigns and their tangible accomplishments by describing building activities, dedication festivals, and the precious materials used by skilled artisans in the work. In keeping with this type of writing that assigns ultimate credit to the king, Solomon is the active subject of many phases of the construction process. Though he enlisted the requisite laborers and skilled artisans, the account records that "Solomon built," "Solomon made," "Solomon carved," and "Solomon overlaid." Such reportorial rhetoric serves not so much as testimony to what Solomon actually did, but as the characteristic means by which credit for the overall accomplishment of this grand project is assigned to the king. Hence, the description of Solomon's building project cannot be marshaled as hard evidence that Solomon was a great builder or was even a wise man. At best, it serves as example of how the biblical tradition was influenced by the ancient Near Eastern ideology that credits the king for his building accomplishments and so contributes to Solomon's legacy.

Exegetical Analysis

The Exterior Temple Structure (6:1-10)

In the opening verse of this construction-site report, we are told that Solomon's project commences "in the four hundred eightieth year after the Israelites came out of the land of Egypt, in the fourth year of Solomon's reign over Israel, in the month of Ziv" (v. 1). The precise dates, "four hundred eighty years since [the Exodus]" and "in the month of Ziv," the old Canaanite name for the second month of the year (April-May), creates an impression of factual concreteness for what follows. Tying Solomon's temple to the Exodus event also conveys the theological import lodged in this account. Indeed, citing the Exodus in the opening description establishes continuity and relationship between past sacral events and the present undertaking. During forty years of wilderness, wandering on the heels of the Exodus, Israel had to make do with a portable shrine for the worship of Yahweh (Exod 25). Now after

480 years, or twelve times forty years, Moses' ideal for worship is coming to fruition in Solomon's temple. At the same time, the Exodus meant liberation from the bondage of slavery for the people. But completion of Solomon's temple project is already requiring the conscription of Israel's own people into months of annual labor to the king. Hence, a theological question looms large over this construction report. Will Solomon's temple be the culmination of Israel's salvific story of liberation from bondage up to this point? Or will the imposition of forced slavelike labor herald the beginning of the reversal of salvation history?

The description that follows immediately sketches a portrait of the building's exterior. It is made primarily of stone with some cedarwood appointments. Ninety feet long and thirty feet wide, three chambers divide its rectangular space. The vestibule, a porchlike entry in front of the building proper, measures twenty feet long. Two adjoining rooms divide the interior of the building into the nave and the inner sanctuary. Two staircases join the three levels of its forty-five feet of height. Windows with recessed frames are incorporated. Like the windows of the Phoenecian temples whose design was likely influential, these windows are probably cut in at the very top of the walls. Here they function not so much to let light in but to let the smoke from the sacrifices out and thus provide ventilation. An undefined structure surrounds the three sides of the building that probably serves as a support to the outer walls.

The description of the construction of the building's stone exterior is followed and completed by some final woodworking in cedar (v. 10). The supporting structure is connected to the temple proper with cedar planks, and the building is roofed "with beams and planks of cedar" (v. 9). Over time, these wooden appointments would weather, change color, and thus blend with the gray hues of the stark stone facade.

Though it is impossible to be definitive about the architectural character of Solomon's temple, the tripartite design and division of the space is typical of some of the Canaanite temples that have been excavated in this region. However, unlike these temples, the house Solomon built in the name of the Lord was not located in the middle of his capital city. Rather it stood on a slab of rock near the outer edge of Jerusalem, a site that today is regarded as holy by Moslems and known as the Dome of the Rock.

Only once during this rather unembellished, straightforward description are we distracted by a parenthetical aside. In verse 7, we are told that the stone used to build the temple is hewn or dressed at the quarry. The reason given, "so that neither hammer nor ax nor any tool of iron was heard in the temple while it was being built," conveys the impression that Solomon and his workers are paying attention to Deut 27:5-6. This tradition bans the use of iron tools, perhaps, as a taboo against the use of imports from foreign countries in the house of Israel's God. However, it is also possible that as the traditions in Josh and Exod suggest (Josh 8:31; Exod 20:25), the prohibition against dressing the stone blocks on site may have simply been out of respect for the sacredness of this place and space. Hence, even in the midst of a rather informational report, we hear concern for attention to statutes and observances associated with the covenant.

Divine Revelation to Solomon (6:11-13)

Although somewhat out of sync with the surrounding report of activities at the construction site, the attention to an observance associated with the covenant in verse 7 does not stand alone. At the conclusion of the report on the exterior of the temple (v. 9), and just before the tour of the building's interior (vv. 14-38), another such disruption in the account occurs. However, unlike the brief detour in verse 7, the narrative in verses 11-13 appears completely disconnected from the surrounding material. The genre is that of a revelation. The formulaic introduction, "Now the word of the Lord came to Solomon . . . " alerts us to the shift. Reports of construction progress cease, and instead God is going to speak directly to Solomon. The opening of the revelation, "Concerning this house that you are building . . . " fits the story's progression and gives the impression that God is going to address Solomon regarding the temple project. However, what follows disrupts and disturbs such expectations. The divine reference to Solomon's enterprise as "this house" rather than "my house" suggests a disconnectedness between God's relationship to this project and Solomon's purpose. Next, an if-then formula follows that bears no grammatical or semantic relationship to the opening clause concerning the temple. "If you will walk in my statutes, obey my ordinances, and keep all my commandments by walking in them, then I will establish my promise with you, which I made to your father David" (v. 12). Rather, the outcome of the condition that demands attention to God's ordinances, statutes, and commandments is a commitment on God's part to keep the word promised to David. The explication of that word follows, reiterating that God will be present among the people of Israel. Located here in the midst of a report on temple construction, the promised outcome for obedience to laws, commandments, and statutes of Torah is more than curious, or simply out of place. God's direct summons to Solomon at this juncture is a serious matter, and the divine promise of presence lodged here is in thick tension with the surrounding account.

According to the revelation, the promise of God's presence depends not upon the availability of an elaborate temple in which to dwell, but upon obedience to God's laws and walking in God's ways. Moreover, even if Solomon is faithful and obedient, God makes no mention of being present in the temple but rather promises to dwell among the people. Though God makes reference to the temple construction, any note of divine approval for Solomon's project is glaringly absent in this revelation. Instead, the tone of the divine words subtly approaches admonishment and puts Solomon on warning. Caught up in the complex domestic and international negotiations as well as the related politics for materials and laborers, Solomon's commitment to his God may well have become compromised or even derailed. Though carried out in the name of the Lord, the planning, managing, and building of such an elaborate architectural undertaking over the course of seven years may blind this king to what God really wants. Juxtaposed between descriptions of the exterior and interior of this elaborate building project, the revelation functions like a blinking yellow light to both Solomon and the reader. For Solomon, it warns that his exterior actions and words might be disconnected or even at odds with earlier interior commitments.

For the reader, who perhaps is amazed by the exterior of Solomon's temple, it signals to proceed with caution into the inner sanctum in the following verses. It warns against the danger of becoming hypnotized by the splendor and extravagance of Solomon's glittering decor within and thus, like Solomon, also risk distraction from what it is that God really wants.

The Temple's Interior Decor (6:14-38)

The repetition, "Solomon built the house and finished it" in the opening verse of this section (v. 14) echoes verse 9 and summons attention back to the tour of this spectacular building. The repeated refrain brackets the intervening revelation (vv. 11-13) as if it were a distracting digression that for now can be quieted and contained. The description of the interior of the temple follows and surpasses in detail and extravagance the account of the exterior of the building. Inside the building, precious woods and gold overlay stone. We hear of cedar wall panels, cypress floorboards, olivewood doors, and golden chains and carvings. Unlike the simple straightforward design of the building's outside, elaborate ornamental carvings of flowers, palm trees, and cherubim adorn the inside. The highly decorative glittering interior contrasts sharply with the austere appearance of the gray exterior.

The account focuses the majority of its attention upon a description of the inner sanctuary. That the ark of the covenant would eventually be located there (v. 19) explains the special attention. This is the space where God would dwell. The room is located in the deepest recesses of the building, adjacent to the nave and farthest removed from any outside public entrance. Constructed as a perfect thirty-foot cube, it is the most holy space in the temple. The entire room is overlaid in gold (v. 20) and two compelling figures—cherubim—occupy and dominate about half the space. Cherubim are large winged creatures that appear half animal and half human. Here their wingspan is so great that it extends wall-to-wall in the Holy of Holies. Often the biblical traditions describe the function of these creatures as guardians and chauffeurs for the deity. For example, in Ps 99:1, God is portrayed as enthroned upon their backs.

Since the inner sanctuary becomes a very restricted space that only the high priest can enter, this lengthy, detailed description is particularly captivating as it affords the only glimpse at a mysterious, off-limit area. Moreover, that it follows on the heels of the revelation to Solomon where God reiterates the divine promise to "dwell among the children of Israel" (v. 13) on the condition of Solomon's obedience to Torah is intriguing, if not perplexing. Is there a theological dispute lodged in this tradition? Does God's presence in the temple represent God's dwelling among the people? How can God dwell in the temple's inner sanctum from which the people are barred? Do only the royal elite with their priestly intermediaries have direct access to the almighty power enthroned upon the cherubim or does God really live among the people? Will the reigning theology reflect that of Torah, where God was present and moved with the people, or does the construction of a Temple represent an alternative, conflicting understanding of the divine?

The description of the temple precincts and its interior design comes to a tidy but unsatisfying close (v. 38). It reiterates that the temple was completed in seven years in the Canaanite month of Bul, probably November on our calendar. However, it leaves unanswered the hounding question of Yahweh's presence in Israel for the future. Is Torah still the governing force in the religious sphere or will the temple supplant it?

Solomon Builds His Own Palace (7:1-12)

Chapter 7 now turns attention away from the temple and unexpectedly fixes upon another of Solomon's building projects, the palace complex. The introduction to this description, reporting that the palace complex took thirteen years to build, contrasts sharply with the conclusion to chapter 6 reporting that the temple was a seven-year project. Initial impressions might argue that the temple was this king's priority. Thus it received most attention and was completed speedily and first. However, the brief sketch (vv. 2-12) of the state buildings and the king's own house challenges such easy assumptions.

The description of the palace moves quickly through five buildings without the kind of attention to decorative detail and dimensions that the report on the temple afforded. We are given only official names of the buildings and a few principal measurements for two of them. We hear the most about the House of the Forest of the Lebanon, probably a large reception or banquet hall approximately 150 feet long and 75 feet wide (vv. 2-5). Paneled extensively throughout in cedar, it stands as high as the temple, with many windows and doorways. Other buildings in the complex include the Hall of Pillars (v. 6), the Hall of the Throne (v. 7), Solomon's own house (v. 8), and a house for Pharaoh's daughter "whom he had taken in marriage" (v. 8). Following, the description catalogs the materials used in the construction (vv. 9-11). Incalculable amounts of cedar transported from Lebanon and costly, carefully hewn stone are the primary building materials.

When compared with the account of the temple, the lack of detail here surrounding the construction of five buildings could at first suggest their lesser importance. However, what little detail we find conveys another message. The scope of the palace complex far surpasses the scope of the temple construction. This necessarily implies a great deal more materials and laborers are required for the work on these state buildings. The size of the House of the Forest of the Lebanon alone (150 x 75 feet) is reportedly much greater than the size of the temple (90 x 30 feet). That this was just one of at least five structures suggests that the palace complex dwarfs the temple as an architectural achievement. Any notion that the house of the Lord approached the likes of some contemporary towering synagogue or landmark cathedral is quickly discounted. When assessed in relation to the palace, the temple is more likely equivalent to what in the ancient world qualified as a king's private chapel.

Both the account of the building of Solomon's palace and its location here in the text is a problem. The report in 7:1-12 not only puts in question the importance of the house of the Lord, but interrupts the report on the temple and its furnishings. How are we to understand building reports so illogically sequenced? That the account of the palace buildings (7:1-12) divides the account of the temple's exterior and interior (6:1-38) from the description of its furnishings (7:13-51) could suggest that Solomon's own energies were divided. That this report on the palace complex distracts attention from the temple structure could also subtly begin to implicate Solomon as distracted from focusing on Yahweh.

The Furnishings for the House of the Lord (7:13-51)

The report on Solomon's projects now returns to the temple. This concluding account details the bronze and gold objects that make up the furnishings. Divided into two segments, verses 13-47 itemize and describe the objects made of bronze, and verses 48-50 review those implements cast in gold. Hiram from Tyre is named as the skilled craftsman responsible for the elaborate bronze work. Not to be confused with the king of Phoenicia named earlier, an important note identifies him as son of an Israelite mother, a widow from the tribe of Naphtali in the north. His work includes the two pillars, the molten sea, and ten stands and basins, along with miscellaneous pots and shovels. It is difficult to determine the significance and precise function of all these objects in the cult. For example, the naming of the two pillars Jachin and Boaz is the subject of much conjecture. In Hebrew, *Boaz* means "with strength" and *Jachin* is probably derived from the Hebrew verb "to be firm, established." Hence, the titles may have functioned as emblematic claims on the temple for Yahweh. Or perhaps these names were literally the first word of an inscription etched upon the front of each of them.

Just before the transition to the description of the gold work conducted by Solomon (vv. 48-50), a concluding postscript on Hiram's work qualifies the production and the role of this skilled craftsman. Credit is transferred to Solomon for the work. As elsewhere in the narrative about the temple, Solomon becomes the subject of the activity on the temple. "In the plain of the Jordan the king [Solomon] cast them" (v. 46). Hence, Solomon is ultimately assigned credit for even the bronze work here.

The brief account that follows continues in the same vein. Solomon crafts the altar, the table of bread, and other implements for the temple cult all in gold. Six times in these three verses we hear about the gold works of this king. He spares no cost and functions as if the wealth of the state is limitless.

Finally, we hear that Solomon is finished with his work on the temple. Though we have heard this before (6:14, 38), this time, he is really finished. He brought what his father David had dedicated, "the silver, the gold, and the vessels" (7:51) and stored them in the temple storerooms. The conclusion provides an appropriate transition to the next chapter. The temple and all its glory are ready for dedication.

Theological and Ethical Analysis

In the course of the unfolding account describing this grand project, the narrative speed has slowed dramatically. Its unhurried pace has allowed us to linger in the temple precinct for an extended period, affording us a chance to take in both the outside and inside of this religious center. From the description of the imposing outer framework reported at the onset, to the individual bronze and gold implements within the building described at the conclusion, the account bespeaks a king who left nothing to chance.

The sketch of the temple is elaborate and breathtaking. Its use of costly imported materials (6:15), elaborate ornate decorations (6:18, 29, 32, 35), along with the unrestrained gilding, testifies to a commitment to excellence. The monumental sculptures (6:23-26; 7:15-16), the incalculable use of bronze and gold for the implements and vessels, as well as the excessive attention to the design and decor of the Holy of Holies could be understood as a reverent obsession for every detail. Without a doubt, the overarching impression here is that the narrator intended all who read this report to gasp with awe and wonder at Solomon's accomplishment.

The report of the temple is not only the center of the Solomonic narrative but the crowning achievement of his reign. As the pinnacle of his career, it plays the largest role in earning Solomon his great fame, honor, and reputation as a skilled builder. The account paints a bigger-than-life portrait of Solomon as personally and ultimately responsible for the temple. Coupled with attention to Solomon is a concern that the covenantal traditions and the law be observed during the process of construction. This focus is expressed both directly and indirectly. As we have seen, in keeping with the observances in Deut 27:5, nothing is permitted to violate the sacredness of the space. All noise associated with the dressing of the stone is to be completed before transporting the building blocks to the temple space. The employment of Hiram, the bronze-metal worker, is carefully qualified by identifying him as the son of an Israelite mother to guard against any accusation that an outsider crafted the cultic objects of the temple.

Description of some of the furnishings and decor suggest a tie with other traditions and embedded expressions of Israelite faith. The familiar figures of the cherubim are constructed to be the recognizable signs of divine presence in the temple. Additionally, though, they symbolize God's presence; they do not symbolize God's confinement. The swiftness of their steedlike bodies connotes God's continued mobility, as in earlier sacral traditions. The extravagant attention to the measurements, decor, and furnishing of the Holy of Holies bespeaks the reverence and confidence that Yahweh will indeed take up residence here.

Other connections between this account of the temple and earlier Israelite religious and theological traditions are also interwoven here. The constructed pillars designated as Jachin ("to be firm") and Boaz ("with strength") probably bear witness to confidence in the power of Israel's God. Perhaps even the incorporation of flowers, pomegranates, and palm trees etched in artistic appointments proclaim God's domain over the earth and its fertility, an arena so often assigned to the Baals. Similarly, the incorporation of the molten sea, a well-known symbol of the god of chaos in the ancient Near East, is here contained and dwarfed by its surroundings in the house of God.

Even the bookends of the narrative that announce the beginning and herald the conclusion of this massive project link the enterprise to sacral traditions. The temporal clause in 6:1 ties the commencement of the work to the central saving event in Israelite history, the exodus. The account concludes by noting that as the work was finished, Solomon brought to the temple the treasures that David, the paradigmatic king of Israel, had set aside for the house of God. The mention of the exodus at the beginning and

David at the conclusion further roots and authorizes this elaborate and extravagant undertaking in the cherished memories of old. These links suggest an intentional association of temple with covenant, election, and other familiar religious stories.

Still, disquiet hangs over the narrative. For all the attention to detail in the construction, to the alignment of the building process with fidelity to covenantal law, to connecting the account with key events or persons within the sacral tradition, the temple is no guarantee of God's enduring presence among the people. Though a national sign of God's presence, the temple could not certify that God is present. Only Solomon's obedience to covenant law and statutes (6:11-13) could accomplish that. This conditionality of divine presence creates tension in this account.

In keeping with the story line, we might marvel at the temple as a staggering achievement. But to do so, we must sideline any thoughts that God might choose not to dwell there. We must edit any musings about whether building a temple constituted a break with ancestral tradition that Yahweh would have no central shrine in which to dwell. In addition, when as readers we praise Solomon's incredible achievement, we must stem all considerations as to how he could afford it. Though the story suggests that Israel was a fledgling nation, Solomon spared no expense. With an excess of extravagant materials and an abundance of skilled laborers, he went about his work. But at what cost? Contemporary examples from oppressive regimes forward an answer. Such extravagance is all too often funded by the surplus of the wealthy derived from the sustenance of the poor.

When the interruption of the account on the temple building with the brief description of Solomon's palace project (7:1-12) occurs, we must look past the differences in the projects. Solomon's palace far exceeds the size and scope of the temple building. Moreover, according to the story, the time it takes to complete Solomon's house is far longer that it takes to build Yahweh's dwelling. Indeed, the temple stands as proclamation that Israel's God is a very great God. But the Solomonic complex competes and perhaps overshadows this theological proclamation and claims instead that Solomon is a very great and powerful king. Indeed, the king is supposed to be God's agent! However, given the brief comparative glimpse of these two houses, Solomon lives less as the divine agent and more as Yahweh's landlord (G. Auld, 48). On display here are the fame, honor, and riches that God promised to Solomon. However, it is disturbingly noteworthy that wisdom is not attested here.

1 KINGS 8

Chapter 8 records the culmination of Solomon's reign as king and his most noteworthy accomplishment in that capacity. The account of the temple dedication that gathers all Israel in Jerusalem records festivity that lasts for seven days. Great feasting, lavish sacrifices, and extended prayer mark the event. Years of planning and labor by many within and outside the kingdom have led up to the momentous event. Indeed, much of the narrative thus far has anticipated this finale.

As climax of the narrative buildup, the account of the dedication here assigns the temple its rightful significance as the central religious site of Israel. Moreover, the dedicatory rhetoric imbues it with layers of theological meaning. Throughout the narrative, Solomon oversees and officiates at this historical event. As a result, the account of the celebration surrounding the temple serves as notice of the king's greatness and the triumph of his reign. Whereas the account features the dedication of the temple as the supreme dwelling place for God, it also exalts Solomon and his accomplishment.

Literary Analysis

A complex compositional history underlies the tradition reporting the dedication of the temple. Although prayer constitutes the most recurring form comprising this chapter, shifts in subjects and objects, as well as the presence of some incongruities, indicate that the account is composed of a variety of traditions. Even as the chapter opens, signs of disarray are evident. In verse 1, Solomon is positioned as active subject assembling Israel. However, before

---

the end of the first sentence, a strange prepositional phrase has Solomon assembling the people "before King Solomon." In addition, as the account begins, Solomon gathers "the elders of Israel" for the dedication. One sentence later, the description reports that "all the people of Israel assembled to King Solomon." Besides these shifts in language, the juxtaposition of opposing theological traditions, as well as evidence of unresolved tensions surrounding topics such as divine presence, suggest the struggles across generations leading to the final form of this account.

Despite these difficulties, a narrative flow from beginning to end obscures the seams and disjunctions here. An order befitting so great a moment as the dedication of the temple of the Lord reigns across this account. The ceremonial events take place here between two sweeping actions. The opening (vv. 1-2) is marked by the gathering of the assembly of Israel. The closing of the festivities is signaled by the dismissal of this great assembly (vv. 65-66). In between the description of these two movements of the whole people, a five-part report centers upon Solomon and his prayer. First, the ark, the tent of meeting (tabernacle), and the sacred vessels are transferred to the temple (vv. 3-13). Next Solomon turns and blesses the people. His words are grounded in an elaborate theological exposition that recalls Israel's sacred history (vv. 14-21). A third part follows, fashioning the major portion and center of the narrative in which Solomon sets forth a seven-petition prayer before God (vv. 22-53). Next, the king again blesses the assembly and accompanies his blessing with great theological commentary (vv. 54-61). Finally, the fifth section describes the offering of an immense number of sacrifices (vv. 62-64).

The chiastic structure of the passage lifts up Solomon's dedicatory prayer (vv. 22-53) as the heart of this celebration. The peoples' actions of gathering and departing (vv. 1-2, 65-66), the ritual actions of transporting the ark and offering the sacrifices (vv. 3-13, 62-64), and Solomon's recitation of a blessing over the people twice (vv. 14-21, 54-61) converge toward this centerpiece (vv. 22-53). With a seven-petition prayer, Solomon dedicates the temple. Hence, the great national celebration involving the movement and action of all Israel pivots around an action that features Solomon alone.

Political matters and religious concerns are not easily distinguished here. What is set forth as an account of a great national religious celebration is laden with political overtones. The dedication of the temple serves to illuminate the greatness of God before the people assembled. However, it also spotlights the greatness of Solomon. This dual focus is just the tip of the iceberg of oppositions and hostilities building across the well-ordered account. Embedded in the report of an apparently flawless ceremony lies evidence of political, religious, theological, and social struggles that have been mounting en route to the momentous celebration. In the exegetical analysis that follows, we will unveil and map some of these tensions.

Exegetical Analysis

Introduction and Assembling the People (8:1-2)

Like the account of its construction (1 Kgs 6–7), the report of an event so important as the dedication of the temple begins by dating the occasion. The weeklong celebration commences in the month of Ethanim, the seventh month according to the ancient Canaanite calendar. This places the dedication in the fall of the year either eleven months after its conclusion or, more likely, one month before the actual completion of the temple, as reported in 6:58. The end of chapter 7 gives the impression that the conclusion of the temple building overlapped with the dedication ceremony. In 7:51, Solomon is transporting all the treasures and vessels that his father David had dedicated to the Lord. Consistent with this activity, chapter 8 opens with the transfer of the treasure of treasures (vv. 3-13) as the ark of the covenant is moved to the temple. Moreover, in the other biblical witness to these events, the Chronicles account (2 Chr 5–7:11), the completion of Solomon's project occurs after the dedication of the temple. Just as 6:38 reports that the temple was completed "in all its parts" before the account of the completion of the interior decorations and furnishings (1 Kgs 7:12-51), so too it is possible that the dedication, described in chapter 8, also occurred within that same seven-year time frame (1 Kgs 6:38). The month of dedication, Ethanim, immediately precedes the month of Bul, when the temple was reportedly completed, thus arguing in favor of such a chronology.

The chronological problem often overshadows other difficulties in these opening verses. First Solomon assembles an impressive list of dignitaries: "the elders," "all the heads of tribes," and "the leaders of the ancestral houses of the Israelites" (v. 1). However, the report recoils from this select guest list in verse 2 and records that "all the people of Israel assembled to King Solomon." The complex character of the introductory account may suggest a social tension that existed over the growing class distinction of the new Solomonic order—a tension between the ruling elite and the more communal assembly of "all Israel" reminiscent of the early days. Compounding the issue further, the references to "elders of Israel" and "leaders of the ancestral houses of the Israelites" hearkens back to the tribal designations and traditions that Solomon's redistricting (1 Kgs 5) sought to eradicate. Hence, the erupting tensions between the old communal order and the new hierarchical framework, as well as between Israel's self-understanding as a tribal community versus Israel as a nation-state, are suggested in the seemingly innocuous introduction to this great festival. That it fell within the fall of the year and lasted for seven days (v. 65) possibly indicates its coincidence with the Feast of Booths. During this seven-day observance, also known as the Feast of Tabernacles, Israel recalled and renewed its covenantal commitment. Dedication of the new temple, the architectural symbol of the Solomonic nation-state, in concert with the old feast of covenant renewal hearkening back to the people's encounter of God at Horeb, may narrate monarchic diplomacy binding the old and the new, the past and the present. Or it may be a textual remnant of the oppositions festering between these alternative perspectives.

Installation of the Ark and the Offering of Sacrifices (8:3-13)

The report on the transporting and installing of the ark of the covenant in the temple (vv. 3-13) unfolds in orderly fashion. First, the ark is moved from the city of David up to the temple mount on the outskirts of that city (vv. 3-4). Second, both Solomon and the people carry out a great deal of sacrificing (v. 5). Next, the sacred box is brought into the temple and placed in the Holy of Holies (vv. 6-9). Following, we hear of several familiar indicators manifesting divine presence (vv. 10-11). Finally, Solomon offers a prayer (vv. 12-13). Despite its reportorial character, the account of the transfer evokes the only drama within this lengthy chapter. Recollections of the previous traditions narrating the relocation of the ark of the covenant interject suspense into an otherwise uneventful account. Earlier, when David moved the ark into Jerusalem, one of his officers, who touched it, lost his life (2 Sam 6:6-7). Other traditions report foreign deities falling to the ground before the holy ark (1 Sam 5:1-5). Whether this revered container, the symbol of God's presence, can be moved without incident stirs interest, if not rapt attention, in a relatively action-less story. The interjection of the notice that innumerable sacrifices were conducted simultaneously with the movement of the ark suggests the exhaustive measures taken to ensure safe transport.

Although accompanied by a large cadre of various cultic officials, the priests alone carry the ark. Unlike David's decision to move the ark on a cart made for such occasions (2 Sam 6:3), the priests carry the ark up from the city and into the temple precinct on poles, reminiscent of the tradition that the priests first carried it across the Jordan as Israel entered the land (Josh 3–4). Additionally, the narrative reports that only the two stone tablets that "Moses had placed there at Horeb" (v. 9) are contained in the ark. Hence, images from cherished sacral stories serve as familiar points of contact with the past, easing the transition to a new regime in the present.

As the ark is firmly positioned under the lengthy wingspan of the cherubim, parallels with other ancient Near Eastern deities begin to retheologize Israel's understanding of its God. In those instances, the deity was elevated and enthroned on the backs of the cherubim with a boxlike structure such as the ark as a footstool connoting a sense of the deity's stability and permanence.

That the uneventful move and placement of the ark in the temple signals divine approval is further confirmed by what follows. As the priests begin exiting the Holy of Holies, a cloud envelops the holy place and "the glory of the LORD filled the house of the

LORD" (v. 11). As if to interpret the unfolding events, Solomon now speaks. He reports that God will dwell in "thick darkness" and that this house that he, Solomon, has built will be God's dwelling place forever.

Across this account, the melding of images from the past and from the present suggests the weaving together of different theological traditions. However, these differences may indicate more than a complex compositional history. They also suggest growing divisions in the community as well as mounting theological tensions in the story. The familiar cloud symbolizing the presence of Israel's God is being reinterpreted by Solomon in the tale as a "thick darkness," probably associated with the remoteness and exclusivity of the Holy of Holies, God's new dwelling place. The reference to the ark on poles that "are there to this day" lacks congruity with the ark's placement below the cherubim. In the wilderness, Israel's God, represented by the moving ark, journeyed with the people as the Lord had promised. Now, Israel's God is permanently housed in the temple, enthroned on high with the ark as a footstool. God is remanded to the Holy of Holies, a larger but nevertheless boxlike enclosure (10 x 10 x 10 cubits) where according to Solomon, "you [will] dwell in forever" (v. 13).

Solomon Blesses the People (8:14-21)

With the ark safely in place, Solomon turns toward the whole assembly of Israel to bless them (v. 14). This action parallels the same move on his part later in the account (v. 54) framing the lengthy prayer of dedication within (vv. 22-53). The portrait of Solomon turning to the people, then to God, and then back to the people illustrates the role that the king of Israel is to assume. He is to be a vice-regent with the responsibility of mediating between God and the people and between the people and God.

However, what starts out here as a blessing on the assembly standing before him abruptly shifts to a prayer in praise of God. Solomon extols the Lord, because from the earliest times of the exodus up to the time of David God has made promises that are now being fulfilled. In particular, the promise that David's son would build a house for God (2 Sam 7:1-17) is highlighted as now realized during this king's reign. Subtly, the praise of God shifts and attention turns again to Solomon. The blessing upon the people that became a prayer of praise to God now becomes a rhetorical legitimization of Solomon and his kingship. The address that praises God for fulfilling the promises made to David at the same time honors Solomon for this great achievement.

The shift in focus from the people to God and then from God to Solomon is accompanied by a shift in theology. In Solomon's previous oration (vv. 12-13), he identified God's presence with the darkness of the Holy of Holies and with the temple as an eternal dwelling place. God was envisioned as enthroned on the backs of the cherubim with the ark as a footstool. Now, Solomon makes clear that neither the temple nor the ark can actually contain or confine God. Rather, the temple is built for God's name as fulfillment of the promise under Solomon. Yet Yahweh's enthronement ritualized by the placement of the ark in the temple (vv. 3-13) becomes overshadowed by an emphasis upon Solomon's enthronement and reign. In concert with this shift, Solomon's recitation here is weighted with ideology of legitimacy for both his kingship and the Davidic dynasty. Hence, theology is put to the service of politics.

Solomon's Prayer (8:22-53)

This whole chapter serves as the centerpiece of Solomon's reign, his dedicatory prayer (vv. 22-53) constitutes the literary center of the chapter. Some even argue that the high theology expressed in this oration makes it the pinnacle of the whole book of Kings. Still, whereas it may emerge as the literary center, it is not completely in synchrony with all the surrounding narrative themes and theological underpinnings of the stories leading up to this event. After considering the prayer itself, we will return to consider some of these dissonances and tensions to which it gives rise.

The account begins by describing the king's solemn gesture as the prayer commences. Solomon turns to the altar, raises his outstretched hands toward heaven, and begins to pray. Four parts structure his entreaty. In the first part (vv. 22-26), Solomon extols the greatness of God. Acknowledging God's uniqueness in heaven and on earth, as well as God's utter fidelity to covenantal promises, his prayer quickly narrows its focus and fixes upon David. In particular, Solomon beseeches God to be faithful to the promise made to his father that a successor would always be on David's throne. He concludes with a request that God confirm this word.

In the second part of the prayer (vv. 27-30) Solomon again extols the incomprehensible nature of God's presence. The words of his supplication suggest that God's presence eclipses the limits of heaven and earth and hence most certainly the material limits of the temple. However, that the temple is built in the name of the Lord makes it the right place to call confidently upon God and be granted a hearing. With this admission, Solomon's prayer abruptly turns toward a prayer for himself. Employing the term *servant*, previously used to refer to his father David, Solomon beseeches God five times to hear and to heed his requests.

Seven petitions make up the third and longest section of his prayer (vv. 31-51). Two parts, the circumstances and the petition, work to structure each plea (Long, 101-2). Until now, the prayer has spotlighted God's utter fidelity to covenant. Here, Israel's persistent waywardness to the covenant is presumed. As each petition rehearses familiar disasters as the consequences of disobedience to the covenantal relationship, Solomon beseeches God to "forgive." In contrast to the focus upon God and the king up to this point in Solomon's prayer, the driving preoccupation here is ensuring the well-being of the people. The petitions echo clearly the Deuteronomist's understanding of divine justice. They also bespeak Israel's utter dependence upon God. The great God who is referenced as residing in heaven high above the earth in every one of the seven petitions (vv. 32, 34, 36, 39, 43, 45, 49) is also the One intimately turned to in search of forgiveness, and confidently counted upon to "hear" their prayer. Moreover, the rhetoric of the petitions ("If your people go out to battle . . ." "When . . . [your people] have sinned against you . . ." "When your people . . . are defeated before an enemy . . .") conveys the expectations of God's complete involvement. In any and all situations, God can be called upon and expected to hear their prayer.

Two of the petitions deserve special attention. The fifth petition (vv. 41-43) asks that God attend to the prayer of a foreigner. Israel's self-understanding as "the light to all nations" and of Zion as the gathering place of all peoples (Isa 2:2-3) finds expression here. God's answer to the foreigner is one stop on the way to Solomon's later petition that "all the peoples of the earth may know your name and fear you" (v. 43). Given the persistent antagonism between Israel and other peoples in much of the tradition, this prayer for the foreigner is striking. The quest for God's care and forgiveness upon Israel is here extended to all.

The last petition (vv. 46-51) is also worthy of note. Coming at the end of this series of seven petitions, it is the longest and most emphatic. The repetition of two similar sounding words in Hebrew (*shub* and *shubah*) give way to a word play that creates this emphasis. *Shub,* meaning "repent or return," and *shubah,* meaning "to be carried away," oscillate back and forth across this plea urging God to receive the sinner who returns with a contrite heart after being carried away by an enemy as punishment for sin. The images surely refer to the Israelite exiles. Hence, the prayer of Solomon extends even to those who will be driven from the land many years after this king and his reign. Whereas it is easy to argue for the Deuteronomic editor's influence here, the text extends an invitation to read this curious conclusion to Solomon's petitions in the final form in which we receive it. In this way, the concluding plea unwittingly places the indictment of this king and his successors on his own lips. Exile is a foregone conclusion; but the plea discloses more. From the heights of the Solomonic era to the depths of bondage in exile, Israel can still have confidence that they can call upon God, and also that God will still "hear."

Solomon Blesses the People (8:54-61)

After the preceding lengthy oration, Solomon concludes with actions and recitations paralleling his gestures and words prior to the seven-petition prayer. He rises from facing the altar, stands, and again blesses the assembly. Throughout the blessing of the people, he beseeches God in the name of the people for the continued company of divine presence and for protection. In turn, he urges the people to be faithful to the covenant and all its laws and statutes. The Judahite covenant theology, featuring David and Zion, which was the focus of the earlier blessing (vv. 14-21), is here balanced with reference to the Mosaic covenant, the predominant tradition among the northern tribes. Moses, like David, is referred to as "servant," the term Solomon uses to identify himself before God.

Next, Solomon grounds this call to faithfulness in the Mosaic covenant. Israel must be obedient so that all people will be drawn unto God. Once again we hear the radical universalistic overtones characteristic of the fifth petition. Israel's role in the world as fashioned in earlier traditions (Gen 12:1-3; Exod 19:6) and reiterated later in the prophets (Isa 2:2-3; 49:6) is echoed here. This people have been designated as the means by which, in the words of Solomon's prayer, "all the peoples of the earth may know that the LORD is God; there is no other" (v. 60).

More Sacrificial Offerings (8:62-64)

Parallel to the ritual actions that accompanied the ark's move to the temple at the opening of this chapter, Solomon and the people again offer sacrifices. Like the previous extravagance, "sacrificing so many sheep and oxen that they could not be counted" (v. 5), the sacrifices after the dedicatory prayer are also numerous. Offering sacrifices of well-being to the tune of twenty-two thousand oxen and one hundred twenty thousand sheep, "the king and all the people of Israel dedicated the house of the LORD" (v. 63). So great and numerous were the animal and grain offerings that the activity had to be moved to the middle court; the bronze altar could not accommodate them all. Like the offerings made earlier to curb the danger associated with the transfer of the ark (v. 5), the sacrifices here are also offerings of well-being, that is, peace offerings directed to enlist the deity's assurance of protection for all participants. Accordingly, Solomon's prayer for the prosperity of the community (vv. 54-61) is followed by an account of these sacrifices of well-being. Word and deed are joined together here.

Some have argued that this second account of elaborate sacrifices offered by Solomon and the people is indicative of a much more extensive practice. These ritual offerings may have been going on constantly during the seven days of festivities. Whether the sacrifices were continuously offered throughout the celebration or were a twice-repeated extravaganza, the vision Solomon receives in the following chapter qualifies the value of all this pageantry and excess.

Dismissal and Conclusion (8:65-66)

The monumental celebration now draws to a close. The opening verse (v. 65) recaps the festivities ("Solomon held the festival at that time, and all Israel with him . . .") while stressing the extent of its scope. It records that the participants came from as far away as "Lebo-hamath to the Wadi of Egypt" (v. 65). The reference to the entrance to upper Syria in the northeast (Lebo-hamath) and to a water depression in the Sinai on the way to Egypt in the southwest (Wadi of Egypt) portrays the kingdom of Solomon as vast and far-reaching. Peoples from these farthest corners had assembled for this historic event. The ark had been successfully transferred and placed in its permanent dwelling. With blessings, speeches, sacrifices, and prayers, the dedication of the temple is complete. On the eighth day, the feast draws to a close. Solomon now dismisses this great assembly. The celebration was a memorable success. The tone of the concluding exchanges between monarch and assembly is notably joyful. The dedication fostered mutuality and goodwill. As the king sends the people on their way, they bless their king.

The narrative summary concurs with this assessment. When the people departed, they "went to their tents, joyful and in good spirits because of all the goodness that the LORD had shown to his servant David and to his people Israel" (v. 66). Still, a question lingers. Was God's goodness to David to be understood as extended to his dynasty? Or is this a subtle insinuation that all that has unfolded here has more to do with David's fidelity than anything having to do with his son Solomon?

Theological and Ethical Analysis

The chapter leaves little doubt about the importance of the temple in the life of Israel. Throughout the book of Kings, the temple's role is central and serves as a principal touchstone for the evaluation of the Judahite rulers. Those who corrupt worship and import apostasy into the temple precincts are judged as having done what is displeasing in the sight of the Lord. Those who faithfully conduct their ritual in the temple, ensure the centralization of all worship there, and occasionally cleanse it of foreign influences are consistently judged as righteous.

Central to the life of the community, the temple is also tied to the destiny of the people. Its destruction signals God's ultimate punishment for the peoples' infidelity. Later, its rebuilding symbolizes new life and confidence in the community's restoration by God. In all periods, it stands as material evidence of God's promised presence to Israel.

But how is God present to the people? The matter of God's presence is emblematic of covenant. Still, divine presence is not easily grasped. It is and continues to be a theological problem with which both believers of ancient Israel and those of the modern world must grapple. Chapter 8 sets forth an exquisite theology in this regard that wrestles with the immanence and transcendence of the divine. The priestly theology of God's glory filling the temple is coupled with God shrouded in the darkness of the Holy of Holies. Though God resides in the heavens, God also dwells among those obedient to the law. Although God hears prayers in the temple bearing the divine name, the Holy One is not confined there. God invites Israel to call for assistance in this holy place, yet God resides beyond even heaven and earth. Promising to be present to protect or to punish, God is "the beyond" within Israel's midst. This theological exposition is profound. Without defining God, it offers trustworthy insight about the nature of the divine. Namely, it discloses the unfathomable nature of the Holy One of Israel. The great God on high is at the same time caught up in the life of Israel.

Chapter 8 serves as catechetical statement regarding Israel's understanding of faith in God. In addition to expounding upon how God is present, it also narrates how God acts. The promise of divine presence is conditioned upon obedience to the covenant. Failure to obey reaps calamity and devastation. Still, God's invitation to repent brings with it the prospect of restoration.

Throughout this chapter, the Deuteronomist's theology has fashioned a compelling notion of the divine as well as has set forth a portrait of the idyllic relationship between Israel, the king, and this God. However, the ideal does not account for the real. Embedded in the narrative are hints that all is not well in this relationship. References in the story anticipate trouble on the horizon.

Whereas God appears to accept sacrifices, obedience is what God most wants. Solomon's excess in sacrifice here risks obscuring the importance of covenantal fidelity. It promotes and privileges extravagant, public religious formalism. Eventually, such practices will become the basis for the prophets' denunciation of cultic sacrifices and offerings as Israel's participation in spiritual bankruptcy (Amos 5:21-22; Jer 7:21-23). In another instance, when Solomon blesses the people, his prayer, "incline our hearts" toward God (v. 58), creates a disquieting parallel to what follows. Just a few chapters later, where that same verb occurs, we hear that Solomon actually "inclined his heart" toward his pagan wives and toward other gods.

Probably most disturbing of all is the concluding image of the people joyfully returning to their tents. The next time the people respond to the summons "To your tents, O Israel!" (1 Kgs 12:16), it will not be with joy; rather, it will signal the division of Solomon's kingdom. We have remarked how this dedicatory event constitutes the pinnacle of Solomon's reign. As high point it also contains its own warning. From here on out, things will be on the decline.

1 KINGS 9

Like the dream at Gibeon (1 Kgs 3:1-5), Solomon experiences another divine revelation in this chapter. Despite the abrupt change in form and content from the previous material, the account of the revelation joins this narrative with the preceding story of the temple's construction and dedication. In this revelation to Solomon, God affirms both the temple building project and Solomon's prayer of dedication, and sanctifies all that has been done. However, what is new and perhaps unexpected here is the accompanying declaration of the conditions upon which the temple and all that it signifies will remain acceptable. In addition, the conditions upon which it will be destroyed are given extended attention. Once again, the covenantal relationship between the Davidic successor and God is revisited and reiterated. However, this time the covenantal agreement appears to have become increasingly conditional. The rehearsal of the terms of the covenantal relationship juries the forthcoming verdict concerning all the deeds of this king, both at home and abroad.

Literary Analysis

Following the brief introduction (v. 1) that rehearses once again the completion of all Solomon's building projects, two distinct literary units structure this chapter (vv. 1-9, 10-28). First, a dream revelation reminiscent of Solomon's experience at Gibeon (1 Kgs 3:1-15) unfolds. Three parts organize this nighttime encounter (vv. 3, 4-5, 6-9). Initially, God acknowledges Solomon's prayer and confirms approval of the sanctuary by consecrating the temple (v. 3). Second, God reiterates the promised succession of the Davidic line *if* Solomon remains faithful to the covenant and its statutes (vv. 4-5). The third and final part (vv. 6-9) of the revelation details the unhappy consequences *if* Solomon and his successors depart from covenantal fidelity. In particular, worship of other deities carries catastrophic consequences not only for the king, but for the whole people Israel. As the account of Solomon's revelation progresses, rhetoric increases incrementally across these three parts. Hence, the third section is not only the longest; the detailing of the consequences for infidelity to the covenant for this king becomes the most extended and elaborated narrative of the entire revelation.

The second half of the chapter (vv. 10-28) turns its attention to a series of various supplementary reports concerning Solomon's other governing activities and projects. These read as a miscellany of five notices warranting recording but not elaboration. Although scholars agree on the rather disjointed nature of this series, the reports do work together. As a collage, they afford a variegated view of this king's other domestic activities and involvements apart from the temple and palace construction.

Exegetical Analysis

Another Dream Revelation (9:1-9)

Whereas the narrative of the dream revelation departs in form and style from what precedes it, the opening verse establishes a link between the two chapters. It reminds us that God appeared to Solomon after Solomon had "finished building the house of the LORD and the king's house and all that Solomon desired to build" (v. 1). This creates a sequential though not necessarily chronological relationship between these events, suggesting that the dream revelation is related to and perhaps even essential to what comes before. For in this dream appearance to Solomon, God confirms and sanctifies the temple and its dedication. Previously, God had not directly approved the project. Hence, the narrative tension remaining at the close of the otherwise joyous events of chapter 8 is now finally resolved. As chapter 9 opens, God's revelation to Solomon not only provides firsthand evidence of the divine endorsement but also brings the account of the temple's construction and dedication to its successful culmination. All that has been done as previously recorded has found acceptance with God.

This second epiphany (v. 2) recalls the previous dream revelation at Gibeon (1 Kgs 3:1-15). In both instances God appears to Solomon in a dream. As the divine disclosure unfolds across this narrative, the parallels and contrasts between the two accounts afford further insights. In the first of this three-part revelation, God not only approves of the temple dedication but also confirms that all Solomon has asked and prayed for has been granted. Like the account at Gibeon when God responds affirmatively to Solomon's request, in this second revelation God answers Solomon's earlier plea by accepting the temple and "consecrat[ing] this house that you have built" (v. 3). The parallel between these two revelations extends further. Like the account in chapter 3, what God grants exceeds what this king asked for. In chapter 3, Solomon asked for "understanding" with which to govern the people (1 Kgs 3:9). In response, God promised Solomon much more. Here Solomon asked for God's name to dwell in the temple. In like manner, God assures him that the holy name will dwell here, then reveals that the divine heart and eyes will be there "for all time" as well (v. 3).

In the second part of the revelation, God turns attention away from the temple and focuses upon Solomon himself. The familiar "if-then" format we have come to associate with the terms of the covenant shapes this disclosure. If he observes the statutes and remains obedient to all that God has established, then Solomon will be the recipient of divine blessings. As at Gibeon, Solomon is assured that his royal throne will endure forever. However, unlike the revelation at Gibeon, the promises of wealth, prosperity, and international fame are absent. One could argue that the promises to Solomon have been reduced to a guarantee of unending successors to the throne, since he has already received the gifts of prosperity, wealth, and international renown. However, another line of understanding would allege that as this king has been preoccupied with his projects and his empire, he has gradually lost sight of the covenant. Consequently, the promise of a successor to the throne is itself threatened and thus has become exceedingly urgent. Hence, it moves to center stage alone. The prospect of wealth, prosperity, and international renown are moot points if the promise of an eternal successor of David's house is cut off. Hence, in this second part of the revelation, the promises to Solomon have been reduced to that upon which all others hinge. Accordingly, Solomon's fidelity becomes the criterion upon which the continuation of the Davidic line depends, as well as the basis upon which the fate of the whole people Israel hinges.

The third part of the revelation departs dramatically from the previous dream encounter at Gibeon. Although the "if-then" format continues, an exposition of curse replaces the focus upon blessing. In addition, whereas Solomon continues to be addressed, the "you" of this direct address shifts to second-person plural in the Hebrew, which is further specified as "you or your children" (v. 6). Solomon and his successors are promised comprehensive dismissal and punishment for infidelity. Moreover, the violation of covenant is named specifically as "serv[ing] other gods and worship[ing] them" (v. 6). The elaboration of the consequence for this abrogation exceeds in description and details the promised blessing.

The extent of the punishment for such violations serves to under-mine the confidence that the blessing might have cultivated. The language—"cut Israel off from the land"; "cast out of my sight"; "Israel will become . . . a taunt"; "this house will become a heap of ruins; everyone passing by it . . . will hiss" (vv. 7-8) ; and so forth—draws a disquieting pall over this revelation. Now the exposition of blessing is far overshadowed by the extent and gravity of the curse. A decision for infidelity and its consequences parades itself disturbingly before Solomon and his successors as if it lingers very near. In addition, the weight of punishment for the king's waywardness rests heavily upon Israel. Moreover, in the course of the revelation, the God of the covenantal relation-ship discloses in unequivocating terms who this Holy One is. Faced with Israel's infidelity, the God who consecrates the temple and promises that the divine name will dwell there is quite capa-ble of demolishing this human-made artifact and scattering the people.

Solomon's Domestic Activities (9:10-26)

With the temple as the primary focus of Solomon's reign, most of his undertakings as head of state have been defined thus far pri-marily by his building projects in Jerusalem. Still, many other mat-ters also occupy a king. The miscellany report in verses 10-25 read as a secretary's records of some of these activities. The notations are incomplete, offering only snippets of some of the king's many projects and business dealings. Nonetheless, these tallies of his domestic projects, along with the brief snapshots to follow in chapter 10 of his international involvements, together sketch a sweeping portrait of Solomon and his reign.

The first notation (vv. 11-14) concerns Hiram, one of Solomon's enduring international partners in trade and commerce. Recall that Hiram supplied cedar, cypress, and other materials to Solomon for his building projects (1 Kgs 5:10). In this report, we hear about a dimension of those transactions previously left unnoted. In exchange for timber and gold, Solomon had evidently promised his Phoenician friend twenty cities in and around Galilee. When Hiram travels to the area to take possession of these territories, he is not satisfied. The report records that as a result the cities are called "the land of Cabul," a term of undetermined but likely derogatory significance. Far removed from the capital and the Judahite center with which Solomon identified his kingdom, these northern territories may have been considered readily expendable. Moreover, a New Testament reference suggests the low esteem with which these villages in and around Galilee continued to be regarded centuries later (John 1:46). That Hiram is not pleased appears to be the substance of the report.

The second notice concerns the conscription of laborers for other building sites throughout the kingdom. Construction at Hazor, Meggido, and Gezer are mentioned as well as "storage cities, cities of his chariots, the cities for his cavalry, and whatever Solomon desired to build, in Jerusalem, in Lebanon, and in all the land of his dominion" (v. 19). Here concern seems fixed not upon accuracy of where and what Solomon develops, but upon the extent and buildup of his vast empire. As the scope of his kingdom grows, so too does his need for cheap laborers to carry out the work. As if to qualify earlier reports recording the enlistment of Israelites as laborers for the building of the Jerusalem complex, this account notes the enslavement of Israel's alien residents. Foreigners living in Israel's territories are reduced to involuntary labor force for Solomon's public works. The tally of this laboring class includes the Amorites, Hittites, Perizzites, Hivites, and Jebusites, approximating the list of conquered peoples destined for extermination in the conquest of the land (Deut 7:1; 20:16-18). Whether this is a formulaic roster of people commonly considered expendable or an attempt to make Solomon appear lenient for having "spared" those destined for annihilation, the overarching effect raises concerns we will address in the theological and ethical analysis to follow.

On the heels of the report noting Solomon's treatment of foreigners, we hear of one foreigner who receives special treatment. In verse 24, another reference is made to Pharaoh's daughter, who had become Solomon's wife. She goes up to the house in the city of David that Solomon had erected especially for her (1 Kgs 3:1).

Earlier, the report on Solomon's labor practices indicated that the Egyptian pharaoh paid him a dowry in the form of the captured city of Gezer (vv. 16-17). For kings, the practice of betrothing foreign wives is a matter of economic exchange and political negotiations.

The fourth segment of this menagerie of reports shifts attention to Solomon's official role in religious matters (v. 25). It reports that three times a year he offers up sacrifices of well-being in the temple he built for the Lord in Jerusalem. The reference to the three sacrifices paints the impression of this ruler's observance of the three feasts marking Israel's liturgical year: the Feast of Tabernacles, the Feast of Weeks, and the Feast of Covenant Renewal (Deut 16:16-17; Exod 23:14-17). Though brief, this passing mention of Solomon officiating at these religious celebrations lends legitimacy to the temple and the capital city in which it stands. Moreover, the image of the king as official high priest reinforces the notion of religion as a function of and at the service of the state.

Finally, the last of these miscellaneous notes returns us to where they began. Another business partnership between Solomon and Hiram is recorded—as if Hiram's earlier dissatisfaction over the twenty cities offered in payment for his materials has been resolved. Now these two rulers have set out on a naval expedition to Ophir, a city in southern Arabia with a legendary reputation for its gold. Hiram's control over the major ports of Phoenicia on the Mediterranean makes him an attractive partner for Solomon's novice naval ambitions. Moreover, the pursuit of more gold coheres with the kind of extravagance to which this king has become accustomed. These archival jottings conclude the sketch of Solomon's activities at home and serve as a transition to the reports that follow. As chapter 9 concludes, Solomon ventures forth from the home front on these seaward expeditions; chapter 10 will provide a report on his international involvements.

Theological and Ethical Analysis

A surface reading of Solomon's activities conveys the impression of a successful and established statesman. Beyond the ambitious construction of the temple and palace complex, he undertakes other extensive building projects throughout the country. His capacity to carry these out so successfully bespeaks political and economic savvy. He has command of a vast number of conquered peoples at home. His progress on the domestic front necessarily implies his successful forging of trade and commerce connections internationally. And indeed this is the case. The overriding portrait here is that God's promises of wealth, wisdom, and fame have been fulfilled. But as the consequences of each of Solomon's enterprises are examined more closely, one might wonder whether Solomon has fulfilled his promises.

The record shows that Solomon offered to pay Hiram with twenty cities from the northern territory of Israel. Whereas the focus of the narrative fixes upon Hiram finding the cities unacceptable, there are other aspects of this agreement embedded in this account that are even more unacceptable. Within these cities are whole populations, presumably Israelite, with tribal, ethnic, and familial connections. These are being offered as economic capital in exchange for building materials. No mention is made of the change of these groups' life circumstances entailed by the land exchange. The severing of their tribal roots seems not to be considered. The alteration of their national identity appears utterly ignored. The notion of covenant community appears expendable to this king when weighed against the merits of trade negotiations and economic advancement.

The conscription of laborers to carry out Solomon's national projects is also reported in a matter-of-fact fashion. The report seems to paint the impression that only conquered peoples were members of the laboring class. Unlike the temporary civil obligation of Israelites who built the temple and palace (1 Kgs 5:13-16), the conscription of conquered peoples is explained here as permanent. Solomon's policy might even be dubbed "praiseworthy" given the religious warrant. After all, Deut prescribes that such groups of foreigners be destroyed. Hence, Solomon's enslavement of these groups destined for annihilation appears lenient. However, history has taught us to be wary of the annihilation, oppression, and ill-treatment of others that is founded upon any sort of religious justification. In addition, the reality constructed by the record here is challenged when Solomon's son attempts to ascend the throne. As those occupying the northern territory will make clear, the classist society developing under Solomon's regime is built not solely upon the backs of outsiders. Israelites themselves will resist and revolt against the slave labor practices that have harnessed their families and their communities. Such practices begun under Solomon's tutelage suggest once again his attitude toward Israel. The covenant community is easily expendable if it yields economic advantage. Even if the theological notion of covenant community is sidelined, such practices by those with unmitigated power evoke the lessons history has taught us. The expansionistic ambitions of powerful rulers are often realized in the shadow of policies that diminish the value of human beings and refuse them treatment with dignity. Often an insatiable appetite for wealth accompanies this quest for power.

Following on the heels of all the gilding Solomon ordered during the interior decorating of the temple and the new naval expedition is the first of many references to Solomon's pursuit of gold (1 Kgs 10:2, 10-11, 14, 16-18, 21-22, 25). Indeed, God promised Solomon the gift of great wealth. Is Solomon's growing treasury an expression of that gift or of the king's unbridled greed? In its prescription for limits on royal authority, Deut 17:17 explicitly warns against acquiring great amounts of silver and gold. Hence, we are left to wonder whether Solomon's pursuit of wealth in tandem with his hunger for power is in excess of God's gift.

Deuteronomy's warning regarding the accumulation of gold is accompanied by a warning against acquiring many wives (17:17). Both of these pursuits are considered distractions that will lead the king's heart away from the Lord and ultimately down the road of apostasy. That the records reference Solomon's pursuit of and possession of both many wives and much gold should put us on alert. In addition, this mention of Solomon's Egyptian wife is not especially assuring as to Solomon's character. This wife of Solomon is the daughter of the Egyptian pharaoh. Although this is the third time we hear of her presence in Solomon's royal court, not once is mention made of any fondness, much less love, which Solomon has for her. She, like the Israelite community itself, is cited because the relationship establishes some political connection, economic advantage, or is prompted by one of Solomon's military expeditions.

Finally, in the midst of all the questions raised about Solomon's commitment to covenant and to the community of Israel as the expression of covenant, the account of this king officiating at the three annual sacrifices in the temple is disconcerting, if not contemptible. In concert with the reigning conditions of injustice and human oppression, Solomon's officiating in the temple hauntingly foreshadows a crisis of cult and worship in the days ahead. Alongside unbridled pursuits of wealth at the expense of people's well-being, the image of this king as cultic high priest invites a disquieting preview of the later prophetic warnings (Amos 5:22, 24).

In the opening of the chapter, we wondered about any connection between the reports in 9:10-26 regarding Solomon's domestic involvements as king and the dream revelation in 9:1-9. Indeed, they are more intimately related than they first appear. In the dream revelation, God makes clear in the most unequivocal terms the conditional nature of covenant as well as the absolute warrant for fidelity hovering over this king. Though only bits and pieces of reports narrate his reign, when measured against this yardstick Solomon's faithfulness to the covenant appears wanting.

1 KINGS 10

The exposition of Solomon's accomplishments continues in this chapter. Solomon has already ventured beyond the confines of his own kingdom with seafaring expeditions (9:26-28). Now the chapter turns to his international involvements and the consequent recognition such affairs bring him. An account of a meeting with another ruling monarch, the queen of Sheba, along with a series of reports attesting to this king's wealth, wisdom, and fame, depict Solomon as a world marvel. The queen of Sheba's testimony followed by the tally of the king's riches and international connections invite assent to the biblical narrator's unqualified conclusion. "Solomon excelled all the kings of the earth in riches and in wisdom" (v. 23). Yet irony works here too, raising suspicions whether all the grandeur assigned to this remarkable king is really so well deserved.

Literary Analysis

Two distinct literary segments constitute chapter 10. First, an account of the queen of Sheba's visit to Solomon in Jerusalem opens the chapters (10:1-13). Different in form and content from what has preceded and what follows, this up close encounter between two world rulers is not unrelated to the surrounding collections of records and briefings attesting to Solomon's greatness. The queen's visit serves to illustrate in word and deed what the incomplete inventories surrounding this narrative report. Notations of her arrival and her departure (vv. 1, 13) signal the clear literary demarcations of this narrative unit. Arriving in Jerusalem to see for herself whether this king's reputation is credible, she has come "to test" Solomon. What the queen of Sheba hears, sees, says, and does mark the divisions of this brief story and build a rhetorical case supporting the claims of fame and greatness accorded this king. First, she hears the king's answers to her "hard questions" (vv. 2-3). Next, she "observed all the wisdom of Solomon" in terms of his great wealth and the signs of prosperity in his kingdom (vv. 4-5). Third, she proclaims with a profusion of superlatives her personal testimony to the greatness of Solomon (vv. 6-9). With eulogylike effusiveness, with blessing, and with praise, her speech functions as an affidavit fashioning the legacy of Solomon in legendary proportions.

Finally, actions confirm the queen's words. Following her speech, the queen of Sheba presents Solomon with gifts as extravagant as his reputation. "Then she gave the king one hundred twenty talents of gold, a great quantity of spices, and precious stones; never again did spices come in such quantity as that which the queen of Sheba gave to King Solomon" (v. 10). This in turn prompts the king's shower of presents upon the queen. The narrator's notation of her departure (v. 13) signals the conclusion of both her visit and this literary unit.

The second section of this chapter, verses 14-28, matches in form the catalog-like notations recording Solomon's accomplishments and involvements in 9:10-28. Initially, the verses read like a collation of various briefings gathered together for "the record." However, a threefold purposefulness can be discerned in this apparently random arrangement. Attention to Solomon's wealth serves as the structuring device. First, verses 14-15 offer a glimpse of the income Solomon generates, especially in gold, from his international contacts. Second, an account of how he uses this income and what he makes with these incredible amounts of gold follows (vv. 16-21). Finally, the record notes how such an unbelievable income, particularly the vast amounts of gold, is maintained (v. 22). This tripartite account of Solomon's portfolio serves as a literary drumroll leading up to and justifying the acclamation of Solomon (vv. 23-25) as a renowned ruler. Solomon "excelled all the kings of the earth" (v. 23) in his wealth and his wisdom, and "the whole earth sought the presence of Solomon" (v. 24). Finally, an addendum (vv. 26-29) brings the chapter to a close. Chariots, horses, silver, cedar, and imports from Egypt and Kue, as well as trade deals between northern and southern kingdoms with Israel acting as "broker," give further specificity to the great wealth and wisdom for which Solomon is reputed.

With the authoritative eyewitness of a queen to certify the evidence, followed by data from official-sounding records, chapter 10 leaves little doubt as to Solomon's reputation for wealth and for wisdom. It is tempting to be awed by such pronouncements of Solomon's accomplishments. However, whereas most of the record marshals abundant data of Solomon's vast riches, there is curiously little evidence of his wisdom. Perhaps such great wealth is viewed as a sign of great wisdom. One could only acquire wealth and reputation by being wise. However, the quantity of wealth Solomon possessed and the ways he acquired it may qualify the kind of wisdom that is attributed to him. Moreover, the use to which he put his wealth raises further questions as to whether Solomon possessed wisdom at all.

Exegetical Analysis

The Queen of Sheba Visits Solomon (10:1-13)

The queen of Sheba comes calling upon the king of Israel with real intention. This is not some casual social visit between two friends who happen to be rulers. The identity of the queen and even Sheba's location remain the subject of debate. That we do not know her name suggests the diminished emphasis upon her actual identity. Sheba, located somewhere in the Arabian Peninsula, is also hardly a point of emphasis in this story. As soon as the introductory verse alerts us to the arrival of this royal woman in Solomon's city, we learn of her motivation. She has come to "test him with hard questions" (v. 1) so as to verify or discount the fame of Solomon of which she has heard.

Immediately, the notion of testing signals some tension. This is a rather novel occurrence across the Solomonic material. Since the account of Solomon becoming king (1 Kgs 1–2) most of the narrative has been reportorial in nature, lacking the drama characteristic of a good story. Only the tale of the two mothers requesting a seemingly impossible decision from the king (3:16-28) built the kind of suspense we associate with a memorable plot. Just so, the opening of our story in chapter 10 creates expectations that a similarly riveting tale is about to unfold.

As the narrative continues in verse 2, the potential excitement that such an encounter might generate begins to erode. The queen has brought with her a vast array of spices, gold, and precious stones. Ready with gifts galore, this queen obviously anticipates a positive outcome and is well prepared to honor the king for his successful responses to her testing. Swiftly, in a one-sentence summary (v. 3), the test is conducted and the outcome reported. We do not hear the substance, the number of questions, or the kind of interrogation that was staged. The queen asked all that was on her mind and Solomon answered all her questions. That's it! As quickly as the prospect of suspense is introduced into the plot with the queen's plan to test Solomon, the potential drama fizzles. Whereas the account of the visit of the queen of Sheba before Solomon spans verses 1-13, the "test" lasts for only three verses

(vv. 1-3). Moreover, early in the story, the unfolding of events suggests that although the story will spotlight the queen of Sheba and her visit before the king, it turns out to be Solomon's tale.

What the queen concludes from listening to Solomon is reinforced by what she observes in his capital city. She notes his royal palace (v. 4) and observes the lavish character of the food, clothing, and seating provided for Solomon's officials, as well as the number of servants in attendance (v. 5). She also beholds the burnt offerings that Solomon offers at the house of the Lord (v. 5). If the number and size of these offerings is anything like we have heard of in the past (8:5, 63), the extravagance expended here must also be mind-boggling. The sum effect of her investigations leaves the queen breathless, "there was no more spirit in her" (v. 5).

Whereas most of the preceding narrative describing Solomon's activities has been devoted to the preparations, the gathering of materials, and the construction and dedication of the temple, the queen's investigation takes no specific note of this accomplishment. No attention is given to the temple of the Lord. Although the excessive cultic sacrifices offered by Solomon in the temple precincts are a source of marvel for the queen, the temple itself is not.

Based upon what she hears and sees, the queen embarks upon the third and final phase of her investigative visit. She showers the king with profuse praise. With summary exaltation, beatitude, and blessing, she honors Israel's monarch. First, she extols Solomon for his accomplishments and his wisdom while expressing her own incredulity (vv. 6-7), which warranted this on-site investigation. Next, she recognizes and memorializes the consummate bliss of Solomon's wives and his servants with a formal beatitude. "Happy are your wives! Happy are these your servants, who continually attend you and hear your wisdom!" (v. 8). Finally, her speech climaxes with a blessing that turns into a theological exposition. Here she ties all that has come to Solomon—his success, prosperity, and wisdom—to the Lord, the God of Israel. This is a strange pronouncement on the lips of a foreigner, and presumably a worshiper of another deity. She not only extols Solomon, but declares that his God, the God of Israel, is ultimately responsible for all the honor and success that comes to this king.

The conclusion to her pronouncement is especially attention grabbing. She not only summarizes God's commission to Solomon to "execute justice and righteousness," but also discloses the divine motive prompting Solomon's election to kingship by God. "Because the LORD loved Israel forever, he has made you king" (v. 9). In a moment, we will consider whether the commission to execute justice and righteousness founded upon God's love of Israel has been the foundation upon which Solomon's success and fame have been grounded.

Finally, the queen concludes her visit with an extraordinary presentation of gifts. She provides the king with one hundred twenty talents of gold, precious stones, and an abundance of extravagant spices. The narrator notes that "never again did spices come in such quantity" as the queen's gift to the king (v. 10). Although remarkable, such quantity is not unprecedented. In an apparently extraneous note that follows, the size of the gift is qualified. The quantity and quality of almug wood and precious stones that the fleet of Hiram brought back from Ophir to Solomon is also beyond belief. "No such almug wood has come or been seen to this day" (v. 12). Without a doubt, Solomon is the recipient of unbelievable amounts of rare and precious gifts. The account of the queen's visit now concludes with a note that Solomon also gave her gifts out of his "royal bounty" and then "she returned to her own land, with her servants" (v. 13). The queen's visit serves as an up close testimony of what the surrounding bits and pieces of records have reported. That the testimony came from the mouth of another powerful ruler apparently rubber-stamps the credibility of the assessment.

Further Evidence of Wealth, Fame, and Wisdom (10:14-29)

The second section of this chapter adds further support to the theme of Solomon's success as a ruler, specifically in terms of wealth, wisdom, and fame. Here his wealth is addressed from three angles: what he possesses, what he uses it for, and how he maintains this level of income. First, we hear that Solomon has accumulated an unprecedented amount of wealth. As an illustration of his great wealth, the weight of "six hundred sixty-six talents of gold" (equivalent to an exceedingly large sum of money in the ancient world) has come to him in one year (v. 14). His business negotiations with traders, merchants, and even kings of Arabia and governors of the land accounts for his burgeoning revenue. The second notation (vv. 16-21) parades a litany of some of the uses to which Solomon puts this economic excess. He makes several hundred large gold shields that he uses to decorate the House of the Forest of Lebanon (vv. 16-17). Built at the top of six steps, his own ivory throne, with a rounded back and two armrests each guarded by a lion, is overlaid in gold. Other uses include the gilding of all the vessels of the House of the Forest of Lebanon. All of these details sketch the impression of glittering wealth and extravagance. Even Solomon's drinking vessels are made of gold (v. 21). The third report concerning Solomon's incredible fortune summarizes how he maintained such an income. Again we hear of his fleet of ships of Tarshish at sea with Hiram's fleet. The mention of "ships of Tarshish," a distant port, encourages admiration for how far and wide Solomon's trade ships journey. The notation of the remarkable and exotic cargo (gold, ivory, and rare animals) that this naval fleet deposits every three years on the shores of Solomon's ports furthers this impression.

This repository of information regarding Solomon's inexhaustible wealth contributes the final reasons that have been amassing across these two chapters (9 and 10), justifying the praise and acclamation that follows (vv. 23-25). In the most unqualified language, a summary observation assigns Solomon a stature and renown unsurpassed in the entire world. "Thus King Solomon excelled all the kings of the earth in riches and in wisdom" (v. 23). Moreover, his fame is not just the opinion of this record keeper. The adulation here is grounded in external evidence. "The whole earth sought the presence of Solomon to hear the wisdom, which God had put into his mind" (v. 24). The shower of costly gifts from each and every visitor—"silver and gold, garments, weaponry, spices, horses, and mules, so much year by year" (v. 25)—lends further credibility to the honor and esteem in which King Solomon was held.

Finally, the chapter draws to a close with an addendum (vv. 26-29). This final memo notes horses, chariots, and the sites built for their storage. The commonness of such items as silver and cedar in Jerusalem magnifies the boom animating the economy of the capital city. Trade deals of horses and chariots with Egypt, Kue, and the Hittites at the going rate conclude this tale of triumph. The mention of horses and chariots as signs of wealth echoes an earlier citation (1 Kgs 4:26) of Solomon's equestrian business. There we noted the shadow cast by Deut 17:16 upon kings with such practices. That Solomon's success in international trade appears tied to the continuation and expansion of accumulating horses and chariots flies in the face of the Deuteronomic warning. That this second mention of Solomon's ongoing transactions in horses and chariots occurs at the end of this account of his glorious acclaim may signal something else. "All that glitters is not gold," or, for that matter, all that glitters does not equal wealth, fame, or even wisdom! This second mention of the forbidden horses and chariots against which Israel's kings are warned not only signals trouble on the horizon; it also serves as a transition to the turn of events that will dismantle Solomon's glittering glory!

Theological and Ethical Analysis

Because it is impartial, the assessment of outsiders is often sought to render an evaluation. The queen of Sheba plays such a role in our story. She verifies and interprets the information about the king that has been amassing throughout these chapters. As an objective observer, she offers an assessment of Solomon that we can trust as impartial and thus credible. Like a good evaluator, her appraisal is not founded upon secondary sources or grounded in hearsay. She comes to Solomon's city, to his palace, and before Solomon himself. She asks questions, she listens, she observes, and only then does she draw conclusions.

Indeed, what Solomon says in response to her questions, what he shows her, and what he gives in gifts to her confirm the surface impression that has been building in the previous chapters. Wealth and fame modify the king's name. The standards of living in Jerusalem are such that they capture an outsider's attention. Not only are Solomon's wives living in noteworthy conditions, but so also are his servants. The food on the royal table, the clothing of palace subordinates, the opulence of the surroundings, and the extravagance of the temple sacrifices all elicit attention and mention. Together they serve as the raw data from which this foreign evaluator makes an appraisal. But what Solomon has said, has displayed, and has provided as gifts for his visitor confirm more than his reputation as a statesman or his international renown as a world force. They also serve as indictment. Amid all the evidence of Solomon's indisputable fame and honor, irony works as a qualifier disclosing the underside of the sovereign's successful standing.

The exchanges between the queen of Sheba and Solomon echo the exchanges between Solomon and the Lord at Gibeon (3:1-15). The queen's testimony about Solomon's wisdom, wealth, and fame confirms that what God promised this ruler has been fulfilled. However, her testimony about Israel's God raises questions as to whether what was required of Solomon has been satisfied. Moreover, the strangeness of her assertion attracts our attention. From the lips of this foreign ruler, who likely worshiped another deity, comes a bold theological pronouncement. Solomon is not only on the throne because of the Lord's appointment. The queen also pointedly summarizes the divine sentiment motivating Solomon's ascent to power. God loves Israel. As if privy to the encounter before God and Solomon at Gibeon, she outlines the divine agenda for Solomon's reign, "to execute justice and righteousness" (v. 9).

Once again, an undercurrent of reservation about Solomon's greatness and success interrupts the buildup of a comely portrait. The juxtaposition in her evaluation is noteworthy. On the one hand, she marvels at the wealth, well-being, and prosperity of Solomon and his royal household concentrated in and around Jerusalem. On the other hand, she says nothing about the well-being and prosperity of the rest of the nation's peoples on whose backs this wealth and fame have been amassed. This silence functions as a serious caveat in the record of the king who was appointed to "execute righteousness and justice" among the people whom God loves.

At Gibeon, Solomon confessed his incapacity to govern a people of such numbers and greatness as Israel. He asked God for "an understanding mind to govern your people, able to discern between good and evil" (3:9). In return God promised that Solomon's request would be granted along with much more—wealth, fame, and success—provided that Solomon walk in the ways of the covenant. Now, many years later, this outsider's words recall the terms of the exchange between the king and the Lord.

Like the account in chapter 9 when God visited Solomon in a dream, the visit from a foreigner not only attests to Solomon's greatness and fame as the result of God's gift, it also echoes the warrant of covenantal fidelity weighing in as we head to the final assessment of the king. Both chapters (9 and 10) remind us of the dream at Gibeon. In the preceding account, the connection is more direct. "The LORD appeared to Solomon a second time as he had appeared to him at Gibeon" (9:2). Here, the connection is more subtly encoded in the words of a foreign visitor. Reminding him of the requirement and promises of that encounter at Gibeon, the queen summarizes, "Because the LORD loved Israel forever, he has made you king to execute justice and righteousness" (10:9).

Both episodes are followed by a loosely edited litany of Solomon's activities and accomplishments. The lists confirm the wealth, power, and fame of Solomon nationally and internationally, but also raise questions concerning his faithfulness. God demanded unflinching fidelity to all the laws and the statutes. By contrast, the litany of Solomon's activities across these lists—foreign wives, excess in sacrifice, increasing accumulation of horses and chariots for business deals, accumulation of incalculable amounts of gold and other forms of material wealth—unmask the specter of Solomon's covenantal waywardness. The assessment of this king is being made not only on what he has done, but also on what he has failed to do.

How precarious are the conditions of success, power, and fame. Though they can become the means by which to foster life, well-being, and prosperity of increasing numbers of people, they can also become a self-aggrandizing addiction. And like the self-destructive cycle of addictive behavior, all that once mattered is willingly sacrificed. The great and numerous people that Solomon confessed being too small to rule (3:7-8) appears to have become expendable. His fixation upon building and dedicating a house for the name of the Lord also seems to have receded in importance compared to his sideshow of sacrifices. Even Solomon's prayerful concern for the well-being and future of the whole people (8:31-53) appears now to have been forsaken, relegated solely to the arena of prayer. Instead, the evidence presented to the foreign queen suggests his commitment has been compromised and his vision has narrowed. Only the living conditions and the people in and around his royal household in Jerusalem weigh in as the measure of his success. Had the queen visited the countryside and the villages of the outlying regions, her assessment might have been different. Indeed, Solomon's success, wealth, and fame are signs that he is gifted with wisdom; but he uses that wisdom in the service of himself and his royal household. Hence, wisdom itself is undermined.

Following the dream at Gibeon, two unnamed powerless women stood before Solomon beckoning him to render a wise judgment concerning the life of a child (3:16-28). His order to sever the child in two did uncover the real mother as well as elicit praise for his great wisdom. But in retrospect, a wisdom grounded in a violent order could chart its own devastating course. Now, toward the end of his career, another unnamed power-ful woman from a faraway place comes to test this king and bear witness to the buildup of that wisdom and its harvest. What at first appears as towering greatness will soon sever the nation.

1 KINGS 11

With chapter 11, all the claims of wealth, wisdom, and fame surrounding Solomon come to an abrupt halt. The apparently praiseworthy characterization prevailing across the preceding chapters concludes with a pathetic portrait of the king. A brief summary of his activities makes Solomon himself responsible for the upcoming divine judgment with the fullness of its catastrophic dimensions—the division of the kingdom. How could the course of what seemed so clearly narrated as the sparkling career of Israel's king come to such a horrific reversal? An undercurrent of suspicion that has continually accompanied the otherwise exceedingly positive appraisal of this king provided hints that this story could end so unexpectedly. But the cause-and-effect relation between Solomon's decisions and the consequence for the nation are clearly spelled out here. Solomon has exempted himself from the statutes governing his covenantal commitments. In doing so, he has quickly succumbed to apostasy, turning away from the Lord. As a result, he reaps God's rapid judgment and punishment. The kingdom will be divided.

Perhaps the attractions and excesses of power and privilege tempted Solomon to believe that in his greatness God would excuse him from such religious obligations. Or perhaps he mistakenly decided that given his status as an international power he was above any kind of strict adherence to the law. Or maybe he naively decided that covenantal observance was a thing of the past, a practice with which only the old tribal Israel was concerned. Whatever his reasons, the Deuteronomist's opinion is clear. The moral and religious decline of one man has shattered the promised destiny of the house of David. Only one tribe will constitute the house of David. The nation will divide.

Literary Analysis

Solomon bears responsibility for God's promised division of the kingdom. This overarching theme cuts across two major sections of the chapter (vv. 1-13 and 14-40). In part one (11:1-13), two subsections delineate the cause of this unthinkable catastrophe. First, the waywardness of Solomon (vv. 1-8) is set forth without qualification. He has turned to many foreign women and made them his wives in explicit violation of covenantal law. Second, the unconditional nature of the covenant grounds the narrative in the second subsection (vv. 9-13). It guarantees judgment and punishment in the face of violations against God's statutes, particularly, the law against apostasy. Swiftly, the narrative introduces God's anger with Solomon and the consequent sentencing of him for such blatant infidelity. This first section ends with a caveat softening the otherwise deadly blow. For the sake of David and for the sake of Jerusalem, God will give one tribe into the hand of Solomon's son (v. 13). Hence, though Solomon will be punished for his covenantal infidelity, God will remain faithful to the covenantal promise; David's line will endure.

Part two of this chapter turns attention to how this sentence and punishment will be carried out. Like the format of part one, two subsections govern this exposition (vv. 11-25, 26-40). The first unit (vv. 11-25) earmarks external threats to Solomon's kingdom that are on the rise. The twice repeated formulaic introduction, "Then the LORD raised up an adversary against Solomon" (vv. 14, 23), introduces two outside threats in this first segment. The fugitives, Hadad and Rezon, who were unsuccessfully hunted by the house of David, have now been dubbed the instruments of God's wrath against David's son Solomon. Their status as fugitives constitutes a threat to Solomon that serves as the instrument of divine punishment that governs the second section here.

In the latter half of part two (vv. 26-40), Jeroboam emerges as the internal stumbling block to the endurance of Solomon's kingdom. His encounter with the prophet Ahijah on the road outside Jerusalem makes clear that all but the tribe of Judah will be handed over to him as ruler. Although no explanation is given whether Solomon knew of the prophet's oracle, the conclusion of the narrative takes an abrupt but logical turn. The king sought to kill Jeroboam. This section ends with the summary that Jeroboam flees and lives as a fugitive in Egypt until the death of Solomon (v. 40). Hence in part two the house of Solomon is portrayed as endangered by both external threats (vv. 11-25) and internal threats (vv. 26-40), both characterized as instruments of divine wrath.

Across the broad literary landscape fashioning the Solomon era, chapter 11 functions as narrative axis heralding a massive reversal of events. As the narrative pinnacle of Solomonic greatness, chapters 9 and 10 pointed to Solomon's national and international renown. Now all that has been overturned. The Solomonic empire is under threat both from outside and from within, and only Solomon himself is to blame. But the realization of the divine sentence lies outside this king's purview. The chapter concludes with a regnal resume accompanied by an obituary notice.

Exegetical Analysis

The Culmination of Solomon's Waywardness (11:1-8)

The opening sentence signals the culmination of the turning away from the Lord that has attracted Solomon during his entire career. "King Solomon loved many foreign women along with the daughter of Pharaoh" (11:1). This final chapter begins by reminding us of the beginning of Solomon's career as ruler. In chapter 3:1-3, Solomon began his rule by taking a foreign woman, the daughter of Pharaoh, as a wife (3:1). However, at the same time, it was also noted that "Solomon loved the LORD" (3:3). Because of the inherent temptation "to serve other gods" enjoined by intermarriage with outsiders, Deut 7:1-4 forbade any union between Israelites and the inhabitants of Canaan. Hence, as a safeguard against apostasy, the law also extended to the prohibition of marriage with any non-Israelite (Fretheim, 63, and Walsh, 70). Thus, right at the beginning of his reign as king, a decision in concert with his love for the Lord or a decision in tandem with his attraction to that which the law forbade pressed upon Solomon. The international security that marriage to an Egyptian princess could provide was already assured instead by God's gifts at Gibeon. Solomon was promised wealth, international regard, and a long life. Therefore he could be free to use another great gift that God provided—the gift of wisdom—in order "to govern your people, able to discern between good from evil" (3:9).

The choice Solomon made again and again over the course of his life is clear. The final assessment that unfolds in these verses (vv. 1-8) is less about breaking one law of Deuteronomy as it is about his repeated choices that now culminate in comprehensive waywardness. Polygamy itself is not the issue. That was a common and accepted practice in the ancient world. Failure to trust in the Lord is the crime here. The involvement with women from Egyptian, Moabite, Ammonite, Edomite, Sidonian, and Hittite kingdoms indicts Solomon. Such intermarriages grew out of inter-

national alliances and treaties by which nations secured themselves before enemy threats. Solomon's guilt lies in placing his
trust in the power of others rather than in God. Moreover, the
number of wives, "seven hundred princesses and three hundred
concubines" (v. 3), even among ancient practices and even assuming some hyperbole, is unconscionable. It bespeaks an excess of
one who has lost touch with reality and with relationships. Here,
no prospect of human relationship or care exists. Women have
been reduced to a commodity to exchange and to possess. The
iteration of his love for foreign women (vv. 1-2) in such numbers
does not convey intimate caring but a recalcitrant attachment to
these women as possession and obsession. Moreover, the unimaginable number of wives coincides with behavior patterns well
established throughout his lifetime. Excess has defined this king's
ambitions. Across this narrative, we have seen Solomon caught up
in amassing luxuries and possessions. His plan to build a temple
to the Lord expanded to a project that included five other buildings, larger and more extravagantly appointed for his own opulent
style of living than the temple itself. In violation of covenant law,
he acquired horses and chariots again and again. He even constructed permanent facilities for them in his kingdom, as well as
brokering their trade between nations. His accumulation of gold
and other precious materials such as almug wood, silver, and precious stones showed no limits despite the warning in Deuteronomy
against the accumulation of wealth. Hence, the unbelievable number of wives he possesses symbolizes more than his insistent violation of the law barring acquiring many wives. It narrates a
man whose heart is driven by excess, an excess that puts him in
violation not only of one statute but of many covenantal laws.

A heart so distracted is necessarily a heart "not true to the LORD
his God" (v. 4). It is only a small step now to actually setting his
heart and attention on other deities. In virtue or in vice, one thing
leads to another, or so the story goes. Solomon's repeated transgressions of the covenant climax with a turning away from God.
The Solomon who "loved the LORD" in the beginning of his career
now follows "Astarte the goddess of the Sidonians, and Milcom
the abomination of the Ammonites" (v. 5). In addition, he builds

high places and cultic sites for the worship of other abominations, Chemosh and Molech.

The evaluative tone of this concluding account of Solomon's career is unmistakably negative. There is no mincing of words here. Indeed, "Solomon did what was evil in the sight of the LORD" (v. 6). All the infidelity and immorality that had been dressed in luxuries, appointed in gold, and hiding behind an unmerited reputation has come to light. Now, at the end of his life, Solomon's sinfulness is before him. Its consequences will craft his legacy. Divine judgment and punishment swiftly follow.

Divine Judgment (11:9-13)

The narrative of Solomon's actions in the first part of the account (vv. 1-8) sets the stage for the judgment that follows (vv. 9-13). However, God is not angry with Solomon merely for his marriages to foreign women and the associated idolatry. Rather, the problem is more pervasive and comprehensive; Solomon's heart has turned away from the Lord. How could this happen?

Twice the Lord privileged Solomon with personal encounters (3:3-15; 9:4-9). On both occasions God impressed upon Solomon the need to keep the covenant, the laws, and the statutes. However, the laws were not ends in themselves but the means to intimate covenantal relationship with God. Keeping the laws and the statutes makes kinship with this God possible. Solomon is punished not just because he has broken the law or even a whole host of laws; rather, it is the cumulative effect of his violations of the laws that have led to this judgment. Small choices against covenant over the course of his life have eventually mushroomed to their fullest effect—the king's complete and total about-face. The man who at the beginning of his career once "loved the LORD" (3:3) is now the man who at the end of his reign has "turned away from the LORD" (v. 9).

There is no choice even for a merciful God. In the face of such a lifelong habit of decisions against covenant, judgment must come. The kingdom will be torn from Solomon's hand and given to another. That it will be given to his servant draws attention to the severity of both the crime and the punishment. Solomon, to whom all divine promises of prosperity, fame, and riches had come, turned away from the Lord. As punishment, the kingdom will not be turned over to another powerful ruler or to an international figure equal in stature to Israel's great monarch. Instead, the kingdom will come into the hand of a "servant." The one who will usurp Solomon's sovereign place is but his servant.

Still, the promise made to David tempers the severity of the Lord's anger and punishment. Two caveats soften the sharpness and gravity of the divine blow. First, God promises that a tribe will be spared and put in the charge of Solomon's own son. But this is for the sake of David, not Solomon. At the same time, the reference to "tribe" suggests God's recognition of the tribal configuration of Israel from the past as well as chastisement of Solomon's redistricting of the land (9:10) (Walsh, 136). Second, the punishment is further mitigated. The kingdom will be "torn away" only after Solomon's death. Still, it is small consolation to a powerful king to know that all that he has amassed in a lifetime and that is associated with his name is going to be dashed and dismantled soon after his death. The seriousness of the divine punishment carries its own commentary. There can be no doubt about the gravity of Solomon's misdeeds in the Lord's assessment. A heart so utterly turned away from the Lord explains so comprehensive a sentence.

External Threats (11:14-25)

God's punishment is swift. The pronouncement of the divine judgment meted out to Solomon has hardly come to a close when we hear of the instruments of the Lord's punishment being stirred. Immediately, this next section narrates the Lord raising up two adversaries against Solomon (vv. 14, 23). The international renown of Solomon that only a chapter earlier seemed uncompromisingly secure now appears endangered by two external threats.

First, we hear about Hadad of Edom who, according to the story, had earlier survived a deadly campaign against his own countrymen led by David's military chief Joab. The episode likely refers to 2 Sam 8:13-14, an account of a crusade bent upon exterminating vast numbers of Edomites. The scant account narrates that Hadad, then only a child, escaped by journeying through Midian and Paran on the way to Egypt. Like a replay of previous tales, Pharaoh looked favorably upon the youth, providing a house, land, provisions, and even a member of the royal family for him as a wife.

Hearing that David and Joab are dead, Hadad now moves to renounce his Egyptian refuge. He is determined to leave behind security, well-being, and luxury of life in the royal household in order to return to his native land. Though a foreigner, Hadad's determination before a resistant pharaoh to forego the safe sanctuary of Egypt suggests a man of integrity.

The account concerning Hadad is quite brief and the actual role he will play is never clarified. Nonetheless, some unmistakable parallels between this Edom fugitive and God's chosen leader Moses from earlier days warrant attention to Hadad's role in the narrative. As Hadad escapes to Midian to escape the wrath of a king, so too did Moses seek safe haven in that north Arabian oasis. As Hadad was raised and gifted by the generosity of an Egyptian pharaoh, so too was Moses nurtured within the royal Egyptian household. And as Hadad now seeks to leave Egypt in the face of a resistant pharaoh, so too did Moses seek to exit the land of the Nile against the wishes of the ruling sovereign. Although the information never specifies in what way Hadad will be the Lord's instrument of punishment, the parallels between Hadad and Moses craft the clear impression that external threats to the Solomonic kingdom are the result of divine causation.

In a similar fashion, Rezon, introduced and described as Solomon's adversary, parallels another great Israelite figure, David. Rezon is described as a leader of a band of outlaws. Like David, he was not only servant to a king, but also ended up fleeing from his overlord. Later, he returns to Damascus, captures the city, and eventually is elevated as its king. The parallel with David, who returns after Saul's death to capture Jerusalem and eventually reign as king there, is sharp. Once again, it remains undefined just how Rezon will function as God's punishment against the house of Solomon. However, that he parallels another agent appointed by God to carry out the divine plan clearly depicts him as an instrument in the divine scheme of judgment and punishment upon the house of Solomon.

An Internal Threat (11:26-40)

The preceding brief presentation of Hadad and Rezon establishes them as external threats to the well-being of the Solomonic kingdom. Their account is counterbalanced by an extended narrative introducing Jeroboam as an internal affront to the king. Jeroboam is identified as the son of Zeruah, a widow. Although the lack of patrimonial designation is unusual in the introduction of important figures in the biblical tradition, the absence serves to direct our attention to another dimension of his identity, his tribal origins. Jeroboam is an Ephramite. Ephraim is located in the southern portion of the central hill country, the region where most of the tribes of Israel settled. It was reputed for its rich, fertile lands that were geographically better protected than most of the other tribal locations. Ephraim had an immensely important role throughout Israel's history. The old sacral worship centers at Shiloh, Bethel, and Shechem were located in Ephraim. Therefore, it had served as a familiar place visited in the past by Israelites from other tribes. That some of Israel's key leaders such as Joshua and Samuel came from Ephraim establishes a precedent for the role that Jeroboam is about to play. Immediately after this brief biographical sketch the record notes that Jeroboam rebelled against Solomon and declares that what follows sets forth the reason for his revolt.

As the account of Jeroboam unfolds, the relations between Solomon and Jeroboam appear, at least initially, more than amicable. Solomon regards Jeroboam as a man of valor (*gedol hayil*). He entrusts the young Ephramite with the job of foreman over a core group from the house of Joseph. They are presumably working on the Millo (9:15, 24), a type of support construction for a building or even parts of a city often adjacent to surrounding walls. All is set to go right between this king and his appointee—except that it doesn't. The unexpected encounter between Ahijah the prophet and Jeroboam reverses the expected cooperation between Solomon and Jeroboam.

Ahijah is introduced as a prophet from Shiloh. This is the first time since the appearance of Nathan in chapter 1 that we encounter a prophet and the role prophets play in ancient Israel. Across the two books of Kings, prophets emerge as the contrasting counterpart to kings. At the beginning of these tales, David's prophet Nathan figures prominently in the close of David's reign and the rise of Solomon to power. Prophets are crucial to kings throughout these narratives. However, the relations between kings and prophets are often characterized by tension and sometimes erode to the point of enmity. Prophets were intermediaries between God and kings and God and the people. They supported and were critical of kings. Monarchs both consulted prophets and viewed them as threats. More often than not, the words the prophets spoke and their interpretation of events from God's viewpoint formed a sharply contrasting alternative to what kings said and did.

The characterization of Ahijah as a prophet from Shiloh generates a sense of tension in regard to the Solomonic kingdom. Shiloh was the old northern shrine. It was a center of the sacral Mosaic tradition and its understanding of tribal Israel. Thus, as cultic center, Shiloh is Jerusalem's rival. Characteristically, the prophet employs both deed and word in the delivery of the divine message. First, the prophet takes hold of his own new garment and tears it into twelve pieces in the presence of Jeroboam. The enlistment of the word *tear* here facilitates the obvious connection to the Lord's promised punishment to Solomon, "I will surely *tear* the kingdom from you and give it to your servant" (v. 11). The twelve pieces anticipate the return to the tribal division that had been erased with Solomon's districting policies. Further, the Hebrew consonants of the word *garment* (*slm*) closely resemble the consonants of Solomon's name (*slm*). Like the prophet's garment, Solomon's house will be ripped apart and divided once again into twelve tribes.

The word delivered by the prophet Ahijah is equally compelling. His oracular pronouncement in verses 33-39 focuses upon what has been and what will be. First, the prophet rehearses a summary of Solomon's past. In short, Israel's king has forsaken the Lord, culminating in the worship of a whole litany of foreign deities. He has ignored the statutes and laws and thus turned away from covenant. The prophet's speech here not only rehearses the past but also justifies the punishment the Lord is about to set forth. As if to mirror the two parts into which the kingdom will now be divided, Ahijah divides his pronouncement of what will be into two parts. First, he indicates that one part of the kingdom will go to Solomon's son. The area in and around Jerusalem will be the domain of the Solomonic heir. However, the prophet makes clear that it is only for the sake of David and for the sake of God's own name worshiped there that the Jerusalem region is being preserved. Though the kingdom is severed, God's unconditional promise to the house of David is maintained.

In the second part of the pronouncement about the future, the prophet assigns to Jeroboam the rulership of the ten tribes. Jeroboam will be king of Israel and, like previous rulers, is bound by the covenantal language of obedience. "If you will listen to all that I command you, walk in my ways, and do what is right in my sight by keeping my statutes and my commandments, as David my servant did, I will be with you, and will build you an enduring house, as I built for David, and I will give Israel to you" (v. 38). The conditional nature of the promise to Jeroboam echoes the terms bridling Solomon's kingship. However, the promise of presence, "I will be with you . . ." reminds us of the cadences of the Mosaic and Davidic traditions and God's continual assurance of dwelling among the people.

Ahijah's speech ends by reiterating God's determination to punish disobedient descendants of David. However, like the caveat that mitigated the impact of the punishment to Solomon, once again, the addition of the qualifier "but not forever" discloses the wellspring of divine mercy. Even in the face of the utter and complete disobedience of Solomon and his house, God's wrath does not persist.

The account of Jeroboam's election as king of the soon-to-be northern Israel ends with a narrative summary of Solomon's determination to kill Jeroboam. Although nothing in the account indicates that Solomon is privy to this encounter between Jeroboam and Ahijah, as the story closes Solomon knows of such sentiments. The amicable relations between the king and his servant have now turned sour. Such enmity prompts Jeroboam to flee to Egypt. The geographical reference and the familiarity of this course of events put Jeroboam in the line of other great leaders from Israel's sacral past. Joseph was received in Egypt where he rose to greatness. Moses, too, lived and was nurtured among Egyptian royalty before becoming the liberator of the people. And David's rise to power was preceded by his days as a fugitive, though not in Egypt. The stage is set for a new era of leadership in Israel to begin. The obituary that follows, recording the end of Solomon, also signals the beginning of new leadership.

The Death of Solomon (11:41-43)

This closing unit introduces what will become the formulaic summary characterizing the close of the reign and the death of subsequent kings across these two books. Such a scheme will vary in its elements but typically serves as a concluding abstract of the sovereign's reign. It can include a brief resumé, a theological assessment of their standing before the Lord, a chronological reference, a note on their successor, or an occasional citation of other sources where more information is recorded about their reign.

The summary on Solomon opens by referring to such a source, that is, the Book of the Acts of Solomon, where the rest of his acts are recorded. The number of years Solomon reigned in Jerusalem is recorded as "forty" here. Concluding remarks locate his burial in the city of David and designate as successor his son Rehoboam. However, particular to Solomon's regnal summary, here is a final mention of wisdom. The reference of a resource recording the rest of Solomon's acts as king suggests that additional accounts of his wisdom can be found there. On the heels of the preceding narrative of Solomon's waywardness, the reference to further accounts of "all his wisdom" serves as a subtle indictment leveled by history itself. For as we have seen across these chapters, the accumulation of the deeds of this king qualify—in a most derogatory fashion—rather than exalt the kind of wisdom Solomon exhibited.

Theological and Ethical Analysis

Ungodly oppressive policies along with apostasy are often ear-marked as Solomon's crucial lapse in judgment. In the biblical tradition, turning to other gods is always marshaled as an explanation for the catastrophic end to what was supposed to be a glorious reign. Years ago some even referred to the tenure of this king as the age of Solomonic Enlightenment, tarnished only by an understandable but unfortunate decision to accommodate the deities of his foreign wives. When weighed against all his magnificent accomplishments, a bit of defensiveness is readily conjured on behalf of this king. Perhaps the divine punishment was too harsh, even impulsive, given all that Solomon had done. However, as we have attended to all the hints disclosing the underside of Solomon's accomplishments across these chapters, perhaps it is precisely on account of *all that Solomon had done* that the sentence at the end of this eventful career was utterly justified as well as long overdue. Perhaps the judgment against Solomon, long in coming, manifests not so much the harshness of God's judgment, but rather witnesses to absolute mercifulness and patience on the part of the Lord.

Apostasy was not simply Solomon's one-time sinful choice meriting divine punishment at the end of an otherwise faithful life. Rather it was the culmination of a series of choices symbolizing Solomon's gradual but nevertheless persistent turning away from the Lord. At the end of his reign, the indictment of apostasy narrates as well as climaxes a lifelong series of decisions to pursue other powers, to become caught up in other preoccupations, and to succumb to other attractions apart from covenantal relationship with the Lord. What began as a few minor transgressions, left unchecked, eventually mushrooms into a full-blown about-face. Hence, at the end of his career, those repeated pursuits in directions away from the Lord and the covenant to which Solomon was bound yield a judgment of apostasy.

Early in his reign, we heard that Solomon had some fundamental choices to make that would govern not only the course of his kingship but the course of his relationship with God. Indeed, he "loved the LORD" (3:3). This is the heart of covenantal faith. But in Israel, love of the Lord could never exist as some sort of spiritual abstraction or philosophical conviction. Elaborated across the covenant statutes, it is always transposed into demands insisting upon "love of neighbor." For one who was Israel's king, that private devotion of loving the Lord must be realized in very specific public manifestations. Love of the Lord must be transposed into concrete economic, social, and political expressions of care for the other. In principle, Solomon seemed to understand this. When he comes before the Lord, both in the dream at Gibeon and in the temple at its dedication, the people and their well-being are the focus of his prayer. At Gibeon, he asks to have an understanding mind to govern this great people. God grants him that and more, promising him riches, honor, and length of days. With such divine insurance for his own well-being, wealth, and honor, Solomon is free to set his attention on governing the people with a wise and understanding heart. At the dedication of the temple (chapter 8), Solomon again makes the people the focus of his prayer. He asks God to ensure Israel's well-being, that is, protect its people from famine, enemies, and sickness, and to grant forgiveness if they sin, as well as restoration if they are driven from home by their enemy. However, when the substance of his prayer life is compared with the account of his public life, a portrait of spiritual bankruptcy emerges.

Across these eleven chapters, the detailed account of what Solomon did to ensure his own well-being and that of his royal household in and around Jerusalem stands in stark contrast to the narrative's silence as to exactly what he did to ensure the well-being of the people of Israel. In addition to the temple, we know what lavish palace buildings Solomon erected for his royal family and the affairs of state. However, we know nothing of the kind of housing in which the people in the hill country dwelled. We are provided accounts of the elaborate food provisions available to Solomon and his royal house for each day (4:22-23), and we hear of the elaborate provisions made available to Hiram in exchange for cedar and cypress (5:10-11). However, we hear nothing of what the people of Israel ate or whether they had the necessary provisions for themselves and their families after they had provided for the king. The excess of gold, silver, spices, and precious imports such as almug wood could become the stimulus to grow an economy that would benefit all. But instead, we hear nothing of economic planning that provides much beyond the glittering lifestyle of those associated with Solomon's royal house. Indeed, even the queen of Sheba comments that Solomon's servants fare very well. But of the quality of life characterizing the majority of Israelites, we hear very little. When they are referenced, they are going out to labor in one of Solomon's projects for one quarter of their year, or some of their towns and villages are being handed over as payment for Solomon's imports.

Indeed, Solomon loved the Lord. But the public manifestation of that private devotion exposed his spiritual orientation as mere facade. Over the course of a lifetime, an insatiable hunger for power and privilege amassed. Eventually the cumulative effect of such an orientation exposed itself as sin. Apostasy is its name. Oppression is its tactic. Greed is its dynamism. Social inequities are its product. God's punishment will level the unevenness of these circumstances. The power of the ruler will be torn away by one without power. The office of the sovereign will be handed over to his servant. The nation upon which he built his fame will divide.

1 KINGS 12

With the close of Solomon's reign and the concluding note of his death and burial, the promised consequences for his inattention to the covenantal statutes begin to materialize. The impression of political stability and national unity during his reign quickly disclose themselves as mere appearances. When Rehoboam moves to ascend the throne, he unwisely refuses to lighten the people's burden. Immediately, in fulfillment of the prophet's word, the people rebel, making Jeroboam king of all Israel except for the tribe of Judah. But the events that unfold exceed the divine plan. Chapter 12 offers a snapshot view of not only how Jeroboam initially succeeds but also why he ultimately fails as the leader of the people.

Literary Analysis

Two uneven segments structure this chapter (vv. 1-24, 25-33). The first and major portion of the narrative (12:1-24) is devoted to the fulfillment of the prophecy of the Lord spoken by the prophet Ahijah (11:31-39). The kingdom would be torn to pieces and ten of the former tribes would be given to Jeroboam to rule as king. The second major section (vv. 25-33) records a fast-moving exposition of the activities Jeroboam undertakes to secure his reign.

The first section is marked off by an introduction (vv. 1-2) and a conclusion (v. 24) that set up and then reverse the circumstances narrated here. In the opening of this section, Rehoboam has gone to Shechem. All Israel, along with Jeroboam who has returned from Egypt, has assembled to make him king. In the conclusion, Rehoboam and all his troops bent upon attacking Jeroboam and the northern tribes are commanded by God to disperse and go home. In the opening of the story, Rehoboam is king before the people and before Jeroboam, who had earlier fled to Egypt. In the conclusion of the account, Jeroboam is king and Rehoboam must flee.

The story of Jeroboam's ascent to kingship unfolds across a story centered upon Rehoboam, Solomon's son. Following the introduction, a series of three vignettes (vv. 3-16, 17-20, 21-24), which feature the character and action of Rehoboam, give rise to and confirm Jeroboam's rule. In the opening scene, a cycle of exchanges first between Rehoboam and Israel and then between Rehoboam and his advisors positions northern Israel to rebel. In the first encounter (vv. 3-5), Israel headed by Jeroboam approaches Rehoboam and asks him to lighten the load of hard service they carried under his father Solomon. Rehoboam orders them to return in three days for his response. Next, a set of consultations takes place (vv. 6-7, 8-11). Rehoboam initially consults the older men who had served under Solomon, then with the younger men he grew up with whom he has evidently elevated to royal office. The latter advise Rehoboam to be far harsher than his father as a show of strength and as a means to ensure the people's subservience. In the fourth and final exchange of this first scene (vv. 12-16), Israel returns after three days. Rehoboam informs them of his unsympathetic decision, which instigates a response in word and deed on the part of Israel, bringing the first scene to a conclusion.

In the next scene (vv. 17-20), Rehoboam reigns over all Israel and determines to secure the people's compliance by a show of force. However, the narrator concludes the section by noting that all the tribes followed the newly established King Jeroboam instead—except for the tribe of Judah.

Finally, in the third scene (vv. 21-23), Rehoboam rallies the troops in and around Jerusalem as well as those he controls in the territory of Benjamin. Determined to restore his power over the whole kingdom, he plans to fight against the house of Israel. But as this final scene closes, Rehoboam, who went to Shechem at the beginning of the story to become king of Israel, returns home to Jerusalem as the king of only Judah (v. 24). It is curious that a story explaining the rise of Jeroboam is so fixed and navigated by the character of Rehoboam and his deeds.

The second section of the chapter (vv. 25-33) offers some explanation for this strange focus. What follows is a short exposition of Jeroboam's activities to secure his kingship that at first glance appears innocuous. However, the importance that might have been assigned to the rise of Jeroboam's kingship is quickly diminished by what he does to ensure his reign. In the series of archival-like notes, the narrative reports on his activities: building projects, setting up cultic sites, earmarking festivals, offering sacrifices—projects that parallel the kinds of work characterizing Solomon's reign. However, in contrast to the delayed reprimand following the lengthy, detailed exposition of Solomon's activities, the condemnation of Jeroboam comes quickly. What Jeroboam did is evaluated as sinful (v. 30). Hence, whereas the story sets out to describe the rise of Jeroboam's kingship, it quickly anticipates his downfall. Whereas it narrates how he succeeds in rising to kingship, it also makes clear why he ultimately fails.

Exegetical Analysis

The Northern Tribes Secede the Nation (12:1-16)

The story opens by introducing Rehoboam and Jeroboam (vv. 1-2). Rehoboam has gone to Shechem in order to be confirmed as king before all Israel. That Jerusalem is the capital city, the site of the temple, and the place where the king's royal palace is situated, makes Rehoboam's three-day journey to this old northern cultic center curious as well as revelatory. It suggests that the dual identity of Israel and Judah that was supposedly merged under David and cemented under Solomon may not have been quite as unified as it seemed. Rehoboam's kingship cannot be presumed. He must travel north to Shechem in order to secure public support for his rule. Though son of Solomon and heir in the house of David, Rehoboam's kingship is not automatic.

In that same introductory opening, Jeroboam, who had fled from Solomon and escaped to Egypt, returns when he hears Rehoboam has gone up to Shechem. That Jeroboam returns and is present at the Shechem assembly suggests his lack of fear of Rehoboam. In the first round of exchanges (vv. 3-5), he and the assembly of Israel confront Rehoboam. Their collective oration has the character of a showdown or even an ultimatum. First, they indict Solomon. "Your father made our yoke heavy" (v. 4). What we suspected in the Solomonic era has now been confirmed. The greatness of Rehoboam's father and all his accomplishments was at the expense of the lives of countless laborers and their families. Now the people make clear their requirements for Rehoboam's rule over them. "Lighten the hard service of your father and his heavy yoke that he placed upon us, and we will serve you" (v. 4). Rehoboam's kingship over this people is not guaranteed. Their allegiance to him is contingent upon terms that they themselves name. Rehoboam takes time and counsel before responding. He tells them to return in three days for his answer.

A series of two consultations follow. First, Rehoboam takes counsel with the older men, likely Solomon's own advisors, regarding how he should respond (vv. 6-7). "How do you advise me to answer this people?" (v. 6). Their identification as "older men" conjures expectations of wise counsel. Though their leniency encourages this impression, in the end it reveals itself as a sham. They urge Rehoboam to be of service and speak good words to the people for the sole purpose of securing the people's perpetual service to him. After all, that's what this is about. The people constituting the labor force are resisting and must be coaxed back into submission. But Rehoboam disregards the elders' advice. He is interested in securing the people's servant status in his labor camps. He is not interested in being their servant. So Rehoboam seeks further advice.

In the second round of consultations, Rehoboam turns to "the young men who had grown up with him and now attended him" (v. 8). Rehoboam consults them because he "disregarded the advice that the older men gave him" (v. 8). He evidently had confidence that these younger peers would tell him what he wanted to hear. As "younger men," they, like Rehoboam, were inexperienced. The story conveys the impression that these young members of the Solomonic royal class were indulged youths with a strong sense of entitlement. That they "now attended him" implies not only favoritism in their appointments but that their jobs could depend upon the counsel they gave.

Moreover, the advice Rehoboam now seeks from the younger men subtly contrasts with what he sought from the older men. Previously he inquired as to the manner of responding to the northerners. "How do you advise me to answer this people?" (v. 6). Not having received the answer he was looking for, Rehoboam asks the younger men exactly *what* to say. The rhetoric of question underscores his dependence upon them, "What do you advise that *we* answer this people . . . ?" (v. 9). The use of the first-person plural "we" also indicates his insistence that the decision appear as the product of a powerful united front. His request encourages the young men to advise a policy of intimidation.

Prompted by Rehoboam's question, the younger men's counsel is harsh and vulgar. They script an answer for the king filled with crude images intended to drive home the gravity of their threatened response. Rehoboam is told to say, "My little finger [likely a reference to the male sexual organ] is thicker than my father's loins" (v. 10). Such a strategy bespeaks their brashness and machismo. Inexperience yields what might be expected. Characteristic of young men endowed with power they did not earn, they urge Rehoboam to take a hard line in responding to the people. Rehoboam is directed not only to acknowledge Solomon's oppression of them, "Now, whereas my father laid on you a heavy yoke . . ." (v. 11), he is to hold that standard up as a benchmark about to be surpassed with his new regime. The assigned speech, "I will add to your yoke" indicates their labor will be increased, not decreased. And "I will discipline you with scorpions" signifies that the discipline for those who might resist will be ever more severe.

The final exchange between Rehoboam and the people takes place when they return for his response. Fortunately, he recites only part of the script provided to him by the younger men. Still, his words both acknowledge the oppressiveness of his father and his own intention to be yet harsher. Narrative tension increases, then diminishes when the narrator interprets Rehoboam's refusal to listen to the people as fulfilling Yahweh's plan. The reference to Ahijah, the prophet, specifically connects the foretold rise of Jeroboam to kingship with the obstinacy of Rehoboam before Israel.

The encounter between Rehoboam and Israel comes to a conclusion. With word and deed Israel responds to Rehoboam's recalcitrance. First, with poetic words they disassociate themselves from the house of David. In the first couplet, they repudiate any alliance with the Davidic rulers. The harshness of their lives warrants their collective rejection of Rehoboam's claim on them. In the concluding couplet, the expression "To your tents, O Israel!" (v. 16) enlists the language of separation. The closing pronouncement, "Look now to your own house, O David" (v. 16), resounds as an over-the-shoulder rejoinder that makes clear the divisiveness that now reigns in the land. Their words are followed by their deeds. "Israel went away to their tents" (v. 16). With this pronouncement and gesture Israel turns its back on Rehoboam's despotism. The northern tribes take their first step toward seceding from the nation.

The Northern Tribes Rebel (12:17-20)

In the second scene featuring Rehoboam on the way to Jeroboam's rise, the new king of Judah tries to assert control over the northern people. Immediately, his lack of experience and ineptness as a ruler lead to the expected disastrous results. Resorting to both the tactics and the persons who proved effective under his father's reign, Rehoboam sends Adoram to the north as "taskmaster over the forced labor" (v. 18). Adoram had success-fully held the same position under Solomon during the various building projects of the past (4:6; 5:4). Since his threatening words proved ineffective before these rebels, Rehoboam now resorts to threatening them with the harshness of taskmasters. But this is a new era. When Adoram goes north, the people seize him and stone him. Rehoboam, who is also present, quickly mounts his chariot and flees for Jerusalem. Adoram is left to die while the new king saves his own life. The narrator's note suggests that such episodes were not an exception but defined the nature of the future. "So Israel has been in rebellion against the house of David to this day" (v. 19).

The narrative tension brought about by Israel's rejection of Rehoboam begins to diminish with the report of Jeroboam's return (v. 20). As the story continues, they call an assembly and make Jeroboam their king (v. 20). At first this verse raises some confusion with reference to the assembly at Shechem recorded in verse 2. There the narrative records that Jeroboam had returned from Egypt and was already among the people who confront Rehoboam. However, the NRSV translation likely creates this complication by translating two different Hebrew words in verses 2 and 3 and verse 20 as "assembly." Hence, it is possible that an earlier account intended to portray two different groups that met for two different purposes. Moreover, in verse 20, when "all Israel heard that Jeroboam returned," it need not be referring to his return from Egypt. It may also be read as his returning from Shechem. In any case, the second scene ends with Jeroboam as king over all Israel. In tandem with this event the narrator offers the concluding note that no one followed Rehoboam, except the tribe of Judah alone.

Rehoboam's Planned Attack Is Thwarted (12:21-24)

Having fled from the northern territory upon the death of his foreman Adoram, Rehoboam is now safe at home in Jerusalem.

But the notion of a divided nation is unthinkable to the new king. He assembles an army of incredible numbers (180,000) from both Judah and Benjamin. According to tradition, Benjamin was a tribe on the northern border of Judah. Saul was a Benjaminite, suggesting that early on the northern insurgents who resisted consolidation of the north and south under David were probably from this region. Hence, it is likely that the Benjamin territory had to come under direct control earlier for the successful establishment of the house of David and the subsequent continuation of that house under Solomon. Whereas sentiments in Benjamin were likely with the north, the mention of Rehoboam drawing troops from Benjamin as well as Judah suggests the continuation of that control. The mention of Benjamin here also fulfills the rest of Ahijah's prophecy regarding the one tribe that will remain under the control of Solomon's son (11:32).

As Rehoboam musters his troops for a campaign northward to restore the kingdom, Shemaiah, a man of God, is introduced into the whirlwind of preparations. God commissions Shemaiah to inform Rehoboam that he is not to go up against Israel. All that has taken place is according to the plan of the Lord. Hence, Ahijah's earlier prophecy that foretold the division of the kingdom is paralleled here by the word of another man of God. Shemaiah confirms that the present tearing apart of the kingdom fulfills the divine plan. The king and the people's response confirmed the credibility that such a man of God's word had. This first narrative section ends by reporting that "they heeded the word of the Lord and went home again, according to the word of the Lord" (v. 24).

Jeroboam's Kingship and the Golden Calves (12:25-33)

As the second major section of the chapter opens, its narrative focus shifts. Finally, Jeroboam, the newly claimed king of the northern tribes, becomes prominent in the narrative. Jeroboam has been granted an abundance of reliable evidence upon which to move forward confidently as king. While he was still working in Jerusalem (11:29-39), the prophet, as the intermediary of God, confirmed the Lord's plan and consequently the approval of Jeroboam's kingship. Moreover, he has "all Israel's" support.

Jeroboam's rise to kingship is one of the most trouble-free and uncontested recorded in the accounts of the northern monarch in the books of Kings. Still, before his retreat to Egypt, Jeroboam served under Solomon. He may well have known the military capacity residing in Judah. He likely knew of the value religion had in creating allegiance and building statehood. Moreover, anyone with the slightest amount of political savvy knows the fickleness of people when it comes to standing behind their national leader. Hence, some of Jeroboam's early gestures as king are defensive moves.

First, he establishes a residence for himself at Shechem and then builds up Penuel. Immediately, he constructs two cultic centers at Bethel in the south and at Dan in the north as national shrines. He obviously understands the symbolic value and attraction of the temple in Jerusalem. The creation of two new high places is a clear, stopgap measure designed to discourage the interest in Jerusalem by cultivating the identification and allegiance of the people with these new centers and with the associated king. The convenience of one in the north and one in the south might have been attractive, or might even have been in response to past complaints from the people of the northernmost hill country who had to travel all the way to Jerusalem. Moreover, Dan and Bethel were important, ancient tribal Israelite sacred sites. For example, according to early traditions, Israel's great ancestor Jacob built an altar at Bethel (Gen 28:10-22; 35:1-7). Hence, Jeroboam's building activities at these locations may not have been perceived as instituting something new, but as reviving and thus respecting old sacred traditions and the places with which these northern settlements identified.

Next, Jeroboam made and set up two golden calves in each location. In the ancient Near East, deities were commonly portrayed as riding or sitting on the backs of large animals. Even in the Jerusalem temple, the cherubim served as the Lord's throne in the Holy of Holies. In addition, Jeroboam appropriately employs priests at each cultic center, institutes festivals rivaling those in Judah, and oversees sacrifices and other familiar activities associated with shrines. Jeroboam himself goes up and burns incense in

Bethel. One gains the impression of a king who, like Solomon, gets right down to the important business of religious obligation—minus the extravagance and excesses for which his predecessor was known. Moreover, Jeroboam's flurry of activities in establishing these alternative national shrines is indicative of his political wisdom. Fostering national religious identity through the establishment of cultic centers and identification with a particular deity were all decisive political moves in the buildup of statehood. These infused a sense of national unity and helped cement popular support. Religion had a clear and powerful role in any successful political system in the ancient world. Jeroboam appears to act in order to build upon these understandings.

However, whereas Jeroboam's moves may conjure the impression of a quick-thinking, wise, new ruler whose actions merit praise, the account also introduces elements that qualify these credits. When he establishes the golden calves at each cultic site, the account offers the only quote we hear of Jeroboam speaking to the people. "You have gone up to Jerusalem long enough. Here are your gods, O Israel, who brought you up out of the land of Egypt" (v. 28). As rapidly as the reputation of Jeroboam began its ascent, it starts a perilous fall to its demise. Echoes of a previous tradition that led to God's angry destruction of the people resonate across this brief account. In Exod 32, Aaron fashioned a golden calf for the people to worship against the clear mandate of the first and second commandments, "You shall have no other gods before me" (Exod 20:3), and "You shall not make for yourself an idol, whether in the form of anything that is in heaven above, or that is on the earth beneath, or that is in the water under the earth" (Exod 20:4). According to this story, as a result of this misconduct, a large number of people were slain in the camp (Exod 23:28), and God promised to obliterate from the divine register the names of those who did such sinful deeds.

Jeroboam may have been gesturing to the area above the golden calves when he proclaims the presence of God to the people. But this account appears to parallel the account in Exod 32. This close relationship may have actually developed in the telling and retelling of this story. Although we have two separate traditions here, over time the telling of the sin of the Aaron tradition gradually qualifies and redefines the account of what Jeroboam was up to. When later editors prepared the final story of Jeroboam's deeds, the parallel in words and deeds of these two separate stories leads to an indictment against Jeroboam, his cultic centers, and golden calves. The resonances with the Exodus tale redefine this new king's activities as identical with Aaron's. Significantly, in the reference to the setting up of the calves in Bethel and Dan, the narrator notes parenthetically that "this thing became a sin" (v. 30). That it "became" a sin suggests that what Jeroboam did initially may not have been sinful, but rather was acceptable. However, over time, either because of cultic distortions, the incorporation of worshiping additional deities, or simply in the telling and retelling, what he did became sinful.

Theological and Ethical Analysis

Though providing an account of Jeroboam's ascent to divinely ordained kingship, much of this chapter's attention is fixed upon Rehoboam. When we finally focus upon the newly appointed royal leader of the north, his early actions reap indictment and condemnation. Why were Jeroboam's initial actions to establish his reign in the north met with such rapid judgment? Would not the establishment of cultic sites be appropriate ways for the people to worship Yahweh as they had in earlier times? If Jeroboam's setting up of the golden calves was initially a legitimate religious gesture to foster the worship of Yahweh, how did it "become" a sin?

The short catalog of events leading up to Jeroboam's recognition as king in the north was met with divine approval. One man of God prophesied that the kingdom would be torn away and given to Jeroboam (11:31-38). Another man of God (12:22-24) confirms that the tumultuous events leading up to his ascent were according to divine plan. But quickly something went terribly wrong, as Jeroboam does what we might expect a king to do in going about his early business as a new sovereign.

Even for new kings, religious actions are empty formulations if they are not grounded in heartfelt and faith-filled motives. Given

Solomon's disaster, Jeroboam's heart needed to fix on the Lord. Instead, other concerns distract him. He fears that the people will resort to Rehoboam (v. 26), and this anxiety does not stop there. The account allows us to eavesdrop on Jeroboam talking to himself. Though we have no evidence for what is fueling his worries, we hear him express fear that the people will kill him (v. 27). Whether his anxiety was legitimate or not, fear rather than faith seems to motivate what Jeroboam does. But it is not fear of the Lord. It is on the heels of these expressions of worry that Jeroboam sets up altars in the high places. Determined to compel popular support and favor as well as secure his own well-being and safety, Jeroboam establishes cultic sites. There is no hint that what he does he does for the Lord. His actions are driven by the political expediencies of his new role and imagined potential threats. They are an expression of his faulty confidence in exterior accoutrements as insurance of his popular reception as king.

Though Jeroboam "the servant" has replaced Solomon "the sovereign," when garbed in the role of "king" they look disturbingly alike. Solomon's building projects, temple construction, sacrifices, and accumulations of wealth and power turned out to be a major distraction and a cause for his turning away from the covenant fidelity to which he was called. Jeroboam appears to be journeying down the same path, despite the promised dead end. Religious formalism devoid of a heart set on the Lord leads one to the catastrophic outcome of personal and national demise. The establishment of cultic sites, the performance of cultic actions, and the participation in cultic prayer guarantee nothing before the Lord if backed by ulterior political motives. Political savvy and spiritual authority are difficult companions when resident in the same human heart. What Jeroboam has done becomes a sin. Accordingly, the fate of Solomon, whom the Lord authorized him to replace, will eventually become Jeroboam's own destiny.

1 KINGS 13

A man from Judah delivers God's condemnation of the altar at Bethel to Jeroboam. A whole series of signs confirms his pronouncement. The message is further iterated to the prophet at Bethel. Both the king and a Bethel prophet respond to this Word of the Lord. The contrast in their responses portends Jeroboam's future. The desecration of this altar serves as prelude to the condemnation of the king and his whole household.

Literary Analysis

As chapter 13 opens, it continues the context and builds upon the occasion with which chapter 12 ended. Jeroboam has gone up to Bethel to offer incense. The narrative that follows is a complex literary piece that unfolds in two parts (vv. 1-25, 26-34). Two major scenes craft part one of the chapter (vv. 1-10 and 11-25). The man of God from Judah figures centrally in each vignette. Parallels across these two sections loosely ally the two scenes. A prominent figure associated with the cultic shrine in the north (a king in scene one and a Bethel prophet in scene two) is central to each. In both instances the presence of the Judahite prophet occasions confirmatory signs of the word of the Lord. On both occasions hospitality is extended to and rejected by the visiting Judahite prophet. The pronouncement of the word of the Lord recurs significantly in each. The frequent iteration of "the word of the LORD" and the Hebrew word for "return/turn" across these sections anticipates the message lodged here. The word of the Lord beckons people to turn from their waywardness and return to the Lord with all their heart.

In scene one (vv. 1-10), King Jeroboam is officiating at the altar that the Judahite visitor condemns. When the king orders that the intruder be seized (v. 4), his own hand withers and he relents. The splitting apart of the Bethel altar (v. 5) along with the subsequent healing of the king's hand (v. 6) confirms the word of this man of God. According to his pronouncement, the altar at Bethel and its priesthood will be desecrated in the days of Josiah. The scene ends with the man of God's rejection of Jeroboam's compensatory invitation to dine and to receive a gift. Obedient to God's command, he departs by means of a different route from that by which he came.

In scene two (vv. 11-25), an old Bethel prophet determines to find this man of God from Judah and bring him to his house.

Aided by his sons, the prophet sets out on the donkey they provide and finds the man of God sitting under an oak tree. The prophet of Bethel extends an invitation of hospitality to the visiting messenger similar to that of the king's. Again, obedient to God's command, the Judahite refuses. However, when the Bethel host identifies himself as a prophet also and declares that the word of the Lord commanded him to extend this offer of hospitality, the man accepts. Unbeknownst to the Judahite messenger, the narrative record informs us that the Bethel prophet lied.

Upon returning to the Bethel prophet's home, the two men eat and drink. At the conclusion of this respite, the word of the Lord reveals itself to the Bethel prophet, condemning the Judahite visitor's unwitting disobedience. Death will be his punishment, followed by a burial outside his ancestral tomb. Exactly according to the Lord's word, when this man of God departs on the donkey saddled for him, a lion attacks and kills him. However, his body is not utterly destroyed. With the lion and donkey standing beside it, the mangled corpse becomes evidence of his death as well as the fulfillment of God's word concerning his prophet.

Now two short concluding reports follow, recording the contrasting responses of this prophet and this king to the word of the Lord as proclaimed by the now deceased man from Judah (vv. 26-32, 33-34). The first reports the prophet's belief that the Lord has condemned Bethel and all the high places in Samaria (vv. 26-32). The second recounts that Jeroboam evidently does not believe (vv. 33-34). As conclusion to the narrative, the account adds that the king's refusal to amend his ways will have dire consequences. His own house will be cut off and destroyed from the face of the earth (v. 34).

Exegetical Analysis

Jeroboam Encounters the Man of God from Judah (13:1-10)

The opening of this first section occurs at the altar at Bethel, the setting with which the preceding chapter closed. However, now the narrative camera, equipped with a sensitive microphone, zooms in. We watch the details and hear the voices of a tense exchange taking place at the cultic site. A man of God from Judah has come to

Bethel and is publicly disrupting Jeroboam's preparations to offer incense on the altar. His disturbing message foretells the day when another king will desecrate the very altar before which Jeroboam is about to officiate. Identifying that king as Josiah, the messenger's pronouncement that "the priests of the high places [will be sacrificed] and human bones shall be burned" (v. 2) on the altar anticipates and approximates the description of Josiah's vast cultic reform three centuries later (2 Kgs 23:15-20). It is important to note that the messenger does not condemn Jeroboam but the *altar*, the centerpiece of a cultic site. Whereas God desires the worship of the king and his servants, the potential of these cultic sites to distract many from true worship is at the heart of this condemnation.

Next, the messenger follows his proclamation with two confirmatory signs. The first is prompted by Jeroboam's resistive outburst and attempted show of power. The hand of the king stretched out authoritatively with an order to seize the disruptive scoundrel withers (v. 4). In Hebrew, the word for hand (*yad*) also means power. Thus when the king extends his hand he extends a show of power to silence the man of God. Ironically, a greater force overpowers him. Immediately following, this same power of God delivers another sign. The altar is broken down (v. 5). Recognizing the legitimacy of the man of God and his message, or perhaps desperate to regain power, the king entreats the visitor to intercede for his healing before the Lord. As a third sign, the king's hand is restored (v. 6). However, the king needs more than a physical healing. As we will see, Jeroboam's devotion and attention to the Lord needs to be restored so he can return to faithful relationship with his God.

The king, in turn, invites the man to come and dine with him as well as to receive a gift (v. 7). Professional prophets often earned a living by receiving payment in the form of wages, food, or other commodities for their pronouncements. That the prophet turns down the invitation of the king only strengthens the legitimacy of what he has pronounced. This man of God delivers the message for the Lord rather than for a living. Moreover, he cites the commandment under which he is bound when he rejects the king's invitation (vv. 8-9). He may not eat or drink in Bethel according to the word of the Lord. In the ancient Near East, sharing a meal was a means to express kinship and oneness with another. Such a gesture would obscure the sense of estrangement from the Lord that is at the heart of his message. In work and in action, the prophetic messenger seeks to move the king to return to the Lord.

A Prophet from Bethel Meets the Messenger from Judah (13:11-25)

In the next scene, an old prophet of Bethel is brought news of the man from Judah and all that he has proclaimed concerning the altar at Bethel (v. 11). That prophets were associated with cultic sites and often earned their living at these shrines explains the old man's interest in this messenger and his message. Having inquired as to the direction in which the Judahite set out, the prophet orders his sons to ready a donkey for him. When the prophet from Bethel finds the man of God sitting under an oak tree, he asks him to confirm his identity. "Are you the man of God who came from Judah?" (v. 14). That the old man asks the visitor to identify himself as a man from Judah suggests there are political overtones to the pursuit of this intruder. Pronouncements of doom against Bethel by one from Judah could be readily understood as a political act with no religious or theological grounding from the Lord. With reason, this old man is suspicious of the southerner and his message.

When the prophet of Bethel invites him to come and dine at his house, the man of God refuses, repeating the explanation given to the king's offer of hospitality (vv. 16-17). Now the old man makes use of his recognized status as a prophet. He claims that "by the word of the LORD" a divine messenger instructed him to bring the man from Judah to his home and offer him food and drink (v. 18). The narrative confirms our suspicions. The old prophet is deceiving the man. Faithful to what he believes is the word of the Lord, the man from Judah returns with the prophet of Bethel and eats and drinks in his home (v. 19). Now the old prophet does receive a word from the Lord that makes him responsible for the dire consequence that is about to befall the visitor who has unwittingly disobeyed God's command. When the man from Judah dies, his body will not come to rest with his ancestors.

Immediately, the man from Judah sets out on his way and is killed by a lion (v. 24). The lion, an instrument of God's punishment, acts uncharacteristically. Whereas the animal does take the man's life, it stands alongside the man's donkey, hovering over the dead body on the roadside (v. 24). As if to guard the evidence, the lion's watch preserves the body as mute testimony that what the Lord foretold has been fulfilled. As the consequence for his disobedience, the man from Judah dies in a foreign place with no prospects for burial among his ancestors. At the same time, his death becomes a sign that he was indeed a man of God and his message was legitimate.

It is easy to become distracted by the failed obedience of the Judahite. Taken on its own apart from the larger narrative, this peculiar little scene invites us to fix upon the consequences of obedience and disobedience. However, the parallels and subsequent contrasts between the king's encounter with his man of God and the prophet's interactions with him disclose other insights. Though not exact, the parallels establish connections between the two scenes, inviting us to read them together. Both the king and the prophet have direct interchanges with the man. Though the man of God delivers his message in the king's presence, the prophet also receives a report of all the man said from one of his sons. Both king and prophet exercise some negative gesture of power over the man. The king orders to have the man seized. The prophet manipulates the man's commitment to the word of the Lord by deception. Both king and prophet extend an invitation to the man to eat and drink. And finally, both the king and the prophet receive confirmatory signs that what the man proclaimed was indeed from the Lord. Although their parallel experiences with this visitor are distinct, both king and prophet are positioned to respond to the confirmed word brought by this man of God. The two short reports that follow record their responses.

The Prophet of Bethel Responds to the Man from Judah (13:26-32)

Immediately following the account of the man from Judah's death on the road, the news is brought to the old prophet. He responds in word and deed. First, he proclaims his belief that all that has taken place is according to the word of the Lord. "It is the man of God who disobeyed according to the word of the LORD . . . and killed him according to the word that the LORD spoke to him" (v. 26). His words represent his own conversion. Discounting the man when he was living, the prophet deceived him. Now at the news of his death, the prophet believes him. The man's death becomes evidence that witnesses to his message concerning Israel and its backing as "the word of the LORD."

Next, the prophet responds by retrieving the dead man's corpse (vv. 28-29). The narrative records that he "took up the body," "laid it on the donkey," "brought it back to the city," "mourned" the man, and finally "buried" him in his own grave (vv. 29-31). His actions speak clearly to his changed attitude and heart toward the man from Judah and his message. But the prophet goes even farther. He orders his sons that upon his death they are to bury his own bones beside those of the Judahite (v. 31). The opposition between the man from Judah and the prophet from Bethel in life becomes kinship and oneness in death. Moreover, the prophet manifests his inward turning to the man and his message by his own proclamation, pronouncing his own conviction that the word of the Lord against the altar in Bethel and in all the high places throughout Samaria will come about (v. 32).

The King Responds to the Man from Judah (13:33-34)

In one sentence, the parallels collapse between these two officials associated with the cultic site at Bethel. Both king and prophet encountered the man and heard his word. Both witnessed confirmatory signs. Since it was the prophet's role to advise the king, it is even likely Jeroboam not only had the signs displayed before him by the man of Judah, but also knew of the confirmatory disclosures received by this prophet of Bethel. But as the account of Jeroboam's response opens, we hear that "even after this event Jeroboam did not turn from his evil way" (v. 33). Not in word or in deed did Jeroboam "return," or much less, believe. Indeed, his refusal to believe casts a judgment upon the sincerity of his earlier gestures toward the man of God. His offer of hospitality and his promise of a gift were merely bribes or attempts to cajole him.

Any speculation that Jeroboam took seriously the pronouncements concerning the altar in Bethel and the high places throughout the north are quickly disappointed with the concluding report. Not only did Jeroboam not retreat from what he had been doing, but he promoted the involvement of others in these condemned cultic machinations.

The conclusion to the account records that the king allowed anyone who wanted to become priests to officiate at the high places. Such indiscretion manifests an utter lack of concern for the quality of religious officials responsible for the important work of cult. It also cultivates disregard and thus disrespect for the lineage to which the office of priesthood had been subject. However, there is something even more reprehensible in Jeroboam's policy. The permissiveness encourages others' association with the cultic sites, with which he himself has been identified and that are now clearly forbidden by the word of the Lord. The consequence for one's own sin before the Lord assures punishment. But the consequence for leading others to sin assures the absence of any sign of divine leniency or compassion. Jeroboam and his house will be cut off and destroyed "from the face of the earth" (v. 34).

Theological and Ethical Analysis

The complexity of this chapter raises several difficult and awkward theological questions. We could fix on the man from Judah and be challenged by the apparently uncompromising obedience required of those called to serve the Lord. As a moral lesson, such a reading would be harsh and incompatible with other stories of disobedience. Upon broader theological reflection, such a conjecture seems incompatible with the many instances where God extends compassion in judgment even to the likes of one like Solomon. Though his kingdom would come to an end as punishment for his life of increasing sin culminating in apostasy, the Lord granted that not all the tribes would be torn away from his son.

The notion that in this instance the story sets out to teach a kind of unflinching obedience to God's command that is met with death even if one unwittingly disobeys is difficult and unpersuasive. The role of the man of God is really secondary to this tale, a story that is about Jeroboam and his reign. However, the role of the man of God does offer a lesson to ponder in a story that is fixed upon the king.

God makes overtures to Jeroboam in order to curb the policies and practices of this new king. The Lord sends a messenger in an attempt to persuade the monarch to consider another path. In this instance, the Judahite messenger does not condemn Jeroboam but the altar at Bethel and the other high places. Moreover, the Lord even offers signs via this emissary to urge the king to take a different course in his reign and to "return" to the Lord. In addition, this messenger engages the prophet of Bethel, the one who might have had some leverage with royal power. He, too, not only is informed of what the man of God said, but is offered confirmatory signs that cost the visitor his life. Hence, the servant is the expression of God's desperate quest to win Jeroboam back. In life and in death, the servant of the Lord witnesses God's invitation to the king to "return."

Sometimes it requires an outsider like this man of God to offer an appraisal that can be trusted, or to express the Lord's invitation for us to come back. But every agent of the Lord is still characterized by human affiliations. These can become the stumbling blocks or the excuses easily latched onto in order to disqualify the message or the messenger. That the man was from Judah made it possible for the king to discount his message of condemnation as political. That he was a man of God made it necessary to consider the truth of what he said and did. The prophet turned from his skepticism and disbelief. He assented to the message and the man as sent by the Lord. The king, however, continued on his path of sinfulness. Moreover, he led others in that waywardness. After the Lord's overture and invitation to "return" that cost the servant his life, the reservoir of divine compassion is depleted. Jeroboam will reap the unconditional judgment of the Lord. He and his family will be cut off and dashed from the face of the earth.

1 KINGS 14

Chapter 14 sets forth two summary evaluations of the reign of Jeroboam and Rehoboam, the two kings of the now divided kingdoms. In the course of the account, we are reminded of their enmity and continual war with each other. Yet, despite their hostility and opposition, they appear remarkably alike in one respect. They both do what is sinful before the Lord.

Literary Analysis

Concluding information and a final evaluation of Jeroboam's reign (vv. 1-20), followed by that of Rehoboam (vv. 21-31), organizes this chapter. Whereas the literary character of each of these evaluations differs, both evaluations leave us with the same conclusion. Neither king has been successful in the eyes of the Lord.

The evaluative account of Jeroboam is presented as a story. In the opening (v. 2), the illness of Abijah, Jeroboam's son, creates a crisis, demanding resolution. A twice-repeated pattern of command-fulfillment language encloses the tale (vv. 2-6, 12-18). Jeroboam commands his wife to disguise herself, and armed with food gifts go consult the prophet Ahijah as to the fate of the child. Accordingly, Jeroboam's wife goes, disguises herself, and consults the old, blind prophet who, even before she stands before him, recognizes her as Jeroboam's wife.

In the conclusion of the story (vv. 12-18), Ahijah the prophet arms the woman with pronouncements and the promise of a sign for Jeroboam, and then instructs her to return home. Once again, the woman carries out the command. She gets up and returns to Tirzah. As she arrives at the threshold, the child dies, serving as another sign for the king and fulfilling the word of the Lord spoken to her by the prophet.

In between this opening and concluding command-fulfillment narrative pattern, the intervening speech of the prophet Ahijah (vv. 7-11) governs the story. The characteristic oracular formula, "Thus says the LORD" (v. 7), introduces his pronouncement. Three parts structure the ensuing revelation. First, the prophet rehearses what God has done for Jeroboam (vv. 7-8). Next, he summarizes what in response Jeroboam has done (v. 9). The contrast of the benevolence on the part of God and the sinfulness on the part of Jeroboam anticipate the third segment of the oracle. In this final pronouncement (vv. 10-11), the prophet discloses the divinely decreed punishment. Though Jeroboam sought an oracle concerning the fate of his ill son, he will receive an oracle about himself and the fate of the nation. Following this final judgment against the house of Jeroboam, a regnal summary (vv. 19-20) closes the book on his kingship.

In the latter portion of the chapter (vv. 21-31), two summary statements enclose an overview of Rehoboam's reign. The opening summary (v. 21) records personal biographical information. The concluding summary (vv. 29-31) further amends this resumé. Between these two frames, the record preserves two brief accounts that at first glance seem not to focus upon Rehoboam. In verses 22-24, the people of Judah are described as evil in the sight of the Lord. With no segue, a second account, seemingly unrelated to what preceded, is set forth. During the fifth year of Rehoboam's reign, King Shishak of Egypt came to Judah and evidently overpowered Rehoboam's forces.

Although these two unrelated accounts offer no direct evaluation of Rehoboam, his effectiveness as a ruler and his own influence as a leader of the people before Yahweh are disquietingly clear. In one fell swoop, a foreign power not only trounces upon and carries off the treasures that were the lifework of his father Solomon, but also unveils the utter contrast between Rehoboam's weakness and his father's power among the nations. Moreover, the deep-seated and widespread character of Judahite religious violations directly indicts Rehoboam for his own infidelity and nonattention to the matter of covenant. The account of the close of his reign instills little confidence in the prospect of a return to the Lord.

Exegetical Analysis

A Final Evaluation of Jeroboam (14:1-20)

A crisis introduces the concluding evaluation of Jeroboam. His son Abijah has fallen ill, so ill that Jeroboam sends his wife to the prophet Ahijah for word concerning the child's fate. Jeroboam's concern could well stem from his paternal concern for the child. That he sends for word from the man of God who foretold Jeroboam's rise to kingship suggests the king's concern about dynastic succession as well.

The significance of the name Jeroboam gives to his son should not be overlooked. "Abijah" means "Yahweh is my father." It suggests that at one point, perhaps earlier in his reign, this king did understand himself in faithful kinship with Yahweh. Here, however, the grave illness of the child may signal the endangerment of that relationship. Death of a child named "Yahweh is my father" may mean more than the loss of a son or even a threat to the continuance of the dynastic house of Jeroboam. Given the infidelity of this king, it may portend the end of his relationship with the Lord.

Jeroboam instructs his wife to disguise herself, take loaves, cakes, and honey, and seek a word from Ahijah the prophet concerning the stricken child. Instructing her to masquerade herself suggests tension or trouble in Jeroboam's relation with the man of God, who foretold this king's reign in Israel. A quick glance back reminds us that the Lord, through the prophet, called him to "listen to all that I command you, walk in my ways, and do what is right in my sight by keeping my statutes and commandments, as David my servant did" (11:38). The concluding evaluation will confirm that the king failed to do what he was called to do.

Though his blindness and her disguise should doubly hamper Ahijah's recognition of Jeroboam's wife, human pretense poses no challenge for this faithful prophet of the Lord. The prophet had already received the word of the Lord about this visitor and what to say to her before she arrives. At the sound of her feet crossing the threshold of his doorway, the prophet addresses her as Jeroboam's wife. Before she can even make a request, he redefines the purpose of her visit. He has "heavy tidings" with which he will burden her (v. 6) that include the fate of her son and much more. Here the story shifts. The crisis that governed the plot thus far is about to be replaced by a new crisis. Narrative speed slows to a halt in order to give full attention to the prophet's pronouncement.

"Thus says the LORD, the God of Israel"(v. 7) shifts the narrative direction as well as introduces the prophet's oracle. First, Ahijah recalls what God has done for Jeroboam (vv. 7-8a). Jeroboam had been exalted and readied by God for the great work he was called to do. Being made the leader, he was bequeathed responsibility. God's inheritance, the people of Israel, was torn away from the house of David and entrusted to him. However, Jeroboam has turned away from the work to which he was commissioned. He has not fulfilled the responsibility and trust bestowed upon him.

In the second part of the oracle (vv. 8b-9), the prophet enumerates the many ways that Jeroboam has gone astray. Jeroboam has not kept the commandments or set his heart upon God. It is no surprise that his lack of an interiority governed by the covenant has materialized in all kinds of evil. He has gone after other gods, cast images of idols, and provoked Yahweh's anger. In sum, Jeroboam has turned his back upon the Lord and embraced apostasy, the very sin in which all of Solomon's evil ways culminated.

Hence, the third and final section of the oracle (vv. 10-11) manifests both the consequences reaped by Jeroboam's covenantal delinquency as well as the heat of divine anger. With graphic and vulgar images, the punishment for sin is detailed. The Hebrew for "every male" (v. 10), literally translated "every male who pisses against the wall," is coupled with the image of the house of Jeroboam being burned as "one burns up dung." Such graphic language suggests the Lord's disgust toward all those affiliated with the house of Jeroboam. Moreover, the disquiet of this death sentence is surpassed by what follows. In the promised punishment, anyone belonging to Jeroboam, whether they die in the city or countryside, will be left unburied. Their corpses will serve as food for the scavengers of nature. Thus the scourge of no burial further exacerbates the shame of annihilation. At the conclusion of the oracle the prophet does address the fate of the sick child about which the wife of Jeroboam came to inquire. He orders her to return and only then discloses to her the heartbreaking news that the child will die upon her arrival. However, all Israel will mourn and bury him because he has been found pleasing to the

Lord. Hence, in these newly prophesied circumstances, the feared fate of the sick child becomes a blessing. The child who is about to die is granted the peace and rest of proper burial and mourning on account of the Lord's favor. By contrast, those males of the house of Jeroboam that are living are about to die unmourned and unburied on account of the Lord's anger.

Abijah will not be the heir to the throne of Jeroboam. Instead, Yahweh will raise up a descendant who will cut off the house of Jeroboam. Additionally, Israel itself will not have rest but will go into exile. Images of an uprooted reed in the water, along with a description of Israel banished outside the land given to its ancestors and scattered beyond the Euphrates, narrate the extension of the Lord's anger to those who have followed this king in his sinfulness. Enumerating their evil, the prophet points to Israel's making of the *asherim,* or sacred poles, as one of the many ways they cooperated with Jeroboam's apostasy and provoked the divine wrath. The prophet's pronouncement sketches a network of sin that in its cause and effect is both complex and comprehensive. It ensnares Jeroboam, his household, and ultimately the whole people of Israel.

The woman follows the prophet's command. She gets up and returns home (v. 17). According to the prophet's word, as she approaches the threshold of the house the child dies. This then becomes another sign to Jeroboam, along with the king's own withered hand (13:4), the breakup of the altar (13:5), and the death of the man of God from Judah (13:26), credentialing the word delivered by these men of God as truth.

The account of the reign of Jeroboam closes with what we have come to recognize as the typical regnal abstract. For further information on how Jeroboam "warred and how he reigned" (v. 19), we are referred to the other record of the northern kings and their deeds, the Book of the Annals of the Kings of Israel. Jeroboam reigned twenty-two years. His son Nadab succeeds his father.

The Final Evaluation of Rehoboam (14:21-31)

Thus far we have heard little to commend Rehoboam and his kingship in his efforts to reign. Failing to respond positively to

Israel's plea for more equitable labor practices, Rehoboam instigates the northern territories' rebellion. When he tries to curb
their revolt, Rehoboam's own official is slain while he himself hurries to escape to his city. Planning to war against the northern
rebels, his plan is cut short by a word from the Lord. In the course
of his reign, the nation was divided, a northern kingdom arose,
and according to this final account, things at home in Judah
appear less than praiseworthy.

As this final assessment of Rehoboam's career as king commences, the focus and framework of the unit (vv. 21-31) separates
it from the preceding evaluation of Jeroboam. Two summary
statements regarding his personal data (vv. 21, 29-31) frame two
reports (vv. 22-24, 25-28). These internal briefs offer the only
close-up clips of events during the term of this king.

First, the record begins by rehearsing Rehoboam's age when he
began to reign, as well as the length of his royal term in
Jerusalem—seventeen years (v. 21). It is noteworthy that here the
attention upon Rehoboam shifts momentarily to Jerusalem, qual-
ifying it not as the seat of Rehoboam's reign but as the "the city
that the LORD had chosen out of all the tribes of Israel" in order
to establish the divine name there. This reminder becomes especially important when considered in relationship to the brief
upcoming account summarizing Judah's religious behavior and
the ransacking of the temple by Shishak. Finally, Rehoboam's
mother, Naamah the Ammonite, is named. Her mention reminds
us of the cultic violations of his father. Solomon's habitual pattern
of taking foreign wives culminated in his worship of many foreign
deities.

There are also other subtle reminders of the parallel between
Solomon's career and that of his son. The account of Solomon's
kingship closed with a two-part grand summary of his reign.
Chapter 9 reported how the nation was faring at home under him.
Chapter 10 indicated the success of this king on the international
scoreboard. Similarly, but in much more abbreviated fashion, two
briefs clips here (vv. 22-24, 25-28) offer a glance at the state of the
union in Judah under Rehoboam as well as suggesting the caliber
of his dealings with international powers.

First, at home Judah's activity in regard to the Lord is summarized point blank. The Judahites "did what was evil in the sight of the LORD" (v. 22). What follows offers a tally of just what this evil includes. Provoking the Lord to jealousy, building high places and the prohibited *asherim* (sacred poles), and accommodating male temple prostitution number among the abominations of which they are accused. That Judah exceeded "the abominations of the nations that the LORD drove out before the people of Israel" (v. 24) suggests it as a nation that deserves to be driven out itself. The destiny of exile pronounced by the prophet concerning Israel parallels the fate of Judah insinuated here. As a reflection upon the reign of Rehoboam, the state of Judah before the Lord offers an assessment of this king. The people's widespread violations serve as a commentary on Rehoboam's own leadership and delinquency.

In the second summary clip, we turn attention to his international dealings. The short account in verses 25-28 offers a rather uncomely sample. Shishak, king of Egypt, has invaded Judah and plundered the temple. Though Rehoboam's father Solomon had amicable relations with Egypt, symbolized by his marriage to the Egyptian princess and the construction of her palace, these diplomatic ties have rapidly unraveled under Rehoboam's watch. The humiliation is further extended when Shishak carries off all the treasures of the king's house and the house of the Lord (v. 26). In addition, he confiscated the gold shields that Solomon had made. This sample of Rehoboam's international position suggests further the lamentable nature of his status as king. Moreover, in both the description of Judah's religious activity and Shishak's attack on the capital, the importance of Jerusalem as the "city that the LORD had chosen out of all the tribes of Israel" (v. 21) is gravely diminished. Rehoboam, king of this city and its people, is responsible.

The account of Rehoboam concludes with another summary statement (vv. 29-31). Again, we are reminded of a source, the Book of the Annals of the Kings of Judah, where other activities of Rehoboam are recorded. In addition, continual war between Rehoboam and Jeroboam is noted. Finally, Rehoboam's son Abijam is named as his successor. (Whereas the name "Abijam" occurs in the Hebrew text, the parallel account in 2 Chr 12:16, along with a later Greek history of the Jews [Josephus, *Antiquities of the Jews* 8.9.1], identifies the son as Abijah.) As a final note, his mother, Naamah the Ammonite, is named again, recalling one more time the Solomonic roots of Rehoboam's failure.

Theological and Ethical Analysis

"There was war between Rehoboam and Jeroboam continually" (v. 30). In addition to the various involvements that the record here attributes to these two rulers of the small states of Israel and Judah, Jeroboam and Rehoboam will be remembered as enemies of each other. Moreover, their opposition will not confine itself only to the years of their royal tenure. Except for a few intermittent kings in the years to come, their enmity will continue for the life of both nations. Founded upon these hostilities, land borders will be challenged. Militias in each state will be built up. Labor obligations upon citizens will necessarily increase. And each nation's emerging sense of identity will be, in part, at the expense of the state to the north or to the south constituting the hostile "other." In the end, both kingdoms will succumb to an onslaught of foreign powers beyond them. Hence, a well-seeded spirit of enmity and hostility is the legacy of both Jeroboam and Rehoboam.

Ironically, these rulers with their all differences are remarkably alike. The very invitations and failures that lead up to this enmity actually constitute their kinship. Both Rehoboam and Jeroboam's establishment as kings was by divine design. While the kingdom was being torn away from Solomon, divine compassion mandated that one tribe remain and be handed over to his son. Thus God's promise to the house of David was realized in Rehoboam's succession to the throne in the southern nation of Judah. The Lord even more directly commissioned Jeroboam's appointment. The prophet of God, Ahijah, sketched the Lord's plan of appointment for Jeroboam in clear, definitive terms. He would be the servant to whom responsibility for the ten tribes would be designated. But the similarities between Rehoboam and Jeroboam do not stop there.

Both kings were in a position to address the wrongdoings that Solomon had promulgated. The people came to Rehoboam asking him to diminish their labor and to institute a policy that was more compassionate than his father's program. Jeroboam also was specifically commissioned to correct the ills of the past. He was appointed to assume rulership of the ten tribes because Solomon had fallen into apostasy and not kept the commandments and statutes of the Lord (11:33). However, both Rehoboam and Jeroboam fail. Rehoboam not only refused to listen to the people's plea for leniency in labor obligations, but he determined to increase their burden. For his part, Jeroboam was commissioned to rule because of Solomon's covenantal infidelity. Still, Jeroboam quickly laid the foundation for his own covenantal infidelity by the establishment of high places. Moreover, the people in both Israel and Judah became involved in forbidden religious practices because of these kings. Apostasy was rampant and both kings were responsible.

That the stories of both kings end in failure is utterly lamentable. Their parallel failure surpasses even Solomon's reprehensible end. These two kings were situated to succeed by learning lessons from the past. Both rulers were in a position to fashion a reign alternative to their predecessor, to refuse to duplicate Solomon's mistakes. Both kings failed abysmally, not only because of their own infidelity or even because they both caused the people to turn from the Lord to apostasy; their failure is founded upon their cultivated hostility toward each other.

How is it that such archenemies as Rehoboam and Jeroboam, with all their differences and constant warring, could appear so markedly alike? Perhaps that question prompts a lesson. Though they were staunch enemies during their reign, in retrospect, they appear remarkably similar. The narrative's prolonged attention to their lamentable downfalls warrants that we not miss the instruction. The one viewed with contempt and identified as the opponent may turn out to look a lot like oneself. Moreover, the prospect of being in covenantal relationship with God can never coincide with maintaining and fostering enmity and opposition. Such an insight moves beyond the ancient context and urgently challenges us with its instruction today. As individuals and as nations, those we define as enemies may disclose a great deal about ourselves. Moreover, the prospect of living in covenantal relationship with God today resides outside contemporary frameworks of opposition, hostility, and war.

1 KINGS 15 AND 16

The warring begun between the northern and southern states under Rehoboam and Jeroboam finds its fruition in the accounts of the subsequent kings. Chapters 15 and 16 offer a bird's-eye view of the successors to these two thrones during the next forty years. Set forth as isolated summaries, the reign of six rulers of the north and two rulers in the south testify to the inevitable long-term effects of the earlier fraternal opposition. The hostilities seeded under Rehoboam and Jeroboam reap a harvest of increasing instability within each nation-state. Across these chapters, accounts of internal strife over the question of succession in the north accompany the ongoing conflicts between Israel and Judah. Moreover, the summary of each of these kings and their troubles is corroborated with a review of their standing before the Lord. The assessment, for the most part, is not optimistic. The legacy of Rehoboam and Jeroboam continues to leave its unfortunate imprint in the hopelessly sinful course taken by the subsequent kings of each nation.

Literary Analysis

Eight discrete regnal units synchronically sketch the contours of these chapters. The first two regnal accounts (15:1-8, 9-24) set forth summaries of two kings, Rehoboam's son, Abijam, and Ahijam's offspring, Asa, who rule in Judah during the next forty years. Six more summaries follow each, offering reviews of the six northern kings—Nadab, Baasha, Elah, Zimri, Omri, and Ahab—who rule after Jeroboam for approximately the same forty-year period (15:25-32; 15:33–16:7; 16:8-14; 16:15-20; 16:21-28; 16:29-34). Easily identified, each regnal account is demarcated by an introduction and concluding summary. Although the concluding summaries vary in content, the introductions consistently identify the new ruler of that state in relationship to who is ruling at that time in the other kingdom.

The recurrence of the familiar elements that compose these regnal resumés create a rhythmic, iterative retelling across the eight units. Whereas not every one of the summaries bears all these features—the time of the reign, the identification of parentage, the duration of the reign, the reference to other sources for further details of this king's deeds (Annals of the Kings of Judah, Annals of the Kings of Israel), the place of burial, and identification of their successor—a composite made up primarily of these elements composes the regnal brief on each and every king.

Despite these common elements, other narrative materials are included intermittently, adding detail, distinctiveness, and sometimes low drama to these otherwise rather formulaic accounts. The resumé of Asa, king of Judah, is expanded with details describing conflict with Israel at Ramah (15:16-22). Nadab's regnal summary is punctuated with a brief allusion to the murder and intrigue often characterizing the establishment of kingship in the north (15:26). A reminder of a prophet's words adds tension to Baasha's file (15:29). A passing summary of an internal struggle for the throne precedes the introduction to Omri's reign (16:21-22).

Though each of these summaries appears to open and close independently from one another, literary devices work to create links across the units and establish a sense of their simultaneity. As already mentioned, the consistent citation of who reigns in the other kingdom at the time of the featured king's introduction is the most obvious technique synchronizing events between Israel and Judah. In this regard, we note that King Jeroboam reigns in the north for the entire tenure of the first Judahite successor to Rehoboam, Abijam, his son, as well as during the first year of Abijam's successor, Asa. In turn, Asa remains king in Judah during the reign of all six kings (Nadab, Baasha, Elah, Zimri, Omri, and Ahab), who follow Jeroboam in the north. Although any attempt to map an accurate chronology from the citation of each individual king's length of tenure fails, these opening citations successfully craft an impression of simultaneous periodization.

In the course of the summaries, periodic reference to the deeds of the king in the other nation also creates a sense of the coincidence of these events. This subtle literary device, known as "resumptive repetition," rehearses segments of one king's story outside its actual account. For example, portions of Baasha's story recorded in 15:33–16:9 are elaborated apart from his regnal summary. Conflict with Baasha is elaborated in the resumé of Asa (15:16-22), and again in the course of Nadab's file (15:25-31). The overall effect creates the impression of contemporaneous events. Though the individual units recording the reigns of each king are isolated and separate, the events narrated within each are not. They coexist, interact, and have a determining impact within the unfolding of each king's tenure. Additionally, this interface of individual accounts underscores a further, more important notion. Whereas indeed the kingdom has been divided, the overarching story is not. The account of what now has become two nations remains a single story of God's people in the course of the same salvation history. Moreover, the persistence of this God across all divisions is etched in each regnal unit. Although varying elements characteristic of the regnal resumé craft the distinctiveness of each king's summary, a divine assessment of each individual ruler persists throughout.

This theological appraisal makes these regnal briefs more than narratives with modest historical value. The assessment of each king before the Lord reminds us that this is theological history. As theological history, the story of the kings, summoned to special relationship with the Lord, witnesses to God's persistent invitation to covenantal fidelity. As the account progresses, the emerging description narrates a grave increase in the unevenness in this relationship. While the Lord remains patient and faithful to covenantal promises, the kings continue down the path of infidelity in the form of apostasy.

Exegetical Analysis

The Reign of Abijam in Judah (15:1-8)

In the opening regnal unit, we are introduced to Rehoboam's successor and son, Abijam. Remembering that the chronology represented here may not conform to our calculations, this narrative brief records that Abijam rules for three years during the eighteenth year of Jeroboam in the north. The identification of his mother as "Maacah daughter of Abishalom" (v. 2) creates some unsolvable problems for the historian. Abishalom might be a variant of Absalom, Solomon's deceased brother (2 Sam 14:27). In this instance, Maacah would be Rehoboam's cousin as well as his wife. Such an arrangement is conceivable. Ancient practices among ruling families encouraged kings to marry their cousins or half sisters in order to protect the royal line. However, the chronicler's account (2 Chr 13:2) identifies Abijam's mother as Micaiah, daughter of Uriel of Gibeah. Such discrepancies leave the matter of Abijam's maternal origin in question.

At first glance, the report on Abijam's reign appears fairly formulaic, with virtually no narrative intrigue. However, the account sets up a comparison here in this first of regnal units that should not be overlooked. Although we do not know what sins he commits, the evaluation of Abijam is immediately and comprehensively negative. Directly after his introduction, the indicting assessment follows that "he committed all the sins that his father did before him; his heart was not true to the LORD his God, like the heart of his father David" (v. 3). The comparison with David is familiar. David has served as a frequent model by which previous kings have been assessed. In the monarchic traditions, his rule keeps cropping up as the benchmark of what constitutes fidelity before the Lord. However, unlike previous citations of this kingly standard, here a reference is also made to David's own sinful downfall in the midst of his faithful reign. The account recalls that he did stumble in the matter of Uriah, the Hittite whom David had murdered to cover his adulterous activity with the man's wife Bathsheba (2 Sam 11:14-21). Such a qualification adds depth to the comparison, as well as refines the challenge to subsequent kings. The faithfulness of a king's heart does not depend upon a life of perfection but upon a life governed by repentance and return. David, who sinned, paid for his evil choice and set his heart on the Lord once again. Thus, the comparison goes deeper here than King David who was faithful versus Abijam who is not.

The comparison sets forth what will become significant as the royal parade of powerful men continues on a perilous path of apostasy—sin is inevitable, but repentance and return remain a possibility before the Lord.

Asa, King of Judah (15:9-24)

As the continuation of the Davidic line, Asa, son of Abijam, ascends the throne during the final years of Jeroboam in the north and reigns for forty-one years. The question of Macaah's identity becomes even more complicated as here she is recorded as the mother of Asa. This, of course, would make Asa and Abijam brothers rather than father and son. We are left only to conclude that confusion surrounds the notation of the mother of these two kings.

Immediately, Asa receives a review that contrasts his ways with the ways of his father. Asa "did what was right in the sight of the LORD" (v. 11). However, the report on this king and his activities qualifies the good that he does. The review is a mixture of positive and negative.

First, Asa initiates a cultic reform. He abolishes what had evidently become a generally accepted practice of temple prostitution. He corrects the path of apostasy of his predecessors by removing the idols they had made. He even dethrones the queen mother in conjunction with the image of Asherah she had installed. Cutting down the wooden image, he burns the idol in the Valley of Kidron. Such cultic housecleaning would place Asa among the ranks of two subsequent kings about whom the Deuteronomic narrative has praise, namely, Josiah and Hezekiah. However, all this good is modified by the concluding observation that the high places are not dismantled. Asa takes positive steps, but does not go far enough in his efforts at cultic reform.

Next we hear the assessment again that his heart was true to the Lord all his days (v. 14). This is reinforced by the subsequent description. He returns to the house of the Lord the votive gifts that his father had removed. In addition, Asa adds his own votive gifts of silver and gold to the Lord's dwelling place. However, no sooner has the good been recorded than it gets qualified again.

Asa continues to battle with Israel, now ruled by Baasha. To curb Baasha's affront at Ramah, the northernmost border of Judah, Asa calls on the support of Aram, a small state north of Israel. Under political pressure, Asa shows exactly where his allegiances lie. He is quick to trust in a foreign military power rather than to trust in God. He removes the treasures from the Lord's house and uses them as collateral to make an alliance with this foreign power. Hence, his goodness is short-lived.

The follow-up report records that Aram is victorious over Israel, capturing some of its northern cities at Ijon, Dan, Abel-beth-maacah, Chinneroth, and Naphtali, as well as forcing Baasha's retreat from Ramah. Once again, Asa seems to be the recipient of divine favor and approval, though this time, less directly. But the Lord's favor may be qualified, as is the assessment of Asa, by what follows. The victorious king issues a proclamation ordering all of Judah to dismantle the stones and timber at Ramah. With these materials he builds the cities Geba and Mizpah. His order echoes the labor practices under Solomon from which the people recoiled under Rehoboam. Though Asa's regnal summary concludes with the characteristic citations about his death, place of burial, and successor, an uncharacteristic notation precedes it. "But in his old age he was diseased in his feet" (v. 23). As disease was commonly viewed as divine disapproval, Asa's positive review in the eyes of the Lord remains a question at the conclusion of his summary.

Nadab, King of Israel (15:25-32)

Nadab, the son of Jeroboam, ascends the throne in Israel and reigns for only two years. Asa is king in Judah during this time. The regnal summary opens with the familiar theological review. Nadab, like his father Jeroboam, does evil in the sight of the Lord and also causes Israel to sin. But the resumé digresses and reports less about what Nadab actually did and more about what happened to him. Baasha, son of Ahijah, who we already know will menace King Asa at Ramah, now conspires to destroy his own kinsman, Nadab. Not only does Baasha strike Nadab down, he utterly wipes out the whole house of Jeroboam.

This rapid unraveling of Jeroboam's dynasty fulfills the prophecy of Ahijah (14:10-11) but it also does more. It discloses the stark difference between how kings arise in the north and how they ascend in the south—a difference that will persist in the upcoming successions. In Judah, the Davidic line determines each succeeding king with little or no disruption. In the north, the process of ascension remains unclear. Some have argued that kings arose in the north by means of affiliation with a powerful prophet, as was the case with Jeroboam and as will be the case with Jehu (16:1). However, narrative scenarios suggest a process governed by raw power battles between intertribal groups. This certainly seems to be the case in the upcoming ascent of Baasha in place of Nadab. Moreover, though the account of Baasha's slaughter of Nadab and the whole house of Jeroboam disrupts the typical individual summary in this history of kings, digressions narrating the bloody struggles and murder between households vying for the throne will become emblematic in the files on the northern kings.

Hence, though the report on Nadab's short tenure as king is brief, it signals much about the future course of kingship in the north. Consistent with the shift in focus that has interrupted this report, the record on Nadab ends with no information on his burial or successor. Rather, the warring between Asa and Baasha about which we have already been alerted is reported to be continual.

Baasha, King of Israel (15:33–16:7)

During the third year of Asa's rule in Judah, Baasha comes to power in Israel and reigns for almost a quarter of a century. His twenty-four years as king suggests the strength of his rule. But Baasha, too, did what was displeasing to the Lord (15:34). Once again the brief formulaic account of this king's reign is expanded with details that suggest its complexity. King Baasha, who destroyed the whole house of Jeroboam, as was foretold by the prophet Ahijah, is here prophesied as about to be destroyed himself.

Without narrative warning, Jehu, son of Hanani, pronounces a word against Baasha and against his whole house. Whereas the account records Jehu's declaration, "the word of the LORD" (16:1), it is not until the end of the regnal resumé that Jehu's status as prophet is confirmed (v. 7). Now the parallels between Jeroboam and Baasha and their destinies become revelatory as well as compelling. As Ahijah predicted the fall of Jeroboam and his house (14:7-16), Jehu the prophet foretells the demise of Baasha and his house (16:1-4). Even the format of the prophets' pronouncements against the two kings matches. Both rehearse what God has done (14:7-8; 16:2a), and then describe how each king has responded (14:9; 16:2b). Both pronounce the divine judgment drawing upon the same horrific images (14:10-11; 16:3-4). Baasha and Jeroboam are evil in the sight of the Lord and both are judged even more severely because they cause others in Israel to sin as well. Finally, the fate of Baasha is narrated with the same language as the dreadful destiny of Jeroboam and his house (14:11). His corpse and those of his family will be food for the dogs and a diet for the wild scavengers of the field (16:4). Irony dominates in this report of powerful Baasha and his rule. Though Baasha destroyed the whole house of Jeroboam, he will encounter the same fate. As Jeroboam's dynasty ended when his son Nadab was slain, so too, will Baasha's house meet its doom with the assassination of his son Elah.

Elah, King of Israel (16:8-14)

With Elah's establishment on the throne in Israel, the house of Baasha becomes a dynasty replacing the first dynastic establishment under Jeroboam and his son Nadab. Hope for a stable government in the north is quickly dashed, however. Following the standard introduction to Elah, son of Baasha, whose short two-year reign is recorded to coincide with the twenty-sixth year of Asa's tenure as king in Judah, a brief summary records his rapid overthrow. Though the details of the revolt headed by Zimri are few, the account leaves little doubt that corruption within the kingdom is rampant. The plot to dethrone Elah comes from within the ranks of his own royal officials. Zimri is entrusted with the charge of half of the king's chariot forces. Functioning within the official ranks of this Baashan dynasty under Elah, Zimri has evidently learned well the tactics of a coup. He duplicates Baasha's monstrous acts by assassinating not only the king but every male of the Baashan household (v. 11).

The narrative account invites little sympathy for the victims. Besides the standard information set forth in the regnal resumé, the narrative reports only that King Elah lived at Tirzah and was "drinking himself drunk" (v. 9). Disdain for this dynasty is further made evident in the description of its destruction. The record of the destruction of the royal family reverts to the same derogatory language ("every male who pisses against the wall" [v. 11]) used in the condemnation of Jeroboam and his house. Moreover, the report draws an explicit link between Zimri's successful conspiracy against Elah and his whole house and the prophecy that Jehu spoke against the house of Baasha (16:3-4, 7). Further, it specifies the sin for which the king is judged. Elah, along with his father Baasha, angered the Lord with the idols they had made and thereby caused Israel to sin (v. 13). The account pays its final disrespect to this pathetic king by omitting all information about Elah's death, burial, or successor to the throne.

Zimri, King of Israel (16:15-20)

The standard opening records that during the twenty-seventh year of king Asa in Judah, Zimri is on the throne in Israel for only seven days. The duration "seven days" anticipates the report of a revolt that immediately follows. Israel's army remains in conflict with the Philistines at Gibbethon. However, when they hear of Zimri's successful coup and the murder of Elah, they counter this new candidate's claim to the throne with their own contestant. They crown Omri, who unlike Zimri is evidently with them in the battle encampment as the commander of the army (v. 16). Little notoriety surrounds Zimri and his short reign. What is recorded indicates an utter lack of public support for the rise of this new ruler. The army's acclamation of Omri as their king is followed by action against Zimri's would-be rule. The troops leave Gibbethon and surround Tirzah, where Zimri has taken up residence. However, Zimri gives them no opportunity to dethrone him. Instead, he commits suicide. He burns down the house in the king's quarters with himself inside (v. 18). Not unexpectedly, the theological evaluation of Zimri follows suit with his predecessors, even those he destroyed. He did what was displeasing in the sight of the Lord, sinning just like Jeroboam and causing Israel to commit iniquity. Again, like Elah's account, this disquieting summary omits the formulaic record of Zimri's death, burial, and successor. Instead, we learn of those things through the story of Zimri's conspiracy.

Omri, King of Israel (16:21-28)

The summary of Omri's reign digresses briefly from the standard opening format. Though the preceding verses reported that Zimri had killed himself as the army proclaimed Omri king, the rise of a ruler over all Israel has grown increasingly conflictual. Hence, a civil war has broken out over whether Omri will be king or whether Tibni, son of Ginath, will ascend the throne. The transition report (vv. 21-23) disrupts the paradelike summaries of kings and their careers, thus mirroring the mounting disruption to the continuity in succession that such struggles for the throne pose in Israel. Moreover, jostling for power is not confined to "wanna-be" kings and their constituencies. As the account opens, we hear that the people of Israel were divided into two parts. The divisiveness among the would-be candidates and their tribal affiliates has become divisive for the whole community. We learn that half the people followed Omri and half followed Tibni. The date of Zimri's reign as coinciding with Asa's twenty-seventh year (v. 15) and Omri's actual uncontested ascent to kingship during Asa's thirty-first year (v. 23) indicates that the civil strife in the north lasted four years. Such long conflicts were destabilizing and costly. Most significantly, they always cost opponents their lives. Thus, when the report confirms Omri's kingship, it also confirms Tibni's death (v. 22).

Omri rules for twelve years in Israel. The dating here is difficult to verify but the record may include the years of civil conflict as part of Omri's reign. For six years as king, Omri lives in Tirzah. However, he also establishes a city at Samaria. Buying a piece of land from Shemer, Omri fortifies the hill and establishes a city that will become the capital of the north. Centrally located and geographically protected by its elevation, the eventual designation of Samaria as capital city could lend some unifying force to the discordant relations among tribal factions that resided in Israel at that time. Moreover, centering government in one capital city would better define Israel as a nation. Establishing a residence in a well-fortified location also paved the way for Omri's sons to succeed the throne with less contest. Indeed, this was the case. His was to become the longest and most enduring of northern dynasties.

However, the conclusion to Omri's resumé still logs the standard negative evaluation of these northern kings. Omri is described as surpassing all the previous kings by his iniquity, being likened to Jeroboam. As if to verify this assessment, all the accusations leveled against previous kings are gathered here in an itemized fashion, lending support for this indictment of Omri. He walked in the way of Jeroboam. He caused Israel to sin. He provoked the Lord's anger. He resorted to idols (v. 26). On the heels of this comprehensively negative scorecard the account of Omri closes. However, unlike his predecessors, Omri's death and burial as well as his successor are recorded.

Ahab, King of Israel (16:29-34)

Ahab's reign begins during Asa's thirty-eighth year as king in Judah. Though the opening of Ahab's summary is standard, he is identified three times in the first three sentences as "the son of Omri." Initially it might appear that such repetition intends to emphasize that the house of Omri continues. However, in the account of Ahab's activities as king that follows, the connection may be more pejorative. It is not simply a matter of a son who walks in his father's footsteps. Rather, it anticipates a son who surpasses his father. Omri, who is considered the most evil of kings thus far, will be outdone in sinfulness by his very own son.

Precisely when Ahab's account turns away from this standard opening, the sinfulness receives elaborate explication. Living at Samaria, Ahab takes a foreign wife (v. 31). As if no lesson had been learned from Solomon's weakness for foreign wives, his apostasy, and his eventual downfall, Ahab marries a Phoenician princess, Jezebel. She is the daughter of Ethbaal, king of Sidon. The family name already signals the overt danger Ahab is risking. Jezebel's father's name, "Ethbaal," which means "Baal is," declares belief in the power of this deity. Even Jezebel's name is likely a derivative of Baal. Hence, this family's identity is itself founded upon a profession of faith in Baal.

Baal is the deity who in agrarian society was thought to be responsible for the rain and the fertility of the soil. With elaborate ritual the people in these ancient agricultural societies worshiped Baal in order to support life on the land. As might be expected, when the narrative tallies Ahab's activities as king, it is wholly negative because of the king's idolatry. After Ahab marries Jezebel, he himself serves Baal. He worships Baal, erects an altar for Baal, and sets up a house for Baal. Finally, he erects a sacred pole, an *asherah* (v. 33), probably as Baal's consort. It is no surprise that the summary evaluation on Ahab is that he exceeded all the kings, including, we presume, his father, in his provocation of Yahweh (v. 33).

When we expect this regnal resumé to close, it takes an unexpected turn, offering a parenthetical report that further magnifies Ahab's iniquity. The report describes how Hiel of Bethel, likely under Ahab's command, went about rebuilding Jericho. In the process, Hiel's two sons, Abiram and Segub, die while overseeing major segments of the construction. Years earlier, according to tradition, Joshua (Josh 6:26) had condemned anyone who would dare rebuild Jericho after its demise. Hence, the death of the two sons fulfills that curse according to the "word of the LORD, which he spoke by Joshua son of Nun" (v. 34).

Evidently the storyteller wants to create the impression that Jericho's reconstruction was attempted under the auspices of Ahab. Inclusion of the report here as part of Ahab's regnal summary argues this king's failure in religious matters. Not only does Ahab appear to provoke the Lord with his attention to the Baal, but he also dismisses the binding significance of the sacral past in such traditions that eventually comprise the book of Joshua. Unlike the brief resumés of the preceding kings, Ahab's account does not end here. Instead, it continues in the chapters ahead, intertwined with the stories about Elijah the prophet and the conflict erupting between them.

Theological and Ethical Analysis

The formulaic presentation of these reports on the reigns of the eight kings of Judah and Israel during these early years of separation makes for a rather unimpressive legacy. Though the individual accounts lack luster and drama, the repeated sinfulness and covenantal infidelity narrated throughout each summary beats like a warning drum. Such unchecked apostasy does have consequences. When these summaries are read together, the growing heap of deeds displeasing before the Lord crafts a subtle narrative tension that assumes the form of a question. How long will the Lord tolerate the apostasy and the turning away from the promises of the covenant?

The nations are in disarray. The warring begun between Rehoboam and Jeroboam continues during the reigns of the successive rulers. Civil strife wreaks havoc within individual states. The report of further building projects at Geba, Mizpah, and Samaria offers no indication that the burdensome labor practices that the people suffered under Solomon have been abandoned. The struggle for the throne in the north enjoins violence and deception. Conspiracy, murder of entire families, and even suicide determine succession. In these struggles over power and the related power politics, brutality emerges as royalty's closest companion. The consequences for these rulers before the Lord unfold in the unraveling of the nations. With the growing tensions surrounding the direction of each state, the question sounds again. How long will the Lord tolerate apostasy and a turning away from the covenant?

As each king ascends the throne, he descends more deeply into iniquity than his predecessor. In many of the theological evaluations, the individual ruler is not only deemed to be displeasing before the Lord, but he is often assessed as repeating the sins of Jeroboam. Nadab, Baasha, and Zimri are all compared to this template of evil. Recall that because he built high places, altars, and led the people to sin against the Lord, the summary on

Jeroboam's era accorded him the reputation of being the pinnacle of sinfulness. As sentenced before the Lord, he and his family were cut off from the face of the earth. But now things have grown even worse. Omri, who also is said to have walked in the ways of Jeroboam, earns the reputation of surpassing all his predecessors with his evil ways. Moreover, the account of Omri's son Ahab leads the narrative to its height of tension. Ahab is said to have provoked the anger of the Lord, the God of Israel, more than had all the kings of Israel who were before him (16:33). Again, the question urges itself upon readers of these narratives. How long will the Lord tolerate apostasy and a turning away from the covenant?

Across these accounts, the theological assessment has repeatedly announced God's displeasure. But the repetitive refrain "did what was displeasing in the sight of the LORD" discloses more than divine dissatisfaction. "The sight of the LORD" suggests God's constant vigilance and watchfulness over these events, as well as implies a divine vision of how things would be. The vigilance reminds us that the Lord persists in the covenantal promise to be present to Israel. The vision of how things would be suggests a divine plan for humanity and God in covenantal relationship. Though God has remained present to the people, the people continually turn away. Though the Lord envisioned a faithful relationship with this people, the people seem only to know infidelity and a turning toward idols. How long will the Lord tolerate apostasy and a turning away from the covenant?

1 KINGS 17

In previous chapters, the stories of kings dominate the narrative focus. One by one the records document each ruler's personal data, deeds, and standing before the Lord. While the course of kings and their histories unfold, the course of salvation history becomes more and more of a crisis. The recurring formulaic theological evaluation "he did what was displeasing before the LORD" occurs as a persistent fixture in these records, contributing to an overarching negative impression regarding the future. But this is more than an impression. Another element in the stories also justifies the pessimistic review. The intermittent appearances and messages of prophets (Ahijah, the man of God from Judah, Shemaiah, and Jehu the son of Hanani) communicate directly the divine dismay.

In chapter 17, the rising prophetic affront to the reigning king, Ahab, overtakes the narrative and becomes as dominant as it is prolonged. With this chapter, a cycle of stories riveted upon Elijah the prophet governs the story line, only to be replaced by another prophet, Elisha, when the second book of Kings opens. Hence, the weight of the narrative focus as we have known it thus far shifts from kings who are on occasion confronted by prophets, to prophets who are now more often than not in conflict with kings.

Literary Analysis

With chapter 17, a cycle of stories begins that interrupts the parade of synchronistic accounts of the kings of Judah and Israel. Though the narrative of Ahab's reign continues, he is no longer the protagonist. Instead, a prophet assumes center stage in interacting with this king, along with many other characters who had served namelessly as mere literary props in the tale of kings and all their greatness and waywardness. The stories unfolding here are legends. As such, they narrate the marvelous attributes and heroic actions of a dominant figure, in this case, Elijah. However, as legends, they also function to reflect the lives of peasants in the ninth century B.C.E. As portrayed in the preceding tales, these are the people sidelined thus far who carried out Solomon's laborious projects, who complained to Rehoboam seeking relief from the forced work, and who built Jeroboam's cities and cast his golden calves. These tales depict Elijah the prophet confronting royal power at the top while caught up in the lives of the peasants and the poor—people who have suffered under these ambitious kings—and the conflicts resulting from contests for the throne.

The chapter abruptly commences by introducing Elijah the Tishbite from Gilead (v. 1). This programmatic opening to the stories that follow takes the form of an oath challenging King Ahab. Identifying himself with the God of Israel, Elijah swears that there will be neither dew nor rain in the land except at the prophet's command. Immediately three stories follow (vv. 2-6, 7-16, 17-24), related in different ways to one another and to this opening proclamation. Each manifests its own literary integrity as a separate story. Each tale begins with a crisis that builds narrative tension before it is eventually resolved.

In the first account (vv. 2-6), the word of the Lord commands Elijah to go hide by the Wadi Cherith, east of the Jordan. The prophet's own preceding proclamation of "no dew or rain," signaling drought and eventual famine, creates a crisis for the prophet himself that the Lord addresses. Another food crisis introduces the second story (vv. 7-16). Elijah is commanded by the Lord to travel beyond Israel to a widow at Sidon. The drought has extended to this village of Zarephath, creating future conditions of famine; once again, the Lord provides.

In the third story (vv. 17-24), Elijah is living with a widow. Whether it is the same widow as in the previous account remains unclear. However, again a life-threatening crisis ensues when the son of the woman becomes so ill that "no breath is left in him" (v. 17). Elijah prays to the Lord and the child's life is restored.

Despite the separateness of each tale, thematic threads unite the stories. In each account, a crisis erupts over conditions that jeopardize life—Elijah's sustenance in the wadi, the starving widow and her son, and finally the severe illness of the widow's son. In each instance, the word of the Lord develops in scope and recognition. In the first account, the word was proclaimed to Elijah (v. 2). In the second story, not only is the word proclaimed to the prophet again (v. 7), but he also becomes the instrument of its proclamation (v. 14). Finally, in the third tale, the woman witnesses to the proclamation of the word and its truth when Elijah presents her with her son now cured by the Lord (v. 24).

From a literary standpoint there is also a gradual development across the three stories in Elijah's character and in his relationship with the Lord. Initially, as the recipient of the Lord's command who follows orders, Elijah is passive. In the second story, Elijah is again obedient to the Lord's command but now also acts to involve the widow in the resolution of a crisis over food. In the third account, Elijah assumes full responsibility and prays insistently to the Lord to address the threat of death hovering over the child. Hence, the chain of three stories crafts an unfolding portrait of Elijah as prophet. Even the geographic shifts across the three tales—from the gully depression of a wadi, up to the widow at Zarephath, and finally to his ascent to the upper room with the child in order to beseech God—facilitate the rise of the Elijah character. Hence, chapter 17 initiates an account that through a cycle of stories allows us to glimpse the evolving relationship between God and this prophet. Moreover, Elijah's activity on behalf of those oppressed by powerful kings and rulers will also evolve. Often he will stand for an alternative source of power than that of the monarchy. Challenging the power of state, he will serve as a sign of the God who is deeply concerned about those oppressed.

Exegetical Analysis

Elijah at the Wadi Cherith (17:1-7)

Elijah, whose name means "Yahweh is my God," appears out of nowhere and confronts King Ahab. The narrative description identifies him as a Tishbite, referring to his place of origin in Gilead. Although the exact location of Tishbe remains unknown, Gilead refers to the northeastern region of Israel. However, when Elijah speaks, he identifies himself not by place but by virtue of the God of Israel before whom he stands. Coupled with this identification, he employs one of the strongest forms of speech to confront Ahab. Elijah pronounces an oath that there will be neither dew nor rain except at his word.

The promised drought is a direct challenge to the king and the god upon whom he and his father Omri have set their hearts. Married to Jezebel, a worshiper of Baal from Phoenicia, Ahab has built an altar and a temple to Baal in Samaria (16:32). Following in his father's footsteps, he has entrusted the well-being of Israel to Baal. Baal is the storm god whose rain brings life upon the earth. For many who lived in the Fertile Crescent at that time, all that lived, grew, and thrived depended upon Baal. Hence, Elijah's oath challenges more than just the king. It expresses a radically alternative worldview contesting the reigning mind-set about the very source of life in Israel.

It is not difficult to imagine that such a pronouncement puts Elijah in danger. If a drought does occur, the king will hold Elijah responsible. If it does not occur, the scoundrel and his threatening oaths need not be tolerated. Immediately, however, the God before whom Elijah professes to "stand" acts to protect him. The word of the Lord commands this prophetic renegade to hide in the Wadi Cherith. A wadi is a gully depression that fills in the wet season. Cherith is probably located somewhere east of the Jordan. Because its waters are seasonal streams, one cannot count on the wadi for water in an extended drought. Hence, though it might be a good place to hide, it is not a good place to live. It is no surprise that God, who has been endlessly patient with kings, now provides for Elijah in unexpected ways. God commands ravens to bring food to Elijah in his seclusion. Moreover, these birds of prey bring bread and meat not once, but twice, daily—abundant provisions for a fugitive. In addition, streams supply water for him in this hideout. The image yokes itself with the feeding stories from Israel's sacred past. The God who provided bread, meat, and water for the people in the wilderness is the God who does the same once again for Elijah. This first introductory scene manifests the kinship between God and Elijah. God protects and provides for Elijah. In turn, Elijah—in word and in deed—makes clear his fidelity to God. Not only does he profess his identification with the God of Israel, but when the Lord tells him to go hide in the Wadi Cherith, Elijah immediately acts to obey the command.

Elijah Is Fed by the Widow at Zarephath (17:8-16)

As this second story opens, another crisis ensues. The wadi where Elijah has been hiding has dried up. Ironically, it is Elijah's own proclamation before Ahab that brings about another crisis for him. This notice acts as a transition to the next story and anticipates another account of divine intervention on behalf of the prophet. The word of the Lord comes to him a second time and orders him to go to Zarephath, where a widow will feed him. The command-fulfillment format that governed the previous tale structures this account as well. However, now the two-part pattern frames not only God's and Elijah's exchange, but also will script Elijah's word to the widow and her response to him.

Elijah obeys and goes to Zarephath, a town located on the shores of the Mediterranean, six miles south of Sidon. There he meets a widow. Widows in the ancient Near East were destitute figures. As the poorest among the poor, they ranked alongside the orphan and the sojourner, and were often objects of charity. However, the encounter between Elijah and the widow discloses that her circumstances are even more dire than her low social standing leads us to suspect. The drought and subsequent famine proclaimed by Elijah before Ahab have also materialized here in Zarephath where they threaten this woman's life. The earliest effects of famine are always visited upon the poor. It is most significant that Zeraphath, just six miles south of Sidon, belongs to the same region from which Jezebel and her Baal prophets had come. However, Baal the storm god seems to have been rendered ineffectual against the word proclaimed by Elijah, servant of the God of Israel. Drought and famine have affected even Baal's own domain.

When Elijah first meets the woman she is gathering a few sticks, a sign of her poverty. Elijah initiates the encounter, commanding her to bring him some water. The woman, in turn, follows this stranger's orders as if obedience were second nature to her in her lowly status as widow. Then Elijah calls after her, extending his request. Now he asks for "a morsel of bread in your hand" (v. 11). It is this request that prompts her to interact with him. With an oath, she swears by Elijah's God that she has "only a handful of meal in a jar, and a little oil in a jug" (v. 12). In addition, she acknowledges she is resigned to death, as is characteristic among the poorest of the poor. She and her son will eat what is left and then they will die.

Elijah meets the woman's oath with his own challenge. Using an oracular formula, he introduces the God of Israel's promise to her. "The jar of meal will not be emptied and the jug of oil will not fail until the day that the LORD sends rain on the earth" (v. 14). He who has been fed by God in the wadi is a credible witness to such a promise. The widow is first invited to believe and then challenged to act upon that faith.

Narrative tension resolves when the widow goes and does according to Elijah's request. She prepares bread for Elijah, herself, and her son. And as promised, the jar of meal was not spent, nor was the jug of oil emptied for many days, according to the word of the Lord spoken by Elijah. Once again, God works wonders in unexpected and life-giving ways. But the real miracle is not only the endless supply of flour and oil. That this lowly woman finds the courage to give up her status as victim, makes a decision to believe, and acts in the interest of life is truly extraordinary.

Elijah plays an important enabling role in this whole process. He who has been fed by God in the wilderness now enjoins others to experience that same divine care and nurturing. Armed with the power of faith, Elijah becomes an agent of empowerment for the poor. He sets before the woman the choice for Yahweh accompanied by a promise of plenty and a promise of life over and against her current situation of poverty and resignation to death. But he does not provide for her. She must choose and act in the interest of life herself. When she does, the widow, her whole household, and the prophet live with limitless provisions according to the word of the Lord.

Elijah Raises the Widow's Son (17:17-24)

The third story is introduced with the transitional phrase, "After this" (v. 17), which invites hearing it in conjunction with the immediately preceding account. The opening reference to "the woman" who is later referred to as "the widow" (v. 20), as well as references to her son and to her house, all urge connecting this separate story with the characters of the previous narrative. Moreover, the impending death in this tale fashions continuity with the two previous stories and encourages reading them together.

The son of the woman has fallen ill. His condition is so grave that "there was no breath left in him" (v. 17). In the ancient world, life was in the breath. Hence, one whose breath was shallow was judged to be leaving this life. The widow blames Elijah (who is evidently lodging with her) for this malady. Acknowledging his religious authority, she not only addresses him as "man of God," she also demonstrates knowledge of the theology upon which his faith is founded. The God of this prophet metes out reward and punishment according to a person's own goodness and iniquity. Hence, she connects the child's sickness to her own sin and charges the prophet with courting God's judgment upon her household by his presence there.

Elijah does not respond to her accusation but charges her to give him her son. Taking the child to the upper room where he is staying, he levels against God the accusation that the widow charged Elijah: "O LORD my God, have you brought calamity even upon the widow with whom I am staying, by killing her son?" (v. 20). Elijah lays him on his own bed and stretches himself out upon the child. This was not an unfamiliar practice in the ancient world, which believed that contact between a healthy body and that of an infirm one could bring about a healing (see also 2 Kgs 4).

Elijah raises his voice to God a second time. This time, petition replaces reproach. He pleads with God on behalf of the child. "O LORD my God, let this child's life come into him again" (v. 21). The narrative reports a successful outcome. The child revives and the prophet returns the child to his mother announcing, "See, your son is alive" (v. 23). The account closes with the woman's profession of faith in Elijah and in the word of the Lord that is in his mouth. This conclusion qualifies the oath uttered by the prophet at the opening of this chapter. Elijah, servant of the Lord, God of Israel, proclaimed that the dew or rain in the land would be at the control of his word (v. 1). The story concludes as the widow recognizes that Elijah's word is true—indeed, is the word of the Lord. Elijah's command over the forces of life—whether over the dew and the rain, his own sustenance in the wadi, the food provisions for the widow and her household, or even the restoration of the life of the widow's son—is all by virtue of the power of the word of the Lord.

Theological and Ethical Analysis

Since the opening of this first book of Kings, accounts of the power struggles, ascent to the throne, buildup of military forces, and the building projects of Solomon, followed by all the subsequent rulers of the northern and southern kingdoms, have dominated the story line. The records of these kings and their national celebrations, international dealings, and governing enterprises, as well as the records of their cultic excesses, religious indiscretions, and blatant apostasy, have commanded center stage. With the spotlight riveted upon monarchs, other characters and their stories have, at best, merited only a superficial and brief mention. At worst, the glorification of the king has been at the expense of lesser characters that have been sidelined or ignored altogether. Dispensable lives—forces in the royal armies; nameless foreign women imported as wives to please these kings; people living in land exchanged as collateral for gold, timber, or other goods for government projects—these are the masses shouldering the burden of the monarchs and their reigns. Across these accounts, the narrative's attention to the privileging of the powerful and the empowering of the privileged has overshadowed the implied people of these kingdoms.

With chapter 17, all this has been challenged and all this has changed. The focus shifts abruptly away from the king. First, the protagonist king is upstaged by the now protagonist prophet, Elijah. Next, Elijah's opening oath challenges Ahab's royal authority to the core. Dew and rain, forces upon which the productivity and success of Ahab's reign in his agrarian culture depend, will respond only at the prophet's word. Over the course of three stories, Elijah's word with which he swears before this king is disclosed as the word of the Lord. Hence, the power that this king must now more directly confront is God's power made manifest in the prophet. In addition, the power of God's word manifests itself as a life-giving force to the poor, to foreigners, to the prophet, and even to those near death. God's word acts on behalf of the people, most especially the peasants that have thus far been sidelined. No longer will the Lord hold back. The kings have met their match. Just as the power of evil left unchecked gives way to further evil throughout the reigns of rulers, so too does the power of God's goodness unchecked give way to increasing goodness.

Introduced in the first story, the power of God's word not only commissions the prophet to seek protection and nourishment in an unlikely place, but it miraculously provides for him in the wadi. Nourished by the power of God's word, the prophet now becomes its agent. Elijah proclaims the word to a poor widow in a foreign land. Upon her belief, the word becomes life-giving not only for herself but for her son and for the prophet as well. The word does not remain the prerogative of the prophet. A widowed woman, who has directly experienced God's word as manifest by the prophet, herself witnesses to the power of God's word. Now she recognizes God's presence in the very utterances of Elijah. From God's proclamation of the divine word to Elijah to the widow's recognition of the word in Elijah's mouth, the word of the Lord has been an omnipresent manifestation of goodness. In the process of challenging the power of kings, it has been about the business of reversing the circumstances of the poor.

Kings and their antics posed no challenge to the God of Elijah. This God is not merely the opponent of Baal. Indeed, in the recesses of a wadi, the Lord of the prophet manifests control over the forces of nature. In times of famine, the same God also sees to the provisions and sustenance of the poor in a foreign village. Finally, God discloses divine control of the primordial force of death itself. This is the God of life!

1 KINGS 18

The command-fulfillment pattern navigates the story line of this chapter but with a twist this time. In the opening account, the Lord commands Elijah to show himself to Ahab because God is about to send rain upon the earth and end the drought. Straightaway, Elijah shows himself to Ahab, but the promised rain is delayed as the intervening contest on Mount Carmel complicates the otherwise clearly defined course of the story. In the process, the religious fidelity and authority of the prophet threatens to be compromised by the impending political and social exigencies.

Literary Analysis

As chapter 18 opens, a transitional statement establishes continuity with the preceding events. The opening words, "After many days," signal that the upcoming account follows on the heels of the previous stories. In addition, the phrase suggests that the conditions of drought pronounced in the previous chapter have grown steadily worse.

Governed by a command-fulfillment scheme, an introduction and conclusion frame this chapter. The introduction (v. 1) once again features the word of the Lord. God commands Elijah to go and present himself to Ahab before whom the prophet previously swore an oath declaring control of the dew and rain. At the same time, God declares that rain will come upon the earth. In the conclusion (vv. 41-46), Elijah is in the company of Ahab, running ahead of the king's chariot to the entrance of Jezreel. According to the Lord's promise, heavy rains fall upon Israel. Four scenes (vv. 2b-6, 7-16, 17-19, 20-40) fashion the heart of the intervening narrative. Each involves an encounter between two parties—Ahab and Obadiah, Elijah and Obadiah, Ahab and Elijah, and Elijah and the Baal prophets. Dialogue more than action moves the story toward its conclusion. Taken together, the four scenes function distinctively in the development of the plot. Rather than furthering the narrative movement to its destination, these encounters delay and even complicate the fulfillment of the divine promise and command.

In the first encounter (vv. 2b-6) King Ahab commands his steward, Obadiah, to go throughout the land seeking springs and wadis where grass might still exist. This first story concludes with the king and Obadiah going their separate ways in the land—and perhaps departing in their hearts as well. The second encounter follows (vv. 7-16) when Obadiah unexpectedly stumbles upon Elijah, whom the king has been hunting. The chance meeting ends when Obadiah agrees to obey the prophet's order. He must inform King Ahab that "Elijah is here" (v. 11). The third encounter (vv. 17-19) is brief. Elijah does appear before Ahab, thus fulfilling the command of the Lord at the opening of the chapter. Their meeting is unfriendly and the language is hostile. As a result, a fourth and final encounter is unexpectedly introduced.

Elijah will meet the Baal prophets on Mount Carmel (vv. 20-40). In the logic of the story there is nothing warranting this encounter. Elijah initiates the meeting without explanation or reason. Moreover, Elijah's challenge moves beyond hostile verbal exchanges. The confrontation becomes a contest. Conflict between Ahab and Elijah now materializes as a showdown between Yahweh and Baal. But this is more than a contest between deities. It rapidly reveals itself as a contest between prophets, with significant social and political consequences.

Finally, the account of the rains (vv. 41-46) signals the fulfillment of the divine promise as well as the conclusion to the chapter. In the opening of the story, God ordered Elijah to present himself before Ahab, who sought to destroy the prophet. Now, Elijah is ordering Ahab to go to Jezreel because God's promise of rain is about to be fulfilled. The drought ends with Elijah running ahead of Ahab's chariot, heralding the coming of the storm. In the course of these encounters, roles have changed and allegiances have shifted. Unflinching fidelity to the Lord on the part of even God's prophet shows itself to be faltering.

Exegetical Analysis

Introduction (18:1-2a)

The introduction reports that the drought has continued for three years. Such conditions have dire consequences in agricultural societies since life depends upon the land and its bounty. The well-being of both humans and beasts is at risk. The repeated cycle of seasons without rain also bears religious overtones. It fuels skepticism about the viability of faith in Baal and the associated cult, and, simultaneously it raises questions about the king, his queen, and the reliability of the divine backing of this royal regime and its prophets. Drought threatens the well-being of the agrarian-based nation.

With the opening of the chapter, the word of the Lord that previously showed itself victorious over the forces of death acts again in the interest of life. God promises to send rain upon the earth (v. 1). But the promise is preceded by a command. First, the prophet

Elijah must present himself before the king. This is not a particularly safe option. In this set of dire circumstances, Ahab, no doubt, is desperate to find a cure for the rain and a cause for the blame. Elijah is an easy target.

Obadiah and Ahab (18:2b-6)

As the first scene unfolds, the anticipated encounter between Elijah and the king is delayed. Instead, the narrative features Ahab and his chief of staff, Obadiah. The initial sentence establishes the setting. "The famine was severe in Samaria" (v. 2b). Although the consequences of the drought are felt throughout the land as far away as Zarephath (17:9), the narrative camera zooms in on Samaria, Israel's capital city. The lack of harvest in the land reaps a grave political harvest for this king. National famine means a crisis in the capital.

That the king is desperate becomes clear in the short account that follows. He summons his chief officer who is in charge of the palace, Obadiah, to accompany him in a search for any overlooked water throughout the land. As if delirious from heat stroke, the king himself is out looking for springs. A campaign to save some of the animals is at the heart of his pursuit. Perhaps the waters of some wadi have been missed where a little pasture for the mules and horses still grows. Denial is a common response on the part of those who have yet to confront a crisis head-on. The king determines that he and Obadiah will divide the land between them. He will set off in one direction and Obadiah in another.

Despite his minor role in the story, Obadiah receives a great deal of attention. He is fashioned as a complex character who must negotiate the incompatibility of his work life and his faith. Though he is a servant of the king, his name, "Obadiah," means "servant of Yahweh." Trusted by the king, he "trusts" in Yahweh ("revered the LORD" v. 3). As a servant of the king, he accompanies Ahab in his effort to save the livestock. However, he also has saved the lives of one hundred prophets of Yahweh who were threatened by Jezebel's murderous campaign. Obadiah helps the king look for fodder for the animals, but he also secretly provides bread and water for the prophets of the Lord. Hence, before the king, Obadiah lives up to his job description and his duty. Before the Lord, Obadiah lives up to his name. The risks he takes in his fidelity to the Lord form a stark contrast to Ahab in this scene. As an agent of the Lord, Obadiah acts to save human lives. By contrast, the narrative paints Ahab's behavior as ludicrous. As king of the people of Israel, Ahab acts to rescue the animals. When the scene concludes, the king and his servant are scurrying throughout the land. The different directions they take coincide with the cross-purposes at which they work.

Obadiah and Elijah (18:7-16)

Though Obadiah and Ahab go separate ways, they both eventually encounter Elijah. First Obadiah meets the elusive prophet. The opening verse of this first encounter accomplishes a great deal with few words. In one sentence, the narrative reports that Obadiah sets off on his journey through the countryside, is met by Elijah, and immediately recognizes him. With a rhetorical question Obadiah acknowledges the prophet, as well as expresses his surprise. "Is it you, my lord Elijah?" (v. 7). With an economy of words, Elijah confirms his identity and gets to the matter at hand. He orders Obadiah to go tell Ahab that he has found Elijah. Again, Obadiah responds with a question. "How have I sinned, that you would hand your servant over to Ahab, to kill me?" (v. 9). Understanding the life-threatening consequences for himself if he is to fulfill the prophet's order, Obadiah responds much like the widow who accused Elijah of bringing home the consequences of her sin when her son teetered on the brink of death. His fear is so intense that this command response will need to be recited twice more in the narrative (vv. 11-12, 14) before Obadiah acts upon it.

Next, Obadiah launches a two-part wordy oration in an attempt to convince the prophet to change his mind and his command. First, he tries to instigate fear in the prophet (v. 10). Ahab has not only been searching the countryside of Israel for Elijah; his hunt for the fugitive prophet has extended to other countries as well. The king has even required an affidavit from these foreign powers swearing that they have not granted Elijah refuge there.

Obadiah's report of Ahab's far-reaching pursuit of the prophet is intended to dramatize just how desperate and irate this king is. Having sketched such threatening conditions, Obadiah repeats Elijah's command as if to illustrate the absurdity and danger of Elijah's appearance now. Moreover, he adds the possible complication that the spirit of the Lord could carry Elijah away, endangering Obadiah. Again he repeats his fear of being killed. All these efforts at persuasion are evidently to no avail. Although we are afforded no report of Elijah's response, that Obadiah tries a different tack suggests the prophet remains unwavering in his resolve. He is determined to fulfill the Lord's command and appear before the king. Obadiah will act as herald of this dangerous epiphany.

In the second half of Obadiah's speech, he marshals evidence of his own good deeds on behalf of Yahweh's prophets. In contrast to Jezebel's slaughter of the prophets, Obadiah has not only risked hiding them in caves, he has also provided them with bread and water during this time of drought and famine (v. 13). Once again, Obadiah repeats the prophet's command to announce Elijah's presence to Ahab, and repeats the presumed outcome for himself. This time, the juxtaposition works to highlight the inequity between the good that he has done and the undeserved punishment of death that awaits him.

Elijah remains unpersuaded. However, he recognizes that Obadiah needs some further assurance. Hence the prophet swears an oath that he will indeed present himself before Ahab. The oath is evidently disarming to Obadiah. He is finally at a loss for words. The narrative reports that without further delay, Obadiah goes and reports to Ahab that he has found Elijah.

Obadiah's fear concurs with his compromised status in life. Privately, according to his own claim, he has been faithful to the Lord from his youth (v. 12). Publicly, he must appear faithful to the king as his steward. Elijah unmasks those mixed allegiances. He refers to Ahab as Obadiah's "lord" (v. 8). Moreover, the prophet's command requires Obadiah to go public with what he harbors in the privacy of his heart. His instruction to Obadiah to proclaim "Elijah is here" translates literally from the Hebrew *(hinneh 'eliyahu)*, "Behold, Yahweh is my God." Hence, the prophet is requiring of this servant much more than the disclosure that Elijah has been found. The prophet requires of Obadiah what he will eventually require of the people of Israel—to proclaim a faith in Yahweh and thus denounce a pledge of fidelity to this royal power and its Baalistic backing.

Ahab and Elijah (18:17-19)

Unlike the prolonged meeting between Elijah and Obadiah, the encounter between Ahab and the prophet is brief and to the point. The hostilities that have been accumulating for the three years of the drought are right at the surface. There is no mincing of words when the two parties meet. Ahab greets the prophet by accusing him of being the "troubler of Israel" (v. 17). Elijah retorts by reversing the accusation and extending it to include both Ahab and Ahab's father's house. Moreover, the prophet cites evidence to support his name-calling—the king's family has forsaken the commandments and followed the Baals. The opposition erupting from this verbal exchange is grounded in more than mere interpersonal conflict. It represents the antagonism between two opposing worldviews. One assumes that the accumulation and control of political power directs the course of human events. The other recognizes the Lord as author and director of life's unfoldings. In Ahab's perspective, Elijah, who is responsible for the drought and famine that is so costly, threatens his kingship and power before the people. In Elijah's view, Ahab, who is responsible for the sinfulness in the form of apostasy, threatens Israel's relationship with God.

The polarities are not only decisive but also divisive. They are life-threatening on both scores. An immediate resolution is necessary. Hence, Elijah proposes a remedy in the form of a challenge with which Ahab evidently concurs. The king is to marshal his religious might by assembling the four hundred fifty prophets of Baal and the four hundred prophets of Asherah, Baal's consort, on Mount Carmel. A contest on Mount Carmel will bring about a resolution to this conflict.

The Contest on Mount Carmel (18:20-40)

At the outset, a religious issue lies at the heart of this contest. Who is God in Israel? But as the story unfolds, other matters are also at stake. In ancient Israel and its Near Eastern context, religion was never an isolated matter. It was intimately intertwined with politics and the surrounding social environs. As kings' political decisions and social rulings reaped religious consequences, so too did religious officials' and prophets' actions have political and social ramifications. Hence, the contest that unfolds on Mount Carmel will have more than a theological outcome regarding who is God in Israel. It will also have social and political consequences for both king and prophet.

The literary frame of the tale suggests that a dramatic change is about to take place. What begins on the heights of Mount Carmel (v. 20) will end in the depths of the Kishon Valley (v. 40). The shift is not only geographic, however. Secondary borders disclose that another change is also taking place, a change in the hearts of the people. In the beginning of the narrative, Elijah confronts all the people assembled on the mountain with the question,. "How long will you go limping with two different opinions?" (v. 21). The prophet then clarifies the choice he is setting before them. They must either claim Baal or the Lord as their God. But the people remain silent before his invitation. Perhaps they do not even understand the question in a world where polytheism was the familiar religious framework. However, in the conclusion of the contest, all this is reversed. The people declare their faith, acclaiming, "The LORD indeed is God; the LORD indeed is God" (v. 39). The contest and its outcome evoke this comprehensive change of heart.

The test of power between deities on Mount Carmel unfolds in three parts (vv. 22-25, 26-29, 30-38). In the first section, Elijah dictates the terms of the competition (vv. 22-25). After pointing out the unevenness of the circumstances—Elijah, the only prophet of Yahweh, versus the four hundred and fifty prophets of Baal—the prophet orders that two bulls be provided for them (v. 23a). Next, he specifies the preparations of their individual sacrificial animals that he and the Baal prophets will undertake. Each will prepare the bull and arrange it on the wood but not set fire to it (v. 23b). Following, each side will invoke their respective deities (v. 24a). Here, the prophet's language changes unexpectedly. Now he includes the people's participation in the closing set of instructions. With the second-person plural form of address, he directs the assembly, "You call on the name of your god and I will call on the name of the LORD" (v. 24). His instructions suggest that the people side with Baal. It also indicates the prophet's assessment of the people's earlier unwillingness to make a decision for the Lord or for Baal. No decision is a decision for Baal.

The next part of this dramatic story (vv. 26-29) reports on the preparation and outcome of the Baal prophets' sacrifice. The description of their preparatory actions is brief and to the point. "They took the bull that was given them, prepared it, and called on the name of Baal from morning until noon" (v. 26a). In contrast to the lack of details involved in their readying the sacrifice, the account of the Baal prophets' offering focuses much more prolonged attention upon the outcome of their efforts. Immediately, it is reported that "there was no voice, and no answer" (v. 26) to their sacrifice. But the magnitude of their failure is dramatized by what follows. First, Elijah mocks them. Then they try to intensify their efforts to attract Baal's attention by performing a ritual dance around the altar they had made. Next, they urge a response from Baal by ritually cutting on themselves. All efforts fail. The iterative character of the concluding report makes the negative outcome unequivocally clear. "There was no voice, no answer, and no response" (v. 29).

The third and final part of the contest turns attention to Elijah. As he begins, we cannot help but notice the contrast between the very elongated account of Elijah's preparation of the sacrifice (vv. 30-37) and the brief sentence that described the Baal prophets' preparatory efforts (v. 26a). The narrative report slows dramatically, riveting our attention on every detail of the prophet's activities. First, he invites all the people to come closer to him, and they respond by gathering around. Next he rebuilds an altar, which had been broken down, in the name of the Lord. This may be an act of reverence but it also may signify more. Respectable social standing and public credibility were often granted prophets by virtue of their association with a cultic shrine or site in the north. Elijah may be reclaiming a cultic site for the Lord, but he may also be establishing a name for himself. Taking twelve stones according to the twelve tribes of Israel, he credentials his gestures with reference to the sacral traditions stemming from Israel's remembered beginnings (Josh 4:1-9). Next, he makes a trench around the altar large enough to hold two measures of seed. He arranges the wood, cuts up the bull, and arranges it on the wood.

The sacrifice is still not ready. Now Elijah orders that four jars of water be poured on the offering and it is carried out according to his word. He repeats the order two more times so that the prepared sacrifice is ultimately drenched with twelve jars of water. In addition, the narrative relates that the water fills the surrounding trench. This use of water goes well beyond the agreed upon conditions of the contest and seems particularly odd in a time of drought. However, if the fire of Elijah's God does ignite the sacrifice, these dampened conditions will surely verify and magnify the absolute power of this deity. Moreover, the references to dirt, seed, bull, wood, and water are surely intended to suggest an assemblage of the familiar elements in agriculture upon which the people's lives depend.

Now Elijah steps forward and invokes God's participation with a two-part prayer. Grounding his petition in the ancestors— Abraham, Isaac, and Jacob—Elijah first asks that the Lord be made known as the God in Israel. Then he adds a second petition. Elijah requests endorsement of himself as a servant of the Lord who has carried out everything according to God's commands. Pleading with God further, he cries, "Answer me, O LORD, answer me" so that the people will turn and be converted.

This prolonged cultic preparation has built immense narrative tension and fueled high expectation. When the fire falls from heaven, it does not disappoint. The description of the grand finale is elaborate. As the fire descends, it not only burns the combustibles—wood and burnt offering—it also envelops and consumes the stones and dust as well as licks up the water in the trench. Hence, not only did the fire of the Lord envelop the holocaust, but the stone altar that the prophet had rebuilt was destroyed by the inferno. There is no question about who is God in Israel. The people's comprehensive acclamation confirms this. "The LORD indeed is God; the LORD indeed is God" (v. 49).

However, a cloud of ambiguity hangs over the close of this dramatic event. That the altar rebuilt by the prophet was destroyed could indicate the spectacular and comprehensive nature of the divine response. It could also raise questions about this prophet and his cultic excess. Whereas the people may have received confirmation about who is God in Israel, the prophet may be the recipient of divine chastisement. Elijah's sacrificial preparations went well beyond anything agreed upon with the Baal prophets. Reclaiming a cultic site for Yahweh also affords the prophet notoriety. Since shrines and altars elevated their builders, as well as the builder's deity, the destruction of this altar may be a subtle reproach of the prophet who constructed it. With Elijah's insistence that not only God be known in Israel but that he be recognized as this God's prophet who has done everything according to divine command, he complicates and even compromises the objective of this event. The contest between deities has become a contest between prophets. Elijah's follow-up action confirms this. As the episode closes, Elijah orders the Baal prophets to be taken to Wadi Kishon where he slaughters them. Hence, the victory of the prophet's Lord on the mountaintop ends in a murderous act by the Lord's prophet in the depths of a valley.

The Coming of the Rain (18:41-46)

The divine promise of rain with which the chapter opened is about to be fulfilled in these concluding verses. The devastating effects of the drought have been mounting across the stories since Elijah's commission. The story of the widow at Zarephath (17:7-16) indicated that the famine had spread beyond Israel to the territory of Phoenicia. The king, along with his servant Obadiah, was out desperately searching for any overlooked fodder for the animals. This is about to be reversed; torrential rains will overturn the drought. The mention of rain three times (vv. 41, 44, 45) anticipates the coming of the welcomed waters. But as this chapter concludes, other more significant reversals are also evident. The antagonism between king and prophet appear to have dissipated. Elijah, who earlier was in hiding, now runs in front of the king's chariot. Ahab, whom Obadiah implied was quite fearsome and whom Elijah had previously done his best to avoid, no longer appears very threatening. Indeed, Ahab's dreaded power over Elijah's life now seems as illusory as Baal's power over the forces of life. Moreover, the king who was previously barking orders concerning Elijah is now following the prophet's orders.

First, Elijah instructs the king to go up and eat and drink on the mountain. Immediately Ahab concurs with the prophet's command (v. 42). The eating and drinking signals the king's confidence in the prophet's pronouncement. Rain is on the way (v. 41). Following, Elijah commands his servant to "look toward the sea" seven times while he himself assumes what is likely a posture of intense prayer, with his head between his knees. When a puff of cloud is finally spotted on the horizon by the servant, Elijah issues Ahab another order to which the king obediently responds. The king is to go down in his chariot to Jezreel or he is liable to be stranded and drenched. Again the king's new confidence in the prophet is evident by Ahab's compliance.

As the narrative closes, it swells with descriptions assuring that rain has finally come. The heavens darken, the clouds and wind come up, and heavy rains begin to fall. The finale closes with Ahab riding his chariot to Jezreel preceded by Elijah. Running in front of the royal entourage, the prophet heralds both the approach of the rain and the arrival of the king.

Theological and Ethical Analysis

The magnitude of the display on Mount Carmel turns the hearts of the people back to the Lord. Fire, the image in the early traditions that signaled the presence of God to Moses at Midian, once again manifests itself, this time before the gaze of the whole community. The awesome holiness of the Lord conveyed by the wonder and terror of an all-engulfing fire wins the people's conversion and their confession of faith. Such strategy on Elijah's part displays the prophet's cunning.

Across these chapters of 1 Kings, rulers' inclinations have increasingly leaned toward apostasy. Even worse, the kings' infidelity toward the Lord has been multiplied by their concomitant influencing of the people in this same wayward direction. Ahab is rated the worst in this regard for having made a home and established a cult for Baal in the precincts of the nation's capital. Religious syncretism is so well entrenched within Israel under Ahab that when Elijah asks the people to choose between Baal and the Lord their silence suggests a failure to understand the legitimacy of the question. If Elijah's work is to redirect the unfaithful course that the kings have navigated for the people back to the Lord, it must be at the grassroots level. Hence, Elijah ignores Ahab's infidelity and begins with the people. After all, it is their assent and allegiance upon which the kings depend. Thus, it is no surprise that when the fire falls, the people's confession of faith in the Lord occasions Ahab's immediate willingness to have confidence in the prophet and the Lord as well.

As politics are caught up in matters of religion, so too is religion influenced by the course of social and political forces. Likewise, the prophet himself as religious agent is subject to the political and social ramifications of his work. Hence, prophetic conflicts engaged disputes deeper and broader than religious matters. What began as a contest between deities on Mount Carmel was at the same time a competition between prophets. A complex network of social issues fueled the rivalry. Such conflicts were characteristic and erupted between persons of essentially the same public identity and social standing. As potential members of the court, prophets were always in line to become royal officials who offered kings counsel. Recall the crucial role Nathan played as counselor to David on the king's deathbed (1 Kgs 1:11-40). Moreover, since court prophets often descended from cultic guilds, it is not surprising to find these royal advisors engaged in cultic activities (Newsom, 7). The Baal prophets are a good example. The Baal prophets' kinship with the king and queen, as well as their cultic performance on Mount Carmel, confirms their twofold status. This coveted position in both court and cult could instigate competition between prophets. Thus, conflict between prophets necessarily involved competition for authority, status, and office within the community.

Whereas the Mount Carmel episode was directed to address a theological issue, it also occasioned this kind of dispute between prophets. As members of the same social group, Elijah and the Baal prophets not only needed to resolve a religious matter, but their own power, status, and recognition before the people and before the king were also on the line. Elijah's elaborate cultic actions were undoubtedly tied to his fidelity to God. Nonetheless, the reestablishment of this site for God would automatically make him its cultic official. Indeed, his prayer that God's presence would be manifested before the people demonstrated Elijah's commitment to his prophetic call. Yet, other petitions also fashioned his prayer. He asked that the people be made to recognize him as the prophet in Israel. He also requested that they know all he had done was according to the command of this powerful God. Though Elijah orchestrates a stunning defeat of his opponents, the Lord's fire falling from the heaven does not conclude the episode; rather, Elijah's slaughter of the Baal prophets caps it.

With this league of four hundred and fifty court prophets obliterated, the prospects for the public endorsement of Elijah as well as the people's return to the Lord are high. Elijah's social position has shifted dramatically from a prophet in hiding to a significant public presence. Even the king's hostility toward Elijah seems diminished. When the chapter ends, the king is not only obeying Elijah's orders and adhering to his counsel, but Elijah himself is running ahead of Ahab's chariot as they enter Jezreel together. The lesson before us is sobering. Religious motivations can become compromised by self-serving tendencies. Even the most devoted of religious officials are not exempt from inclinations toward public recognition or professional advancement. Religious workers then and today are always faced with temptations to social opportunism lodged in their ministries. The struggle to keep the Lord at the forefront of religious activities and commitments is not only the challenge before Elijah; it is the challenge before us today.

1 KINGS 19

Elijah, the true prophet of Yahweh, opposes the false prophets of Baal in chapter 18. The apostasy of Ahab's court contrasts with the piety of this prophet. The infidelity of Israel is countered by the fidelity of Elijah. Yet, the upcoming representation of Elijah's retreat to the wilderness is charged with conflict. Political, professional, and social oppositions isolate him in the wilderness. Indeed, Elijah's very sojourn in the wilderness contradicts the expectation of his prophetic office. Prophecy cannot be carried out in a desolate desert. Rather, it must be manifest within a community, and manifest specifically among God's people. Elijah struggles with an interior crisis as well as exterior threats to his life. Though he tries to escape, he cannot evade God's call. Though he seeks to abandon his prophetic commission, God does not abandon him.

Literary Analysis

Four separate scenes constitute the narrative movement of this chapter (vv. 1-3, 4-8, 9-18, 19-21). The first scene (vv. 1-3) functions as a transitional account. Ahab rehearses for Jezebel the comprehensive slaughter of the Baal prophets that Elijah has carried out. The king's summary provides a link to what has preceded in the Mount Carmel episode and explains what follows in the account of Elijah's sojourn in the wilderness. When Jezebel hears of Elijah's mass murder of her religious officials, she makes an oath to end his life. Her pronouncement prompts Elijah's first journey, his rapid flight southward to Beersheba, beyond the borders of the northern kingdom.

The second section (vv. 4-8) of the narrative takes place in the wilderness, a day's journey beyond Beersheba. Elijah's flight from the homeland immediately leads to despair in the wilderness. But a messenger of the Lord readies him for the forty days and forty nights he travels until he reaches Horeb, the mount of God.

The third scene (vv. 9-18) begins as Elijah arrives at his destination and spends the night in "the cave," presumably the one where Moses lodged when he encountered God (Exod 33:22). God's repeated questioning of Elijah's presence in that place divides the scene into two parts (vv. 9-13a, 13b-18). The first part fixes upon a series of three theophanic-like signs anticipating a divine manifestation to Elijah. However, this buildup ends in a rather obscure and even disappointing finale that raises suspicions as to whether Elijah experienced any theophany at all.

In the second part of this scene, introduced by the same question (v. 13b), a voice inquires again as to the reason for Elijah's sojourn in this wilderness place. Now the Lord's word is manifestly clear. Elijah is given three mandates. He is to anoint Hazael as king over Aram, Jehu as king in Israel, and Elisha as prophet to succeed him. More significantly, he is commanded by the Lord to leave the security of the wilderness and begin the journey back.

This travel itinerary initiates the fourth and final scene (vv. 19-21). Elijah sets out from the wilderness and finds Elisha, son of Shaphat, who is plowing in a field. After an exchange that evidently constitutes a conferring of the prophet office, Elisha sets out and follows Elijah. Hence, the chapter begins with Elijah traveling to Horeb, apparently following in the footsteps of Moses. When the chapter closes, Elisha, who has become the servant of the prophet, sets out to travel in the footsteps of Elijah.

Exegetical Analysis

Elijah on the Run (19:1-3)

The story opens with a report of Elijah's comprehensive victory—a report that at the same time summarizes the fate of the advocates of Baal. "Ahab told Jezebel all that Elijah had done, and how he had killed all the prophets with the sword" (v. 1). The introduction, which highlights the king, the queen, and the prophet, leaves little question as to the comprehensive nature of the prophet's prowess. Any report of Yahweh's fantastic fire falling from the heavens on Mount Carmel has been surpassed by this summary of Elijah's bloody finale. Such a report reinforces impressions of Elijah's daring determination. Ordinarily, such achievements not only won recognition in the community, but a promotion both in the cult and in the court might be expected. A competition such as Elijah's with the Baal prophets was a means of expanding one's sphere of influence, gaining public endorsement, and increasing one's professional status (Fry, 46). This opening sentence, which pairs the prophet with the king and queen, could nurture such expectations.

However, Jezebel's oath quickly ruptures any illusions of grandeur for Elijah. She sends a message to him swearing "So may the gods do to me, and more also, if I do not make your life like the life of one of them by this time tomorrow" (v. 2). In addition to disabling Elijah in his role as prophet, her oath addresses the inherent social agenda lodged in the conflict between prophets. Elijah's "life" and its implied social standing will not be elevated at the expense of her prophets' "lives." She will render them all on equal footing. Cut off from life, her prophets have lost all social position and identity. As a fugitive on the run, Elijah's potential for social elevation will be similarly dashed. Had Jezebel intended to kill the prophet, she might not have sent a warning. Hence, the scheme of the queen, who at best enjoys a dubious reputation across the traditions, overshadows the prophet and his actions. She accomplishes her goal without bloodshed. Her oath sets the prophet and the tale in motion. "He was afraid; he got up and fled for his life, and he came to Beer-sheba, which belongs to Judah; he left his servant there" (v. 3).

Ironically, fear, not fidelity to the Lord, governs Elijah's actions in this story. The description not only narrates the prophet's flight, it reverses the direction of the larger narrative tale. In 1 Kgs 17, Elijah had been commissioned in the wilderness to present himself as a prophet before the life-threatening king. Now the prophet retreats from that royal audience to avoid the same threat. The narrative betrays his motive. Elijah's obedience to the word of the Lord (18:1) has been compromised by a concern for his own "life" (v. 3). At the same time, the tale discloses the social estrangement that the prophet's actions incur. Beersheba marks the southern limits of Judah, beyond the jurisdiction of Ahab and Jezebel. Having arrived at the outer limit of the Judean nation, Elijah has not yet arrived at his intended destination. This first section closes with the notice that he leaves his servant there.

Elijah's Sojourn in the Wilderness (19:4-8)

As the next scene opens, the prophet's seclusion intensifies as he moves beyond Beersheba. Having departed from his servant, Elijah journeys alone into exile. "But he himself went a day's journey into the wilderness, and came and sat down under a solitary broom tree" (v. 4). A day's journey accomplishes geographical separation from all others. The vagueness of "a solitary broom tree" reinforces the lack of destination. Irony dramatizes the social consequences for the prophet. If competition for recognition and social status played a role amid his religious responsibilities on Mount Carmel, the outcome has now yielded isolation in the wilderness.

Elijah's first-person account of his plight reports despondency and desperation. "It is enough; now, O LORD, take away my life, for I am no better than my ancestors" (v. 4). This is the first time Elijah speaks to God since the contest on Mount Carmel. There he asked to be publicly endorsed as God's prophet: "Let it be known this day . . . that I am your servant, and that I have done all these things at your bidding" (18:38). In the isolation of the wilderness, he now requests to die. The repetition of the word "life" (vv. 2, 3, 4) is revealing. The prophet who fled for his "life" now wishes to die. This expression of a desire for death may be related to a frustrated ambition for recognition and authority. Elijah wants to die but he does not want to be killed.

After wishing for death, the prophet lies down and seeks consolation in the unconsciousness of sleep. Entering a dream state that in Hebrew conception hangs midway between life and death, the prophet moves into further isolation. The narrative cooperates by departing from its previous geographical moorings and becomes highly symbolic. Two encounters structure the dream that follows (vv. 5-6, 7-8). First, an angel touches Elijah. The introduction of an angel, the same Hebrew word (*mal'ak*) used for the messenger that Jezebel sent to him, builds momentary suspense. Is this mysterious visitor an instrument of death or life? The angel's invitation for him to get up and eat helps allay the tension. At his head are a cake baked on hot stones and a jug of water—rather sumptuous fare for the wilderness. But the despondent prophet will not be easily revived by food and drink. As soon as he eats and drinks, he lies down again.

Again, the messenger touches him and speaks to him. This time the messenger is identified as "the angel of the LORD" (v. 7). Elijah is again instructed to eat and drink. Now a motive is given for the nourishment. He is about to set out on another journey, and so "he got up, and ate and drank" (v. 8). Images of the past intermingle with a replay of snippets from the present. The feeding story before a journey reaches back to previous events. A miraculous feeding prefaced Elijah's journey to Sidon. There, a widow miraculously fed the prophet before his encounter with Ahab at Samaria (1 Kgs 17:7-16). In addition, parallels with an even earlier tradition begin to resonate here. Events from the Moses tradition work to coincide with the contours of this story. Once, Moses killed an enemy and fled to the wilderness in order to escape those who sought his life (Exod 2:11-15). On another occasion Elijah's great ancestor came to a bush and encountered a divine messenger (Exod 3:1-6). In another story, Moses wished for his own death in the wilderness when he was overcome with the burden of his commission (Num 11:15). And again, God fed Moses and the people in that desert setting (Num 11:31-32).

As the tale continues to resist the anchor of real time, these Moses-Elijah parallels become more explicit and determine the destination of the prophet and the direction of the story line. The second scene closes with Elijah journeying in the wilderness forty days and forty nights until he reaches Horeb, the mountain of God.

Elijah at Mount Horeb (19:9-18)

Upon arriving at the mountain, Elijah enters a cave (v. 9) where he spends the night. The Hebrew reads "the cave" (*hamme'ara*). The presence of the definite article sustains the analogy with Elijah's great ancestor Moses. Moses hid himself in "the cave" to shield himself from the glory of God (Exod 33:22-23). Such parallels cultivate expectations of an upcoming Moses-like theophany for Elijah. Yet, a fundamental difference separates Elijah from his ancestor. As prophetic intercessor, Moses journeyed to the wilderness to plead on behalf of the people. By contrast, Elijah flees to the wilderness on his own behalf. Recall, "He was afraid; he got up and fled for his life" (v. 3).

The formulaic introduction, "Then the word of the LORD came to him," (v. 9) suggests an upcoming prophetic commission for Elijah. Instead, the divine issues an inquiry, "What are you doing here, Elijah?" (v. 9). Though his retreat to the cave is analogous to that of his ancestor Moses, Elijah's sojourn is questioned. God's brief and straightforward query contrasts with the prophet's extended response. Elijah explains that he is very zealous for the Lord, the God of hosts. Then he recites a litany of allegations against the opposition. The Israelites have abandoned the covenant, broken down altars, and slain the prophets. The enumeration of these hostilities momentarily obscures Elijah's own antagonistic actions. Elijah's description of the children of Israel's slaughter of the prophets is ironic. His language employs the same words that Ahab used to report Elijah's red-handed deed against the Baal prophets (v. 1). Thus, the prophet's own speech dispels the difference between himself and his opponents. Their brutality in conflict establishes their commonality. Both Elijah and the children of Israel have engaged in a murderous enterprise.

Further, Elijah's response may reveal the deeper conflict hounding the prophet. Instead of being a prophet like his ancestor Moses, the social temptation to advancement surrounding Elijah's exercise of his prophetic role has ostracized him from the community. The opposition experienced was not confined to the king and queen or the cultic arena of Baal prophets. His reply here to the "word of the LORD" suggests the scope of the opposition to him has broadened. The alienation Elijah encountered before Ahab and Jezebel, as well as before the Baal prophets, now widens in his perspective to include the community of Israel. "They are seeking my life, to take it away" (v. 10).

Moreover, the poetics of his answer disclose a contradiction surrounding even the ideological portrait of Elijah as a faithful follower of the Lord. He professes his extreme zeal for the Lord at the beginning of his reply. But the conclusion of his response betrays this prophet's ongoing concern for himself. "I alone am left, and they are seeking my life, to take it away" (v. 10). Elijah's flight from Jezebel was instigated by a concern for his life. His despair in the wilderness motivated a request that his life be destroyed. Now Elijah explains his retreat to Horeb as an act of self-defense. "They are seeking my life" (v. 10). Concern for his own life continually governs the actions of this prophet. Thus, the prophet's zeal for the Lord is enmeshed with zeal for his own life.

Anticipation builds toward a theophanic encounter as the climactic and concluding parallel between Elijah and his ancestor Moses. Elijah is instructed to go stand on the mountain "for the LORD is about to pass by" (v. 11). The ensuing parade of familiar theophanic images—a great wind, an earthquake, and fire—fosters expectation of a divine epiphany. Nonetheless, the threefold, sonorous, negative cadence "the LORD was not" summarily dashes all hopes. The familiar theophanic triad does not manifest the divine. The stateliness of nature's description contrasts with the tumult nature creates. Ironically, this parade of violent upheavals climaxes with the ambiguous quietude that follows. The actual translation of the Hebrew here is highly disputed. The NRSV translates it as "a sound of sheer silence" (v. 12), rendering whatever it manifests imperceptible. This combination of contradictory words *sound* and *silence* fashions a chilling anticlimax in the place of the anticipated theophany.

Elijah's response mirrors that of other great religious figures who are about to receive a revelation. "He wrapped his face in his mantle" (v. 13). Mohammed enveloped himself in his cloak when he received his first visions in a cave on Mount Hira. Similarly, Moses was covered when the divine passed by (Exod 33:20). But once again a subtle difference disrupts the parallel between Moses and Elijah. In the Exodus account, the Lord covered Moses so Moses would not die. By contrast, Elijah covers *himself* to preserve himself from death. The gesture continues Elijah's ongoing concern for his own life, as well as demonstrates his expectation of a revelation from God. But what Elijah prepares for is not what he encounters. Instead, he hears only a familiar voice repeating a familiar question. "What are you doing here, Elijah?"(v. 13). Once again, Elijah's location in the wilderness is questioned. In verse 9, this voice is identified as the word of the Lord. Thus, it is the same voice that has been continually beckoning Elijah. The word of the Lord made itself known to the prophet at Cherith (17:8), at Sidon (18:1), and at Mount Carmel. Once again, the persistent word of the Lord pursues the conflict-riddled prophet even into the wilderness. Despite the prophet's determination to abandon his responsibilities, the Lord tends to the prophet and refuses to abandon him.

The points of contact with the Moses-like images of prophecy begin to collapse. No grand theophany erupts on Horeb for Elijah. Even the symbols associated with Moses as covenant mediator are negated. The wind, the earthquake, and the fire are devoid of divine presence. Moreover, the illusive "sound of sheer silence" renders the significance of any occurrence a point of debate even to this day. When questioned again about the reason for his sojourn, the monotonous repetition of the prophet's earlier response corroborates the lack of any encounter. Unlike the transformation of one's person that characteristically results from an encounter with God, nothing has changed for Elijah, nor has Elijah changed. The best he can do is repeat himself. The despondency of Elijah hiding out in the desert and riddled with conflict persists. Moreover, the social pressures and conflicts surrounding his prophetic office have harvested a more internal struggle. Elijah is stuck in his self-righteousness. The monotonous repetition of his previous reply serves as evidence.

A divine commission arranges for the succession of both kings and prophets (vv. 15-16). The characters at the opening of the story are about to be replaced. Hazael of Aram will replace Phoenicia (hence, Jezebel) as the northern threat to Israel. Jehu's dynasty will overthrow Ahab's house. Finally, Elisha will replace Elijah as prophet. The replacement of Elijah by Elisha artistically climaxes the threefold mandate. Elijah will be relieved of his prophetic post. But this new complex of characters evidently will not diminish the social upheaval of the era or the conflict. "Whoever escapes from the sword of Hazael, Jehu shall kill; and whoever escapes from the sword of Jehu, Elisha shall kill" (v. 17). Though the language here cannot be pressed too literally, its message is clear. The players on the sociohistorical horizon will change. The struggle against Baal worship will continue, and a prophet's religious struggle will remain connected to the political and social strife. Conflict will preside. Amid this turmoil, the sojourn in the wilderness ends with a note of consolation, however. Elijah is really not alone. There are others residing in Israel who are faithful to the Lord. The Lord has preserved seven thousand faithful who have never worshiped Baal. Elijah has reason to take heart as he returns. Others exist in Israel who support his work and might even be a means of edification for his wavering faith.

Elijah Seeks Out Elisha (19:19-21)

Elijah's fourth and final trek concludes the chapter. Unlike his entry into the wilderness, described as "a day's journey," or his move to Horeb where he entered "the cave," no details describing this last movement introduce the scene. He sets out from "there," and immediately finds Elisha. This raises expectations that Elijah has finally returned to the business of fulfilling the Lord's word and carrying out the three tasks to which he was commissioned. However, in what follows, Elijah only initiates action on one of the commands, the anointing of Elisha. Whether or not he does so completely or according to the word of the Lord remains a question.

Elisha, whose name means "God is salvation," is identified as the son of Shaphat. The earlier reference (v. 16) indicated that his family was of Abel-meholah, a place in Israel referenced elsewhere (Judg 7:22; 1 Kgs 4:12) but the location of which remains uncertain. When Elijah encounters him, Elisha is working as ploughman behind a yoke of twelve teams of oxen, a possible indication of the family's wealth. The image also reminds us of the agricultural character of Israel and the people's utter dependence and identification with the land. Instead of actually anointing Elisha when he comes upon him, Elijah throws his mantle over him. Whereas the meaning of the gesture is uncertain, the prophet had used the mantle to preserve his own life at Horeb (v. 13). Perhaps now the same mantle is cast over Elisha as a way of making a claim on another's life for the service of the Lord.

Still, it is important to note, there is no mentioning of any anointing of Elisha as successor to the prophet. Instead, Elisha "follows" Elijah and later is described as the prophet's "servant" (v. 21), not his successor.

There is further dissonance with what we might have expected in the prophet's commissioning of his replacement. When Elisha requests leave to go and bid farewell to his mother and father, Elijah offers a strange response. "Go back again; for what have I done to you?" (v. 20). Whether Elijah was checking to see if Elisha understood what had just taken place or was retreating from having made any gesture of invitation to Elisha remains unclear. In either case, Elijah's cryptic response hardly qualifies as an encouraging reception of Elisha's willingness to follow.

Elisha, for his part, sets about bringing closure to his former life in order to respond and follow the prophet. First, he kisses his parents good-bye. Then, he slaughters the oxen, and using the wooden harnesses makes a fire and boils their flesh. Finally, he shares the boiled meat with the people, a gesture likely serving as a thanksgiving sacrifice. Together, these actions symbolize an irrevocable decision and a break with his past that readies Elisha to take up a new identity. Hence, whereas Elisha is ready to succeed the prophet, Elijah gives no indication he is ready for a successor. Instead, Elisha follows Elijah as a servant, replacing, perhaps, the servant whom Elijah left at Beersheba before his journey into the wilderness (v. 3). As the chapter closes, Elisha has joined Elijah, but not yet as his replacement. Moreover, nothing in the brief scene suggests an especially amicable relationship between the two. In fact, a hint of tension can be detected. In contrast to Elisha's willingness to go along with the prophet, Elijah still seems unwilling to go along completely with God's plan to replace him as prophet.

Theological and Ethical Analysis

It is not difficult, even for the contemporary reader, to relate to Elijah's flight and sojourn in the wilderness. The desperation and desire to give up when his efforts and religious activities took an unexpected turn and failed to yield the fringe benefits he might have expected are all easy to understand. God had commissioned the prophet to a difficult task. Elijah had to confront the recalcitrance of a king and the apostasy of the people. The people had to be put back in touch with their need for God. As the prophet orchestrated their insight and their subsequent conversion to the Lord, he was also harvesting a set of opportune social circumstances for himself. If Elijah's role in the community and at a cultic shrine could be established, the people's dependence upon him would elevate his importance and indispensability. Moreover, the idealized portrait of Moses in the traditions of the past verified and encouraged a notion of prophetic authority to which the community was subject. Then and today, the exercise of religious authority in the community has secondary but very real consequences for leadership. Whereas it is an opportunity for service, it can also be an occasion to upgrade one's social position or illuminate one's social importance.

In the case of Elijah, the competition between deities that urged competition between prophets became a means to reinstate his position in the public arena of Israel, but the resultant conflict also enjoined risks. Participation in this religious conflict with an eye to his personal agenda set a prophet in conflict with his religious commitment. And as we might guess, such polarization risks reaping a more costly and intrinsic schism. The prophet could be at odds with God.

In the wilderness, Elijah appears in conflict with himself and with his God. He flees for his life, but seeks that his life be taken in the wilderness. He sleeps in response to despair. He alleges that he is the only one left and that the people want to take his life. Finally, he prepares (perhaps presumptuously) to encounter God as Moses did. Covering himself to save his life, he encounters only a "sound of sheer silence." When he does hear something, it is the same word of the Lord inquiring again why he is in the wilderness. Prophecy cannot be carried out in the seclusion of the isolated environs of nature. Despite the threats to his life, he must go back. In the course of a threefold commission, Elijah is commanded to replace himself as prophet. Moreover, the word of the Lord makes clear that Elijah is not the only faithful follower.

When Elijah does return, he fulfills only one of the tasks to which he was commissioned. He calls upon Elisha, his designated replacement. However, the significance of throwing his cloak over Elisha is unclear. Whether this is an obscure cultic gesture of appointment or a gesture delaying the actual anointing of Elisha in his place remains a question. The obscurity of the gesture's meaning coincides with the cloud that has begun to muddle Elijah's prophetic commitment. What is clear and instructive here is that the response to one's religious commitments and responsibilities houses at the same time an occasion for social opportunism. Though committed to elevating God in the hearts of the people, leaders can end up devoting themselves to advancing themselves or inflating their own importance. Distraction by such incentives not only sets a person in conflict with religious commitments, but can even confound his or her relationship with God. Elijah's disquiet matches our own. Though united in their struggle to win back the hearts of the people, God and the prophet are positioned at the opposite boundaries of the narrative in this endeavor. Literary contrast discloses the discordant actions that have eroded the mutuality of their cause. The divine activity at the conclusion of the story (v. 18) contrasts with the prophet's conduct reported in the introduction (v. 1). God is preserving the faithful (v. 18) while Elijah has slain the Baal prophets (v. 1).

1 KINGS 20

Chapter 20 marks an abrupt shift in the narrative while portending the beginning of the end of Ahab's reign. Though the prominence of Elijah in the narrative disappears, prophecy does not. Thus, the accounts that follow continue to counter Elijah's claim of being the only prophet left and move us closer to the end of his prophetic career. Ahab, who has been remanded to the background for the previous chapters, now moves front and center. However, his renewed role as a major player in the narrative functions in an account that moves toward his death as foretold by the word of the Lord. Amid all these shifts in characters on the scene of human history, God's promise of presence and manifestation of divine power continues to persist and to preside.

Literary Analysis

Three scenes divide and organize this chapter (vv. 1-21, 22-34, 35-43). The first two segments recount battles in which Israel is attacked at Samaria by the Syrian forces. In both cases, Ahab appears victorious. In the third scene, a prophet offers an assessment of Ahab. An unexpected negative evaluation counters and qualifies the preceding positive military outcomes. Though Ahab has been given victory, the king is still condemned to death.

In the first battle account (vv. 1-21), Ben-hadad, king of Aram (Syria), musters a coalition of thirty-two kings in order to besiege Israel's capital and king at Samaria. A series of rhetorical exchanges between Ben-hadad and Ahab, Ahab and the elders, and Ahab and a prophet structure the account. In the end, Israel is victorious, accomplishing an unbridled defeat of the Arameans.

With little transition, the second battle scene commences (vv. 22-34) with a notice to the king from the prophet to prepare again for another confrontation with Aram. This time, the affront is as much directed toward Israel's God as it is toward the king. Once again, a man of God confirms for Ahab that victory will belong to Israel so that "you shall know that I am the LORD" (v. 28). When the Aramean king surrenders, Ahab offers to spare him on conditions that Israel be granted trading privileges with Damascus and the towns in the north be restored.

The third and final scene (vv. 35-43) appears to depart dramatically from the previous two battle accounts. Commanded by the Lord, a prophet employs a ruse to prompt the king to proclaim a judgment against himself. As the scene closes, the king sets out for home, resentful and downcast.

At first glance, the proper execution of holy war, with its warrant to exterminate captives, appears to be the immediate issue joining the battle accounts together with this final scene. Contrary to the war code, Ahab had released the captive Ben-hadad. However, the narrative shift in this chapter with its focus upon

Ahab suggests that another matter may be at hand. Here begins the final overarching assessment of Ahab and his reign.

Exegetical Analysis

Battle at Samaria (20:1-21)

Verse 1 sets forth the instigating problem. Ben-hadad, the king of Aram, along with an impressive allied coalition of thirty-two kings, has besieged Israel's capital, Samaria. The historical details in this chapter are insufficient to determine which Ben-hadad this is, or whether these thirty-two kings were actually chieftains of small northern settlements. Other discrepancies in chronology and historical details warrant paying attention to the assessment of Ahab's kingship lodged here, rather than expecting any kind of accurate historical account.

On the heels of the alert regarding Ben-hadad's assault, a series of four exchanges follow (vv. 2-6, 7-8, 9-12, 13-14). These pave the way to the actual battle account (vv. 15-21). In the first exchange, Ben-hadad sends his messengers to Ahab demanding his wealth, wives, and children. Ahab's response to the Aramean overlord suggests Syria's sovereignty over Israel. Ahab agrees to turn over his gold and silver, as well as his family. Moreover, he refers to Ben-hadad as "my lord, O king," indicating Israel's vassal status. But Ben-hadad demands more. He will exceed the relationship of sovereign-vassal by also plundering the capital to his heart's content. The foreign tyrant threatens to send his servants to Ahab's palace and the homes of his royal class with a license to take whatever they want. This time Ahab is silent.

In the next round of exchanges, Ahab consults his elders (vv. 7-8), who lend him their support. He portrays Ben-hadad as "seeking trouble" (v. 7), the very characterization with which Elijah once characterized Ahab (1 Kgs 18:18). He alleges that Ben-hadad is involved here in a form of intentional provocation. After the king reports the demands of their northern enemy to the elders, the narrative indicates that they urge Ahab to resist. Moreover, the account goes on to relate that not only "all the elders" but "all the people" support opposing this threat.

The third round of exchanges (vv. 9-12) resumes the rhetorical impasse between Ahab and Ben-hadad. Ahab's servants carry the message of his willingness to pay tribute according to the first demand, but his refusal to allow more. Ben-hadad returns a reply in the form of an oath that swears to decimate Samaria in the next twenty-four hours. His recitation and threatened attack carries the frightful image of so large a militia that there will not be enough dust left in Samaria for each soldier to carry away a handful of dust from the ruins. As this verbal battle continues, Ahab replies with a proverb. He warns Ben-hadad to resist boasting of victory before he has actually fought and achieved the prize. This rhetorical cross fire ends as Ben-hadad gives orders for his Aramean troops to prepare for the real military confrontation.

A fourth and final dialogue (vv. 13-14) precedes the actual battle. This exchange is both unexpected and unprecedented. An unnamed prophet approaches Ahab with a word from the Lord. Ahab has become accustomed to pronouncements of judgments from the prophets. By contrast, this time the prophet promises victory for Ahab. However, this is not because of anything the king has done or because he deserves it. A follow-up declaration in the word of the Lord identifies a theological motive underwriting the victory at hand. God guarantees deliverance so that "you shall know that I am the LORD" (v. 13). This promise of victory carries with it the implicit indictment of Ahab's political foul play. Ahab's foreign policy in the form of tribute paid to Ben-hadad, whom he addressed as "my lord" (v. 4), has been misguided. The only one deserving that title is Israel's sovereign Lord.

When the battle begins, Ahab takes advantage of Ben-hadad's drunken stupor. According to the instructions of the prophet, Israel's king sends the young men of each district as captains into battle. They execute a preemptive strike upon the unsuspecting Arameans. The startled enemy and their intoxicated king are no match for Israel in this surprise attack. By the time they get their battle strategy together, they have been defeated by the Israelites. The account closes with a report of the slaughter of Aram's troops and Ben-hadad's flight on horseback.

Battle at Aphek (20:22-34)

The second battle account begins with the prophet's counsel to Ahab. Warning that the king of Aram will do battle with him again in the spring, he urges the king to be prepared. Immediately, the narrative shifts to an account of Aram's preparations that are well underway for this confrontation (vv. 23-25). Aram is proceeding on the theological misconception that Israel's God is a god of the hills. According to this miscalculation, a battle against the Israelites in the plain will surely guarantee victory.

Just as the prophet foretold the king, the narrative reports that Ben-hadad and his forces go up against the Israelites at Aphek. The site injects the story with some drama. Aphek is located in the plain of Philistia, where in Israel's earlier traditions they lost both a battle and the ark of the covenant to their long-standing enemy the Philistines (1 Sam 4:1-11). Moreover, the tension surrounding the confrontation increases further with the image used to describe Israel's encampment. They are portrayed as "two little flocks of goats" (v. 27) in contrast to the Aramean forces that are filling the countryside around them. This time, the conditions of the battle appear exceedingly uneven. One can only wonder if Ahab really took the prophet's warning seriously and heeded his advice to prepare for this military confrontation (v. 22).

Fortunately Israel's fate is not dependent upon its king but upon God. The man of God once again speaks to Ahab and, despite the apparent lack of readiness for battle, guarantees victory. The theological incentive for the battle's outcome is set forth again in even more explicit terms. This is not about Ahab or about God's favor toward him. This is about making clear that the Lord's identity is not limited to a god of the hills or of any other force of nature with which the multiplicity of gods are associated. Moreover, this victory will confront Ahab so that he will have to face what he seems not to know or believe yet. Simply but profoundly, the Lord is God (v. 28). As this oracle regarding God's self-disclosure ends, the battle account begins.

Though the Arameans outnumber the Israelites, on the seventh day Israel overpowers them. Israel's miraculous power is easily identified as the result of the Lord's intervention. When twenty-seven thousand of the enemy soldiers escape into the city of Aphek, they meet their death as the wall of the city falls upon them. Images of similar initiatives by God on behalf of Israel arise in the narrative. God's miraculous power at Jericho (Josh 6:15-27) seems to revisit the scene here at Aphek. The battle outcome is surely moving in Israel's favor.

Once again, Ben-hadad escapes the threat of death that such warfare inflicts. He hides in the city only to be addressed by his own servants who advise his surrender. Still, the Syrian forces continue to work with what strategy is left to them. Their confidence in their own military expertise is now replaced with confidence in the mercy of the Israelite king. They plan to tie sackcloth around their waists and rope around their necks in a last-ditch effort to save their lives. Sackcloth will signify their sorrow and the rope will imply their subservience and surrender.

Like the opening of the first battle, three rounds of exchanges between Ben-hadad and Ahab follow to bring the account of the second battle to its close. However, now the roles of the rulers are reversed. Ahab is in a position to dictate the terms of vassalship and Ben-hadad's posture is that of subject.

In the first exchange (v. 32), Ben-hadad's servants, who have appeared in sackcloth and rope before Ahab, accomplish the communication. Referring to Ben-hadad as Ahab's "servant," they appeal for his life with the language of vassalship. Ahab's unexpected response, "He is my brother," modifies the relationship of the treaty partnership. Subject and sovereign have become brothers. In the second exchange, Ben-hadad's servants seize the opportunity that the language of equanimity affords. They agree, "Yes, Ben-hadad is your brother," and immediately they follow Ahab's subsequent order to go and bring the fugitive king before him. The third and final exchange takes place directly between Ahab and Ben-hadad without the intermediary work of servants. Ben-hadad appears well prepared for the encounter. Immediately he offers to open trade routes and to restore to Israel the northern towns that had been confiscated. Upon this agreement, Ahab sets Ben-hadad free.

Ahab's acceptance of Ben-hadad's offer and his agreement to these terms may appear politically suave and economically expedient, but they also show Ahab's character as theologically pathetic. Though the roles of Ahab and Ben-hadad have been reversed across these exchanges, the Israelite king has not changed. The outcome is the same. At the beginning of the first battle, Ahab agreed to pay the tribute required by Ben-hadad, suggesting the vassalship under which Israel was then residing. In the conclusion, this king continues to secure Israel's political and economic life with the terms of a treaty. Whether with a foreign sovereign or a prisoner of war, Ahab makes deals that bespeak his dependence upon other powers rather than his dependence upon God.

The Assessment of Ahab (20:35-43)

This third scene opens with a series of exchanges between members of a company of prophets. Though the presence of prophets suggests a connection to the two preceding scenes, the specific narrative relationship of this scene to the foregoing battle account is not readily apparent. When one prophet refuses to inflict injury upon another prophet, even though it is at the command of the Lord, the resistant man of God comes under a curse. A lion will meet him on the road and he will be killed. Immediately, the deadly fate is realized. Next, another man is asked to afflict the prophet and he does so without hesitation. Then the wounded prophet disguises himself and waits at the roadside for Ahab to pass by. When the king comes along, the disguised man explains to the ruler that during the battle he was commissioned by one of the soldiers to guard a captive at the price of his life or a fine of a silver talent. As if seeking an executive pardon for a legitimate excuse, he goes on to explain that the prisoner escaped when he was busy "here and there" (v. 40). Immediately, the king reiterates the punishment promised to the man by the commissioning officer. As soon as the king repeats the judgment against the delinquent guard, the prophet removes his disguise and pronounces the same judgment upon the king. His oracle makes clear that Ben-hadad was the released prisoner. Though the Lord gave victory against the enemy to Israel's king, he released the enemy at the conclusion of the battle. The man whom the king released and with whom he made a treaty is the man devoted to destruction under the Lord's ban.

The point of this prophet's ruse before the king becomes clear. As Nathan coaxed David into enunciating a judgment and punishment for his crime with a parable (2 Sam 12), so too the prophet here sets up Ahab to pronounce the verdict and sentence upon himself for his behavior in battle. The Lord had delivered Ben-hadad into Ahab's power at Aphek. However, Ahab was more interested in political and economic securities. He still trusted Ben-hadad rather than the Lord to provide for the nation. He let the captured Aramean king go free in exchange for access to the markets of Damascus and the return of the northern towns that had been conquered by the tyrant's father. In doing so, Ahab ignored his obligation to the requirements of the *herem,* or ban, during holy war (Deut 20:10-18). Now the king's life will be the price for Ben-hadad's freedom, and the lives of Israel's people will be the price for the lives of Aram's people. Once again, Ahab's misdeeds have catastrophic consequences, not only for himself, but also for all of Israel. When Nathan confronted David with his crime and his punishment, he was repentant and filled with remorse. The contrast between kings levels the judgment on Ahab. When a prophet confronts this king with his wrongdoing, Ahab trudges toward home "resentful and sullen" (v. 43).

Theological and Ethical Analysis

As we know well, in life, appearances can be deceptive. This is certainly true of the conditions surrounding human existence. This is also true in regard to the choices we make and the motivations accompanying them. Things are not always as they seem.

Ahab's willingness to pay tribute at Ben-hadad's initial demand appears as wise diplomacy on the part of one who was a vassal to the northern superpower. In light of Israel's subservient status and the need to protect domestic well-being, Ahab's willingness to meet Aram's first demand seems prudent. However, when Ben-hadad's second demand is made, the ulterior motive behind

Ahab's initial decision is disclosed. Initially, Ahab is willing to surrender whatever it takes to safeguard what he most values. However, when that is threatened, his docility as a vassal subject disappears. The nation will go to war to safeguard his prized possessions.

Again, the king's willingness to listen to one of the prophet's declarations of the word of the Lord in regard to battle plans appears as an expression of the king's faith and obedience to a higher authority. Moreover, in each instance of warfare, the prophet proclaims the purpose of victory as explicitly theological, "So that you shall know that I am the LORD" (vv. 13, 28). But the story quickly reveals the limits of Ahab's fidelity to the Lord and the shallow motivations behind his superficial acts of compliance. The open trade routes and the economic gain with which this king would be credited determine just how far his obedience to God will go. Political and economic expediency motivate the release of the captured king, despite the mandate of holy war whereby this enemy is to be delivered up for destruction. Hence, Ahab's obedience to the prophet's word shows itself to be grounded less in fidelity to God than in advancing his own plan of victory. Despite the demands of holy war, Ahab uses his God-given military success to reclaim lost territories in the north, as well as to ensure economic advantages in Damascus. Though Ben-hadad was under God's ban, Ahab frees the captured prisoner on terms that advance his own self-serving but shortsighted economic and political enhancements.

To the modern reader, this holy war ban that demands offering up to destruction everything and everyone in battle is morally difficult to accept, if not repugnant. It narrates a kind of warfare we stand against and a kind of theology that is a far cry from the God in whom we believe. Of course, holy war was not just about vengeance and violence, but was a measure for ensuring that Israel did not turn to other gods. Still, the practice remains a stumbling block for modern readers. Nonetheless, woven into the layers of this text is a lesson that beckons us to self-examination. Here we are called to evaluate not so much our choices or our actions but rather the motives behind what we do. It is possible that our own choices, while appearing moral and of high standards, are actually motivated by that which is personally expedient or self-serving. On occasion, our deeds of mercy might really be acts of self-aggrandizement. Even the actions that serve as public expressions of both a kinship and fidelity to God might, actually, turn out to be betrayals of the very faith to which they purport to witness. Although the practices of warfare narrated in this story are quite removed from what we can accommodate under just war theory, the lessons that can be learned from the character Ahab are close at hand.

1 Kings 21

The story of Naboth's vineyard occasions the reappearance of Elijah in the narrative. The prophet who became distracted from his commitments now has the opportunity for redress. The account that unfolds here is more than a dispute over land. It is, once again, another representation of the two opposing systems operative in Israel polarizing the king and the prophet. As the agent of the God of Israel, Elijah must confront Ahab again. This time, the prophet will deliver a judgment and a sentence, and this time the king will respond.

Literary Analysis

The chapter opens with a brief introduction that establishes only a vague connection with the preceding account. Two parts divide the story that follows. Part one (vv. 1-16) narrates Ahab's desire for land and the subsequent murder of the landowner, Naboth. Part two (vv. 17-29) sets forth Elijah's confrontation of the king on his criminally acquired land parcel and the subsequent condemnation of this ruler.

A series of dialogues interlaced with action structure part one (vv. 1-16). A conversation between Ahab and Naboth, a citizen of Jezreel, establishes the problem (vv. 2-4). Ahab wants Naboth's vineyard and offers in exchange a fair price or another comparable plot. Naboth's refusal and oath before the Lord ends the discussion. In the next dialogue (vv. 5-7), when Jezebel asks him what is wrong, Ahab explains how Naboth thwarted his desire for the coveted vineyard. Following, the narrative tallies a series of actions by Jezebel making good on her word (vv. 8-14). She writes letters in the name of Ahab, seals them with his seal, and sends them to the elders and nobles in Jezreel where Naboth lives. These written orders deceive and eventually lead to a false judgment against Naboth that costs him his life. The action concludes with another dialogue between Jezebel and Ahab (v. 15). She communicates to Ahab that Naboth is dead. As part one closes, Ahab is heading down to the vineyard of the dead man in order to take possession of it (v. 16).

Part two (vv. 17-29) unfolds as a dialogue between Elijah and Ahab. Upon the Lord's command, Elijah pronounces judgment upon the king. Next, the prophet delivers the sentence. The life of Ahab and his entire household will be cut off in Israel.

When Ahab hears the prophet's words, he tears his clothes, puts on sackcloth (v. 27), and begins to fast and repent. As the account concludes, the Lord speaks to the prophet one more time (vv. 28-29). Pointing out Ahab's unprecedented turn toward the Lord, God promises to lighten the punishment. Disaster against his house will not be realized in Ahab's time, but in the era of his sons.

In part one, Jezebel's confrontation of Ahab and her plan on his behalf introduce a moral tension that cultivates an injustice. In part two, Elijah's confrontation of Ahab and pronouncement of God's punishment against the king address this crime. This narrative resolution is reinforced by the description of Ahab and Jezebel in relation to eating and fasting. In the opening of the tale, Ahab's recalcitrant refusal to eat expresses his frustrated wish for Naboth's vineyard. In the conclusion of the story, the king manifests his observance and repentance before the prophet's pronouncement by fasting. In contrast, Jezebel urges Ahab to eat while she enacts a plan to take possession of the vineyard for Ahab. However, in the conclusion of the story, Elijah foretells that it is Jezebel's corpse that will be eaten by the dogs. In the process, Jezebel's procurement of land for Ahab turns out to be a source of death for the king. Elijah's pronouncement of a death sentence for the king and his household yields a repentance that prolongs Ahab's life.

Exegetical Analysis

Naboth versus the King (21:1-16)

The opening dialogue between Ahab and Naboth, a resident of Jezreel, gives rise to a dispute. Ahab wants Naboth's vineyard, but Naboth refuses to capitulate to the king. What appears as the king's fair offer turns out to be an unfair request. Though Ahab offers a reasonable price or another vineyard of equal or greater value, he puts Naboth in a very difficult position. Naboth must either violate his family's identity and inheritance or refuse the king's request. According to Israelite tradition, the land belonging to Naboth is a possession of his family. It is their inheritance that constitutes their identity. They belong to the land as much as the land belongs to them. The land was tied to the original identity and integrity of tribal Israel. It was a sign of the inheritance that God had entrusted to Israel. Hence, Ahab's request is asking much more of Naboth than a mere plot of land. He is asking Naboth to violate his ancestral religious obligation. He is requiring Naboth to harm both his family and its past.

Moreover, if carried out, the violation is further exacerbated by Ahab's plan to turn the vineyard into a vegetable garden near his palace. Deuteronomy 11:10 contrasts the vegetable gardens of Egypt, the land of Israel's oppression, with the promised land. Vegetable gardens are associated with Israel's time of oppression and enslavement. By contrast, vineyards, which take years to grow and require constant tending, are symbols of the promised land Israel received from God when it was liberated from Egyptian bondage. Israel itself is often portrayed as a vineyard constantly cared for by the Lord and not to be traded for another people (Isa 3:14, 5:1-7; Jer 12:10). Hence, this dispute narrates much more than a disagreement over a vineyard. It discloses opposing views between the king and the people concerning issues of land and identity. For Ahab, the land is a commodity to be apprehended, divided, and traded. It can be used as collateral to serve the economics of government or even to gratify the king's personal whims. Conversely, for the people, the land is tied to the traditions of the past. It signifies the Lord's gift: their inheritance, their family identity, and their identity as God's people. Naboth's audacious oath refusing the king's request both rehearses this significance and ends the discussion.

As Ahab returns home, his response to Naboth's refusal initiates another dialogue. His sullen, resentful demeanor along with his refusal to eat prompts Jezebel's inquiry (v. 5). Ahab describes the dispute to Jezebel, a dispute culminating in Naboth's refusal to turn over his vineyard. Though Jezebel chides the king for being passive and impotent, he may actually be setting her up to act for him. When he recounts Naboth's response, he does so with significant omissions. Reporting only the refusal, Ahab never mentions Naboth's reference to the land as his "ancestral inheritance" or that his response before the king assumed the form of a sworn affidavit before the Lord: "The LORD forbid . . ." (v. 3). Thus, Ahab renders Naboth's observance of a religious obligation as a belligerent refusal of the king's fair and simple request.

This incites an instant response from Jezebel. Because she operates outside this religious tradition concerning the land, she is perfectly positioned to do whatever it takes to claim possession of Naboth's vineyard and acquire for Ahab what he desires. She schemes a ruse. Sending a letter in Ahab's name to the elders and nobles of Naboth's city, she instructs them to call a fast (v. 9). Though no reason is designated in the story, public fasts were initiated usually in the face of a great calamity or crisis impinging upon a community. Often a fast followed upon the heels of great sin in order to try and avert the anticipated punishment.

Jezebel's instructions then tie the fast to Naboth. He is to be brought before the assembly and charged with treason and blasphemy. Two scoundrels, the witnesses required by the law, will bring the charges against him. They are to allege that Naboth cursed both God and the king, a crime punishable by death according to Israel's covenantal code (Exod 22:28; Lev 24:16). Immediately following this judicial charade, the narrative reports that all of the royal orders are carried out, culminating in

Naboth's stoning. Though the letter was sent in the king's name, the news of Naboth's death is reported to Jezebel. In turn, Jezebel informs Ahab that he can now take possession of Naboth's vineyard. Then she gives the reason. Naboth, the impediment to the fulfillment of the king's wish, has been eliminated. Ahab, responding as if he has been waiting for this outcome, functions indirectly as an agent to this whole plot. As soon as he hears, without delay or further inquiry into these events, Ahab goes down in order to take possession of Naboth's vineyard (v. 16).

Elijah versus Ahab (21:17-29)

The word of the Lord comes to Elijah for the first time since his return from the wilderness. The commission is similar to the very first command the prophet was given at the opening of his career (1 Kgs 17:1). Once again, he is to come before Ahab and confront him with his misdeeds. The Lord's commission to the prophet is very specific. He is told exactly where to find the king of Samaria. Ahab is in the vineyard of Naboth, having gone there to take possession of it. The prophet will address the king in the midst of the object of his crime. The prophet is also instructed to cite both offenses—the murder and the taking possession of another's property. Following the accusation, Elijah is to pronounce the divine judgment and sentence. Ahab's fate will match the fate of the man he murdered. The dogs will lick up his blood (v. 19).

When Elijah meets Ahab, the king's salutation makes clear the terms of the relationship. At the Mount Carmel encounter, the king characterized the prophet as the "troubler of Israel" (1 Kgs 18:17). Now, the terms of hostility are much more personal. Ahab refers to Elijah as "O my enemy" (v. 20). Swiftly, and without even invoking the familiar oracular formula, "Thus says the LORD," Elijah launches into a summary indictment on Ahab: "Because you have sold yourself to do what is evil in the sight of the LORD" (v. 20). Immediately, he follows it with an elongated description of the promised punishment. The prophet minces no words. The Lord is going to "bring disaster," "consume," and "cut off from Ahab every male, bond or free, in Israel." This will not be just the end of Ahab. It will be the end of his whole household and dynasty. The prophet likens this ruler's evil to that of Jeroboam and Baasha, names that have become the benchmarks for the gravest iniquities before the Lord in Israel thus far. Like these two ill-reputed kings, Ahab has angered the Lord and caused Israel to sin. But that is not the end of the punishment. Jezebel will also suffer a deadly fate. Indeed, anyone and everyone related to Ahab by blood or marriage will be food for the dogs within the city and food for the birds in the country (v. 24). The image intends to assure that no one will escape this devastating destiny. The scavengers of the earth will consume their corpses. There will be no rest for them even in death.

The parentheses of the NRSV that follows in verses 25-26 offer a later editorial note that reinforces the prophet's harsh assessment. It reaffirms this critical judgment against Ahab and his whole household, and conjures a note of uncompromising finality. Ahab is indeed the worst king we have encountered thus far. As if Elijah's comparison of Jeroboam and Baasha did not quite capture how evil this king really is, the editor compares him to one of Israel's own enemies, the Amorites. These were the people the Lord judged so unworthy that they were driven from their territory (Judg 11:4-33). Now, the king who unjustly confiscated a plot of private property from one of his citizens must, like the Amorites, be expelled from the land. His crimes have been many and have amassed to the point of divine intolerance. The murder of one of his own citizens for the purpose of acquiring this man's vineyard was the final blow. Ahab's own dynasty will be brought down.

The story seems to have come to a close. But an addendum adds an unanticipated twist (vv. 27-29). When Ahab hears the words of the prophet, he does the unexpected. He tears his clothes, puts on sackcloth, and begins a personal fast. Such gestures of repentance, although characteristic of other biblical characters across the tradition, are most unprecedented for this king. Whether motivated by supreme remorse or self-interest, Ahab's actions cannot be ignored. God does not assess Ahab's motivation but summons Elijah to take note, drawing attention to the unimaginable about-face that can take place even within the greatest of sinners. Elijah's pronouncements in the name of the Lord have actually evoked a turning of the heart of this king. Hence, the divine punishment will be delayed. The immediacy of the threat against the king is modified. The end will still come to Ahab's house. However, it will be postponed until the days of his sons' royal tenure. Such an addition to the narrative serves both a theological and historical purpose. Theologically, it narrates what the ancient believers likely understood as Yahweh's graciousness even to such a sinner as Ahab. Historically, it also served to bring the predicted end of Ahab's household more in line with the actual end of his dynasty during the upcoming reign of his sons.

Theological and Ethical Analysis

This story clearly narrates two systems of authority at work in the service of Israel. The political and economic authority of those in government has the responsibility for the immediate material needs of the people. The authority of religious officials and tradition has the responsibility for the well-being of the people before God. Whereas it is possible for these to work together for the good of the community, more often than not they are at odds with each other.

Naboth, a citizen who owns a parcel of land, tries to be faithful to his inheritance and that of his ancestors. He refuses the king's request out of obedience and respect for his religious tradition and ancestry. The king, who is entrusted with the responsibility to promote justice among the citizens regarding economic and political matters, ends up perverting it and instead promoting the spread of injustice. He covets that which is not his. He allows another to promulgate a gross manipulation of the law to procure what is not his. Finally, he takes possession of that which belongs to another.

In the process, his crimes spin a web of further injustices entrapping others in his snare of evil. A religious practice, fasting, is employed for ill intent in the community. Thus, religious action is polluted. Citizens are enlisted to turn against fellow citizens in false testimony. Others are enjoined in the stoning of an innocent man. When political authority undermines religious tradition and meaning, it reaps deadly consequences. The buildup of community erodes, meriting God's condemnation and judgment. Authority that does not author the care of its citizens, the promotion of justice, and the fostering of a people's well-being cannot stand. It is at cross-purposes with the Lord.

Such abuses of power so costly to the least among citizens or even to the average peasant like Naboth are not confined to ancient Israel. In our own world, this same misuse of power discourages the buildup of the human community. Large corporations often manipulate legal codes and practices in order to squeeze small businesses out of existence. Powerful governments slash budgets, depriving citizens of basic needs while satisfying the desire for further luxuries among those at the top. First-world countries already controlling a great deal of the earth's natural resources often negotiate inequitable deals or exert military pressure in order to control even more resources belonging to the needy two-thirds world.

When authority is exercised for the promotion of justice, it is the work of God. But if authority is merely used to wield power and to satisfy the already ingratiated whims of the politically and economically well endowed, its long-range outcome is assured. It will surely reap the same judgment the prophet set before the king. Moreover, those who continue such practices while counting on the kind of last-minute graciousness God showed to Ahab are likely making unwise bets. As the following final chapter of 1 Kings will suggest, there are limits even to God's mercy.

1 KINGS 22

At the close of the preceding chapter, God's graciousness to Ahab modified the divine sentencing of his house for destruction. It would be delayed until the reign of Ahab's sons. Still, two prophets have already foretold Ahab's own death. The appearance of a third prophet in the upcoming chapter anticipates the fruition of these prophetic pronouncements. What opens as an account of another battle between Israel and Aram becomes, instead, the story of the death of the king. Prophecy concerning Ahab reaches its fulfillment.

COMMENTARY

Literary Analysis

Chapter 22 contains two distinct literary units. The first and most lengthy segment sets forth the account of Ahab's death (vv. 1-38). Read in conjunction with the larger narrative begun in 16:29, it brings the extended record of his reign to a close. Following, three regnal summaries (vv. 39-40, 41-50, 51-53) conclude the chapter.

The opening story of Ahab's death is a well-composed literary unit (vv. 1-38). It begins with Ahab presumably in Samaria planning a battle against Aram in order to retrieve Ramoth-gilead. The account closes with Ahab's death from that battle and his burial in Samaria.

Three parts make up this story recounting Ahab's end. Part one (vv. 1-4) establishes the context, introduces a problem, and proposes a battle plan to address the difficulty. Though Israel has enjoyed peaceful relations with Aram for the past three years, it has not received the return of Ramoth-gilead, a land of the Trans-Jordan once occupied by tribal Israel. Enlisting the support of Jehoshaphat, king of Judah, Ahab plans a battle against Syria in order to reclaim this lost territory.

Part two of the tale (vv. 5-28) unfolds as two prophetic consultations. The first is brief (vv. 5-6) and affirms the king's plan. The second is lengthy and elaborate (vv. 7-28), complicating both Ahab's intentions as well as adding a subplot to the story of Ahab's death. The prophet Micaiah comes before the king and delivers what appear to be two contradictory prophecies about the battle plan that work together to construct the truth. Micaiah's two prophetic pronouncements incite two responses (vv. 24-25, 26-27). Representing the prophets present, Zedekiah challenges Micaiah's reception of the spirit and the prophetic message that he speaks (vv. 24-25). Following, Ahab sentences Micaiah to prison, ordering that he be given only minimal provisions until the king himself returns in peace (vv. 26-27). However, Micaiah has the last word here. He calls upon the people to witness to these pronouncements in light of the upcoming events (v. 29).

The third and final segment of the story narrates the actual battle and Ahab's seemingly accidental death (vv. 29-38). Ahab

212

prescribes a battle strategy aimed at securing his own safety. The narrative concludes by recording that despite his effort Ahab dies that evening and is buried in Samaria (v. 37). The account ends with the fulfillment of Elijah's prophecy concerning not only Ahab's death but also its aftermath. The story of this king's end concludes with the unsettling image of the dogs licking up the king's spilled blood just as the prophet Elijah had foretold.

Following the story of Ahab's death, three regnal resumés (vv. 39-40, 41-50, 51-53) bring the chapter to a close. The first summarizes Ahab's reign and serves as a conclusion to the account begun in 16:29. The second fixes upon Jehoshaphat, king in Judah during the final years of Ahab's rule. The third reports the reign of Ahab's son, Ahaziah. Although this characteristic resumé serves to close the first book of Kings, it actually introduces a unit of tradition about Ahaziah that will continue into the first chapter of the next book before reaching its regnal formulaic conclusion in 2 Kgs 1:18.

Exegetical Analysis

A Plan for War (22:1-4)

The opening verse (v. 1) establishes the context and a connection between this chapter and the events of chapter 20. Israel and Aram have been at peace for three years, but that peace is about to be interrupted by Ahab. With two questions, he identifies a problem, conceives a plan, and establishes an alliance. First, he speaks to his servants. With a rhetorical question, the king introduces tension into this otherwise tranquil time. Aram has not returned Ramoth-gilead, a territory once belonging to Israel. Earlier, Ahab had released Ben-hadad, his prisoner in the battle, on the agreement that these northern territories would be returned (1 Kgs 20:34). Ramoth-gilead was strategically important, as it was the border city between Israel and Aram. However, Ahab's question does not point a blaming finger toward Aram, but rather at himself and those he speaks to. "Do you know that Ramoth-gilead belongs to us, yet we are doing nothing to take it out of the hand of the king of Aram?" (v. 3). With sly political rhetoric,

Ahab's accusation plays on the public's sense of national pride. He makes Israel's own passivity about this injustice as problematic as Aram's failure to return the land. Thus his rhetorical scheme garners public support for his battle scheme.

Second, Ahab speaks to Jehoshaphat, who has come down to him from Jerusalem (v. 4). The king of Judah's receptivity to Ahab's plan indicates that Israel and Judah are also enjoying peaceful relations. The ever-present threat of Aram looming at their border likely urged a spirit of congeniality between the two states. Ahab's second question, now directed at Jehoshaphat, is not rhetorical but direct. He asks if this neighboring sovereign will be with him against Aram. An alliance is established for the upcoming battle by Jehoshaphat's pledge of goods, soldiers, and unity of purpose. He promises Ahab, "I am as you are" (v. 4).

First Prophetic Consultation (22:5-6)

As the exchange between kings continues, Jehoshaphat levels a condition upon the plan. Following the protocol for battle in Israel, first they must consult the Lord. It was standard practice in Israel to ascertain an oracle before going off to war (Judg 20:27-28; 1 Sam 14:36-37; 25:1-5; 30:7-8; 2 Sam 5:19). The narrative tension introduced by Ahab's battle proposal is now temporarily upstaged by another problem. Will the Lord rubber-stamp Ahab's preemptive strike in the plan to reclaim Ramoth-gilead? Is Ahab's seemingly justified claim on Ramoth-gilead justified before the Lord?

Ahab does not protest Jehoshaphat's condition, nor does he delay. Immediately, he gathers a group of four hundred prophets. Though they are not identified specifically, their number, "four hundred," ties them to the four hundred prophets of Asherah that this same king summoned to Mount Carmel along with the four hundred fifty Baal prophets (1 Kgs 18:19-20). The latter were slain by Elijah (1 Kgs 18:40). Ahab's question to them is straightforward and to the point. Though Jehoshaphat urges the consultation, Ahab makes the inquiry in his own name. "Shall I go to battle against Ramoth-gilead, or shall I refrain?" (v. 6). The prophets' unanimous affirmative answer, so straightforward and uncomplicated, appears dictated by the king's question. They affirm his plan and they promise victory. Whether it was their identity as prophets of a god other than the Lord, the lack of the oracular formula in their pronouncement ("Thus says the LORD"), or the impression that they serve as this king's cheerleaders, Jehoshaphat is not satisfied.

Second Prophetic Consultation (22:7-28)

The second consultation unfolds in three parts (vv. 7-12, 13-23, 24-28), narrating a lengthy subplot to the story line. First, an exchange between the kings warrants a summoning of another prophet. Without rejecting the other prophets' response or questioning their credentials, Jehoshaphat diplomatically expresses his dissatisfaction with a question. "Is there no other prophet of the LORD here of whom we may inquire?" (v. 7). Ahab responds affirmatively but begrudgingly. Moreover, his response is laden with his reticence. Cooperating with Jehoshaphat's request could complicate his plan. First, Ahab claims that there is only "one other" available, even though we know otherwise. Readers know that Obadiah had hidden the Lord's prophets and that Elijah is back from the wilderness, along with Elisha, his successor.

Next, Ahab tries to derail any further complications resulting from this upcoming consultation. He expresses his own negative sentiments toward this prophet. Further, he indicates that this individual only prophesies disaster in regard to Ahab, raising questions about the legitimacy of what Micaiah speaks. His argument intends to suggest an interpersonal conflict that would question the reliability of this prophet's pronouncements. In the Hebrew, Ahab delays actually identifying this lone man of God until very late in the conversation (v. 8). Only after he has completed his attempt to discredit him does Ahab name Micaiah son of Imlah (v. 8). Jehoshaphat rejects Ahab's disqualification of the prophet, ending the delay in seeking this man's counsel.

Immediately, Ahab summons Micaiah for a word from the Lord. His command to his officer for haste, "Bring quickly Micaiah son of Imlah" (v. 9), conveys Ahab's growing impatience with this impasse. A narrative delay in the prophet's appearance that would fulfill the king's command aggravates the situation and builds further tension. First, the two kings are described as sitting on their thrones arrayed in their kingly attire (v. 10). They are stationed at the city gate, the entrance to the capital Samaria, since all that will take place when the prophet arrives will be very public. Moreover, the prophets present continue to urge the king, as they had done earlier, to go up against Aram. The narrative's camera zooms in close affording a snapshot of the kind of frenzied activity taking place before the kings. Zedekiah, son of Chenaanah, takes horns of iron he has made and with a dramatic gesture of a warrior promises Israel will gore the enemy (v. 11). This demonstrative prophetic activity adds to the crisis growing across the story, as well as adds to Ahab's impatience as we all await the arrival of the man of God who may advise otherwise.

The second phase of this consultation account (vv. 13-23) finally begins with the approach of Micaiah. Just before he arrives, the servant of the king who has fetched the prophet tries to dictate a script for the man of God. He is to speak only favorably and in concert with the other prophets. The alliances are clear and evidently known to most, as his servant indicated. Those who work for the king always agree with the king and what he desires. The servant evidently knows of Micaiah, for he anticipates a complication and tries heading it off in advance. But the prophet will not be given his lines. The first time he speaks in the story, Micaiah's fidelity before the Lord is made clear, and narrative suspense only increases. He insists that he will pronounce only what the Lord speaks to him (v. 14). Micaiah, as prophet of the Lord, has no intention of cooperating with any predetermined outcome or anyone else's agenda.

Ahab now makes a similar inquiry of Micaiah as the one he set before the four hundred prophets. The familiar image of one prophet's word versus the four hundred prophets' pronouncement recalls the contest on Mount Carmel. A similar issue latent at the root of the inquiry is, through whom does the God of Israel work? As if to punctuate his question with a sense of public intimidation, Ahab makes his inquiry in the name of the public assembly rather than in his own name. "Micaiah, shall *we* go to Ramoth-gilead to battle, or shall *we* refrain?" (v. 15). Micaiah's positive response matches verbatim the other prophets' counsel. Minus the oracular formula, he too says, "Go up and triumph; the LORD will give it into the hand of the king" (v. 15). Though his words match what the king desires to hear, it undermines the king's credibility. Ahab had prepared for a problematic response from the prophet. He portrayed the prophet's message as predictable, a charge that would undermine the prophet's word. "He never prophesies anything favorable about me, but only disaster" (v. 8). Now, in this public setting, Micaiah's failure to conform to this predictable portrait, as well as the prophet's positive endorsement of the war plan, spins its own irony. Ahab's own credibility is suspect. Accordingly, he lashes out at the prophet. "How many times must I make you swear to tell me nothing but the truth in the name of the LORD?" (v. 16). Unbeknownst to Ahab, his own prepositional phrase here, "in the name of the LORD," is key. Like the four hundred prophets, Micaiah's counsel to Ahab to go to Ramoth-gilead is not uttered in the name of the Lord. Indeed, as we will see, it is prompted by another spirit.

In response to Ahab's angry outburst, or perhaps in obedience to the king, Micaiah utters further counsel. This time in the form of an oracle, he contradicts his earlier pronouncement. He relates a vision where he saw all Israel scattered on the mountains. Drawing upon the image of sheep without a shepherd, he sketches a scene of a people vulnerable and unprotected. They have no king. Credentialing the elaboration of his pronouncement with "and the LORD said," Micaiah continues to explain that the people were told to go home in peace because they no longer had a leader. Foretelling the end of Ahab, this prophecy delivers to the king both what he asks for and what he fears. As Ahab is quick to observe, Micaiah does just what the king predicted. He delivers a pronouncement of disaster for Ahab. At the same time, this is the third prophetic prediction of the king's demise. This third prophecy signals that the moment of destruction is at hand.

Unsolicited, the prophet then offers an exposition of his two opposing pronouncements (vv. 19-23). Prefacing his recitation as the word of the Lord, he reports a vision of the divine assembly.

God is plotting how to entice Ahab to Ramoth-gilead so that he will fall and be destroyed there. At the divine assembly, a spirit comes forward volunteering to be a deceptive force in the mouths of the prophets. They will counsel Ahab to go to Ramoth-gilead. However, it will be the lying spirit in their mouth speaking. The truth they obscure is the disaster decreed by the Lord for Ahab (v. 23). Informed by the lying spirit, Micaiah, along with the four hundred prophets, advises the king to go up to fight at Ramoth-gilead. Speaking in the name of the Lord, Micaiah's vision foretells the king's death if he follows through on his war plan. In both instances, the prophet speaks the truth.

Two responses to the prophet's presentation serve as the third and final segment of this consultation. First, representing the gathering of prophets, Zedekiah physically assaults the prophet for his pronouncement against the king. He charges that Micaiah alone is the one possessed by the lying spirit. Micaiah responds by foretelling the same destiny for Zedekiah as for Ahab (v. 25). Zedekiah will be in hiding because by implication he will be hunted by the enemy. Next, Ahab himself responds. He orders the prophet to be imprisoned. Perhaps he intends that with such a sentence he will call Micaiah's bluff, causing the prophet to recant his words and in turn assure the king's success and safety in battle. Perhaps Ahab wants the prophet alive and in custody so that when he returns from battle the king can have the last word and the prophet can be more appropriately punished for his prophetic improprieties. Or perhaps Ahab dares not kill the prophet, lest what Micaiah speaks may actually be the truth.

The Death of Ahab (22:29-38)

This closing section of the larger story (vv. 1-38) narrating Ahab's death unfolds on a battlefield. The simply structured account—the mustering of forces, the actual battle, the result—moves quickly. Ahab's military plan is founded upon his secret ambivalence regarding Micaiah's prophecy, as well as his own self-interest. Driven by deception, he disguises himself and urges King Jehoshaphat to wear his royal robes into the battlefield. Immediately we are made privy to the logic behind Ahab's deceptive scheme. The directives dictated to the Aramean forces are focused upon the destruction of Israel's king. They are to bypass Israel's forces and make Ahab their sole target. In ancient warfare, destroying the king or military commander-in-chief was the quickest, surest way to disable an enemy and scatter the attackers.

Following this brief clip on the key elements of both companies' battle strategies, the confrontation begins (v. 32). All details are omitted except those fixing upon the fate of the two kings. First, the enemy spots Jehoshaphat. Thinking him to be the king of Israel, they get ready to attack him. When he cries out and evidently makes clear he is not who they are looking for, they turn back and Jehoshaphat is spared.

Ahab's battle episode is much less noteworthy and melodramatic; yet it is catastrophic. "A certain man" (v. 34) by accident strikes the disguised king and Ahab is mortally wounded. The lack of specificity of the man's identity, and even how the "accident" occurred, marks this king's death as hardly noteworthy. But the contrast set up between the two kings in this alliance is ironic. The one who uses disguise to protect himself dies. The endangered one, clothed in royal robes, is spared.

Now stricken, Ahab asks to be taken out of the battle (v. 34). However, his soldiers keep him propped up in his chariot as a symbol. Their leader is still with them in the fight. At sunset, when he dies, the Israelites scatter, each to his own city. The prophet Micaiah's words are fulfilled.

The narrative closes with a brief notation of the deceased king's burial. When they bury the king in Samaria, the narrative description spotlights not the funeral events, but what ensues. The closing description focuses upon the presence of prostitutes at the pool of Samaria, where the fallen king's blood-stained chariot is washed, and it adds a notation about the dogs there licking up his blood (v. 38). Both images offer a final commentary on the reign of this king. The prostitutes serve as a disquieting reminder of this king's infidelity. The dogs recall the words of the prophet Elijah, which are now fulfilled. A plot to fulfill the prophet's word has supplanted a plot that appeared to be driven by the plan to reclaim Ramoth-gilead.

Three Regnal Summaries (22:39-53)

Summaries of three kings' reigns bring chapter 22 to a close. First, a brief endnote closes the very extended account of Ahab's tenure as king (vv. 39-40). Characteristic of the format we have frequently seen across these chapters, readers are referred to the Book of the Annals of the Kings of Israel (v. 39) for a fuller account of "the rest of the acts of Ahab, and all that he did" (v. 39). The brevity of this closing note on Ahab makes sense given the very full narrative beginning that we have for this king in 16:29. Still, the regnal conclusion adds a twofold, neutral notice about Ahab's building activities. Neither praising nor condemning him, it cites the construction of his ivory house and the building of cities as his accomplishment. It is likely that Ahab's house was not made solely of ivory but of very elaborate stone trimmed in precious materials. History and archaeology do tie him to the construction of the towns of Meggido and Hazor, as well as to finishing work on Samaria, the capital city his father built. Finally, this brief summary closes in typical fashion. It notes that he slept with his ancestors and names his successor—Ahaziah, his son.

The second regnal notice focuses upon Jehoshaphat, king of Judah (vv. 41-50). In typical fashion, we hear about his parentage, the number of years that he reigned, birth and death information, and his standing in relation to the Lord. Son of Asa and Azubah, Jehoshaphat began his rule in the fourth year of Ahab's kingship. Reigning for twenty-five years, he, like his father Asa, did what was pleasing in the eyes of the Lord. However, as in the days of Solomon, the people in Judah still visited high places. Still, Jehoshaphat did make some inroads in purifying the cult. He successfully abolished male prostitution associated with the temple. Although he was noted for dominating Edom and keeping peace with Israel, his maritime expeditions were less successful. Still, the overarching impression of Jehoshaphat's kingship inscribed here is positive. The conclusion records that Jehoshaphat "was buried with his ancestors in the city of his father David" (v. 50). The summary closes with a note that Jehoram, his son, succeeded him.

The third and final resumé opens the file on the next king in Israel, Ahaziah, Ahab's son (vv. 51-53). However, his story will continue in 2 Kings, and thus the brief account here appears only as an introduction. However, it also does more. It functions as a stark contrast to the preceding account of Jehoshaphat's reign. Unlike Jehoshaphat and his father Asa, who did what was right before the Lord, this account sketches an introductory portrait of Ahaziah as being just like his father Ahab. Both did what was evil in the Lord's eyes. Jehoshaphat is recorded as ridding Jerusalem of temple prostitution. In the notation about Ahaziah, Israel's new king, the record describes him as serving Baal and worshiping him. Jehoshaphat, who reigns for twenty-five years, is at his death and burial associated with his forefather David, the model of virtuous kingship in Israel. Ahaziah's reign, which lasts a mere two years, is associated with Jeroboam, the model of apostasy before the Lord. The incomplete account of Ahaziah's reign makes for a strange and abrupt end to this book of Kings. The literary disruption coincides with the chaos and calamity that will ensue during the upcoming reigns of both Ahaziah and his brother Jehoram, our subject in the opening chapters in 2 Kings.

Theological and Ethical Analysis

As the account of Ahab's death closes the first book of Kings, we pause to reflect upon the sobering lesson about faith unfolding over these narratives. Though a king in a world so removed from ours, Ahab and his story of struggles may not be so distant or different from our own. When we adopt a more sympathetic attitude toward this king, we might even be able to see a lot of ourselves in Ahab's religious ambivalence.

On numerous occasions, the Lord was made known to Ahab. Despite the king's attraction to apostasy, God's power was miraculously made manifest on Mount Carmel before the king's eyes and the eyes of the community. At the command of the Lord through Elijah, rain brought an end to the political and economic crisis of Ahab's governance that the drought had occasioned. When he faltered in his obedience to the Lord's commands regarding war practices, a disguised prophet offered Ahab an opportunity to confront his own iniquity before the Lord. Indeed, prophets, as instruments of the Lord's will and word, constantly spoke up before this king. On three different occasions prophets informed Ahab about both his own fate and the consequences for others if he were to continue on his path of infidelity toward the Lord. There was constancy about the divine presence to and pursuit of Ahab, both in word and deed. Moreover, its form was not only judgment and condemnation. God offered signs of presence and power in the forces of nature and made manifest divine knowledge in the prophet's understanding of the struggles of the king's heart. Even in times of judgment, God extended gracious forgiveness to Ahab. God did not abandon him, but instead made abundant overtures to Ahab in this story. Soldiers, true and false prophets, prophets in disguise, the forces of nature—all serve as instruments of the Lord summoning Ahab and beckoning him to return to the Lord.

Despite his overwhelming reputation as unfaithful, Ahab did show some signs of response to the Lord. Though he held the unsurpassed reputation for apostasy and hostile relations with the Lord's prophets, he chose not to ignore them, although he viewed them as a threat. His relationship with Elijah was particularly complex. At one point, it actually seemed to be moving away from the long-reigning hostilities between them toward a more peaceful coexistence as the prophet hurried down the mountain in front of his chariot at the approach of the rains. On one occasion, Ahab even went about the gestures of repentance when faced by God's judgment for his offense. Disguising himself before heading into this last battle suggests that on some level, Ahab, in his own heart, allowed that Micaiah's visions and his pronouncement of God's word just might be credible. Thus, despite his well-earned reputation as wayward, Ahab appears to possess some kernel of faith in the Lord, although that faith was not manifest often and never wholeheartedly. Did Ahab really not understand what God wanted? Or did he perhaps comprehend the divine will but refuse to comply? Why was he so consistently remiss when confronted with persistent overtures and invitations of the Lord alongside the signs of the divine domain and power? If we can identify with his halfheartedness when it comes to faith, how do we understand it?

Human desires are readily and comprehensively tied to the immediate context. The concreteness and certainty that our surroundings offer easily override God's more subtle summons echoing in the deep longings of the heart. This was certainly true for Ahab, and it might also be true of us. The lure of instant gratification offered by the material world consistently works to overshadow and outpace the more enduring houndings of the Lord, which require prolonged effort and attention on our parts. Moreover, like Ahab, we often feel the pressure to be accountable to people in the here and now. Even if that means compromising our faith, it can mistakenly appear far more urgent than being accountable before God. Belief is difficult—especially when it seems that God's will for us interferes with our plans or the immediate pressures of our world. Further, grasping at what is secure or satisfying in the present appears to offer insurance in case the whole faith expedition turns out to be false or futile. The conditions of living lives bent completely upon belief are costly. Nonetheless, as Ahab's story shows, the risks of not doing so are far more expensive and dangerous. Hindsight seems the only venue for gaining certainty about whether this faith journey is worth the risk. In advance of our own end time, hindsight eludes us. Although the story of Ahab does not allow us to look back at our lives, it might be enough to get our attention. The insight it affords might even be enough to rupture our complacency, disturb our uncommitted hearts, and reorient our longings in the direction of the God who has been beckoning us even before the time of Ahab.

COMMENTARY: 2 Kings

2 KINGS 1

As the second book of Kings opens, a new crisis arises in Israel. At first report, it appears to be an international threat: a looming Moabite rebellion. As the story unfolds, however, a national problem presents itself also—conflict between kings and prophets, prompted once again by the king's apostasy. The two difficulties need not be viewed as unrelated. Elijah's prophetic death sentence over the new king, Ahaziah, and its swift fulfillment can only intensify the impending Moabite threat.

Literary Analysis

The opening and closing of the chapter set the international and national crises in relation to each other. In the beginning of the narrative (vv. 1-2a), we hear of Moab's rebellion that threatens Israel and we hear of a life-threatening injury to Israel's new king, Ahaziah. At the end of the chapter, the narrative reports that Jehoram, who will later lose control over rebellious Moab (3:4-27), ascends the throne in the wake of Ahaziah's death from his injury (vv. 17-18). In between this literary framework, Elijah's pronouncement of the king's death and its implementation navigates the narrative. First, the new ruler, who has fallen through the lattice in his upper chamber, attempts to deal with his physical crisis by sending messengers to consult Baal-zebub, the god of Ekron, regarding his fate (v. 2b). Next, the crisis is aggravated when the messengers curtail their inquiry of Baal-zebub and instead return and relate Elijah's prophecy to Ahaziah.

Four encounters follow that build narrative tension while delaying the fulfillment of Elijah's prophecy (vv. 9-10, 11-12, 13-15, 16). In the first three (vv. 9-10, 11-12, 13-15), the king dispatches a captain and his force of fifty men to go and command the prophet to come down from atop the hill on which he is sitting. Twice Elijah responds by calling down fire from heaven, which consumes the men. However, the third time, the captain approaches the prophet and pleads for his life and the lives of his troops. Sparing this third entourage, Elijah obeys a word from the Lord and sets out to appear before the king. In the fourth encounter (v. 16), Elijah reports to Ahaziah the oracle of the Lord. The King will die from his injury.

The narrative closes by recording that the word of the Lord, as spoken by the prophet Elijah, has been fulfilled. The characteristic regnal summary follows, with an explanatory note as to why Ahaziah's brother Jehoram, rather than a son, succeeds him.

Exegetical Analysis

Introduction to Two Crises (1:1-2a)

Chapter 1 opens with a notice that Moab has begun to rebel against Israel. As introduction to the story that follows, this opening at first seems awkward and out of place. However, it is coupled with two other notices: Ahab has died (v. 1); and his son Ahaziah has incurred a serious injury from a fall (v. 2a). The report of Moab's rebellion is positioned between the notice of the death of one king and the report of the threatened death of his successor. The juxtaposition of these seemingly unrelated international and national events urges us to consider their relationship. The international turn of events aggravates the national crisis. Moreover, the reports of both sets of events also create an impression of simultaneity that underscores the crises at hand. While Israel's kingship is in the turmoil and uncertainty of transition, Moab seizes the opportunity to begin a rebellion. Since the time of David, Moab had been under Israel's subjugation (2 Sam 8:12). Now its threatened revolt instigates a new predicament that will have to wait until Israel's government is stabilized.

Ahaziah's Consultation (1:2b-4)

Though Ahaziah's injury appears to be the presenting problem, it does not take precedence in the story. Rather, this king's decision to consult Baal, which is far more problematic, determines the course of the tale. Ahaziah sends his messengers to Ekron to ask Baal-zebub whether he will survive his injuries. Ekron is a Philistine town on the Mediterranean coast about twenty-five miles west of Jerusalem. However, we know little about the religion practiced there. The name Baal-zebub, which literally means "Baal the Fly," is the name for a god that does not occur anywhere else in the biblical tradition. Likely, it was a local manifestation of the Baal that was worshiped in a wide variety of contexts in the ancient Near East. Readers will likely recognize its etymological similarity to Beelzebul in the synoptic tradition (Mark 3:22, Matt 12:24, and Luke 11:14). Whether these two names refer to the same being remains a matter of conjecture. Its significance here has less to do with the specificity of its identity than with its role in manifesting once again the royal family's utter disregard for the Lord, the God of Israel, and their ongoing identification with Baal instead. Ahaziah, just like his father Ahab, automa-tically resorts to apostasy. He steadfastly refuses to acknowledge that the source of life, healing, and well-being in Israel is the Lord.

The king's command to his messengers is matched by the Lord's command to Elijah the prophet. He is to intercept the king's messengers and deliver to them the Lord's pronouncement regarding the king. In this encounter, divine power will meet royal power. As the king sends the messengers to inquire of Baal-zebub about his recovery, the Lord is sending the prophet to make an inquiry of the king about his belief. "Is it because there is no God in Israel that you are going to inquire of Baal-zebub, the god of Ekron?" (v. 3). The king seeks an answer from Baal-zebub that he will live. Instructed by the Lord, the prophet is to deliver the Lord's word to the king that he will die.

Though there is no narrative of the encounter between the prophet and the king's messengers, the record reports that upon receiving his instructions the prophet set out. In addition, the scene that follows (vv. 5-8) describes the messengers relating the prophet's word to the king.

The Messengers' Report to Ahaziah (1:5-8)

As the scene opens, the king questions the messengers who have returned. His inquiry suggests that the messengers have returned too soon. Responding to the king, the messengers report their encounter with a man who asked them about who is God in Israel, and whose prophetic inquiry challenged the legitimacy of their journey to Ekron. They repeat exactly the words of Elijah. They also relate with exacting precision the indictment and sentence delivered by the prophet. That the messengers responded to this man by returning to the king instead of going to Ekron as they were commanded suggests they recognized Elijah's authority. For his part, the king does not respond to the message, but asks further questions regarding the man. The description of a hairy man with a leather belt, coupled with his condemnation of the king, leaves no doubt in Ahaziah's mind about the identity of this troubler. Known well for his condemnations against the Omride dynasty, it is Elijah.

Four Encounters (1:9-18)

Three encounters (vv. 9-10, 11-12, 13-15) between the king's officials and the prophet lead to a fourth exchange (v. 16), this time between the prophet and the king. In the first meeting (vv. 9-10), the king dispatches a captain and fifty men to go up to the prophet, who is sitting on a hill. The location reminds us of prophets' association with cultic sites on mountains, as when Elijah rebuilt the altar on Mount Carmel (1 Kgs 18:30). With a salutation that smacks of mockery, the captain addresses Elijah as "man of God" (v. 9). Following the mocking greeting, the captain then delivers to the prophet the king's order to come down. No explanation is given as to why the king wants an audience with the prophet. Perhaps he expects Elijah to heal him, like his father Ahab; perhaps he intends to silence the prophet by destroying him. However, Elijah obeys God, not the king. Instead of going down with the officers, he responds with a challenge to the officer's sarcastic address. "If I am a man of God, let fire come down from heaven and consume you and your fifty" (v. 10). Again, the climax on Mount Carmel is recalled with the image of fire falling from the heavens as confirmation that Elijah's God is Lord in Israel. According to the prophet's summons, fire does fall and the captain and his men are consumed.

The second encounter is like the first, with one difference. This time, the king amends his order and commands the prophet to "come down *quickly*" (v. 11). Whether the addition expresses the king's own concern that his condition is worsening or his consternation that the prophet is not complying remains a question. Though the king's order is now more adamant, Elijah's response is the same. He ignores the summons and calls down fire from heaven that again consumes the captain and his fifty men.

A third time the king sends a captain and his company up the hill to demand the prophet's presence before the king (vv. 13-15). However, this time the captain does not level an order from the king but instead entreats Elijah. Shifting his allegiance, the captain comes before the prophet on bended knee. He pleads for his life and the lives of his men lest the prophet summon a fiery death sentence upon them. In this way, the captain expresses his own belief in the prophet and his word. Moreover, he makes clear his knowledge of the fate of the two previous companies who had visited the prophet and asks that this time Elijah have regard for their lives. The Lord responds before Elijah. Once again, the messenger of the Lord delivers a summons to the prophet (v. 15): he is to go down to the king. That the Lord urges him not to fear further clarifies the reason for the king's pursuit of the prophet. Like his father Ahab, Ahaziah intends to kill Elijah.

In response to the word of the Lord, Elijah goes down. This fourth encounter is abbreviated (v. 16); we are not told of the actual meeting. The narrative relates only that Elijah speaks just as he was commanded. First, he repeats the rhetorical question that indicts the king for turning to Baal-zebub rather than to the Lord. Then Elijah levels the death sentence. Finally, the account then reports without elaboration that the death sentence has been carried out.

Regnal Summary (1:17-18)

The record of Ahaziah's death begins the regnal summary and concludes the preceding story. The prophet's word has been fulfilled. Apostasy warrants God's judgment. The death sentence has been implemented; Ahaziah has died. In the format typical of these summaries, Jehoram, son of Jehoshaphat and now reigning in Judah, is identified as contemporaneous with the reign of Jehoram, brother of Ahaziah, who succeeded the deceased king in Israel. That Ahaziah had produced no heir to the throne explains his brother's succession.

Theological and Ethical Analysis

The self-contained story in this chapter sets forth a familiar and easily detectable message. Consultation of foreign gods is strictly forbidden in Israel's covenantal relationship. From the Solomonic traditions that opens the first book of Kings on down through virtually all subsequent stories of kings and their reigns, the theme of apostasy echoes. But there is more to learn from this story than first meets the eye. Indeed, it joins the previous accounts in a resounding chorus condemning efforts that search for truth, hope, and help in powers that are finite and false. It also gives us pause to reflect upon the deception and destruction growing out of unbridled, self-serving authority that is tied to false belief.

The deception begins with oneself. Refusal to believe in the infinite power of the Lord, who watches over the course of our lives, easily leads to the notion that we are the ones who are in charge. This refusal to acknowledge God's ultimate reign in all matters encourages delusions that one can manipulate reality. It supports our inclinations to serve our self-interests and to use others to do so.

Ahaziah participated in this kind of deception. First, he believed he could be privy to what is beyond human capacity to know. He refused to acknowledge his human limitations regarding the ultimate questions surrounding life and death. He sent his officers to Ekron to get information from a power that does not exist, for an answer that he could not know—whether he would live or die from his injury. To persist in such a lie about human capacity to know and to control often requires enlisting others' participation. Hence, when Ahaziah's officers return without the answer he believed he could procure, his notion of reality and his false sense of control are disrupted. In addition, his illusion of unstoppable power is threatened. Confronted by his officers with evidence of an alternative power in the form of the word of the Lord through Elijah, the king must make a choice. Either he must give up his self-deceiving belief system, acknowledge his vulnerability, and embrace the Lord, or he must become even more fixed and adamant in his false sense of being in charge.

Ahaziah chooses the latter. Now idolatrous faith and illusions about power enjoin not only deception but also destruction as accomplice. Wielding a kind of power as if no other power exists, the ailing king issues command upon command. He orders his captain and fifty men up the mountain. He commands them to order the prophet to come down before him. When that plan goes terribly wrong, the king sets forth the same order with yet greater adamancy.

When human power competes with divine power it often yields tragic outcomes. The first two companies of men that Ahaziah sends up the mountain are destroyed. Innocent lives are put in harm's way. But to keep the delusion alive, the abuse of power becomes imperative. Others are counted as expendable. The refusal to give up power or even to acknowledge the limitations of his control will require sacrificing others in this great charade. Thus, a third company of men is sent.

Such power that functions without controls, believing it can manipulate reality—even ultimate reality—eventually self-destructs. Ahaziah's death confirmed the prophet's word and thus became a witness to the ultimate truth and power of God's word. But it also teaches something else. It illustrates the relationship between lack of faith in the omnipotent Lord and the human potential for abuse of power. When we lose sight of the all-powerful God who controls matters of life and death, we are drawn to other false groundings for our hope. In turn, putting trust in other false controls over our destiny can breed a misuse of power. Keeping such delusions alive not only leads to using or sacrificing others for our self-interests, but can eventually cost us our own lives as well. Ahaziah's story serves as a witness.

2 KINGS 2

Chapter 2 marks a pause in the progression of stories about kings and the dramas of their conflicts with other kings and prophets. References to events, rulers, and other chronological markers are notably absent. The story of the transition of religious leadership from Elijah to Elisha is fittingly positioned in a kind of liminal space. Elijah is about to leave history and narrative, leaving Elisha to succeed him. The story will climax in a space between heaven and earth. As Elijah ascends upward, Elisha will rise to his new role as prophet. No trace of Elijah will remain except for his mantle. With this symbol of his predecessor, Elisha will take up Elijah's role and begin to exercise leadership with power and authority.

Literary Analysis

Three separate stories (vv. 1-18, 19-22, 23-25) work together here, narrating the transition that brings an end to Elijah's career and legitimizes his successor, Elisha. Movement toward and away from the Jordan organizes the first account, dividing it into three episodes (vv. 1-6, 7-12, 13-18). First, a cycle of three conversations between Elijah and Elisha en route to three locations moves the first episode forward toward the Jordan. Three times Elijah instructs Elisha to remain behind while he travels ahead: first to Bethel, then to Jericho, and finally to the Jordan. On each occasion Elisha rebuffs Elijah's instructions, swearing by the Lord that he will not desert his master. Every time the two arrive at their destinations—Bethel, Jericho, and the Jordan—a company of prophets comes out to inform Elisha of that which he apparently already knows: the Lord is about to take his master Elijah away.

When they arrive at the Jordan, the second episode of the first story begins. Having crossed the river, Elisha asks for a double portion of Elijah's spirit (v. 9). After Elijah establishes the conditions whereby Elisha will know if his request has been honored, a chariot of fire and horses of fire separate them while a whirlwind carries Elijah up into heaven (v. 11).

The third and final episode of this first story begins when Elisha returns to the Jordan (vv. 13-18) and, with the help of Elijah's mantle, miraculously crosses the river. Evidently unaware of Elijah's ascent to heaven, the brotherhood of prophets pleads with Elisha to release a company of fifty strong men to seek Elijah on some mountain or in some valley. When their search is unsuccessful, Elisha uses the occasion to establish his authority and credibility.

The second and third stories narrating the prophetic transition illustrate Elisha's prophetic credibility. The second story demonstrates Elisha's power to heal and restore life (vv. 19-22). He purifies the water supply for the people of Jericho. By contrast, the third and final tale (vv. 23-25) discloses the prophet's power as an agent of judgment and death. In the name of the Lord, he curses some young boys who had mockingly jeered at him. Immediately, two she-bears emerge from the woods and maul forty-two of the boys. Though it is a difficult story in moral terms, it serves to illustrate the scope of divine authority of which the prophet is an instrument. At the word of the Lord, life can be healed and nurtured or life can be cursed and destroyed.

Exegetical Analysis

Elijah's Departure and Elisha's Investiture (2:1-18)

The opening verse informs the reader what Elijah and Elisha are yet to learn. Elijah will be taken up to heaven in a whirlwind (v. 1). The Lord is named as the agent of this amazing occurrence; divine intervention infuses a numinous aura over the chapter. Movement toward the Jordan (vv. 1-7), across the Jordan (vv. 8-14), and away from the Jordan (vv. 15-18) organizes the account of Elijah's ascent and Elisha's assumption of his prophetic office (B. Long, 23-24). A highly repetitive dialogue between Elijah and Elisha accomplishes the movement toward the Jordan. The resistance that characterizes their conversations actually discloses the unanimity of their commitment. Elijah alleges that at God's request he must journey first to Bethel, then to Jericho, and finally across the Jordan. Elisha swears before the Lord his fidelity to Elijah in making his case to accompany the prophet in all three instances. Hence, both invoke the Lord in marshaling their arguments.

No reason is given for the journeys. Perhaps Elijah is determined to face what was coming on his own. However, the lack of logic to the geographical progression of the journeys—from Gilgal to Bethel, Bethel to Jericho, and then to the Jordan, which is near Gilgal, the start of these travels—suggests another motivation. As part of preparations for his final departure, Elijah is testing the steadfastness of Elisha's commitment to follow in his ways, no matter how mysterious the route.

Each time the two arrive at their destination, the brotherhood of prophets approaches Elisha and questions whether he knows that his master is about to be taken from him by the Lord. The Hebrew here, which literally translates "taken from over his head," accommodates several interpretations. It could suggest that Elijah is about to disappear as a result of divine intervention. It could also suggest the demoting of Elijah and his authority in relation to Elisha and the other prophets. Because what God will do and how God will do it is shrouded in mystery, Elisha is called to maintain vigilance rather than a pretense of knowing. Hence, each time the brotherhood of prophets warns him, Elisha orders them to be silent.

The second episode of this story begins as they reach the Jordan (vv. 7-12). Upon arriving at the river, Elijah takes the mantle he had cast over Elisha at his calling (1 Kgs 19:19) and strikes the water. The water parts and the two of them cross over on dry ground (v. 8). Images of Moses' entry into the wilderness and his dividing the waters at the Red Sea flood the narrative. Even the descriptive language, "crossed on dry ground," echoes both the exodus story (Exod 14:21) and the later drama when Israel entered the land under Joshua's leadership (Josh 3:17).

Together Elijah and Elisha depart the settled land and enter the wilderness, the very place where Elijah began his ministry. As if to ensure that nothing has been left unattended, Elijah asks Elisha if there is any last wish he can grant for his successor. In the gravity of the moment and the uncertainty about what is to come, Elisha wisely asks for "a double share" of Elijah's spirit (v. 9). Elisha is not requesting twice the spirit of the prophet. Rather, drawing upon the language of Israel's legal tradition (Deut 21:17), Elisha is asking for the inheritance of the oldest son who must carry on the work of a father. The language here does not carry so much a legal connotation legislating inheritance, but rather narrates the intimacy between them. Elisha respectfully communicates that taking up Elijah's role is like that of an eldest son following in the footsteps of his father. Elijah acknowledges that the request is difficult. Understanding that such favors are within the purview of God alone, Elijah sets out the conditions whereby Elisha will know whether or not he has received what he requested. If he sees Elijah being taken, it will be granted (v. 10).

As the two of them continue on walking and talking, the mysterious climax strikes abruptly, without any forewarning. Chariots and horses of fire come between them and a whirlwind catches Elijah and carries him away. As the fury of fire and storm swoops Elijah up in a tornado-like transport, Elisha emotes a soulful cry, "Father, father! The chariots of Israel and its horsemen!" (v. 12). Although the meaning of the exclamation is uncertain, it is possible to hear Elisha's cry as an attempt to translate the fantastic and frightening moment into familiar terms. He tries to identify the fiery chariot and horsemen as Israel's horsemen and chariots. Elijah, his father, is also Israel's defender and protector. When the momentary spectacle is over, Elisha is alone. It dawns on Elisha that Elijah is really, truly gone. Grief-stricken, Elisha tears his garment.

As he moves back across the Jordan, the third and final episode of the story begins (vv. 13-18). Elisha picks up the mantle of Elijah that had fallen from him as he ascended. Repeating what he has learned from his master, Elisha takes the mantle and strikes the waters of the Jordan. At the same time, his question, "Where is the LORD, the God of Elijah?" (v. 14), echoes his desperation and struggle to grasp what has just taken place before his eyes. Immediately, though, the waters part. Like Joshua, who upon assuming the leadership of Moses crosses the Jordan with the people (Josh 3:17), Elisha crosses the river. With this gesture Elisha begins to embrace the religious authority of Elijah's prophetic office. The company of prophets, who are first to encounter him as he comes out of the wilderness, witnesses to his new office. They profess, "The spirit of Elijah rests on Elisha" (v. 15). Both the parting of the waters and this public recognition confirm that what Elisha requested has been granted. Elisha did behold Elijah being taken up.

However, what Elisha has been privy to, the brotherhood of prophets has not been. Though they know Elijah is gone, they do not know where he went. Earlier, Elisha urged the company of prophets to be silent; now he urges them not to search for Elijah. That they seek Elisha's permission to go look for Elijah is evidence of their early recognition of Elisha's new authority. Their persistence finally persuades him to permit them to search. Not finding Elijah, they return to Elisha in Jericho. He uses the occasion to confront them with their need to acknowledge his new authority. Elijah is gone, just as he told them.

Elisha Purifies the Waters at Jericho (2:19-22)

With this brief story and the one to follow (vv. 23-25), Elisha receives further confirmation of his prophetic authority and power. At Jericho there is good land but bad water. The origin of the problem is unclear. However, the bad water recalls the curse pronounced by Joshua over Jericho (Josh 6:26; 1 Kgs 16:34), thus crafting another connection between Elisha and Joshua. In any case, the water causes barrenness and miscarriages, thus threatening the continuation and future of the people living there. Elisha's authority as a prophet is evidently already public knowledge, for the people approach him for help with their environmental crisis. Paralleling the manner in which Elijah began his prophetic work at Zarapheth with the widow (1 Kgs 17), Elisha enlists the people to fetch what he needs. He requests that they bring a new bowl and some salt to him (v. 20). Having tossed the salt into the spring, he now becomes the bearer of the Lord's word for the first time. It is not so much what he does as what he says that causes the

water to become wholesome. The narrator becomes a witness to
the success of the miracle, declaring that the water remained pure
to the time when the story was recorded (v. 22).

Elisha Curses the Boys at Bethel (2:23-25)

Taken by itself, this is a strange and disturbing story. Mocked
by a group of boys, the prophet curses them, whereupon two she-
bears emerge from the nearby woods and maul the youths. Taken
in conjunction with the surrounding narration of transfer of
prophetic authority, this tale, like the preceding one, works to
confirm Elisha's new role. Like the lack of clarity about the cause
of the impure water, in this story the reason for the children's deri-
sions is not clear. Perhaps the prophet's appearance evoked the
childish taunt of "Baldhead." However, the curse that results in
such a harsh punishment is utterly disproportionate to the misbe-
havior. Some might justify the punishment on the basis of Elisha's
changed status in the community. He is no longer a servant of
Elijah, but has taken Elijah's place. He is due, and must demand,
appropriate respect. To tolerate less is to invite insult. Shouting an
insult to the Lord's prophet approaches hurling an insult at the
Lord. Such behavior warrants immediate chastisement. However,
the outcome of the prophet's pronouncement is still difficult to
endorse. Indeed, the story works with the previous tale of the
purification of water at Jericho to confirm Elisha's new prophetic
position. Whether with blessing or with curse, while restoring life
or bringing death, Elisha is now the true herald of the Lord's
word. Yet, the prophet's condemnation of the youth promotes a
violence that we cannot ignore or simply explain away in order to
absolve Elisha. Overexuberance in one's early ministry unaccom-
panied by self-criticism can do more harm than good.

Theological and Ethical Analysis

The overarching theme of the transition of Elijah's prophetic
office to Elisha has governed the exegetical analysis. But as each
prophet participates in this transfer of responsibilities, each is also
undergoing personal change and transformation. As the chapter

opens, the narrative appears fixed upon Elijah and his departure. The opening verse even alerts us that this is coming; the notice of Elijah's impending end urges recall of his life's work. The journey for this legendary prophet has been demanding, sometimes even precarious. Other times, it has been riddled with strife and despair. His recalcitrance before kings, his private spiritual struggles, and his perseverance to the end give us cause to reflect. Before widows, monarchs, royal officials, and the whole assembly of Israel, Elijah manifested a deep commitment to God and an enduring engagement of the people. Now evidently aware that the time of his departure is drawing near, he conveys a sense of detachment. He prepares to return to the wilderness, where the call from the Lord was first issued. Initially, he resists Elisha's offer to accompany him. However, he ultimately agrees to Elisha's company. Elijah's journeys to Bethel, Jericho, and then to the Jordan have an aimless quality, characteristic of one whose mind and heart are no longer present to his circumstances. He is fixed upon a larger unknown. Even in his final hour Elijah is able to pay attention and express concern for another whom he will leave behind to assume his role. He invites Elisha to ask for anything he can grant him before he goes. Yet Elijah knows well what he can and cannot do. In response to Elisha's difficult request, he must surrender to his powerlessness and leave it to God to grant.

Elisha also undergoes a major transition. Though there is a pointlessness about the journeys to Bethel, Jericho, and the Jordan, he walks together with his master until the final moment. Uncertainty surrounds what is about to happen. It is not clear how Elijah will be taken from him. He even silences others concerning Elijah's fate, perhaps because he cannot believe that he will lose Elijah, or perhaps because he is fearful of what it will mean for him.

As Elijah taught about the spiritual struggles involved in remaining faithful, Elisha occasions instruction on exercising new authority and assuming responsibility. Those who acknowledge anxiety and uncertainty in such circumstances find kinship with this prophet. Whereas he faces the prospect of loss, he may also be riddled with self-doubt. He asks Elijah for "a double share" of his spirit—the share given the son who must assume the responsibilities of a father. Next, Elisha must pass a test for which he cannot even prepare. Whether he sees Elijah parting is out of his control. He must transfer his dependence on Elijah to complete dependence upon God. But God's whirlwind does not grant easy access, nor does the Lord's manifestation in the wilderness afford spiritual comfort. Indeed, Elisha does see Elijah depart, but the whirlwind also blows asunder his safety and robs him of the one who gave him his identity. The whirling upheaval that whisks Elijah from him requires Elisha to surrender the safety of his position as servant to grapple with God as one of God's prophets. He must become the Lord's instrument, delivering the divine word before kings and throughout Israel.

When he returns to cross the Jordan, Elisha's cry, "Where is the LORD, the God of Elijah?" expresses a new dependence as well as a panic and desperation. Plagued with sorrow and uncertainty about his competence, he strikes the Jordan twice. As he crosses the river and is recognized by the brotherhood of prophets as filled with Elijah's spirit, he makes no response. This is all too much too fast. Elisha must grow into the mantle of his master.

Gradually, Elisha comes into his own authority. He shows himself responsive to the people in their very basic need for potable water. When he responds to them, it is the Lord whose power he manifests. At the same time, he appears as a rather unrestrained defender of the Lord. In his assessment, boys who would mock a prophet of the Lord have no respect for the Lord. The prophet's pronouncement results in a very disquieting punishment. The man, who was shrouded with fear and uncertainty, has begun the long and arduous journey of discerning the Lord's will. Like most beginners in ministry, he has much to learn before he will be recognized as an accomplished agent of that plan.

2 KINGS 3

The formal introduction to the reign of Jehoram, begun in 1:17, was delayed by the account of the ascent of Elijah (chapter 2). Though Elijah is gone, his successor Elisha now continues his prophetic work. As the typical regnal resumé of Jehoram picks up here, it offers a qualified portrait of Jehoram. Though he makes some effort at cultic reform, he still continues in the sinful ways of his parents (Ahab and Jezebel) and of Jeroboam. In the story that follows, his response to the word of the Lord delivered by Elisha the prophet justifies the negative assessment.

Literary Analysis

Though the regnal resumé (vv. 1-3) that opens the chapter is often viewed as separate from the story that follows, it can be read as one side of the thematic bookends enclosing this narrative. In the beginning of the chapter, Jehoram is introduced as the Israelite king who tried to make some cultic reform by turning away from one of the Baalistic practices of his parents. However, in the end, his sinful ways make him just like his parents as well as like Jeroboam. Thus, the summary accuses him of doing what was displeasing in the sight of the Lord. In the unfolding chapter, Israel, led by Jehoram, receives divine favor in the form of victory. However, in the conclusion of the tale (v. 27), the victory is qualified because they too do what is displeasing before the Lord.

Between these opening and closing frames of the chapter are two crises and plans to address them (vv. 4-12), a two-part oracle from Elisha (vv. 13-19), and the narrative accounts of two resolutions (vv. 20-24). The two crises governing the chapter are related. First, Moab, a subjugated territory since the time of David, begins a rebellion. Then, when Jehoram with Jehoshaphat's help set out to curtail Moab's revolt, their troops run out of water.

A two-part oracle by the prophet (vv. 13-19) addresses both the plan to attack Moab and the water shortage. He declares that the wadi will be full of enough water for both the animals and the troops (vv. 16-17), and he prophesies that Moab will be handed over to the kings. Then Elisha makes an addition to his prophetic pronouncement. Not only will Israel conquer every city, they will destroy the land, disrupt the water supply, and ruin all the arid ground—military behavior strictly contraindicated by Israel's war code (Deut 20:19-20). Hence, the prophet not only foretells what

God will do but also what the troops led by the king will do in response.

A time reference, "the next day," marks the beginning of the story's final segment (vv. 20-27), narrating the resolutions to these problems. According to the word of the prophet, the water fills the land, the Moabites flee, and Israel attacks the cities and devastates the arid land, thus violating the Deuteronomic prohibition (Deut 20:19-20). In desperation, the king of Moab sacrifices his own son as a burnt offering upon the wall (v. 27). Immediately, a great wrath descends upon Israel and they withdraw from the attack, returning to their own territory. Hence, the story closes as it opens. Divine displeasure with this king in the opening of the story is matched by a display of divine displeasure with Israel in the conclusion.

Exegetical Analysis

Jehoram's Regnal Introduction (3:1-3)

When Ahaziah died from his fall, he left no heir (1:17). Hence, his brother Jehoram ascends as king. In typical fashion, his reign is introduced, summarized, and evaluated here. Citing that Jehoshaphat is still king in Judah when Jehoram assumes his royal office, the length of Jehoram's reign is recorded as twelve years. With the stock Deuteronomistic language used to evaluate the northern kings, Jehoram is described as doing "what was evil in the sight of the LORD" (v. 2), and having "clung to the sin of Jeroboam son of Nebat" (v. 3). Still, some complexity is added to this king's character. A brief caveat draws a distinction between Jehoram and his parents; he instituted a cultic reform that undercut what his father had done. He removed the pillar of Baal that Ahab had made. But that did not bring about the end of Baal worship. Because the reform was not complete, the final assessment is negative. The story that follows is illustrative of this overall evaluation.

Two Plans Address Two Crises (3:4-12)

King Mesha is the Moabite contemporary of Jehoram. A sheep breeder, Mesha had been delivering an annual tribute of lambs and wool to Israel up until the time of Ahab. Now the Moabite ruler seeks to end that subservience. With Ahab gone and the sudden death of his son Ahaziah after only two years of rule, Mesha makes his move. His efforts to wiggle out of the vassalship pose a crisis for Jehoram, the successor to the throne. It is very probable that our text grows out of some historical data on Mesha's revolt during this era. However, the degree and length of the rebellion remains a matter of debate. Although not serving the historical discussion, the literary representation that unfolds here works to illustrate the theological assessment of Jehoram with which the chapter opens.

Jehoram wastes no time responding to the international crisis. He constructs a plan. First, he mobilizes Israel's military forces (v. 6). Then, like his father Ahab, he enlists the assistance of the Judahite king, Jehoshaphat (v. 7). No diplomacy is wasted in the buildup of an alliance with the southern ruler. First, Jehoram names the problem, then he makes his request clear. The king of Moab has rebelled against him and Jehoram asks point-blank for Jehoshaphat's participation in the battle against Moab. The straightforwardness of such strategy pays off. Jehoshaphat responds with the same pledge of complete cooperation he offered Ahab against the Arameans (1 Kgs 22:4). Indeed, when Jehoshaphat pledged to cooperate with Ahab in his quest to retrieve Ramoth-gilead, he did so on the condition that a prophet of the Lord be consulted. Here the Judean king pledges horses and people without the condition that divine counsel be sought before commencing any battle with the Moabites, a condition called for in Israel's war protocol. He even leaves to Jehoram's discretion and authority the battle strategy. Accordingly, the Israelite king determines that the battle march will traverse the wilderness of Edom (v. 8).

The campaign of Israelite and Judean forces from the south rallies the Edomites to participate. Edom was still likely the vassal of Judah (1 Kgs 22:47), so its involvement may have been more by force than by choice. In any case, as the three kings lead the military march northward for seven days, a new problem develops. An unforeseen shortage of water for the vast armies and their animals confronts the kings. This time, Jehoram's response is not so forthright or foresighted; he does not rise to the occasion. Instead, the king of Israel blames the Lord. His outburst not only demonstrates his own personal lack of resourcefulness, but also manifests his utter lack of faith.

In addition, Jehoram links the water shortage to a hopelessly pessimistic assessment of the battle's outcome (v. 10). He surmises that according to the divine plan the Moabites will triumph because of the troops' lack of water. However, the opposite is true. It will be precisely by the miraculous gift of water that Israel will be victorious. Jehoshaphat responds to the problem (v. 11). However, his reaction differs markedly from Jehoram's. Perhaps reflecting upon the important omission of consulting the Lord before heading to war, he inquires whether a prophet is available. His inquiry expresses his dependence upon the Lord for help in times of crisis. His turn to the Lord forms a sharp contrast to Jehoram's loss of hope and villainization of Israel's God. The fact that one of the king's servants has to say whether a prophet is even present among them as they go to battle further emphasizes the king of Israel's halfhearted religiosity.

Elisha, the prophet present for consultation with the Lord, is identified in two ways. He is first named in relation to his family, "Elisha son of Shaphat" (v. 11). Then he is further identified in relation to Elijah. He is the one "who used to pour water on the hands of Elijah" (v. 11). That it was water he poured upon the hands of Elijah, the prophet who had earlier addressed the national crisis of drought and rain in Israel (1 Kgs 18), fosters optimism that Elisha is especially fit to deal with the current shortage. Hence, the kings go down to Elisha.

The Oracle of Elisha (3:13-19)

The contrast in the characterization of the two kings is now continued in the contrasting responses the prophet Elisha makes to them. No account of the kings' approach and inquiry of the prophet is recorded. However, Elisha's opening remarks presume they have set their request before him (v. 13). His sarcastic rhetorical question to the king of Israel conveys both bold audacity and resistance to the Omride rulers' ongoing dependence upon the Baal prophets.

For his part, the king of Israel persists in his despair. Again repeating his previous allegation against the Lord, Jehoram's response verifies the prophet's reservation. Elisha then vows that he is willing to turn to the Lord for these kings only because of the regard he has for Jehoshaphat (v. 14). Hence, the aversion he has for Jehoram and the Omrides contrasts with the respect he holds for the king of Judah. Elisha calls for a musician, and under the influence of music begins to prophesy.

Employing the oracular formula "Thus says the LORD," his oracle first addresses the problem of water shortage. A wadi filled with pools will provide drink (v. 16). But this water will not come about by natural means. A miracle from the Lord that will bypass the usual forces of rain will bring it about. Wind and rain are the elements associated with the Canaanite Baal. Thus, when the Lord provides water, it will come about miraculously outside the forces that some could confuse with the work of Baal.

The other crisis, the Moabite threat, will also be addressed by the power of the Lord. The prophet instructs that the water miracle that God will do for them is only minor compared to what will happen to the Moabites. The Lord will hand them over to the allies. Elisha's prophecy not only foretells what God will do, he also details what Israel will do. Israel's troops will conquer every city and will devastate the land. Contrary to the Deuteronomic war code regulating behavior in battle, Israel will ruin the arid ground, chop down fruiting trees, disrupt the water supply, and thereby undermine the economic base of this vassal state. Hence, while Israel will be given victory by the Lord, it will respond with atrocities strictly forbidden by the law (Deut 20:19-20).

Two Resolutions (3:20-24)

The second crisis, the lack of water for the troops and animals, is briefly addressed first (v. 20). Reference to the morning of the next day, at a time coinciding with the morning meal offering, marks the fulfillment of the prophet's word. The water began "to flow from the direction of Edom" (v. 20). No details are given about where the water originated or the speed with which it came. No mention is even made that the thirst of armies and animals was rapidly or gratefully quenched. Following the brief note on the flow of the water, one further comment emphasizing its miraculous nature is added. The water filled the whole country (v. 20).

Most of the narrative attention is fixed on the resolution of the problem with Moab and Israel's planned attack (vv. 21-24). Upon hearing of the approach of the Israelites, Moab calls up its able warriors (v. 21). From youngest to oldest, the nation marshals a defense. All expectations are that a major battle between the allies and Moab is about to ensue.

Like the resolution of the water crisis, the fulfillment of the promised deliverance of Moab begins in the morning on the next day (v. 22). Water, which is a gift of life for Israel now, becomes a source of death for the enemy. When the Moabites see the water, it appears red from their vantage point. Whether the color was because of the reflection of the sun or because of the red sandstone of the wadis is uncertain. However, the parallel with the plagues of Egypt makes certain that just as the prophet foretold, the hand of the Lord is acting on behalf of Israel. The Moabites' misperception leads them to make a devastatingly fatal move. Thinking that the allied kings have turned upon each other and slain each other in a fight, the Moabites move to seize the spoils of the enemy camp. With this grave miscalculation, they are delivered into the power of Israel, just as the prophet Elisha foretold. As the Moabites are driven back, Israel enters their country and continues the attack.

Conclusion (3:25-27)

However, the battle story does not end as expected, or even as Elisha had foretold. When Israel enters Moab, it attacks every city, but it does more, too. Employing the same descriptive language Elisha used to say what Israel would do, the account portrays the utter shattering of the economic network of the country. All lands, settled and unsettled, are devastated. The description of good trees felled employs the language of the prohibition in Deuteronomy. Such unacceptable battle practices are not without consequences.

As Israel presses on, the king of Moab, whose military tactics are failing, resorts to a religious gesture. He offers his firstborn son, the likely heir to the throne, on the wall surrounding the city of Kir-hareseth (v. 27). Immediately, a great wrath comes upon Israel. Certainly this wrath could not be mistaken as an expression of Chemosh, the Moabite deity, for the author of these texts believes only in the Lord. That the wrath comes upon Israel and Israel responds indicates their perception that indeed this is the Lord's wrath upon them. Though strictly forbidden by Israel's war code, Israel has conducted an unbridled campaign to vanquish the land. In turn, such comprehensive devastation has prompted a foreign king to do the unthinkable, something that is also strictly forbidden by Israel's own God. He sacrifices his own son. Atrocities committed in the name of religion are evidently especially offensive to the Lord. Israel will be held accountable not only for its own deeds, but even for the deeds of its enemy.

In the opening of the story, Jehoram is evaluated as having done what is evil in the sight of the Lord. In the conclusion of the tale, that Israel returns home having aborted its potentially victorious attack suggests a similar assessment.

Theological and Ethical Analysis

All was set for Israel to achieve a military victory and in the process quell the revolt of the vassal state, Moab. That the Lord would deliver Moab into Israel's power was confirmed by the word of Elisha, the prophet. But as the tale hurries to its expected conclusion, an unexpected turn of events occurs. A great wrath overcomes Israel. They retreat. The Moabites are not suppressed. Israel returns to its land, but not the victor as promised. Has the prophet been wrong? Has he misspoken? Or was the promise of divine deliverance conditional?

Read backward, this story of the curtailed military victory against the Moabites illustrates the ambivalence with which Jehoram is introduced in the opening regnal summary (vv. 1-3). Though he makes some effort to rid the cult of the Baal influence, Jehoram never embraces a wholehearted turning to the Lord. Indeed, he turns against the Lord as soon as problems arise.

Moreover, he not only blames the Lord, but also goes on to interpret divine motives as devious. "Alas! The LORD has summoned
us, three kings, only to be handed over to Moab" (v. 10). Though
surrounded by others—another king and a prophet, both of
whom encourage other interpretations—Jehoram persists in blaming God. Speaking before the prophet, he reiterates his faithless-
ness, blaming the Lord for the current crisis. His whining exposes
a faith that rests only upon self-serving beliefs. However, the
instruction is not just about Jehoram's halfheartedness; it also
invites our own self-appraisal.

When bad things happen it is God's fault, but when events go
our way there seems no need to involve the Lord, or so it seems to
those of us like Jehoram. The convenience of a God who assures
our advancement and rubber-stamps our plans for success, while
being sure never to get in the way, can be accommodated in faith.
But if trouble erupts, detours develop, and our best-laid plans are
curtailed, God is not only accused of failing to get involved; we
may even decide that God is responsible for making things go
awry.

Jehoram's faith was much like his father's. Though both go
through the motions of belief—Ahab repents before the prophet's
word concerning his destruction and that of his whole household
(1 Kgs 21:27), and Jehoram rids the cult of the pillar of Baal—in
the end their faith is conditioned by belief in a God who serves
their best interests. They could accommodate a God who could be
managed and who was politically and personally expedient. A
God who makes demands in terms of covenant, who courts us to
trust in difficult straits, whose thoughts are not our thoughts, and
whose ways are not necessarily our ways demands a different kind
of faith.

Second, the story can also be read forward, exposing the relat-
edness of sin, violence, and the self-perpetuating cycle these thrive
upon. The regnal introduction to Jehoram assesses that despite his
effort to dismantle one aspect of Baal worship, he did what was
displeasing in the sight of the Lord. In turn, this sinful king who
leads Israel into battle leads them also into behavior prohibited
by the Deuteronomistic code. Such violence in war incites even

further abomination when in desperation before the ravaging of the land the Moabite king sacrifices his own son. The sacrificed life of one innocent child as a burnt offering is enough to ignite a great wrath against Israel. A sinful king who has led a people into sin and who in turn incites an enemy to commit an egregious abomination must be sanctioned. His God refuses to be a king's national trophy or to be triumphalistically touted as an unconditional guarantee of Israelite victory. Instead, this story exposes a God who is the ground of all humanity's being and whose capacity for mercy is matched by a capacity for wrath. Faith in such a God disarms one of any false sense of security. Instead, we are invited to open ourselves up to enter into the mystery of God's ways and to consider trading our plan for what God has in store for us.

2 KINGS 4

Evidence of Elisha's credentials and authority as an agent of the Lord continues in this chapter. Four stories narrate five miraculous overtures whereby the prophet serves as God's instrument of life. The role of the prophet, so often depicted as advising or confronting kings with their sin, is here revealed as equally and intimately intertwined with the lives of the people.

Literary Analysis

This chapter sets forth a collection of four distinct stories (vv. 1-7, 8-37, 38-41, 42-44). Each displays literary unity governed by a plotline where an opening problem reaches a resolution by miraculous intervention. In the first tale (vv. 1-7), the destitution facing a desperate widow and her children is resolved by the abundant flow of oil. In the second account (vv. 8-37), a barren woman is provided a child, and later when the child teeters on the brink of death, he is miraculously restored. In the third story (vv. 38-41), a pot of precious stew in a time of famine is discovered to be poisonous. With a miraculous intervention, it is made edible again. Finally, in the fourth tale, a servant skeptical about the prospects of feeding a large crowd with a few loaves of bread experiences the multiplication of loaves, which provides enough to feed the multitude present. At first glance, these independent stories appear gathered together categorically because of their similarities as miracle stories. However, these tales actually exhibit many other commonalities that, taken together, prove revelatory not only about the prophet but also about the people.

To begin with, all of the stories lack a precise time reference. No mention of the reigning king or of the year is present. The repeated introduction, "one day" (vv. 8, 11, 18), opening all but the first story, fosters a chronological obscurity. Coupled with this imprecision is the lack of proper names except those of Elisha and Gehazi, his servant. Characters in the stories are described only with reference to their geographical location or other persons in the narrative. The widow is the wife of one of the brotherhood of prophets. The barren woman whose son is later restored to life is identified by her geographical location, Shunem. Those whose poisonous stew is purified are called the brotherhood of prophets. And the man whose bread is multiplied for the crowd is referred to by the place from which he came, Baal-shalishah.

The lack of characters' identities across these stories coincides with their lack of social standing. No king, captain, or royal official numbers among the players. Instead, widows, people who work the land, folk who live in towns, and members of a crowd are the key actors in these tales. They represent the nameless, faceless, collective community that is always in the background in the stories about kings, and is often expended by the ruler. Here they are front and center, never allowing the kings to have the stage, as is evident in an interaction between the Shunammite woman and the prophet. When invited by the prophet to enlist the king or his officials for personal favors or gain, she rejects both his offer and any affiliation with royalty.

These are stories about the people and represent those who are in need. Spotlighting the plight of individuals or small groups rather than the whole amorphous Israel, they convey a more personal sense of the plight of the peasants. These are the people who have struggled under the weight of monarchy. These are the people who have incurred the greatest personal costs to their land and identity resulting from wayward kings in Israel. These are the people whose very lives are under threat. Hence, as the miracles unfold across each of these tales, together they celebrate the power of God as the source of life among the people.

Exegetical Analysis

The Widow and the Abundant Flow of Oil (4:1-7)

The opening story of this chapter unfolds quite simply. Although there is no real character development, a dialogue between the widow and the prophet sets forth the problem (v. 1) and evokes a plan to address the difficulty (vv. 2-4). A widow of one from the company of prophets laments before Elisha. A creditor who is about to act upon her deceased husband's unpaid accounts plans to seize her children as slaves. Legitimatized by the Hebrew legal system (Exod 21:7), slavery for unpaid debts was an accepted practice in ancient Israel. This was a constant threat to the poorest of the peasants throughout Israel's history (Amos 2:6; 8:8; Mic 2:9). Moreover, with no other economic supports than a husband or sons, in a patriarchal society a widow who loses her children is particularly vulnerable. The gravity of her situation parallels that of the widow that Elijah encountered in Zarephath (1 Kgs 17:10).

For her part, the woman does not bank solely upon the possibility that Elisha will have compassion upon her situation or that his deeds will mirror that of his predecessor. She proceeds to marshal evidence that there are good reasons for the prophet to act. She refers to her deceased husband twice as Elisha's "servant," perhaps conjuring up some obligation on his part. More importantly, she explicitly provides the incentive that should prompt the prophet to respond whether he plans to or not. Her husband "feared the LORD" (v. 1). Emphasizing her spouse's faith in God, she also indicates her understanding of what is needed here. It will require the prophet to call upon the Lord for assistance.

Respecting her understanding of the situation, the prophet first asks her what he should do for her (v. 2). He certainly cannot address the problem by undercutting Israelite law regarding unpaid debts. The demand she makes upon him requires that he resort to something inconceivable, indeed, a divine gift. That being clear, the dialogue closes with his instruction to her. First, he ascertains what she has in her house that is marketable. Oil will do the trick. He instructs her to go and scour the neighborhood for vessels. We imagine him urging her to find every pot, pan, vessel, or container—anything that can hold oil. Then she is to shut the door of her house behind herself and her children and "start pouring" (v. 4).

The description of the actual miracle is brief and to the point. It skips over an account relating their search for all and every vessel among her neighbors. Instead, it hurries along in order to focus upon her action. She shuts the door. As the children bring the vessels to her, she pours and pours. Finally, she tells her son to bring another container. He announces that there are no more, at which point the oil stops flowing. Fulfilling the prophet's instructions, the widowed woman has been both the agent of and witness to the miracle.

The tale closes with a further instruction by the prophet. When she goes to Elisha and reports the outcome, he tells her to sell the oil and pay the creditor (v. 7). She will evidently have money left over after paying her deceased husband's debts, for the prophet also tells her to use the rest to support herself and her children. Hence, the woman's crisis is addressed and so also is the cycle of poverty that threatens a widowed woman with children in the ancient patriarchal context. Moreover, the miracle has come about by the woman acting to solve her own problem, thus empowering her to address her own crisis.

Two Miracles for the Shunammite Woman (4:8-37)

Like the previous story, in this tale an unnamed woman is the recipient of and witness to a miracle as the result of an interaction with the prophet. However, unlike the widow, the woman from Shunem makes no request of Elisha. Indeed, she provides for him out of her abundance. Referred to as a wealthy woman, she is probably of some status. She provides meals for the prophet whenever he passes through her town. In addition, she and her husband even build a small chamber on the roof and furnish it for his use whenever he comes there (v. 10).

The first miracle in this tale unfolds when Elisha makes an overture to the woman. In return for all she has done for him, he offers to leverage influence with the king or his army commander on her behalf and according to her wishes. But she rejects his proposal, indicating that she identifies with the people of her town and not with the royal elite. Next, at Gehazi's suggestion, Elisha promises the childless woman a son in the next year. Again she objects to the offer in order not to get her hopes up only to be disappointed (v. 16). She knows the shame of childlessness in a patriarchal society and does not want to be falsely encouraged. When the exchange between the prophet and the woman closes, the narrative reports that what the prophet promised was fulfilled. The woman conceived and bore a son in that year just as the prophet had foretold.

The life of a son miraculously given in the first part of this tale is suddenly snuffed out in the second half. Several years have passed and the child is going out to his father in the field. His only words in the story are to his father. He complains of such a severe headache that his father commissions one of his servants to carry the ailing youngster to his mother. Sitting upon her lap, the child's condition worsens until finally at noon he dies (v. 20).

The woman does not accept her fate. Instead, the quickening of the story's pace narrates the swiftness with which she begins to act. Her actions with the dead child, her husband, the servant, and Gehazi manifest haste and decisiveness. First, she takes the child up to the room of the prophet and lays him on Elisha's bed, closing the door behind her. Next she beckons her husband to send a servant and a donkey because she intends to visit the prophet. When her husband objects that it is not the appropriate time for such visitation—a holiday or the Sabbath—she curtails conversation. Offering no explanation, she assures him it will be fine with a one-word response in Hebrew, "shalom" (v. 23). This same determination is evident in her instructions to the servant. Saddling the donkey herself, she urges the servant to hurry ahead according to her instructions.

When she nears her destination at Mount Carmel, Elisha sees her at a distance and sends Gehazi to greet her. With Gehazi too she wastes no words, responding to his threefold interrogation with, "shalom" (v. 26). Finally, she arrives before Elisha whereupon she catches hold of his feet. Her action replaces any long explanation of her distress and all that has taken place. Immediately, Elisha knows she is bitter and sorrowful. With one utterance, she signals the problem. "Did I ask my lord for a son? Did I not say, Do not mislead me?" (v. 28). With two rhetorical questions, she demands the prophet make good on his promise.

Instantly, the prophet responds. He summons Gehazi to go directly to the boy and to take the prophet's staff in order to lay it on the child's face. He is to duplicate the haste with which the woman came to him. He should greet no one on the way. But the mother is not satisfied. As if to bear witness to Elisha's power as prophet, she insists that he come. With a vow, she swears by the Lord that she will not leave until Elisha returns with her. The woman's adamancy that the prophet himself must respond prompts him to go. And it is a good thing that he does, since Gehazi is completely unsuccessful before the dead child. Having carried out Elisha's order, he reports to the prophet that the child still lies lifeless (v. 31).

Now Elisha is alone with the child in his room with the door closed behind him. Like Elijah who resuscitated a woman's son (1 Kgs 17:17-24), Elisha begins by praying to the Lord. Twice he stretches himself out upon the child. With a resuscitation-like gesture, he warms the child's body. Only after the second attempt does the child sneeze seven times and finally open his eyes. Then Elisha summons Gehazi to inform the woman that her son is alive. Again, she comes and falls at his feet, this time not in grief, but in gratitude.

The Poisonous Pot of Stew (4:38-41)

The third miracle story, brief and anecdotal in style, opens by naming another crisis needing the prophet's intervention. When Elisha returns to Gilgal, there is a famine in the land (v. 38). But immediately this problem of food shortage is complicated by a further dilemma. Elisha has ordered his servant to make a pot of stew for the gathered brotherhood of prophets. One of the men inadvertently adds some wild gourds, not knowing what they are. When the men taste the soup, they cry out that it is poisonous. In this time of famine, a pot of stew that cannot be eaten could mean death.

Once again, Elisha orders the recipients of the miracle to participate in it. They are to bring some flour, which he proceeds to put into the pot. The flour, like salt, cures the harmful substance. Next, he commands that the stew be served. A concluding note confirms as a matter of fact that the stew was not harmful (v. 41).

Multiplication of the Loaves (4:42-44)

The fourth and final miracle story is also about food and an occasion to feed those in need. The preceding context of famine can be presumed to continue as background for this tale. Hence, the man from Baal-shalishah, who brings loaves made from the first fruits of his crops to the prophet, is extremely generous. Whether his gift is a religious offering or food for the prophet, it is particularly noteworthy in this time of famine. Elisha, in turn, takes what is given him and orders it to be shared with others. However, his servant objects that there is not enough to feed the one hundred people present. His objection suggests that there is another scarcity in addition to that of food, namely faith. Despite the objection, the loaves are distributed. That some is left over after the bread was set before the one hundred people resolves both insufficiencies. The people who are in need of bread are fed. The servant who is in need of faith now has reason to believe. The account ends by noting that what occurred here was according to the word of the Lord (v. 44).

Theological and Ethical Analysis

Taken together, this menagerie of tales testifies that Elisha is well established, publicly recognized, and intimately caught up in the lives of the people in his role as prophet. His involvement is vital and active at the grass-roots level. His interaction with the widow moves her from the threat of destitute poverty to solvency. His relationship with the Shunammite woman overturns her barrenness with a child and later renders the lifeless son alive again. Protected from the potentially harmful ingredients in the stew, the brotherhood of prophets is nourished by the prophet in a time of famine. That private action among this guild of the prophet's followers is extended to the larger community when the few loaves of the man from Baal-shalishah feed one hundred people. Before kings, the prophet proclaimed God's word. Before the believing peasant population, the prophet must *be* God's word. However, these stories do more than assert the centrality of Elisha and his prophetic power to minister effectively among the people. They also offer a powerful lesson on how God's word must be ministered to the people.

While demonstrating the authority of the prophet in monarchic Israel, these accounts also reveal the distressful conditions in which the peasants were forced to live, specifically under the Omrides, and perhaps more generally during most of the period of the monarchy. The hierarchical framework of ancient Israel that renders the peasants least in that society makes them the most vulnerable: economically, socially, and politically. Hence, in times of economic crisis, they were the most susceptible to falling into debt slavery. The patriarchal hierarchal social order meant that a woman of wealth was not necessarily a woman with any power. In times of instability caused by political or natural forces such as famine, the peasant population is always the most at risk.

If the prophet is to be an effective manifestation of the Lord's word and presence to this group, it has to be in a form that does not disable them or create further dependence. He has to work among them in a way that does not reinforce their status as vulnerable. Whatever Elisha does, it needs to undercut any notion that the people are victims. He must be an enabler, rather than solely a powerful helper. Thus, in each instance as Elisha serves as an agent of the Lord's power, he does not "do" the miracle for them. Instead, he enlists their participation to do what needs to be done for themselves.

Hence, the miraculous manifestation of the life-giving God grows out of an exchange. It is the cooperative interaction between the prophet and the people that brings about the miracle. Elisha sends the widow and her children off to gather jars and jugs. After they have done so, and the oil has ceased flowing, she returns to the prophet to inform him of the outcome. At this point he again instructs her to sell the oil and pay off her husband's debts, as well as debts in the future, so that she and her children can live. Again, she must act to complete the miraculous action that resolves the crisis.

In the second story, Elisha's promise of a child challenges the Shunammite woman's resignation to her barrenness. She will not even ask for the child for which she has given up hope. Still, the prophet presents her with a miraculous prospect that obviously requires her action and cooperation to bring it about. Later, when her son's life is threatened, she, in turn, challenges Elisha to act upon his promise not to deceive her. She demands that he come and heal her child. Once again, the miraculous manifestation of God occurs as the result of a transactional exchange between the prophet and the woman.

In the third story, the prophet does not resolve hunger in the time of famine with a miracle for the brotherhood of prophets. Instead, he urges them into action, to make stew out of whatever they can find. When, because of poisonous ingredients, the stew is found to be dangerous for consumption, again he requires their participation. They must bring him some flour in order to participate in the miracle themselves.

Finally, in the last story, the hunger of the people is satisfied when loaves are shared with the multitude that has gathered. The skeptical servant carries out Elisha's instructions and passes out the food to the one hundred people present. Again, cooperating with the prophet, the servant helps bring about the miracle that resolves the hunger as well as resolves his own disbelief.

Thus, Elisha's ministry enables and empowers the peasants who are powerless. He does not just solve their problems as they stand by passively watching him; he enlists their participation. In doing so he requires that they abandon their hopelessness and sense of powerlessness. Working with the prophet and with one another they discover that they too have a role to play in making manifest the power of the Lord in their lives. In this sense, Elisha's work is a model for ministry. The effective minister is not one who functions as the axis from which all power and authority proceeds. Rather, the successful minister functions as a pivotal force that empowers others to act, enabling them to heal, to teach, and to cooperate with one another in restoring, nourishing, and even bringing forth new life. When others begin to believe that they can be a source of life and well-being for one another and they actually begin to live their lives accordingly, that truly is miraculous!

2 KINGS 5

Thus far, accounts of Elisha's activities have credentialed him as a prophet. He is well established as an agent of the Lord, particularly among the peasants of ancient Israel. In this chapter, an account of Elisha's interventions on behalf of a military general and on behalf of his own servant are added to the list of his activities. However, this time, a non-Israelite is the beneficiary of a miraculous transformation that not only cures his ailment but also brings about his spiritual conversion. At the same time, Elisha's servant Gehazi succumbs to greed and fraud and as a consequence is the recipient of the prophet's chastisement and becomes afflicted. In contrast to previous stories, this tale develops with the focus less upon the prophet and more upon the theological and moral lessons disclosed in the two characters who are respectively healed and sentenced.

Literary Analysis

Rich narrative texture crafts the story of Naaman's healing by Elisha. Though joined with previous accounts by the continuation of Elisha's role as healer, this tale distinguishes itself in two readily discernible ways. First, the plot is composed with complexity and detail. Second, the characters are fashioned with great depth and vividness.

First, the thick, dramatic plot develops across three acts (vv. 1-14, 15-19, 20-27). Each act is a self-contained narrative, focusing on one of the three main characters: Elisha, Naaman, and Gehazi (Cohn, 35). Each narrates the conditions out of which the subsequent one develops. Thus, they are thematically and sequentially interwoven in a unified and riveting drama.

In act one (vv. 1-14), the introduction of Naaman, a Syrian general afflicted with leprosy, occasions the focus upon the figure of Elisha. In addition to effecting a cure for the Syrian general's leprosy, the prophet's program sets the stage for the spiritual conversion that will be taken up in the second act.

In part two of the drama (vv. 15-19), Naaman, who has been physically healed of his leprosy, undergoes a spiritual conversion. The cure and conversion of this well-endowed foreign officer for which no compensation or payment is exchanged becomes the impetus for Gehazi's greed and fraudulent behavior in the third and final act.

In the concluding scene (vv. 20-27), Gehazi is determined to take advantage of the gifts of silver and garments brought by Naaman's entourage that Elisha rejected. In the end, Elisha, who condemns Gehazi's actions and sentences him for his deeds, confronts him. Now Gehazi becomes afflicted with leprosy. Hence, the conclusion of the third act returns thematically to the opening of the first act. The exploitative Gehazi is in the end afflicted with the same condition from which Naaman is eventually cleansed.

For his part, Gehazi is a servant of Elisha. He second-guesses Elisha's decision to accept no gifts as payment for healing Naaman. His greed leads him to scheme a deceptive ploy to gain those gifts. He exploits Naaman and then tries to cover his tracks by lying to Elisha.

Exegetical Analysis

Elisha Cures Naaman's Leprosy (5:1-14)

The opening introduction to Naaman as a military officer from Aram, one of Israel's archenemies, gives us pause. Why is the story about Israel's prophet opening with such a lavish and positive appraisal of an enemy? Moreover, the lengthy description of Naaman creates even further confusion. He is a military officer of high rank who enjoys not only the favor of Aram's king, but also of Israel's God. We are told that the Lord granted victory to Aram on his account (v. 1). The narrative also relates that he is a "mighty warrior." To make matters even more complex, all this greatness and high social notoriety before both his nation's ruler and Israel's God is qualified by a final notation. Naaman suffers from leprosy.

In the ancient world, "leprosy" referred to a myriad of skin diseases—physical conditions that carried with them various social stigmas. One suffering from "leprosy" was barred from worship (Lev 13-14), or in certain circumstances, might be ostracized from normal social intercourse with the community. The narrative does not give any information about the nature of Naaman's disease or the social consequences resulting from this affliction. However, his response to the prospect of a cure suggests his leprosy was more than just a nuisance. He is willing to travel to enemy territory to be healed. A young, nameless servant girl sets in motion a series of events that will realize this outcome and much more. She is an Israelite captive of Naaman, serving his wife. An agent of hope, she informs the Aramean general's wife of the opportunity for a cure if only Naaman could be in the presence of the prophet who is in Samaria (v. 3). Once the prospect for healing is made known to Naaman, the story moves rapidly to the encounter between Elisha and this Aramean officer. The series of interchanges that lead up to the meeting are related with brevity and little detail. Naaman tells his king of the opportunity in Samaria. The king sends him on his way with a letter to Israel's king. He packs gifts of silver, gold, and garments, and sets out. Finally, he arrives and delivers the letter to Israel's king. Now all activity ceases and we are made privy to the contents of the correspondence (v. 6). Aram's king has commissioned Israel's king to cure Naaman of his leprosy. At first, this seems curious since the servant girl identified the prophet in Samaria, not the ruler, as the source of healing for Naaman. However, Aram's king was likely respecting the Israelite monarch's prerogative to commission the prophet to do a great deed in his name. However, the king in Samaria is not complimented. Rather he is tormented when he interprets the correspondence as pretext for a quarrel intended to lead to war. This misunderstanding momentarily threatens to derail Naaman's efforts to procure health and well-being.

Though the king is not named, we presume him to be Jehoram, not only because in the sequence of stories he is still on the throne, but also because he acts like Jehoram. When he was marching out with the kings of Judah and Edom to attack Moab and was confronted with a lack of water for the troops, Jehoram acted similarly (3:10). He was negative and blaming, the same way he is here. Having read the letter from the king of Aram, he tears his robes in a gesture of grief. Pessimism overtakes his spirit and he imagines the worst. Consequently, he is quick to get things wrong. He assumes that Aram is requiring of him that which he cannot possibly do and thus is crafting a pretext for battle. Though he knows the power of Elisha from at least one occasion, on the battlefield at Edom (3:11-20), he does not even consider this resource. Instead of problem solving, he responds sarcastically with a rhetorical question indicating he still has no idea how God does works in Israel (v. 7). Moreover, his efforts to exonerate himself of any responsibility for what he thinks will be an upcoming battle must have been fairly public. Elisha hears that the king has torn his garments and the prophet's summons indicates he knows why.

The prophet sends a message to the king to send Naaman to him (v. 8). Though the king does not like Elisha, he is evidently willing to have the prophet solve his problems for him once again. Naaman travels to the prophet's house. The royal entourage of horses and chariots accompanying him certifies his high status and commands respect, but Elisha does not respond with decorum. He does not even come out to meet this officer. Instead, he sends a messenger with a rather simple prescription for Naaman's cure. He must wash his flesh seven times in the Jordan, the same number of times the Shunammite woman's son sneezed before he finally began to breathe again. The number seven anticipates fulfillment or conveys the sense of successful completion in the biblical tradition (Lev 14:7, 16, 27, 51).

Instead of being relieved at the prospects of a quick fix, Naaman is indignant (v. 11). He feels ignored and discounted. As a statesman from Aram where rivers like Abana (probably Amana) and Pharpar in Damascus run broader and probably cleaner than the Jordan, he did not need to come all this way to enemy territory only to be humiliated publicly. He had higher expectations. In his mind, it would take something dramatic, something visible, something that was done to him rather than something he would have to do. However, like the previous healings and miraculous interventions, the prophet requires the person to act on his own behalf. Naaman must go and wash himself. Filled with anger, he departs. His servants evidently recognize that he is not setting out for the Jordan. Like the young servant girl, what they say prompts Naaman to act and changes the course of the story. With a wise rhetorical maneuver, they challenge him with a compliment (v. 13). If the prophet had required something difficult of Naaman, surely he would rise to the task, so why not at least go through the motions of this rather simple prescription?

It is to Naaman's credit that his servants are able to make such a suggestion, and perhaps it is to his even greater credit that he is willing to submit to their wise counsel. So Naaman goes down and washes himself in the Jordan, the place where both Elijah and Elisha divided the waters. When he immerses himself seven times as the prophet said, he is not only cured, but the flesh of this great man is restored "like the flesh of a young boy" (v. 14). Indeed, Naaman hoped for a cure, but what the word of the man of God accomplishes surpasses all expectations.

Naaman's Spiritual Conversion (5:15-19)

Naaman's hardness of heart ceases. As his flesh turns to that of a renewed state, so too does his heart turn to a new God. His recalcitrance is replaced by receptivity. Humility replaces anger. Gratitude supplants indignation. Though he had expected the prophet to stand before him (v. 11), Naaman now comes and stands before the prophet (v. 15). He confesses his faith in the Lord, God of Israel. However, he does even more. In an unprecedented clause, Naaman casts his confession as monotheistic. He acknowledges that this God in Israel is also God of the whole earth (v. 15). That he has been the recipient of a great favor from the prophet of the one God warrants a gesture on his part. Hence, he follows up his confession with the offer of a gift for the prophet. Elisha refuses to accept the gift, presumably because God's gift giving cannot be compensated. Moreover, the prophet cannot risk his work on behalf of the Lord being confused with a commodity.

Next, Naaman has some new dilemmas. Having been healed by the Lord and converted in his faith, his concerns have to do with worship when he returns home. First, though he has confessed the Lord as God of all the earth, he evidently recognizes the special significance the land of Israel has as the Lord's inheritance. He who previously disdained the waters of Israel's river now asks for two mule loads of soil with which to return to Aram (v. 17). Whether an altar was to be made of the soil, or to be built upon the soil, Naaman attempts to address the matter of worship of the Lord away from the inheritance of the land. Second, when Naaman returns to Aram, he will continue his job as chief officer to the king. Anticipating that he will have to continue to assist the king when he goes in to pray before Rimmon, Naaman asks the prophet for the Lord's forgiveness in advance. Rimmon is Syria's national deity, functioning like Baal in Israel. Hence, Naaman anticipates that at least in appearance he will have to compromise his unflinching allegiance to the Lord when he resumes his job of serving Aram's king, his other lord. Elisha perceives his disquiet and grants him relief from the unrest, bidding him leave "in peace" (v. 19).

Gehazi's Crime and Affliction (5:20-27)

The third and final act opens by noting Naaman's departure. However, the description, "But when he had gone a short distance" (v. 19), indicates that the story is not over yet. Gehazi, Elisha's servant, is introduced into the narrative. He has evidently been standing by, as he knows that Naaman came with gifts and is leaving with them. We hear Gehazi's thoughts when he decides that Naaman has gotten away too easily, given all that was done for him. Moreover, the justification for the ill he is about to do is betrayed in the way he thinks about the man as "that Aramean Naaman" (v. 20). That an officer from the army of Israel's enemy Aram should receive a healing and get off scot-free makes for an inequity that Gehazi has a right to rectify. Gehazi's oath before the Lord to take something from this foreigner (v. 20) contrasts sharply with Elisha's oath before the Lord to refuse to take anything from Naaman (v. 16).

As soon as Gehazi sets out to find the man, Naaman spots him coming and alights from his chariot, greeting him and asking him if everything is all right (v. 21). Gehazi's hot pursuit is met by Naaman's warm reception. That Naaman immediately receives Gehazi so graciously further suggests that the servant earlier had been silently present, witnessing the man's conversion.

Immediately Gehazi's plan of deception begins. First he lies, telling Naaman that two from the brotherhood of prophets have come and are in need. Next he adds another lie saying that Elisha sent him to ask for a talent of silver and a change of clothes for each. Naaman's response crafts a portrait of generosity contrasting with Gehazi's greed. First, he insists Gehazi take twice the silver requested along with two changes of clothing. Then he packs them in bags for Gehazi. Finally, he even provides servants to ferry the packages back to Gehazi's house.

When Gehazi and the servants approach the city wall, Gehazi dismisses the men and takes the loot into the citadel and quickly hides what he has swindled from the unsuspecting new convert (v. 24). Gehazi has taken full advantage of Naaman's deep sense of gratitude for the healing and his new religious fervor for the God of Israel. So when Gehazi goes and stands before Elisha, he must continue his lie. In response to the prophet's question concerning his whereabouts, he denies going anywhere. However, Elisha has the power to know more than he sees or hears. With a rhetorical question, Elisha juxtaposes Naaman's gracious reception alongside Gehazi's plan for deception. "Did I not go with you in spirit when someone left his chariot to meet you?" (v. 26).

Then with another rhetorical question Elisha gives evidence of his power to know what Gehazi has done. Exaggerating the list of what Gehazi took from Naaman, Elisha tallies what the servant likely planned to purchase with the silver, "olive orchards and vineyards, sheep and oxen, and male and female slaves" (v. 26). Gehazi, servant of the prophet of the Lord, has been unfaithful. As a religious official, his deed is especially reprehensible. Gehazi unjustly sought the inheritance of Naaman. His crime warrants that he be justly punished. Hence, he inherits the very affliction of the man whom he defrauded. So Gehazi becomes afflicted with leprosy—he and all his descendants.

Theological and Ethical Analysis

The contrast in characters across this tale discloses a clear moral lesson. Naaman follows up his conversion with actions that embody his transformed heart and spirit. He greets Gehazi graciously. His focus is upon the well-being of the other—that of both Gehazi and Elisha. Immediately, he responds to need with an unquestioning and unconditional generosity—all signs of a heart now fixed upon the Lord. By contrast, Gehazi, motivated by greed and covetousness, goes after gifts the prophet refused for religious service. On its own, the act of deception is objectionable. That Gehazi makes a profit in conjunction with religious service by taking advantage of the transformed spirit of the new convert Naaman is especially offensive. The national identity of Naaman extends the moral lesson further. Here the Israelite is cursed and punished after the foreigner is healed and converted. The lessons erupting out of such irony give way to theological insight. The scope of the Lord's domain is beyond Israel. It reaches into the lives of foreigners—even so-called enemies of Israel. Moreover, God is not just caught up in acts of healing. The Lord is also busy giving victory to the likes of Aramean officials such as Naaman. The misunderstanding of Israel's election that too easily slips into a false security defined as exclusivity is summarily ruptured. This story bursts the boundaries of such a fallacy and exposes the magnitude of the Lord's power and mercy. However, the power of God not only reaches into the recesses of foreign territory but its scope is recognized and declared by the mouth of an outsider. Naaman professes that there is no other God in all the earth. This foreigner's declaration of monotheism captures in all its radicality the heart of Israel's faith. In contrast to King Ahaziah who looked to the god of Ekron for healing, Naaman, a foreigner, comes to Israel for a cure that leads to his conversation (2 Kgs 1:2). Israel's election is about inclusivity, a call to draw all unto the one true God.

Still, the Lord's inclusivity extends even further in this story. The instruments and agents of the divine plan include not only the recognized religious appointees of cult and the prophets; the servants in this story, the least among the people, are also emissaries of the Lord. A young, nameless girl, a captive of war and a servant in the home of a foreign military officer, instigates Naaman's healing. That she is the primary agent behind Naaman's cure and subsequent conversion argues for a God who often acts outside the structures of the hierarchy and the power of kings or religious officials. Moreover, when Naaman's arrogance and anger almost derailed the opportunity for his healing, it is his own servants who are instrumental in persuading this officer of Aram to do what the prophet prescribed. Beyond our expectations, through persons we might least suppose, the Lord continues to manifest power and healing on the road to winning our confession of faith as well. Since the least among us, the servants, are often God's greatest agents, it behooves us to pay attention to those individuals in our own lives.

2 KINGS 6 AND 7

The buildup of attention and credits to Elisha and his great deeds continue in these two chapters. Though the two tales that unfold here—the rescue of the ax head and the conflict with Aram—are vastly different in scope and focus, the needs of the people continue to precipitate the prophet's activities. Whether in matters great or small, the prophet manifests the hand of God operative in the lives of the people in all kinds of settings. Hence, these tales continue to attest not only to the vast scope of the prophet's work, but they also witness to the boundless terrain upon which God's salvific activity unfolds.

Literary Analysis

Across chapters 6 and 7, two stories (vv. 6:1-7; 6:8–7:20) add to the burgeoning file of Elisha's prophetic activities. One is brief and concerned with mundane matters at the local level. It focuses upon an individual among the brotherhood of prophets. The other story is lengthy and grapples with a complex crisis of international proportions. It is driven by the ongoing conflict between Aram and Israel, hostile relations that are not new.

In the first tale (vv. 1-7), the needs of an individual are addressed when one from the brotherhood loses his ax head in the Jordan River. Elisha miraculously recovers the tool from the flowing waters.

The second story is lengthy and presents itself as a literary triptych (6:8-23; 6:24–7:2; 7:3-20) narrating three different occasions of the ongoing conflict between Israel and Aram. In part one (6:8-23), the planned attack by Aram against Israel's troops is thwarted by the prophet's intervention. In part two (6:24–7:2), Israel is under Aram's siege and Israel's king is shown to be impotent. In the closing section (7:3-20), the siege by Aram is thwarted once again on the occasion of the prophet's intervention. Hence, the opening and closing sections are not only accounts where Aram's plot against Israel is foiled, but where the disruption of the enemy's plan comes about in conjunction with Elisha's involvement. As the three individual sections work to tell the larger story, they are joined together by interwoven themes, reversals, and references that pave the way for what follows. The account of the release of the Aramean army in part one leads to Israel's king pointing a blaming finger and vowing to decapitate the prophet in part two. The king's closing confession of despair in part two precipitates the word of the Lord from the prophet. In part three, an end to the siege and famine occurs, fulfilling that word spoken by Elisha.

Exegetical Analysis

Elisha Recovers an Ax Head (6:1-7)

Up until now the prophet has been involved in assisting the brotherhood of prophets with food. Now he is enlisted to aid their efforts in procuring appropriate shelter. Initially, characters more than locations mark the setting of this story. The brotherhood of prophets and their need for housing create the context for the narrative. The place where the company of prophets dwell is about to be replaced with a larger dwelling to better accommodate their gatherings with Elisha. They ask the prophet for permission to rebuild and to gather logs at the Jordan. He agrees to their plan as well as to the invitation to accompany them in their logging expedition (v. 2). Their destination, the Jordan, is now well established for its significance in the activities of both Elisha and his predecessor Elijah (1 Kgs 17:5; 2 Kgs 2:7-8, 13-14).

They hardly arrive and begin their work when a problem develops. The ax head of one among them falls into the river. Immediately, the fellow summons the prophet for help, noting that the implement was borrowed (v. 5). To the modern reader this may appear as a rather small matter. It hardly warrants troubling the prophet for some action on his part. It is surely too trivial around which to tell a story. However, iron was a rare and valuable material in the ancient world. Moreover, the reference to the ax head as belonging to another suggests the respect for individual property rights as well as the possible consequences for violating this ethos.

Like the other miraculous deeds the prophet performed on behalf of people in need, he does not simply perform a miracle for the man. Instead, he enlists the aid and participation of the person making the request. Though Elisha had the capacity to see and know beyond what was concretely visible, still he requests the man to indicate where the ax had fallen in the water. Having identified the place, Elisha embarks upon a gesture reminiscent of imitative magic. He throws a freshly cut stick into the river—a stick that likely floats. It causes the ax head to surface and miraculously float as well. Then, once again, he enlists the man's involvement by summoning him to recover the iron implement. The story closes with a notice that the man did as the prophet told him, thus confirming the miracle (v. 7). What seems like an account of a rather ordinary occurrence once again testifies to the wondrous, abiding presence of God. It invites the reader to search for God's miraculous ways not only in the dramatic moments of our lives but also in our day-in, day-out routine chores and activities.

Attack by Aram Thwarted (6:8-23)

The presenting problem that opens this first part of the second story is not new. Once again, Israel is grappling with the incumbent threat of Aram/Syria. Following the biblical story line, this conflictual relation is ongoing. Since the accounts of Ahab's reign (1 Kgs 20 and 22), stories continue to document what evidently was a persistent strife between Israel and Syria. As recently as the story of Naaman's cure in 2 Kgs 5, the king of Israel initially interpreted the request from Aram's ruler for a cure for his officer as a pretext for another war. The language describing the Aramean king's new aggression at "such and such a place" (v. 8), along with the description that Elisha alerted the king of Israel "more than once or twice" (v. 10) of these impending threats, gives an impression of ongoing conflict.

We meet the main characters of this opening episode of the larger story through a series of brief initial dialogues. First, during what is introduced as a wartime context (v. 8), the Aramean king in the company of his council issues orders for surprise attacks against Israel. Next, Elisha sends word to Israel's king to avoid these sites and thus avoid Aram's affront. With this brief exposition of opening circumstances, the presenting problem narrows and fixes upon Elisha. That he persistently anticipates Aram's battle strategies puts the enemy at an acute disadvantage.

For his part, the unnamed Aramean ruler seems not to understand the real nature of the problem. He thinks there is an in-house traitor lurking within the precincts of his own courts. However, the Aramean officials know who the meddling informant is. After all, given what he did for the Aramean official Naaman, Elisha has become a household name within Syrian circles. Approaching the humorous, the king's advisors must inform him of Elisha's probable involvement, and when they do, the case they make is rather persuasive. They suggest that Elisha's knowledge is so intrusive that he knows what goes on in the king's bedchamber. Hence, they indirectly suggest how likely it is that he knows what is going on in the council of war. The case they make convinces the sovereign to shift his strategy. Before he can annihilate Israel, he must first assassinate Elisha.

The king is then informed of Elisha's whereabouts (v. 13). The prophet is conveniently located at Dothan, a town twelve miles north of Samaria and due south of the Aramean front lines. The ruler orders his officers to Dothan "to go and find where he is" (v. 13) in order to seize him. The Hebrew here reads literally "go and see." This order will prove an ironic twist when these soldiers themselves later lose their sight. Finally, as if having some idea of the kind of force he is up against when he hunts for the prophet, Aram's king marshals horses, chariots, and a great army for the march to Dothan (v. 14).

The narrative focus upon this campaign then ceases. Instead, a shift in perspective makes us privy to a conversation between the prophet and his servant in Dothan. The servant has evidently caught sight of the approaching Aramean garrison and expresses his fear to Elisha. The brief exchange between the prophet and his servant has two effects. First, it slows the narrative action and builds tension. Second, it creates the occasion for the prophet once again to respond to an expressed need.

Three prayers uttered by the prophet now carry the plot forward. First, the prophet asks the Lord for sight for his servant that will allay his servant's fears. Immediately, the servant's eyes are opened and he is given the vision to perceive that despite the Aramean threat the prophet is surrounded by a host of God's protective forces (v. 17). Next, as the Arameans approach, Elisha prays that the enemy be struck with blindness (v. 18). Instantly bedazzled, the soldiers are unable to see. Now they depend upon Elisha to lead them to the city and to the man whom they seek. After leading the armed forces of Aram right into Samaria, Israel's capital, Elisha utters one more prayer and asks that their sight be restored (v. 20).

We hear nothing from the prisoners. As if to suggest their status of powerlessness, no reaction on their part to this frightening turn of events is reported. Instead, another conversation between Elisha and Israel's king moves this first episode to its conclusion.

Though never named, the Israelite ruler is presumably still Jehoram. Given the history of disagreement between this king and Elisha, it is no surprise that the prophet and the king differ on what to do next. The king intends to have the prisoners killed. However, the prophet counters the plan by insisting that the king has no claim on their lives. Holy war has not been declared and thus holy war observances cannot be enacted. Ironically, though Israel's king and Aram's ruler are archenemies, they show themselves to be quite similar. They both have to be dissuaded from their misunderstandings and shortsightedness by their own servants and advisors.

Next, the prophet urges that the men be fed well and set free. Whether according to ancient war practices this would have been an honorable discharge or a disgrace even greater than death is uncertain. What is clear is that this show of power by Elisha's God overpowers and overshadows the acts of aggression and retaliation of both Aram's ruler and Israel's king. Whether for reasons of fear or a new level of amicable relations, the story ends by reporting that there was peace between the two nations. However, that the endurance of this peace would depend upon two rulers—rulers whose credibilities and positions depended heavily upon always gaining more power—portends a peace that would not last. The end comes quickly, as the beginning of the next segment of our story discloses.

Aram Seizes Samaria (6:24–7:2)

With no more specificity than "some time later" (v. 24), we hear that, indeed, the peace did not last. Between the end of one story and the beginning of another the conflict between Israel and Aram has been rekindled. In the opening verse of this second section (v. 24), the circumstances of this new strife are briefly summarized. Under the leadership of King Ben-hadad, Aram has mustered its forces, marched out against Israel, and laid siege to Samaria. Though it remains uncertain to which Ben-hadad this identification refers, it is likely the son of Hazael who ruled in Damascus at the end of the ninth century and on into the eighth century (2 Kgs 8:14; 13:3-7, 22-25).

Besieging a city was an ancient military war tactic to force surrender. No commerce, goods, or personnel could go into or come out of the town. Soon what was in the city would be used up by its residents. Although the account does not indicate how long the siege of Samaria lasts, the description of some economic and domestic circumstances (vv. 25-30) gives the impression that it has been underway for quite some time. In the marketplace, the foodstuffs of the poor were selling for prices that only the rich could afford. The head of a donkey was normally waste that butchers disposed of. Only the indigent might make use of such wastes to boil broth for a poor person's stew. Similarly, undigested seeds could be rescued from dove's dung by the poorest in society to plant a few stalks of wheat or corn. That these deplorable items are commanding exorbitant prices in the marketplace suggests the gravity of the economic crisis resulting from the siege. What had become unthinkable conditions in the market economy are eclipsed by an even more abhorrent situation on the domestic front.

As the king of Israel is walking on the wall surrounding the city, a woman cries out to him, "Help, my lord king!" (v. 26). The king, presumably still Jehoram, responds in his characteristic fashion. He abdicates responsibility and indirectly blames God (v. 27). He, who is in charge of the nation and its well-being, claims not to be accountable for the crisis at the winepress or at the threshing floor. Moreover, he assumes that the woman is calling for food. Whether it was the harshness of the famine or the presumably emaciated appearance of the woman that made him jump to this conclusion, we do not know. Indeed, the woman is experiencing a crisis surrounding food, but not in the way that the king thinks. When he finally gives her a chance to speak, what she discloses far surpasses the expected plea for food that the king anticipated.

Instead, she reveals that just one day earlier she and another woman agreed to eat their children, so they cooked and ate her son first. Now, when the time has come to do the same to the other child, the other mother has hidden her son (vv. 28-29). It is not clear whether the woman wants the king to force the other woman to make good on her word, or if she is telling the king the story in order to illustrate how grave the famine has become. Though other cases of cannibalism in times of siege are noted in the Bible, such circumstances bespeak of conditions of greatest severity (Deut 28:56-57; Lam 2:20; Ezek 5:10). It is likely that the king's experience of famine is quite different from that of the common people, especially the poor, and that he needed to be made aware of these circumstances.

When the king hears the woman's story, he tears his robes and displays sackcloth underneath his royal garments (v. 30). The sackcloth indicates he is fasting from food. However, his fasting from food suggests something else. As king, he likely has access to food, in complete contrast to these women who do not have the freedom to *choose* to fast. Next, he does what King Jehoram always does in times of crisis. He blames someone else. This time, he points the indicting finger at Elisha (v. 31), probably because the prophet let Aram's prisoners go free in the earlier episode. Thus, he responds to the woman's story of violence with an order for further violence. He vows to behead the prophet.

Now the scene shifts to the prophet's house (vv. 32-33). The conflict between Israel and Aram fixes its attention upon a related conflict, the hostility between the king and Elisha. The prophet is sitting in his house in the company of the town's elders. Aware that the king has dispatched his assassin, Elisha orders the doors bolted against the intruder. However, when the attacker arrives, it is the king himself who appears. Evidently having had a change of heart concerning the prophet, the king confesses his despair at the door of the prophet's house. Once again, he blames God for the trouble.

As the threat to Elisha fades, the prophet foretells an end to the threat posed by the famine. He issues an oracle from the Lord that will take effect the next day. The conditions of the marketplace will be reversed on the way to resolving the crisis. Though the king himself does not respond, his captain sarcastically expresses skepticism. The prophet responds with another oracle. He promises that though this officer will see the end of the siege, he will not take part in the reversed economic conditions of food and plenty (7:2).

The Aramean Crisis Resolved (7:3-20)

As the final part of this triptych begins, we listen in on the conversation of four lepers pondering their fate in these cruel times as they stand together outside the city walls. Certain that death awaits them within the precincts of the starving city, they decide to desert to the Aramean camp. Together they embark upon a twilight trek to the enemy encampment; but on their arrival they find no one there. Now the narrator steps in and reports to us something that not even the lepers know (7:6). The Lord had caused the enemy army camped there to hear what they thought was the sound of approaching horses, chariots, and armies. Concluding that allied forces had joined Israel, the Arameans had fled at twilight. Hence, the lepers had evidently arrived just on the heels of the enemy's exodus.

When the account of the lepers in the deserted camp resumes (v. 8), they are wasting no time getting what they need and much more. Upon entering a tent, they eat, drink, and then abscond with some gold, silver, and garments. They do the same at a second tent. Finally, as if some qualm of conscience arises, or perhaps because having satisfied their famished bodies they can now think rationally and even morally, they decide what they are doing is not right.

Together they agree to a new plan (v. 9). They will inform the king of the good news they have stumbled upon. Arriving before the king's gatekeeper, they describe the tethered animals, the empty tents, and the deserted camp. Though still the middle of the night, this news propels the king into action. As is his habit, the king suspects a trick, and then he acts on the sensible suggestion of his servants. The king sends out two men on horseback as decoys and to scout out the situation. The scouts discover the deserted camp just as the lepers reported, as well as other evidence in the form of the Arameans' belongings strewn all the way to the Jordan.

Soon after the messengers return and report this to the king, the people head out to loot the camp and procure the needed food for the city (v. 16). Just as the prophet foretold, the prices in the marketplace for valuable commodities such as meal and barley fall immediately to affordable levels. This shift signals the end of the dire economic conditions that accompany the famine.

Following, the account concludes (vv. 17-20) with a report that the other word spoken by the prophet has also been fulfilled. The captain who had expressed skepticism at the prophet's oracle did live to see the famine end. However, as the people rushed through the city gates, he was trampled to death. Hence, just as the prophet foretold, this man would not partake in the new abundance. The final summary (vv. 18-20) recapitulates the oracle spoken by Elisha in conjunction with this officer of the king and his expression of doubt as a warning for all those who have ears to hear. Amid the restoration of well-being that is taking place for the city, the dark consequences of doubt and despair dare not be ignored.

Theological and Ethical Analysis

The stories of these chapters offer numerous challenges and theological lessons for the faithful reader. First, the role of Elisha across these stories discloses a compelling lesson to anyone committed to bringing about the household of God. The demands of such a commitment may warrant, at times, attention to the seemingly small or insignificant concerns of people at the local level. As Elisha was called upon to rescue an ax head, we too may be asked to participate in matters that in our estimation are of limited importance or that we may even deem insignificant. Alternatively, we may be summoned to serve causes or respond to crises on a grander scale. Like Elisha's involvement in the conflict between Aram and Israel, we too may have to participate in complex situations where the scope of our actions has broad consequences.

The juxtaposition of these stories of the local concerns among the brotherhood of prophets and the international crisis brewing between Israel and Aram makes this point. Both demand and merit the prophet's attention, and both receive divine intervention. Thus, coupled together, they not only challenge us to recognize the vast spectrum of ministerial concerns to which we can be called, but also set forth a noteworthy theological disclosure. The God revealed here responds to the conditions of our human existence in both great and small matters. No circumstances are too enormous, complex, or hopelessly desperate that God cannot still intervene. For our part, we must believe this is so and act upon that faith. Nothing is too trivial or too great for us to bring before the Lord.

These stories also give us pause in order to reflect upon the horrifying and devastating aspects of war. Across the biblical tradition, war becomes so commonplace that its very existence is easy to take for granted. War is "a given," especially during the monarchy—as if the very nature of kings requires them to conduct war. Since these rulers remain fairly insulated from the actual fallout of their military confrontations, they also remain insulated from the day-in, day-out consequences in the lives of common citizens that result. War devastates towns. It destroys the environment and its watering systems that support life. It interrupts commerce and disrupts the economic well-being of the commoner. It darkens and demoralizes the human spirit. Each time kings go to battle, citizens lose lives, families are destabilized, human relations are compromised, people starve, and strife is cultivated between citizens as they struggle to survive.

In the second story of the siege of Israel by Aram (6:24–7:2), two mothers make a desperate pact and agree to eat their children. Though their story of cannibalism typically invokes disdain and revulsion, they are the ones being consumed. Their lives, destinies, and well-being are being swallowed up as a result of the power struggles going on between Israel and Aram and between Israel's king and the prophet. Those power struggles have led to the siege of Samaria, cutting off food supplies to the women. However, the king takes no responsibility for this consequence, but violates the women further. He fails to address their urgent, desperate need. However, he himself appears to be fasting from what presumably must be a supply of food lest this ritual act carry no significance.

Moreover, he makes the conflict over the life of the remaining child the basis for his own act of violence—a vow to behead Elisha the prophet. Unchecked, violence here rears its serpentine head and leads to further violence. Furthermore, the violence enacted against these two mothers is exacerbated in the way their story functions here. It is but a literary prop used only to contribute to the focus upon the conflict between the king and the prophet. As if it has no value on its own, the mothers' tale is never even finished. We do not know what happened to them or to the remaining child. As in wartime, they are the dispensable, disposable persons whose lives seem not to count before the likes of kings and other important officials. Yet, this unfinished story of the cannibal mothers is a chilling testimony of the moral depravity that invades society in wartime. When something so fundamental as a mother's maternal instinct fails, it portends a world in chaos, on the brink of demise (Camp, 108).

Finally, like the essential role played by the unnamed servant girl in securing Naaman's cure (2 Kgs 5), and like his servants who convince the proud Aramean general to wash himself in the Jordan, minor characters in this story play a pivotal role. Their central and essential part calls us to pay attention to the minor characters in our own society and to acknowledge the role that they play. Four lepers who bear the social stigma of marginalized and ostracized persons are unexpected agents witnessing to the divine intervention. It is ironic that those afflicted with a disease that excludes them from society become the heralds of the good news that will restore that same society to health. The lepers are the ones who make known the supply of life-giving food that will reverse the life-threatening effects of famine. Such a turn of events seems more often than not characteristic of God's ways. The powerless lepers are the agents of the all-powerful God, whereas the leadership of the powerful general of the king diminishes as he is trampled to death on account of his disbelief. Such reversals bid for our attention and reflection on who are God's instruments of life and well-being in our own time.

2 KINGS 8

Earlier chapters highlighted Elisha in his exchanges with Israelite and foreign kings, his encounters with the common people, and the interfaced destinies of Israel and Judah that fashioned the backdrop for his prophetic activity. In this chapter, three separate accounts continue these stories, adding to and advancing what we know about each. Each instance further discloses something about the God who not only propels the work of the prophet but controls the course of history itself.

Literary Analysis

Three distinct and separate literary units (vv. 1-6, 7-15, 16-29) make up this chapter. Though unrelated to one another, all are related to other accounts in preceding chapters. In the first story, concerning the recovery of land by the Shunammite woman (vv. 1-6), temporal references divide the tightly composed tale into two parts (vv. 1-2, 3-6). The first recalls an earlier exchange between the prophet and the woman when he had alerted her to leave her land and home on account of an approaching famine.

The second part of the story (vv. 3-6), narrated in the present, takes place when at the end of the seven-year famine the woman returns from Philistia. Having evidently lost possession of her land and home during this absence, she now sets out to beseech the king to restore her property. Citing Elisha's reputation, Gehazi intercedes with the king on her behalf and she herself gives witness to his testimony. Though not present in the story, Elisha's reputation plays a key role in the resolution of the woman's current problem.

By contrast, Elisha is a key player (vv. 7-15) in the second story of the chapter. Additional changes also suggest the beginning of a new unit. The scene shifts, different characters are introduced, and an entirely new topic drives the plot. King Ben-hadad of Aram has fallen ill. He seeks and receives an oracle from the prophet about his prognosis that is subsequently fulfilled. After the brief opening introduction (v. 7) that situates Elisha in Damascus, in close proximity to the ailing king, the story unfolds over the course of three interchanges (vv. 8-9a, 9b-13, 14).

In the first encounter (vv. 8-9), Ben-hadad summons Hazael, ladens him with gifts, and commands him to go and inquire of the Lord through the prophet whether he will recover from his malady. Again the narrative reports that Hazael did as the king ordered.

The second conversation (vv. 9b-13) takes place when Hazael goes and stands before the prophet. Initially Elisha instructs

Hazael to tell the king that he will indeed get well, but in his subsequent oracle from the Lord the prophet says that in actuality he will not recover. In addition to this ambiguous response, the interchange between Elisha and Hazael discloses Hazael's own future on the throne in Damascus.

The third and final conversation is brief; Hazael returns and reports the prophet's oracle to the king (v. 14). Though he relays the prophet's first answer assuring recovery, on the following morning Hazael smothers him to death. The third and final account of this chapter (vv. 16-29) also distinguishes itself from what happened previously. With characteristic dispassion and abbreviated detail, it presents regnal summaries of the two kings of Judah who have been ruling during this time. First, an account and evaluation of Jehoram, king of Judah during the reign of Joram in Israel, is presented (vv. 16-24). Ahaziah's resumé follows, again offering the biographical information and theological evaluation we have come to expect (vv. 25-29). This is succeeded by a brief summary of the war in which Israel and Judah fought as allies against Aram. Though the chapter ends here, the close of Ahaziah's resumé and death notice lie ahead in the upcoming story of Jehu's revolt (chaps. 9–10).

Exegetical Analysis

The Shunammite Woman's Land Restored (8:1-6)

This first story gives us evidence of that which we already know. There is often much more to the prophets' relations with the people than the record of these short stories reveals. Earlier, chapter 4:8-37 narrated an account of the Shunammite woman's hospitality toward the prophet as well as his favors toward her. He provided her with a son and then after the child's sudden death, restored him to life. The first part of our story here suggests that their relationship has continued. Now we hear that the prophet followed up his previous two favors toward the woman with yet another. Aware of an impending famine, Elisha had advised her to seek refuge from this economic peril by leaving Israel. Convinced of the credibility of the prophet's word, the woman had gone away from Israel and settled in Philistia during the seven years of famine. Her return signals the beginning of the second part of the unfolding narrative. It also signals how the prophet's advice in the past resulted in a problem for the woman in the present.

It is clear that in her absence this once "wealthy woman" (4:8) has lost everything. She no longer has possession of land or a home in her country, Israel. We do not know for certain the legal situation that occasions the woman's crisis upon her return. That she goes to the king to beseech him for its restoration suggests that the crown has claimed the land, as in the story of Naboth's vineyard (1 Kgs 21:1-16).

Just as the narrator announces the woman's arrival before the king, Gehazi makes a surprise appearance in the story. He gives witness before the ruler to all the great deeds of the prophet. As Elisha's servant is recalling the prophet's restoration of the Shunammite woman's child to life, the woman herself appears before the king and bears further testimony. As if a sequel to the earlier story when the prophet offered to use his influence before the king to gain favors for the woman (4:13), under the prophet's influence the king now grants the woman's requests and more. Satisfied with the woman's answers to his questions, the king restores not only all the woman's land but also all the revenue that the crown had evidently gained from the land since her departure. Though Elisha's advice to leave the land caused the woman's problem, his reputation now brings about a resolution to her crisis upon her return. Hence, even in Elisha's absence, the goodness of his deeds continues to bring life.

Death Comes to King Ben-hadad (8:7-15)

Though this new tale is unrelated to what immediately preceded, it rings familiar with some of the characters, practices, and story lines of earlier chapters. Ben-hadad, Aram's king whom we have met on several occasions (1 Kgs 20; 2 Kgs 6:24), is ill. Like Ahaziah who had fallen through the lattice and sought word about his prognosis from one of Baal's prophets at Ekron (2 Kgs 1:1), Ben-hadad summons his trusted official Hazael. He sends

Hazael to go and seek an oracle concerning his chances for recovery. As in the case of Naaman's visit to Elisha, Hazael does not go off empty-handed. Armed with an impressive "forty camel loads" of gifts, he seeks out an oracle from a prophet with a well-established reputation for healing, even in this foreign country. Fortuitously, this man of God, Elisha, just happens to be en route to Damascus, the capital of Aram (v. 7). This opening exchange between king and official paves the way for the second encounter, a more extended meeting between the prophet and Hazael.

Hazael manifests true emmissarial protocol when he makes his inquiry before Elisha. He speaks of the king of Aram as "your son," and indicates his own status as the king's servant when he describes that he has been "sent" to consult the prophet (v. 9). A respectful messenger armed with abundant gifts, he comes and stands before the prophet. Then he raises the question regarding Ben-hadad's recovery, as he is commissioned to ask. The prophet's answer cultivates great difficulty for interpreters. At first Elisha assures Hazael that, yes, the king will recover. Then he follows up that response with a report of what the Lord has shown him: "that he shall certainly die" (v. 10). The ambiguity that occasionally characterizes prophets' responses manifests itself here, as it did with Micaiah in 1 Kgs 22. In its obscurity, the prophet's seemingly contradictory word conveys the complexity of a situation that does not easily accommodate a yes or no answer. Recalling that this man of God, Elisha, is often gifted with foresight might help us here. Thus, in his first response to Hazael, he offers an assessment that indeed the king will recover from the illness currently afflicting him. However, because Hazael's action will undercut the fulfillment of this outcome, Elisha follows the positive assessment with a negative brief that he punctuates with certainty. Even though the king would recover from illness, the king will surely die. This oracular pronouncement suggests that Elisha knows what Hazael knows. At this point the plotline takes a detour. What began as a story about Ben-hadad and his quest for information regarding prospects for a cure now becomes a story about Hazael and his plans that will require Ben-hadad to die.

The encounter between the prophet and the Aramean official is momentarily suspended in silence. A fixed gaze from staring eyes narrates the terrifying pause and mounting tension between the two, broken when they both respond. Their shared knowledge prompts Hazael's shame and Elisha's tears. As if to test just how much Elisha understands, Hazael asks, "Why does my lord weep?" (v. 12). Elisha's response discloses his knowledge that the end of Ben-hadad signals the beginning of an era of Aram's tyranny against Israel. Hazael himself will harass Israel with cruelty, humiliation, and savagery. In an emotionally charged oration filled with horrific detail, Elisha recites a litany of Hazael's deeds against the nation. Drawing upon images of war that are characteristic among the prophets' pronouncements (Amos 1:13; Hos 13:16), he sketches a canvas of death and destruction that spares neither Israel's cities, militia, mothers, nor its children.

When Hazael responds to the prophet, he refers to himself as "your servant" (v. 13), still hiding behind a solicitous facade. His protest alleges that the prophet's words are insulting and, given his status, charges that carrying out such a "great thing" is impossible. However, Elisha makes clear that indeed, Hazael will be quite capable of such deeds. Once again the Lord has made known to the prophet beforehand what he now communicates to the one standing in front of him. Hazael will become king of Aram.

The final exchange of the story is brief and occurs when Hazael returns to Ben-hadad. The king inquires of Hazael concerning his chances of recovery. Hazael's duplicity now manifests itself in his answer and action. He can no longer afford to waste precious time. What has been housed as a plan in the private recesses of his heart is now public by virtue of Elisha's knowledge. He assures Ben-hadad that he will recover, but the very next day Hazael seizes a cloth or netting of some kind and suffocates the unsuspecting king. Thus, he commences his reign of terror and begins to fulfill the prophet's word.

The Reigns of Jehoram and Ahaziah in Judah (8:16-29)

The summaries of two Judahite kings close this chapter. First, a précis of Jehoram's rule is set forth (vv. 16-24). It opens with the familiar biographical detail. Jehoram is the son of Jehoshaphat, who at thirty-two years of age began his eight-year tenure as ruler in Jerusalem in the line of David. His reign in Judah coincides with the reign of Joram in Israel. However, unlike his father, whose royal career receives a fairly positive review, Jehoram's legacy is not praiseworthy. Indeed, he is allied with the waywardness of the kings of Israel, and in particular with Ahab, with whom we associate the Baals and extreme apostasy. Hence, the formulaic evaluation of his northern colleagues that, "he did what was evil in the sight of the LORD" (v. 18), is the crowning evaluation of his own reign. The promise to David is cited as the reason God does not destroy Judah despite Jehoram's sinfulness, in contrast to the fate of the northern peoples. However, an addendum to this resumé suggests that Jehoram is not exempt from the consequences of his misdeeds.

A follow-up description notes the rebellions of Edom and Libnah during Jehoram's time (v. 20). Edom has been a colonized territory since the reign of David. However, now it has been able to throw off the governance of Judah under Jehoram and maintain its freedom on into the future. Although we do not know anything about Libnah, it too was likely a colonized territory, probably located near Israel's western seaboard. It is presumably a revenue producer whose rebellion and ongoing resistance to the Judahite crown had serious economic consequences for Judah (v. 22). After detailing what might be intended as the consequences for Jehoram's infidelity to the Lord, the account closes by identifying his successor to the throne, his son, Ahaziah.

The second summary picks up where the first left off. We hear that Ahaziah, at the age of twenty-two, became king and ruled only one year in Jerusalem. His mother, Athaliah, is mentioned here and identified as the granddaughter of King Omri of Israel. Such intermarriage between the north and south explains the duplication of northern kings' names by southern kings of the next generation, as well as the replication of their sins. The evaluation of King Ahaziah's reign parallels the negative assessment earned by his father. Ahaziah also did what was evil in the sight of the Lord. His relationship as the son-in-law of Ahab suggests an explanation.

The intermarriage between the royal families of the two nations also suggests ongoing connections between Israel and Judah that are not without consequences. The persistent hostility between Aram and Israel has spread to Judah. In the brief exposition of his reign that follows (vv. 28-29), Ahaziah joins Joram, son of Ahab, in the war against Hazael, king of Aram. The kinship between the two kings is further manifested by what follows. When Joram is wounded in battle, Ahaziah goes down from the battlefront at Ramoth-gilead to visit the ailing king as he convalesces in Jezreel. No note of Ahaziah's successor is added here. Instead, the two kings in company of each other serve to preface what will become the announcement of their deaths in the upcoming chapter.

Theological and Ethical Analysis

Democracy in the modern world assumes the separation of church and state. Such distinctions are intended to protect and preserve individual freedoms as well as the integrity of these two institutions from any constraining infringement upon each other. Groups of concerned citizens work to monitor that this distinction is maintained and that violations are addressed. Still, politicians often reference God or a specific religious tradition in the course of their practices. They frequently and publicly call upon God to "bless America." When the nation is at war, condolences are given to families of loved ones who die in combat by assuring them of the nation's prayers. Even the monies manufactured and regulated by our own government—both coins and bills—are printed with the faith acclamation "In God We Trust." Perhaps church and state are really not so separated.

For this reason, religious officials have a responsibility to monitor the frequent exploitation of religious and theological influence. The duty to speak out or take action is incumbent upon officials of churches and synagogues if God or religious traditions are being invoked to rubber-stamp corrupt or dehumanizing political agendas. Furthermore, since the government generates policies that determine the well-being of people, religion and its officials must involve themselves in political policy making, especially when it infringes on human rights.

Though the three separate accounts in this chapter leave a record of three very distinct and unrelated traditions, collectively they serve as a warrant for religion and its officials in just such matters. In the first tale, a woman confronts the king with the economic crisis that is threatening her livelihood and challenges the injustice of her lost land holdings. We do not know what the king might have done had Gehazi not recounted Elisha's deeds. However, the story would have us believe that it was the prophet's influence that prompted his favorable decision. Both the woman's and Gehazi's witness to Elisha's power over life and death in regard to the woman's son appear to have provided the persuasive pressure to motivate the king to do the right thing by restoring the land to this Shunammite woman. Here the assertion of a credible source of religious influence overturns an injustice that may have been promulgated by the crown if left to its own devices. Hence, the impact of religious influence upon the political process rescues the woman from the threat of impoverishment when she returns to the land.

In the second story, religious authority asserts itself more deliberately to confront the wrongful plan of a powerful official of the state. Hazael is about to commit a murder that will commence his reign of tyranny. With full knowledge of the Aramean's plan, Elisha does not back down, but confronts him with the evil he is about to do to Israel. Refusing to succumb to the awkwardness of the encounter, the prophet tallies all the horrific crimes that Hazael will commit against Israel. Even when Hazael counters the accusation, alleging that the prophet insults him, Elisha stands firm and identifies the means to such evil. He declares before this Aramean what Hazael evidently knows privately in his heart. Hazael will usurp the throne in Aram. Even when the ills of political forces seem inevitable, or so strong that they cannot be overturned, the outcry by religious institutions or its officials must continue to sound.

In the third and final account of this chapter, religious tradition plays an evaluative role in the summary of kings and their reigns. In contrast to the previous passage where the prophet confronts the powerful official with the evil he is about to do, here the tradition's religious assessment ("did what was evil in the sight of the LORD" [vv. 18, 27]) condemns kings for what they have done. Though the power-wielding machinations of kings appear mighty and daunting, the religious denouncement of these despots and their practices cannot be silenced. The faithful must continue to decry the infidelity of rulers and their failure in responsibility that has led the people into sin.

Religious voices often sound as countertexts to the sometimes woeful schemes and practices of political leaders. Though most lack the economic backing that would put them on par with the forces they confront, their refusal to be silent has its own power. The voice of conscience retains a persistent resonance in society. The injustices that political systems might author do not go uncontested. Systems or policies that dehumanize or oppress select groups cannot become the unchallenged status quo. Whether in the form of a confrontation, denouncement, or brazen evaluation and judgment, the responsibility of religious officials before the powers of state is clear. Whether in the presence of priest, rabbi, minister, deacon, or the believing faithful, those who serve the state and the political process must always know that "there is a prophet among them."

2 KINGS 9

The Omride dynasty comes to its end in this chapter. With Jehu's revolt, the narrative takes a decisive turn and events unfold rapidly. The death of two kings and a queen quickly follows the secret anointing of a new king. A theological polemic permeates and even condones the violence with which these events are carried out, since we are told that all this is done according to the word of the Lord.

Literary Analysis

The story that unfolds in this chapter turns on the command of one prophet that fulfills the commission and oracles of an earlier prophet. The story opens with the command by Elisha to one of his prophets to deliver an oracle to Jehu and anoint him as king (vv. 1-3). The tale closes with the death of Jezebel (vv. 24-37), which after the deaths of Joram and Ahaziah brings an end to the house of Ahab, as prophesied much earlier by Elijah. The enclosed story of Jehu's revolt and rise to power is not isolated, but finds continuity with the circumstances of the preceding chapter and the events narrated in the chapter that follows. At the end of chapter 8, Joram, Israel's wounded king, is visited by Ahaziah, Judah's ruler. Both are together in Jezreel while Israel's troops are still battling Aram at Ramoth-gilead. In chapter 10, Jehu's coup and the destruction of the house of Ahab continues.

In this chapter three major units structure the record of Jehu's rise to power (vv. 1-13, 14-23, 24-37). Section one, which narrates the making of a king, can be divided into three parts (vv. 1-3, 4-10, 11-13), with the oracle commanding the anointing of Jehu repeated in each segment (vv. 3; 6-10; 12). First, Elisha commissions one of his prophets to go to the battlefront at Ramoth-gilead and anoint Jehu as king (vv. 1-3). Next, the designated prophet goes and fulfills Elisha's command in the privacy of a separate room, pouring oil on Jehu's head while proclaiming the oracle that names him king (vv. 4-10). Third, when Jehu returns to the gathering of his war council, he reveals the prophet's oracle at their insistent questioning (vv. 11-13). They respond with a gesture affirming the Lord's word; Jehu will be their king.

The second major segment of the story (vv. 14-23) sets forth Jehu's conspiracy against the house of Omri, his challenge to Joram's faltering kingship, and his successful rebellion.

The third and final segment of the story (vv. 24-37) of Jehu's revolt records the end of the house of Ahab. Three deaths are recounted. First, Jehu slays Joram during his attempted escape (v. 25). Next, he kills Ahaziah, Judah's king and the great-grandson of Omri (v. 27). Finally, the horrifying death of Jezebel is narrated. In each instance, the prophecies of Elijah are remembered and at last fulfilled. Moreover, the bloody massacre against Ahab's house, which begins here and was prophesied by Elijah, will continue on in the chapter that follows.

Exegetical Analysis

Jehu's Anointing (9:1-13)

Three scenes (vv. 1-3, 4-10, 11-13) lead to the fulfillment of the commission to which the prophet Elijah was called (1 Kgs 19:15-16). When Jehu, a commander in the army of Joram, is anointed king in Israel, the Omrides will be brought to their end. The oracle of commissioning repeated in each of these three scenes makes clear that this change in the ruling house of Israel is by the order and plan of the Lord.

In this opening scene, Elisha delivers the commission to one of his cohorts gathered among the company of prophets. His command to the young man to "gird up your loins" (v. 1) indicates the haste with which this dangerous act needs to be carried out. Joram is still recuperating in Jezreel, and his ally, Ahaziah, king of Judah, is currently with him (2 Kgs 8:28-29). Hence, though their troops continue to fight Aram at Ramoth-gilead, they do so without the defining presence or leadership of either of the two kings.

Elisha's instructions to the young emissary are very specific. First, he is to look for Jehu, son of Jehoshaphat and grandson of Nimshi, among the troops. The inclusion of both the father and grandfather's name here is unusual. Perhaps Nimshi was a clan name and is included here to clarify that Jehu was *not* the son of Jehoshaphat the king of Judah (Seow, 217). When the messenger finds Jehu he is to take him aside privately, and—with word and deed—he is to proclaim him king. Reminiscent of Saul's anointing (1 Sam 10:1), he is to pour the oil on his head and pronounce the authorizing oracle that legitimizes what he does as fulfilling the word of the Lord. Finally, the prophet orders the young man to depart hurriedly after he has completed his task. The prophet's instruction makes clear that this is indeed a dangerous act. This anointing of a new king takes place when there is no vacancy on the throne. Any troops among the military forces at Ramoth-gilead who are still faithful to Joram will view the gesture as an act of treason. Hence, Elisha urges the man that when he has completed the task he should run for his life.

The commission issued by Elisha to a member from the brotherhood of prophets in the first scene is carried out in the second scene (vv. 4-10). The commanders of the army are in a council meeting when the young man arrives. He announces that he has a message for Jehu. With a simple statement he ascertains quickly who is the one he seeks among those assembled. Jehu follows him out to a private location. The men waste no time. Without explanation, the prophet begins pouring oil on Jehu's head.

Up until this point, the young prophet had followed Elisha's instructions exactly. However, when he delivers the oracle he was instructed to pronounce, the messenger goes well beyond what he was instructed to say. His pronouncement not only fulfills Elisha's commission to him, but also makes the anointing the fulfillment of Elijah's oracle of judgment against Ahab (1 Kgs 21:21-23). His whole house will perish, including his sons, and the queen, Jezebel. Moreover, the lessons of history that went unheeded are about to be taught again. The house of Ahab will become like the house of Jeroboam and the house of Baasha, the two other dynasties that followed in the way of apostasy and were subsequently destroyed.

The portended death of Jezebel, which concludes the prophet's speech, is predicted in graphic terms. Death appears to be an insufficient punishment for Israel's Phoenician queen. After all, Jezebel was consistently held responsible for the increased popularity of the Baals in Israel. Hence, she will be denied burial and insulted further when dogs consume what is left of her body. Whether or not her condemnation is legitimate, it remains consistent across the narrative. Still, we must at least entertain the possibility that Jezebel serves as a narrative scapegoat, an outsider blamed for a family's sins and a nation's misfortune. Otherwise, how is it that despite the prophets' intolerance for Omride kings, she, rather than they, receives one of the most damning of punishments?

At the conclusion of the scene, the messenger completes his dangerous mission and obeys Elisha's final instruction to him. He leaves the scene in haste. His departure thus signals the beginning of the third and final scene in the anointing of Jehu, the confirmation of his kingship.

In the last scene, Jehu has returned to the meeting among the military officials. Though their reference to the young prophet as a "madman" (v. 11) is pejorative, they evidently take seriously the information he conveyed. When Jehu reenters the gathering of the council, the officials refer to the man's visit and ask if everything is all right. Jehu's ambiguous response does not convince the assembly that everything is well. They reject Jehu's first answer, calling him a liar, and insist he tell them the truth. Perhaps their curiosity is piqued because Jehu's demeanor has changed, or perhaps it is his oiled head that gives him away. Whatever the reason for their disbelief, Jehu ultimately must report the commissioning. So, Jehu responds honestly to their question, repeating the oracle of the Lord that designates him king.

On the occasion of this third citation of the oracle, the officers respond. Hurriedly, they conduct a private ceremony acknowledging Jehu's kingship. With gestures reminiscent of Solomon's coronation (1 Kgs 1:39), they make a royal carpet with their cloaks, sound the trumpet, and declare, "Jehu is king" (v. 13). Their instant reception of the news suggests they were hoping for someone, perhaps Jehu himself, to seize this opportune moment and exert the authority to overthrow the ailing Joram. After all, though Joram was home safely recuperating in his Jezreel residence, his army was still embattled at Ramoth-gilead. Now the council has it on God's own word; Jehu will replace Joram. Although the assembly initially mocked the messenger of this news, now they wholeheartedly accept the message. Their instant acclamation of Jehu's kingship indicates that the seeds of revolt were likely sown long before these events.

Jehu's Coup (9:14-23)

Official recognition of Jehu's kingship requires more than his willingness to accept his new role. Now he must conspire politically and militarily to take the throne. The introduction to the account of the coup (v. 14) confirms his decision to do so. The description that follows (vv. 14-16) rehearses what we already know and sets the stage for the confrontation between the reigning king, Joram, and Jehu, the challenger. Joram is still in the company of Ahaziah in Jezreel, supposedly recovering from his battle wounds. At the same time, he is well protected from the threats his troops face daily at Ramoth-gilead. The fact that Israel remains on guard there (v. 14) suggests that, unlike earlier days, it currently controls this border town, the site of ongoing disputes with Syria in the past (1 Kgs 22). The success of Jehu's conspiracy depends upon secrecy. Hence, he gives the order that no one is to be allowed to leave Ramoth-gilead, lest the news of the acclamation of his kingship make its way to Jezreel. So as to gain the upper hand in his coup, it is essential that Jehu approach and confront Joram before the news of his claim on the crown does. Jehu wastes no time. The introduction closes by noting that Jehu mounted his chariot and left for Jezreel. However, it is unlikely that this king-elect travels alone. Rather, in order to overcome any resistance he might encounter, a sizable militia probably accompanied him.

In the next scene, Jehu's approach to Jezreel unfolds in a characteristic threefold cycle. We have seen this literary tactic before as a means to build narrative tension. The soldiers made three approaches to Elijah stationed on the mount (2 Kgs 1:9, 11, 13) as the prelude to that story's climax. In another instance, when Elijah prepared to depart from this world (2 Kgs 2), he made three journeys (2:2-3, 4-5, 6) during which he tried to dissuade Elisha from following him. Three repetitions of the oracle of Jehu's appointment precede the confrontation, and the accounts of three deaths follow the threefold approach to Joram at Jezreel.

When the sentinel standing guard at Jezreel spots the approaching party, he informs the king. Joram immediately sends out a reconnaissance man to determine if this is friend or foe. Though the king sends a question about peace, the watchful sentinel can only report that the man sent has fallen in behind those approaching. Hence, no answer as to whether this is a peaceful mission or not can be secured.

When the second horseman is sent out, he also fails to return with an answer to the king's inquiry regarding the business of the approaching party. Like the previous man, he too "falls in" behind the new leader. However, now the approaching party has come close enough that it can be identified. His crazy driving gives him away. It is Jehu! Interestingly, the description "maniac" (v. 20) draws upon the same Hebrew word that was used to characterize the young prophet who delivered the oracle of Jehu's appointment, which set Jehu into action.

Perhaps expecting that Jehu or one of his officials brings news from the battlefront, Joram himself readies to go and meet him. In this third and final cycle of the approach (v. 21), Joram, though supposedly still recuperating, is well enough to ride. He and his guest Ahaziah each set out in their own chariots. Unbeknownst to them, they also set out to meet their respective deaths.

The anticipated encounter with Jehu takes place at Naboth's vineyard. Now the narrative begins to teem with connections. The very site where Elijah first delivered the oracle against Ahab's whole house has become the place of its fulfillment. Jehu becomes the instrument of bringing Elijah's word to pass. Furthermore, Joram finally receives an answer to his inquiry about peace. Yet Jehu's answer moves the question of peace well beyond a reference to this encounter only. As he insinuates, so long as the Omrides are in power, there is no peace in Israel. Moreover, given the family's penchant for "whoredoms and sorceries" (v. 22) there is no peace in the relationship between God and Israel. Once again, Jezebel, whose name has become emblematic of all the apostasy identified with the Omrides, is referenced as the reason there is no peace.

Joram's response suggests he understands the gravity and danger of this meeting. This encounter is not about peace. Immediately he acts in his own defense, turning his chariot around and starting to flee. As he heads off, he shouts a warning to Ahaziah. According to Joram, the encounter is about "treason" (v. 23).

Death Comes to the Omrides (9:24-37)

Three deaths (vv. 24-26, 27-29, 30-37) commence Jehu's bloody campaign against the house of Omri. Joram's quick assessment and flight indicates that he recognized the warning signs. This face-off with Jehu is the beginning of a coup. But his effort to save himself is lost with one shot of an arrow from Jehu's bow. As if his death and what follows are the prescribed ritual fulfillment of Elijah's oracle (1 Kgs 21:17-19), Jehu orders his assistant Bidkar to discard the dead king's body on the ground—ground that he identifies as belonging to Naboth, not the crown. Next, Jehu eulogizes Joram's death by rehearsing the Lord's oracle uttered against Ahab, Joram's father. Joram's death makes final recompense for Naboth's murder and the violation of his property.

The account of the death of Ahaziah that follows is more tersely related. While Jehu is busy killing Joram and making proclamations about his death, Ahaziah evidently has a head start in his flight. From Jezreel, he travels south to Beth-haggan and then farther south to Gur by Ibleam. Though Ahaziah makes a run for it, his effort is not enough to curb Jehu's determination to eradicate all those connected to the Omrides in Israel. Whether it is his affiliation with Joram, his blood relations with the house of Omri, or his own participation in the sins of Israel's kings, Ahaziah is Jehu's next target for extermination. Shot by Jehu's forces, Ahaziah goes as far as Megiddo before dying there. His own officers are evidently left unharmed. Unlike Joram's fate, Ahaziah's body is carried home to Jerusalem where he is buried in the city of David with the other southern kings. The account closes with a biographical note recalling the year when Ahaziah began to reign as king over Judah (v. 29). The statement is as much out of place as Ahaziah himself has been in this story of the struggle for the throne in Israel.

The account of Jezebel's death caps and closes this trio of deadly accounts. When Jezebel hears that Jehu is on her trail, she does not hide or cower. Consistent with her character since her introduction into the story, she appears self-reliant and proud. Not in sackcloth and ashes, but royally adorned and dressed, she readies herself for what lies ahead. She does not wait for Jehu to find her; she faces him as he approaches her window. Sarcastically, she inquires about that which she already knows. Jehu's visit is not about peace, and Jezebel makes that clear when she refers to him as Zimri, linking him with the treasonous upstart who ended the Baashan dynasty.

For his part, Jehu has come to do what he continues to defend as the word of God—to wipe out all persons connected to the

Omride household, Jezebel among them. Jehu pays her no respect by paying her no response. Instead, he makes his bid to those attending her. Like the reconnaissance men Joram sent to inquire of Jehu's approach, these servants of Jezebel quickly abandon any allegiance they have to her and join Jehu. At his command, they throw her down from the window to her death. Then, as if the horror of this scene were not enough, the narrative continues with even more graphically deplorable details sketching her final moments (v. 33).

The utter disregard for Jezebel's death is further drawn when immediately following these events Jehu goes inside to eat and drink (v. 34). Having satisfied himself, he gives orders that the fallen queen be provided a proper burial. After all, as he becomes king he must respect protocol regarding the burial of members of the royal class. Alas, he is too late. Scavengers and hungry dogs have made fast work of her corpse. Jezebel will receive no final respects and no final resting place. Moreover, Jehu is quick to define this dreadful destiny as fulfillment of divine oracle (1 Kgs 21:23). However, his citation of the word of the Lord far exceeds the judgment and punishment of Jezebel specified in the original oracle. One begins to think this sounds more like someone covering his own tracks.

Theological and Ethical Analysis

Though the Omrides and their recalcitrant infidelities are brought to an end in this chapter, there is much violence underwriting Jehu's revolt. Conducted in the name of the Lord, all the war maneuvers are made to appear as fulfilling the prophets' words. These stories and those that follow in the next chapter pose a particular challenge for contemporary readers of these texts. The theological and ethical questions resident here are immense in number and scope. How do we understand a salvation history that achieves its end with violence? Are religious beliefs merely pretexts for forwarding political or ideological programs? Can the loss of human life be justified in the conflict between powerful figures? Are we as readers enlisted or even co-opted to assent to this violence and to the condemnation of those earmarked for blame? Over the course of the next few chapters, we will try to address some of these matters. In this brief reflection, we will fix upon the last question with reference to Jezebel.

We begin with the observation that how we deal with violence and its victims in these texts may be related to how we deal with violence and its victims in our own world. When Ahab secured the Phoenician princess as a wife for himself, he was also securing the throne for the Omrides of future generations. As we know, the matter of succession in the north was an ongoing problem often marked by murder and intrigue. The incorporation of this foreign woman into the Israelite royal family likely ensured the military support of the armed forces of Phoenicia, Israel's powerful northern neighbor, in case of a threat to the dynasty. For all her initiative and presence in the narrative, Jezebel is a political pawn moved across the Mesopotamian game board in an agreement between Phoenicia and Israel. Though her name becomes synonymous with apostasy, when she is first introduced into the narrative (1 Kings 16:31), Ahab, not Jezebel, is the one who appears to be actively pursuing Baal. Ahab "went and served Baal, and worshiped him" (1 Kgs 16:31). It was Ahab who "erected an altar for Baal . . . which he built in Samaria" (1 Kgs 16:32). He also built a sacred pole in the capital, and it was Ahab before whom the anger of the Lord was provoked for these deeds (1 Kgs 16:33).

If Jezebel could be exonerated on the matter of Baal influence and associated apostasy, her iniquity and sentence are often still thought to be justified with reference to her persecution of Yahweh's prophets (1 Kgs 18:13). Again and again, her murderous program against these prophets is the basis for her reputation as apostate and immoral. However, when Elijah slaughtered the Baal prophets (1 Kgs 18:40), a theological justification underwrites and approves his deeds. Though both Jezebel's and Elijah's acts involve the murder of religious figures, one is condemned on moral grounds while the other is justified on theological grounds. Different standards appear to exist for different characters. Though acting out of political or religious zeal, Jezebel, who represents a different culture, set of beliefs, and national identity, is condemned for her murderous actions. Elijah, who also acts out of religious and political zeal, and with whom the ancient and contemporary reader might identify, is applauded for his murderous escapade. The consequences of this contradiction in evaluation and judgment are as difficult as they are clear. The allegiances and affiliations that lead us to read in favor of Elijah do so at the expense of Jezebel. As "the other," Jezebel is dispensable and thus is sacrificed. Moreover, the analogies with our own world and its polarities that seed violence are also as difficult as they are clear. Different religious beliefs, cultural values, and ethnic national identities are at the heart of some of our deepest conflicts. These differences fuel wars, serve as grounds for assassinations, and underwrite programs of brutality against particular groups within the human community.

Violence is as insidious as it is contagious. On the heels of Ahab's execution of the Lord's prophets, Elijah's massacre of the Baal prophets is followed by Jezebel's instigation of further violence. In this intensifying cycle of violent acts, Jezebel's deeds are certainly deplorable. She corrupts the legal system, expropriates land holdings of an Israelite family, and unjustly orders the execution of a citizen. Without a doubt, she appears as the driving force behind the crown's theft of Naboth's land and his assassination. Yet, when he confronts Ahab in the dead man's vineyard, Elijah's view of the scope of violence here reaches beyond Jezebel. Indeed, it is Ahab who receives the core of the prophet's condemnation. The verbal reproach against Jezebel appears secondary and reads like an afterthought (Camp, 103-4). How is it then that Jehu identifies Jezebel at the heart of the corruption, justifying his claim upon the throne? Why is her name uttered in the confrontation before Joram and associated with whoredoms and sorceries as the basis for Jehu's overthrow of the corrupt Omride dynasty? Moreover, how is it that Jehu's coup—as fulfillment of Elijah's oracles against the dynastic lineup of four Omride kings—ends up being associated here specifically with the name of one queen, Jezebel? Jezebel receives the lion's share of the criminal credit, although she is not the primary culprit.

In Jehu's political scheme and in that of the narrator of this story, Jezebel serves as the scapegoat. The days of Omri and Ahab were likely positive memories for members of the royal court. After all, these kings established a capital at Samaria, brought stability to the government, and on the surface, conveyed an impression of domestic well-being, at least among the elite. As the tale unfolds, Jehu unseats the reigning king. At the same time, he must be careful not to curtail allegiance to the notion of kingship itself. Hence, Jehu's political revolt appears to be underwritten as a religious reform of kingship, the apostasy and sins of which he lays at the feet of Jezebel. What a sly move to blame the woman. After all, patriarchal society already positioned her as more susceptible to blame and shame. Moreover, she was a Phoenician, and thus a foreigner, an outsider. As an easy target, Jezebel becomes emblematic of the ills that the coup will address, an exponent of the evil that Jehu must right. It is not necessary to be innocent to be a victim.

Though the story leaves little left with which to reinstate Jezebel's humanity, we the readers can still make a difference in her memory. How we read and understand this text further perpetrates or resists the violence encoded there. The Bible convulses with the names of victims, some less obvious and less innocent than others. The case of Jezebel is an instance of the ease with which outsiders may be vilified. How we read and remember her not only occasions the opportunity to rehearse her misdeeds but to be mindful of the violence done to her. It also invites us to reconsider those identified as the "Jezebels" of our own world: those who suffer the violence of sustained or disproportionate blame; those who incur damaged reputations because of their gender, ethnic identity, or their status as "other"; and those who are excoriated for their wrongdoings and are deemed undeserving of forgiveness.

2 KINGS 10

In this chapter, the account of Jehu's coup continues. Having assassinated three key leaders, this candidate for king now turns his attention to the descendants of the royal family, other loyalists, and potential sympathizers of the Omride regime. Through four additional campaigns of murder and annihilation, this acknowledged revolutionary puts an end to the house of Ahab. The narrative qualifies as one of the most violent accounts in the whole Hebrew tradition. In the process, the question lurking in the minds of many readers intensifies: Was Jehu really fulfilling the word of the Lord spoken by the prophet, or was he fulfilling his own unbridled ambitions for power, no matter what the cost?

Literary Analysis

Four self-contained episodes (vv. 1-11, 12-14, 15-17, 18-27) followed by a concluding summary (vv. 28-36) structure this chapter. The four episodes continue the narration of Jehu's purge of all that is left of the house of Ahab. The concluding summary offers an evaluation of Jehu's reign. Although the four accounts of various phases of Jehu's campaign are independent units of tradition, they are united by a thematic commonality. Jehu is bent on eliminating any and all authority that the descendants or supporters of Ahab might still possess. The order of these individual accounts follows Jehu's geographical progression from Jezreel in the first episode, to his journey en route to the capital city in the second and third accounts, culminating with his arrival in Samaria in the fourth and final campaign.

In the first episode (vv. 1-11), Jehu successfully carries out his plot to exterminate all in Jezreel who were associated with the house of Ahab. In the second episode (vv. 12-14), Jehu journeys from Jezreel to Samaria. This time he assassinates some of the relatives of Ahaziah, the Judean king whom he encounters en route. As this story closes, it offers the same observation as the previous episode: no survivors are left. The third account (vv. 15-17) reports another brief incident while Jehu is still traveling to Samaria. In the company of his new colleague Jehonadab, a religious official endorsing his murderous campaign, Jehu conducts a third in the series of violent assaults against those left in the house of Ahab. Finally, having arrived in the capital city, Samaria, the fourth and final episode reports the last in this series of exterminations; this time targeting Baal worshipers in the service of Ahab. Five commands by Jehu structure and narrate the ruse that becomes the occasion for their execution (vv. 19, 20, 22, 24, 25).

Though we hear nothing more about Jehu's reign, the closing regnal summary suggests its complexity. The Deuteronomistic editor praises Jehu for abolishing all semblance of Baal worship, whereas the evaluation characteristic of these resumés ranks Jehu's overall performance before the Lord as displeasing, likening him to Jeroboam and his sins. The follow-up account of incremental losses of land may be read as evidence of this divine displeasure. As expected, the summary closes by naming Jehu's successor to the throne.

Exegetical Analysis

Jehu's Campaign against the Descendants of the House of Ahab (10:1-11)

The notation that "Ahab had seventy sons in Samaria" (v. 1), which opens this chapter, alerts us to the target of the second phase of Jehu's murderous campaign. Like other instances in the biblical narrative (Gen 46:27; Judg 8:30; 9:2), seventy as a multiple of seven suggests not the actual number but the totality of the descendants targeted. The account of two letters that follow reveals Jehu's strategy.

The first letter issues a challenge to the rulers, elders, and guardians of the sons of Ahab (v. 1). These are no lightweight addressees: the rulers govern the cities; the elders represent the people; and the guardians are the trusted sponsors, teachers, and mentors of any potential rulers of the royal family. The challenge Jehu sets before them, to "select the son of your master" as the next king, also harbors a threat (v. 3). The new appointee and those who support him must "fight for [their] master's house" (v. 3) against Jehu himself. Jehu's rhetoric not only suggests the fairness of the proposal but that the odds are on their side. They have horses, chariots, weapons, and a fortified city.

The response of the addressed officials indicates that they know what Jehu also knows. He has already overcome Israel's king, Joram; the queen mother, Jezebel; and the king of Judah, Ahaziah. In addition, he was a chief officer in Ahab's own army who was well known for the aggressive way he commandeered his chariot

(2 Kgs 9:20). Other officials have already joined forces or fallen in behind him. When the steward of the palace and the governor of the city, along with the elders and guardians, respond, they agree to pay allegiance to Jehu and support his coup. Instead of forwarding an opposing candidate for kingship, they pledge to be his servants. Instead of persisting in support of the house of Ahab, they authorize Jehu to do whatever he thinks is right. The absolute submission by these various groups of royal officials to Jehu's rise as king indicates the threat that he poses as well as the authority that he must already possess.

With the first letter, Jehu coerced their allegiance. With the second letter, he put that allegiance to the test by requiring evidence of their obedience. They must decapitate their master's sons and bring the heads to him at Jezreel the next day. Hence, the ones entrusted with the care and upbringing of the royal descendants must now murder their charges. In response to the first letter, we heard the thoughts and exchanges of those addressed. However, the narrative here relates no report of their initial responses in the face of this chilling command. As if they are stunned and numbed by what it is they must now do, the narrative conveys only their action. Concerning their thoughts or feelings, it falls silent. So they slaughter their charges, the king's sons. Preparing the evidence for transport, they put the heads in baskets. Whether to distance themselves from the crime or to keep their distance from this bloodthirsty usurper, they "sent" (v. 7) rather than brought the evidence before him. Jehu, in turn, orders that the heads be piled in two heaps outside the city entrance until the morning.

The next day, Jehu exonerates the people of Jezreel of any responsibility for the coup. Even though he takes full responsibility for the murder of the king, he does not do so for the murder of Ahab's descendants whose heads are piled high beside him. Instead, he uses the terrifying evidence of the severed heads to argue that a force far greater than himself has been at work. He then cites the word of the Lord to Elijah that prophesied the end of all Ahab's house and descendants (1 Kgs 21:21–22:24). Thus, he suggests that the mass murder was brought about by the power of God. This religious stamp of approval upon his own relentless slaughter of Ahab's house also serves to legitimize his continued campaign against those who remain. The narrative reports that subsequently, Jehu kills all those associated with the house of Ahab who remained in Jezreel. Not only the sons are targeted; leaders, close friends, and priests of Ahab's house are also fair game. Jehu earmarked for destruction everyone who might have sympathized with the overthrown royal house. The narrator's conclusion that in Jezreel, "he left him no survivor" makes clear the thoroughness with which he proceeded.

Jehu Slaughters the Kin of Ahaziah (10:12-14)

Jehu now sets his sights upon Samaria where the descendants of Ahab, with his son Joram, roster among the deceased. Passing through Beth-eked of the Shepherds en route to the capital, he meets a group of Ahaziah's relatives. When Jehu asks them straightaway about their identity, their answer is honest and twofold. They identify themselves as kin of the late King Ahaziah of Judah who have come to visit the royal princes and offspring of the queen mother, Jezebel. Evidently the relatives from Judah have not heard the news of the deadly purge of this household and beyond. Moreover, they apparently do not know that they are about to meet the same fate. Jehu is quite unreceptive and hostile to their peaceful mission. He orders that they be taken alive. Captured, these Judean emissaries are slaughtered en route to Samaria. With this act, Jehu's crusade extends its scope to include potential supporters of Ahab's house from Judah. Like the previous report, the narrator records that Jehu's murderous campaign is thorough. No survivor remains.

Jehu and Jehonadab (10:15-17)

Jehu, continuing his journey toward Samaria, has yet another encounter. As he meets up with Jehonadab, the narrative of killing is momentarily halted by the description of the meeting between Jehu and this son of Rechab. Though we have no preliminary information about Jehonadab, later tradition ties him to a group of religious loyalists passionate for a return to a more primitive form of Yahwism. Jeremiah (35:6) identifies a Jonadab (a possible variant spelling of Jehonadab) of earlier traditions as the father figure of the sectlike Rechabites. As Jehu invites Jehonadab up into his chariot, the extension of his hand is more than just an invitation to alight his chariot; it is also the beginning of a partnership whose business will be the cultic cleansing about to take place in Samaria. Jehonadab will witness and endorse the events ready to unfold in the capital against the proponents of Baal, where Jehu's bloody coup will reach its climax. Hence, in preparation for the final campaign against the last vestiges of the house of Ahab, that is, the religious fanatics of Baal, Jehu allies himself with the ardent Yahwists. As he enters Samaria, Jehonadab at his side, he kills all who have anything to do with the deceased King Ahab. When the narrator cites that all this has been done in accordance with the word of the Lord spoken to Elijah, it is unclear whether this is a pathetic attempt to justify such unchecked wrath or an ironic reminder of Jehu's own earlier justification for his murderous antics.

Cultic Cleansing in Samaria (10:18-27)

The final scenario, narrating the calamitous climax of Jehu's coup, unfolds across five commands (vv. 19, 20, 22, 23, 25). As in the case of the massacre of Ahab's sons (vv. 1-11), he enlists others to do his bidding by means of deception. His first order commands "all the people" (v. 18) to assemble the followers of Baal, with the promise that he himself will offer service to Baal that will surpass anything that Ahab did. His summons is as comprehensive as it is complete. They are to gather the prophets of Baal, the worshipers of Baal, and the priests of Baal. Moreover, they are to be certain that "none be missing" (v. 19) when the throng of Baalists has been assembled. A word play enclosing the narrative description of the first command discloses Jehu's ruse. In the opening of the command to assemble all the Baalists, Jehu professes "to serve" (*'abad*) Baal, but the narrator's concluding summary reveals that in actuality he intends "to destroy" (*'abad*) the worshipers of Baal (v. 19).

With the second command (v. 20), Jehu orders that the service to Baal commence. It is clear that he has public support, or at least public compliance, for his newly claimed position of power. Whether out of allegiance or fear, the populace evidently responds to his command. Having assembled all those as he ordered, Baal's temple is described as "wall-to-wall" people (v. 21).

Next, he speaks to the "keeper of the wardrobe," ordering him to provide appropriate attire for those assembled. Immediately, this overseer of the ritual clothing responds and cultic garments are "brought out" for the assembled. Unbeknownst to them, as these participants are vested for the spectacular cultic undertaking, they are literally "dressed to kill."

Now Jehu turns his attention to the Baal loyalists assembled and issues a fourth command specifically to them (v. 23). He orders that they conduct their own cultic cleansing within their assembly. They are to be certain that no Yahwist infidel mars their assembled ranks. Once it is sure that no worshiper of the Lord is among them, the sacrifice and offering begins.

Finally, having officiated over the sacrifice inside the temple precincts, Jehu now officiates over another sacrifice outside these sanctuary confines. He orders his eighty men assembled outside to destroy the worshipers assembled within (v. 25). Under the threat of death themselves, they dare not allow anyone escape. The need to cooperate as completely as possible under such circumstances compels these executioners. They not only destroy all the Baalists, but also bring out the pillar of Baal and demolish it. They even destroy the temple itself. The narrator's summary renders the remaining rubble a "latrine to this day," indicating both the completeness of the destruction of the site as well as the utter assault to its identity.

The Summary of Jehu's Reign (10:28-36)

While we have a rather extended account of the seven phases of Jehu's violent coup to overthrow the house of Ahab in establishing himself as Israel's ruler (2 Kgs 9–10), we have no account of his actual tenure as king. Instead, a regnal summary closes the chapter. On the one hand, the narrator does briefly rubber-stamp (v. 28) what Jehu did specifically in regard to the house of Ahab. Jehu's activities, in putting an end to Ahab's line, are recorded as allied with what the Lord deems "right," and in accordance with that which constituted the divine heart. On the other hand, this evaluation is undercut by the analysis that precedes and follows it. In the opening assessment and again immediately following the commendation of his destruction of Ahab's house, Jehu is judged as being like Jeroboam. Reference is made specifically in regard to Jehu's maintenance of the high places Jeroboam established at Dan and Bethel. Such an indictment casts a cloud of suspicion over Jehu's cultic cleansing of Samaria. Was it politically motivated rather than a true religious gesture? Moreover, is Jehu, like Jeroboam, indicted specifically because he too caused Israel to sin?

The second part of this summary draws even further suspicions around the brief positive appraisal of Jehu. It reports the gradual loss of territory in the north and attributes this specifically to work of the Lord. The transfer of Gilead and Bashan to Hazael, the powerful Syrian king, was an extremely significant loss for both economic and political reasons. The agricultural riches of these territories provided surplus for commerce. In addition, the loss of lands east of the Jordan could only have diminished Israel's domestic security in relation to the imposing international forces to the north and east. Most significantly, the loss of land was a visible and palpable sign of God's disfavor as well as a threat to the covenant relationship. Land and descendants were the gift and sign of the covenant. Hence, this summary of Jehu's reign lays bare many unanswered questions about his activities. Indeed, the end of Ahab's house was according to divine plan, but were Jehu's motives and strategies to bring about that end contrary to divine ways?

The regnal summary ends without answering these and other questions about this king. Instead, it leaves the brief positive appraisal contested. Perhaps the only clear and reliable aspect of this resumé is the characteristic manner in which it concludes. It indicates that Jehu has reigned twenty-eight years and names his son, Jehoahaz, as successor to the throne.

Theological and Ethical Analysis

Without a doubt, this is a difficult text. Jehu practices a kind of relentless violence until his mission is accomplished. Innocent offspring are beheaded. Those who speak honestly and come peacefully are taken alive then slaughtered, and docile worshipers of another persuasion are herded together, double-crossed, and executed. In the process, violence is given free rein. The circle of those brought into the ring of brutality increases. Growing numbers of persons are voluntarily or involuntarily enlisted as participants in the murderous revolt against their fellow citizens. Caregivers must abandon their nurturing instincts and slay the very ones they have been attending. Those accompanying Jehu on the road to Samaria must become on-the-spot executioners of the Judean emissaries. Under threat to their own lives, officers of this new regime are required to execute hordes of unsuspecting attendees at a religious service. As if the account of carnage is not difficult enough, the record is further complicated by the theological underpinnings. God and the divine word are frequently enlisted as the endorsement for such savagery.

Under this unsettling narrative cloud only a few certainties reside. The word of the Lord as spoken through the prophet Elijah did forecast the end of the house of Ahab. Moreover, Jehu was the anointed of God to bring about the fulfillment of this word. Herein lies the difficulty. Does the achievement of even the greatest good justify such horrific violence as these means? Does authorization as divine instrument license one to wield any kind of authority? The narrator seems to think so. He praises Jehu for ridding the country of Baal and for wiping out the house of Ahab.

Later biblical writers will denounce Jehu's bloodshed (Hos 1:4). Indeed, the current state of our world warrants that we resist the narrator and render a different assessment. At this juncture in human history, stories that enlist a religious stamp of approval upon vile and relentless savagery can only be read as a warning. They challenge us to confront the claims we make about our God, especially when they stand over and against the faith claims of other traditions. Such tales prompt us to address our denial about our own similar capacity for such violence. They awaken us to the catastrophe that always reigns when we humans fail to recognize our limitations in understanding divine will. Stories about violence carried out in the name of God summon caution. They become the occasion to acknowledge humbly that our own self-interests are often enmeshed with religious causes. Such traditions invite us to consider that being a revolutionary in our violent world may mean being nonviolent. Finally, they chasten us to remember that even when we seek to accomplish God's will in our causes and commitments, our ways are not always God's ways.

2 KINGS 11

The crisis of the northern kingdom inevitably spilled over into the south. As Jehu executed the remaining sons of Ahab's royal house, Athaliah, granddaughter of Omri and queen mother of the southern kingdom by intermarriage, set about exterminating all the royal descendants of the deceased Ahaziah, Judah's former king. Though the actions ring similar, the consequences for the south are more dire. Athaliah threatens the continuation of the Davidic line. An intervention by a temple priest undercuts the queen's scheme and accomplishes the ascension of Joash, son of Ahaziah, to the throne.

Literary Analysis

Chapter 11 reads as an extended parenthesis juxtaposed between the preceding account of Jehu's revolt and subsequent reign (chaps. 9–10) and the account of Joash's tenure as king in Judah (chap. 12). It records events unfolding in Judah during a seven-year interim when they were without a king, events simultaneous with Jehu's early kingship in Israel.

Two related stories narrate the events of this liminal time (vv. 1-3 and 4-20) and negotiate a reversal. The chapter opens with the queen mother ruling in Judah, but she will be replaced at its close by a child king. The plot of the first story erupts from a crisis brought about by the news of the death of Judah's king, Ahaziah, son of Athaliah, the queen mother during Jehu's revolt. Athaliah assumes leadership and retaliates by ordering the execution of all the remaining royal family, threatening the continuation of the line of David. The crisis is quickly resolved when

Jehosheba, King Joram's daughter, seizes one of Ahaziah's infant sons and hides him.

The circumstance of the deceased Ahaziah's hidden offspring forms the background for the second related story, the reclaiming of the throne for the Davidic heir (vv. 4-21). Through the actions and orders of a temple priest, Jehoiada, the threat to the Davidic line is resolved. First, Jehoiada makes the young king-to-be's whereabouts known to captains, who are sworn to secrecy (v. 4). Next, he gives elaborately detailed orders for them to secure the royal descendant's safety (vv. 5-9). Finally, Jehoiada himself publicly carries out the coronation of the new king (v. 10-12), and orders Athaliah's execution outside the temple precincts (v. 15-16). A citation that Jehoash, the newly crowned ruler, began his reign when he was seven years old draws an end both to the seven-year interim when no king reigned in Judah, as well as to the chapter (v. 21).

Exegetical Analysis

Athaliah Rules Judah (11:1-3)

Though we have known about Jehu's murder of Judah's king, Ahaziah, for some time (2 Kgs 9:27), we do not know about the events that unfold in Judah on the heels of his death. We first hear Queen Mother Athaliah's reaction. Athaliah is the daughter of Ahab who, through an arranged marriage, became the wife of the Judean king, Jehoram, Ahaziah's father (8:16, 25). Evidently equipped to do so, she sets about exterminating all the remaining members of the royal family. Though her actions parallel Jehu's slaughter of all of Ahab's descendants, the reasons propelling her murderous order likely do not. On the motive instigating her deadly campaign, the narrative is silent. Some suppose that fidelity to her father Ahab's house and the worship of the Baals sets her on a track to end all loyalists of Yahwism, so that she attempts to exterminate everyone associated with the line of David. However, nothing in the text grounds the conjecture that Athaliah was a Baalist. The text's emphasis upon her status as the slain king's mother suggests a more likely motive. The senseless loss of a son in battle, coupled with the savagery of war as conducted by Jehu, is enough to push a mother over the brink of grief-filled insanity. If her son must die, so too must all potential heirs to his throne.

The crisis constructed by this deadly campaign is quickly resolved. Another woman counteracts Athaliah's vengeful grief. Jehosheba, the sister of Ahaziah, seizes one of the youngest of the dead king's children. Like Moses' audacious mother (Exod 2:2), Jehosheba schemes a daring plan to protect the child by hiding him. Thus, the danger posed to the Davidic line by the rage of one woman is undercut and redirected by the daring act of another woman. With the life of the child secured, this story serves as a prelude to the next account where his ascent to the throne is accomplished.

Jehoiada Anoints Joash King of Judah (11:4-21)

A temple priest, Jehoiada, husband of Jehosheba, orchestrates the dethronement of Athaliah and the coronation of the new king. A series of actions and commands by this religious official brings about the shift and structures the narrative. First, he must enlist the involvement of others who hold a similar commitment to restore the Davidic line. He is able to make a binding agreement with the Carites and the guards, putting them under oath before he reveals to them the secret existence of Joash, the son of Ahaziah. Jehoiada's success indicates that commitment and accountability exist among some members of the Judean community (v. 4). Though the Carites' origin and identity is uncertain, they were most likely an elite group, perhaps even a cadre, of influential mercenaries. The guards are royal employees and probably are directly responsible to Athaliah's forces. Hence, their promise of secrecy to Jehoiada's plan, and to that of the boy king's existence, is not without personal danger.

Next, Jehoiada gives orders to ensure the security of the boy (vv. 5-9). The Hebrew here is difficult and since we know little about the configuration of the capital city and the makeup of its military guard, these instructions remain obscure. What seems likely is that Jehoiada assigned at least one-third of the palace guards the responsibility to shield and protect the young king. The remaining two-thirds are subdivided to cover all other duties in and around the palace and temple. This high level of security suggests the risk to both those providing security and to the young king if he is discovered.

Now Jehoiada invests the guards' activity with religious significance. He provides the swords and shields of King David to the captains of these groups. The shields were no doubt etched with some insignia representing the monarchy of that cherished time. Such emblematic military provisions make the guards warriors for the restoration of the Davidic line. Hence, their insurrectionist activities are inscribed with religious zeal.

After seven years, the circle of protection surrounding the young king comes to fruition. Under intense security, Jehoiada commences the coronation. He brings the young child forward to what was probably a carefully selected and scrutinized public. He puts the crown on the child's head and a covenant in his hands. It is easy to imagine that this was likely some charter document that rehearsed the character of the Davidic covenant (Deut 17:18-19) and the king's responsibilities therein. In response, those in attendance show their approval and acceptance of this new ruler with acclamation and action. They "proclaimed him king," "anointed him," and "clapped their hands" (v. 12). When their final proclamation goes up it resounds, "Long live the king!" (v. 12) and attracts the attention of Queen Athaliah, who hears all the noise.

Athaliah's assessment of the assembly is as abrupt as her arrival at the formal gathering. Her cry, "Treason! Treason!" (v. 14) occasions another order from Jehoiada. He commands that she and anyone affiliated with her be put to death. However, out of respect for the Lord's house, her execution does not take place within the vicinity of the temple. Rather, she is taken out the entrance to the king's house. Even her exit functions to discredit her. She is led out through the horses' entrance to the king's house and there on the outskirts of the royal residence her life is ended (v. 16).

The coronation of the new king, Joash, is not the end of Jehoiada's responsibilities. Now attention is turned to the relationship between the Davidic line and the covenant. As priest, he officiates a renewal of the covenant between the king and the

Lord, and between the king and the people, highlighting the ruler's covenantal role as vice-regent. The king is bound to mediate between God and the people and the people and God. In a display of impassioned fidelity to this renewed covenant, the people respond by destroying all semblances of Baal in and around the house of the Lord. Baal's temple, altars, and images, as well as Mattan, a Baal priest, are destroyed. As if to curb any resistance or retaliation among Athaliah's loyalists, Jehoiada posts guards over the house of the Lord. Then, in the company of the guards, captains, Carites, and all the people, the new king is paraded from the house of the Lord to his palace throne. The narrative of the events closes with the stark comparison of the rejoicing that is surrounding the ascent of the new king to the silence in the city that coincides with Athaliah's death.

The end of this account builds anticipation for an upcoming story. In typical Deuteronomistic fashion, the record notes that, "Jehoash [an alternative spelling of Joash] was seven years old when he began to reign" (v. 21). *Began* is the operative word here, suggesting that as this chapter comes to a close, the account of Jehoash's kingship still lies ahead.

Theological and Ethical Analysis

Once again, good appears to have triumphed over evil in the familiar Deuteronomistic manner. Athaliah's ruthless attempt to end the Davidic royal line has been thwarted. Her brief stint as queen ruler seems a mere aberration. Like other scoundrels attempting to disrupt the legitimate line of kings and their Yahwistic endorsement, she is punished by what was assumed a justifiable execution. At the same time, the temple priest, Jehoiada, renews the Lord's covenant with the new king and the people. All semblances of Baal and the associated Baalistic practices that desecrated the Yahwism of the temple are destroyed. A legitimate Davidic descendant is back on the throne and it appears that the kingdom of Judah is back on track. But appearances can be deceiving.

At times, there is more to be gained from the biblical tradition than unfolds on the surface level of the story or as controlled by the narrator. Interpretation that informs the ethics surrounding our human relations often warrants that we pay attention elsewhere in these tales. Much is to be learned not only from those characters and the dynamics of story that are featured, but also from those that are not.

In this account, the plot turns upon the rise of the boy Joash to the crown by a parade of actions and commands of the temple priest, Jehoiada. Athaliah, the queen mother, poses only a threat to this outcome when, upon the news of her own son Ahaziah's death, she orders the slaying of all royal offspring. The initial crisis is quickly resolved by setting one woman's actions against another. Athaliah, who is bent upon slaying the children, is undercut by the actions of Jehosheba, who is motivated to save one child. The suggested odds at which these women work, however, is quite secondary to the real plot of the story. Opposed in their plans, they are but a prelude to the real action—Jehoiada's cunning and commands that bring about the rise of a new king. It is easy to read past the unnarrated contrast between these two women and their commitments. After all, their opposition is not the real point of the story. Even though their opposing interventions in regard to the royal offspring make the upcoming story possible, they have no real place in the tale. Athaliah's role ends in execution outside the royal precincts and no further mention of Jehosheba is made once Jehoiada, her husband, enters the scene. Though their contrasting overtures provide a basis upon which a plotline is built, the story has no place for them. Their opposing efforts are but literary props upon which the story of real importance is built—the story of a king's rise to power by means of a powerful priest and his actions.

Such a configuration of women biblical characters in the service of stories about important kings and powerful patriarchs is not unique here, but echoes across the biblical narrative. Two mothers in strife over the life of a child before Solomon serve to illuminate his wisdom (1 Kgs 3:16-28). Two starving mothers who had agreed to eat their children argue over the remaining child in a tale illuminating a controversy between the prophet Elisha and King Jehoram (2 Kgs 6:24-33). The story of struggle between the ancestor Sarah and her servant girl Hagar works in the service of the dominant plot, God's promise of descendants to the featured patriarch Abraham (Gen 16:1-16; 21:1-21). Even the more thickly drawn characters of Rachel and Leah, who end up as opposing characters, do so in a story where their struggles are subsidiary to the story and focalization of the real protagonist, the patriarch Jacob (Gen 29–35).

In a patriarchal milieu, the actions of women—from a good woman who rescues children to a slave girl who grieves over a dying child—remain secondary to the important story narrating the actions of powerful men. From a queen mother on a throne to harlots before a king, female characters end up easily discarded or ignored. These social and political forces with their potential to diminish or eclipse women, or put them at cross-purposes, are not confined to the biblical narrative. As the biblical text writhes with stories where an ethos of dominating power leads to the erasure of those who do not belong to the dominant gender or culture, so too does our own world. Interrogating and musing with the biblical text on this score may lead us to grasp the challenge before us in our own time.

How is it that stories of women in conflict with one another end up making kings, prophets, priests, and patriarchs look good? Why are stories about women often only an occasion to spotlight the virtue, glory, or fame of a powerful man? Does the endurance of hierarchical forms of governance or even patriarchy itself necessitate that women remain invisible? Is it necessary for the maintenance of the ethos of power and domination that women be portrayed at cross-purposes? To put it another way, do women working together as agents in their own right, acting for their own purposes, pose the most fundamental threat to upsetting and dismantling patriarchy and all its associated forms of domination?

2 KINGS 12

Following the previous chapter's digression from the lockstep reporting on the reign of individual kings, this chapter resumes the characteristic format. No mention is made of Queen Athaliah.

Rather, the reign of Judah's newly crowned king, Jehoash, is situated only in reference to the reign of the Israelite king, Jehu. The central role that the temple priest, Jehoiada, played in accomplishing the succession of this child king continues throughout Jehoash's career. Hence, it is no surprise that the report summarizing the new king's accomplishments fixes upon the temple and its renovations.

Literary Analysis

Two summaries introduce and conclude the narrative account of King Jehoash's reign (vv. 1-3, 19-21). In stereotypical fashion, the opening summary (vv. 1-3) offers further remarks about the king's parentage, identifies the ruler in the north, and offers a positive evaluation of the southern reign. This is quickly qualified by a negative evaluation of the people and their continual apostasy. The concluding summary (vv. 19-21) further undercuts the positive assessment of this king. In reporting the circumstances of Jehoash's death and burial, it discloses the murderous plot initiated by his own servants that brought about his end.

Enclosed between these two regnal bookends are two reports narrating the highlights of Jehoash's rule (vv. 4-16, 17-18). Both stories focus upon the temple, but in different ways, creating an ironic contrast. In the first story, Jehoash must instigate a new plan for the collection of funds for the temple repairs, because the priests seem to be abusing the current system (vv. 4-16). In the second story, Jehoash himself raids the temple treasury for votive gifts and goods amassed by previous kings in his effort to quell the threat of invasion by Hazael, king of Aram (vv. 17-18).

Exegetical Analysis

Introduction to the Reign of Jehoash (12:1-3)

The account of the newly crowned Jehoash commences with the characteristic regnal introduction. Elements typical of these opening summaries form the familiar format. Jehoash's tenure as king is synchronized with the seventh year of the Israelite ruler, Jehu. The length of time that the new Judaite king reigns is recorded as forty years. Just before the expected evaluation of his reign before the Lord, his mother is identified. Instead of mentioning Athaliah, the queen mother who ruled in the interim, before king Jehoash and about whom the narrative is silent, Zibiah of Beer-sheba is named as the king's mother. Although it is not completely uncharacteristic for the king's mother to be identified, it is certainly less frequent. Perhaps her identification is intended to assure the reader that in place of the objectionable Athaliah a new queen mother now resides in Judah. Finally, this formulaic introduction to the reign of Jehoash offers the evaluation of the king. Though he is assessed as doing "what was right in the sight of the LORD," the praise seems not to belong to him (v. 2). Rather, the record accords Jehoiada full credit for the positive favor the king enjoys before God.

Still, despite the watchful eye of a temple priest, the people are sacrificing and making offerings on the high places. This draws connections backward and forward in the narrative of kings, raising a question mark about the positive assessment of Jehoash. On the one hand, the notation anticipates the upcoming reign of Josiah, who will centralize cult and worship in Jerusalem (2 Kgs 22:3-7) and put an end to local shrines. On the other hand, the reference echoes the earlier account of Solomon when the people were still frequenting the high places, as did the king himself (1 Kgs 3:1-3). Across these traditions, each king's actual influence upon worship appears very limited. Even now, with a refurbishing of the temple, the people still offer at the local shrines. That kings would serve to mediate God to the people remains a dimming hope for the future.

Jehoash's Temple Renovations (12:4-16)

Jehoash, who was hidden and raised in the temple as a youngster, makes its renovation the heart of his royal career. The narrative report on this project is structured and subdivided by the commands of this king. First, Jehoash issues a twofold order instructing the priests to collect money and with it finance repairs on the house of the Lord (vv. 4-5). Hence, they are to be the recipients of donations and offerings as well as the financiers of this

313

large-scale operation. We can surmise from Jehoash's order that the temple of Solomon has fallen into disrepair over the years. His directives to the priests also distinguish between the money collected from two different sources: assessments of individuals and voluntary offerings. The money assessed each person suggests some collection procedure similar to the one narrated in Lev 27: 1-8. There a person's religious contribution in silver was determined with respect to their age and gender. In addition, Jehoash expected voluntary offerings from any individuals and in any amount. Exactly when Jehoash gave this order to the priests is not stated. However, the narrative reports an unexpected outcome in the twenty-third year of Jehoash's reign. It records that no repairs had yet been undertaken, though presumably the money had been collected.

The failure of this first system prompts Jehoash to create a second one for the priests to monitor (v. 7). First, he summons Jehoiada, who presumably still plays a central role in his life. Next, the king asks them directly why no repairs on the temple have taken place. Before they can reply, he issues an order that indirectly answers his own question. He forbids them to accept any more donations, implying a charge of corruption. Perhaps because their fraud is so blatant, the priests offer no objection or defense to the king. Instead, they consent to a new plan (v. 8).

What follows is a narrative description of the king's new procedure for financing the renovation. According to this scheme, Jehoiada puts a hole in a chest that is set beside the altar on the right, as one comes into the temple. The description gives rise to some confusion as there was no altar immediately inside a doorway in the Solomonic plan of the temple. However, the plan itself is clear. The priests are not completely excused of responsibility. Several of the temple priests are required to guard the chest as people come and place their offerings in it. When the chest is full, the king's own secretary and a high priest are to count the money, place it in bags for weighing, and then hand it over to the supervisors. These trustworthy foremen are then responsible for paying the carpenters, builders, masons, and stonecutters. The money was also to be used to buy building materials—timber and quarried stone—whatever was needed for the renovations. Hence, oversight of the money will be a joint affair of both the crown and the temple.

Two follow-up notes fill out the record on this temple makeover. First, none of the monies gathered were to be used in conjunction with any work done on the priceless sacred vessels, whether for reasons of cultic observances or out of respect for the previous kings who had deposited the vessels there. The collected funds were only for the workers on the temple itself. Second, though the priests' earlier responsibility for managing the finances for this project has been modified, the king's new plan here still assures that priestly support has not been reduced. The monies received from sin and guilt offerings are not to go for the temple repairs, or even to be brought into the house of the Lord. Instead, they are designated solely as support for the livelihood of the priests. Hence, Jehoash initiates a plan to finance the temple project that is equitable as well as collegial, with a system of checks and balances.

Hazael's Threat (12:17-18)

A second narrative rounds out the report of Jehoash's reign. In a brief account following up his grand plan, the king himself undermines his one recorded accomplishment, the renovation of the temple. Hazael of Aram is on the move and has reportedly already attacked the north during Jehu's final days (2 Kgs 10:32-33). Now he poses a threat to Judah and the capital city, Jerusalem. The invader has moved as far as the Philistine city of Gath, on the Mediterranean coast, and has captured it. In his next campaign, Jerusalem is his intended target. The words of Elisha the prophet, who anticipated this bloody assault years earlier, echo here (2 Kgs 8:12). Any impression that the order and sense of stability of earlier Solomonic times has been reinstated because of Jehoash's temple activities quickly dissipates.

In a highly ironic shift, Jehoash's determination to restore the temple will now be supplanted by his determination to preserve Jerusalem against the threat of invasion. To placate the approaching enemy and offset Hazael's attack, Jehoash ransacks the very temple he has worked to repair. The votive gifts of his royal ancestors—Jehoshaphat, Jehoram, and Ahaziah—are stripped from the Lord's house to buy Jerusalem's security. Jehoash raids the treasures of the house of the Lord to pay tribute to a different lord.

The Death of Joash (12:19-21)

Apparently, the threat to Joash's (again, the alternate spelling appears) rule was not only from the outside. In a characteristic summary recording the king's death, we are afforded some unanticipated information. Relations within the kingdom itself have gone awry. A conspiracy by Joash's own servants brings about his end. He is murdered by two of his men.

The story of rescue and protection of the infant Joash recalls the birth stories of others who become great leaders. Hopes surrounded Joash as the new king who would restore order to the nation and fidelity to the Lord. That Joash's reign was marked by his work on the temple seemed to encourage such expectations. However, though the narrator offers no concluding assessment here of the events that took place, the nature of Joash's death indicts him. The king who restored the temple is also responsible for stripping it of its treasures. Hence, the one who was rescued at birth from the threat of death is, in the end, put to death by his own men. This unexpected outcome draws to a close with the expected conclusion. Joash is buried in the city of David among his ancestors, and his son, Amaziah, succeeds him.

Theological and Ethical Analysis

Two instructive lessons arise from the ambiguity surrounding Joash's reign. Rescued as an infant, Joash's coronation enkindled hope for the renewal of a nation finally free from the encumbering influences of the northern Omride dynasty. With the earlier threat to the Davidic line having been quelled, Joash could take up his role as legitimate heir to the throne and to the promises of the Davidic covenant. That the report of his reign is characterized almost solely by temple restoration urges optimism. His determination to build despite the priests' abuse of funds suggests his piety. His establishment of an alternative policy for funding the project indicates his sense of righteousness and justice. That the repairs were finally carried out attests to his steadfastness. He also made sure that laborers were paid (vv. 11, 12, 14), a sign of his fair-mindedness. Finally, though the priests had initially undercut his plan by their fiscal mismanagement, he maintained policies that attended to their needs, thus demonstrating his responsibility. Proceeds from sin and guilt offerings continued to support these temple officials.

By all appearances, the report of Joash's reign implies a king committed to virtue, obedience, and fidelity to the covenant. However, tenacity of character and loyalty to commitments are sometimes best assessed when confronted with crisis. The threat of Hazael's assault on Jerusalem is the litmus test as to whether or not Joash's public persona of virtue and covenant fidelity was founded upon a deep interiority and attention to the Lord or not. His rapid willingness to trade all of the temple treasures for security lays bare where his real trust lies. Such crises in life confront us as well with the depth or shallowness of our own virtue and the steadfastness, or lack thereof, for our own commitments.

Finally, when Joash transfers responsibility for the collection of funds from the priests it is because of their mismanagement. Though little is said, the very removal of their fiscal responsibility indirectly indicts them for an abuse of temple funds. Yet, so often in human relations, the very weaknesses that we are quick to recognize or criticize in others is the very one to which we are often most susceptible. When confronted with the crisis of Syria's military campaign against the capital, Joash robs the temple of its treasures in order to buy security for Judah. Such lessons should serve as warnings to us. When we are drawn to correct or condemn another for his or her actions, the assessment and correction might very well be leveled first upon ourselves.

2 KINGS 13

Chapter 13 continues the procession-like account of Israel's kings, synchronized with Judah's rulers. Additionally, it narrates the persistent threat that Hazael of Aram poses to Israel. However, amid this familiarity there are hints within the chapter suggesting a shift in the characteristic parade of events. Israel's amicable relations with Judah are to end soon, and the nation's ability to resist the attacks of Aram will not continue indefinitely. The death of Elisha the prophet, the centerpiece of the chapter, also indicates further that change is on the horizon; but the tensions that surface in this report and the changes that they anticipate do not come to resolution until the upcoming chapters.

Literary Analysis

The literary pattern of this chapter unfolds in three parts. In part one, two separate accounts report on the reigns of the second and third kings in the line of Jehu: Jehoahaz (vv. 1-9) and Joash (vv. 10-13). In conjunction with the characteristic features of the first king's resumé, we also hear of Jehoahaz's struggle with the Aramaens and how the Lord rescues Israel. However, the repeated apostasies of Israel eventually reduce the forces of Jehoahaz to impotency, rendering Israel an easy target for future attacks. The report on Joash's reign that follows is much briefer and more characteristically formulaic. The notation describing "the might" with which he fought Amaziah, king of Judah, is the only distinguishing feature in this otherwise stereotypical passage (v. 8). The reader must wait until the next chapter for a report of that confrontation (14:8-14). Though the narrative summaries of these kings' tenure differ in length, they are united by the theological assessment each receives. Like their royal ancestor Jeroboam, son of Nebat, both do what is displeasing in the sight of the Lord.

In the closing part of the chapter, two subsequent accounts add to and amend the two opening regnal reports (vv. 22-23, 24-25). In both instances the looming threat of Aram's oppression is addressed. First, Jehoahaz's reign, though persistently threatened by Hazael, is said to be rescued by the compassion of the Lord (vv. 22-23). In the next report, an emendation to the earlier summary of Joash's reign now reports that this king was also able to resist Hazael not only once, but three times. He was even able to recover some of the captured Israelite cities that were lost under his father Jehoahaz. However, the statement that he was victorious three more times signals that the resistance may be limited by time. The material between the opening (vv. 1-9, 10-13) and closing reports (vv. 22-23, 24-25) on these two kings may offer an explanation.

Nestled between the parallel reports on these two kings resides the account of the final deeds and death of the prophet Elisha. First, King Joash, hearing word of his illness, hurries to visit the prophet. Elisha orders the king to participate in two symbolic actions. Each action specifically addresses the impending crisis cultivated by Aram's threat. In the first instance, when the king appears to comply completely, the defeat of Aram at Aphek is foreshadowed. In the second instance, when the king's action falls short, Elisha foretells that Israel will be able to resist Aram only three more times.

The account then depicts the end of the life of Elisha. His death and burial notice occasion one final event. A marauding band of Moabites forces those burying a corpse to hurry, tossing the body into Elisha's grave. When the corpse touches the bones of the buried prophet the dead man is restored to life, recalling one last time the power behind the prophet in both life and death.

Exegetical Analysis

The Reign of Jehoahaz in Israel (13:1-9)

King Jehoahaz becomes the second in the line of Jehu to ascend the throne. He succeeds his father and reigns for seventeen years simultaneously with the kingship of Joash, son of Ahaziah, in Judah. Immediately he is assessed with the formula that has become almost standard for the northern kings. Like his predecessors, Jehoahaz "did what was evil in the sight of the LORD," (v. 2), an evil allied with the sinfulness of Jeroboam. Each time this formulaic evaluation occurs, we are reminded of the persistent objection to worship sites in the north as alternatives to the temple in Jerusalem. Moreover, that Israel is caused to sin by the king's ongoing maintenance of these cultic shrines aggravates the iniquities.

The account of Jehoahaz's royal activities is brief considering the seventeen years that he was king. Two themes dominate the description that ensues. Jehoahaz persistently draws Israel away from fidelity to Yahweh, and Aram, headed up first by Hazael and then by his son Ben-hadad, continues to invade and oppress the northern nation. These two conditions are not unrelated in the report on this king and his reign.

An account standardized by a familiar Deuteronomistic four-fold framework—sin, punishment, repentance, and rescue—structures the narrative of Jehoahaz's repeated sinfulness. The king and Israel sin not only by the maintenance of the worship at northern shrines, but also in regard to more explicit practices of apostasy. The sacred pole, also referred to here as the Asherah, is maintained in Samaria, dramatizing the consistently compromised state of Yahwism. God responds with punishment in the form of the Aramaeans' invasion. That the Lord handed them over repeatedly suggests that their sin and this cycle were also constantly repeated (v. 3). In a fashion uncharacteristic of other northern kings, Jehoahaz turns and beseeches the Lord (v. 4). This overture to God on the part of the king occasions an immediate rescue. Seeing their affliction, God responds by sending a savior. In the book of Judges, where the cycle of sin, punishment, repentance, and rescue is also characteristic, the savior is typically a new judge. In contrast, here the identity or nature of the savior remains unspecified. Some have assumed it to be another foreign power, Elisha, or even the king himself. However, the lack of specification draws attention away from the savior and toward the fact that God responds to the king's request with salvation. With divine intervention, the Israelites escape from Aram and continue to live in their own homes. Hence, Israel's relation to Yahweh was determinative of Israel's well-being at home and abroad. Still, the account records that Israel continued to sin, suggesting that the cycle repeated itself over and over again. Though God's rescue continues to preserve Israel, with each sinful escapade the nation incurs loss. At the conclusion of this brief report, though still surviving Aram's incursions, Jehoahaz and his forces have been reduced to the brink of impotency (v. 7). No further entreaty for the Lord's help sounds from this king, and no sign of another savior appears on the horizon. As the file closes on Jehoahaz, the summary reports what we expect. The rest of his acts are recorded in the Annals of the Kings of Israel. At his death, Jehoahaz is buried in Samaria with his ancestors. Perhaps his son, Joash, who succeeds him, will function as the Lord's instrument of rescue in the future.

The Reign of Jehoash in Israel (13:10-13)

Jehoash, son of Jehoahaz, also reigns during the time of Joash in Judah. There is little that is distinctive about his sixteen-year tenure recorded in this regnal summary. Like his father and most of the other northern kings, he too is considered sinful for continuing the cultic separatism that stems back to Jeroboam's time. He, too, is criticized not only for his own sinfulness but also for causing Israel to sin. It was the enduring responsibility of these kings for the people's fidelity to the Lord that made this perpetual compromise of Yahwistic faith so egregious.

Though the summary of Jehoash's reign ends with the usual citation of his death and burial in Samaria with his ancestors, other stories about this ruler will follow (vv. 14-19, 24-25; 2 Kgs 14:8-14, 15-16). The interspersion of traditions about Jehoash need not be viewed as disorder in the record but rather as an effective literary strategy. On the one hand, Jehoash's regnal summary here, following that of his father Jehoahaz, maintains the character of historical progression and chronology across reports. On the other hand, this interlacing of upcoming accounts with other reports regarding Jehoash's activities crafts a sense of simultaneity with other unfolding events. Interwoven within this standard regnal summary is an element that anticipates and foreshadows things to come. The mention of the "might with which he fought against King Amaziah, King of Judah" (v. 12) not only raises expectations that there will be a conflict between Israel and Judah (2 Kgs 14:8-14); it also suggests that Jehoash restores the Israelite militia that had been so depleted under his father, Jehoahaz (v. 7). By implication, the threat of Aram's forces must have been curbed by Israel in order for it to be able to turn its hostilities toward Judah. The upcoming story of Jehoash's encounter with Elisha the prophet will pave the way for the confrontation. A report of the victory of Jehoash and his forces over Aram (vv. 24-25) will follow.

Death of Elisha (13:14-21)

On the heels of the summaries of these two successors in the Jehu dynasty comes the report on the events of Elisha's life leading up to his death. As if afforded a clip of the reign of King Joash (an alternative spelling for Jehoash), we hear that the prophet has fallen fatally ill and the king is rushing to visit him. Joash's expression of grief and his cry "My father, my father! The chariots of Israel and its horsemen!" (v. 14) not only echoes Elisha's exclamation when Elijah was about to leave him (2 Kgs 2:12), but also testifies to the loss and reverence with which he now regards Elisha. The meaning of the acclamation remains unclear. Here it resounds as a conventional expression of the king's desperation and fear at facing the future without the power and presence of the one departing. As if this is the case, the prophet responds accordingly.

With two signs, Elisha, despite his impending death, offers the king assurance. First, he issues a series of orders to Joash: "Take a bow and arrows"; "Draw the bow"; "Open the window eastward"; and "Shoot," to which the king correspondingly responds (vv. 15-17). In the course of the exchanges the prophet covers the hands of the king with his own hands as a sign of transmission of power (v. 16). Having completed all that he was commanded to do, the king receives the interpretation of the deed that serves as prophetic pronouncement. The Lord will give the king victory over Aram, which is due east of Israel at Aphek.

Next, the prophet instructs the king to take the arrows, which he previously identified as the Lord's (v. 17), and strike the ground. This second sign is more difficult to understand. Perhaps the gesture signals victory over the stricken ground. Though the king follows the prophet's order, his threefold strike was not enough for the prophet. Elisha chides him for not continuing to strike the ground with the arrow. In conjunction with this enigmatic gesture, the prophet proclaims that although Israel will be successful before Aram, its number of victories over this enemy will be limited to three (v.19).

A brief nondescript note follows, reporting on the death and burial of the prophet Elisha. However, an unrelated set of circumstances unfolds on the heels of this announcement. Apparently, bands of wandering Moabites used to invade Israel in the spring season each year. During the burial of some individual, these invaders were spotted. As those burying the dead man hurried to dispose of his corpse, they threw him into Elisha's grave. Once he touched the bones of Elisha, the man was restored to life. The account is most likely a tale included to convey divine care for the king and his community despite the prophet's death. The prophet, who was a source of protection and power during his life, continues to be so even in his death. This story could also be a warning, however. The power of the Lord over life and death, which was present among them in the person of the prophet, is now gone.

Israel and Aram (13:22-25)

The chapter closes with two follow-up accounts (vv. 22-23, 24-25) regarding events from the reigns of the two kings, Jehoahaz and Jehoash, whose resumés opened the chapter (vv. 1-9, 10-13). Both reports zero in on the conflict between Aram and Israel that has been referenced so frequently throughout this chapter. First, Jehoahaz and his people are rescued from the grip of Aram specifically because of God's graciousness and compassion. Additionally, a reference to the covenant made with Abraham, Isaac, and Jacob (Gen 15, 17; Deut 4:31, 9:27; 1 Kgs 18:36) serves as further grounds for the divine intervention against Israel's enemy. From the beginning, God keeps promises to Israel.

In the second account (vv. 24-25), Israel under the rule of Jehoash is able to overpower Aram. After Ben-hadad replaces his father Hazael, Jehoash succeeds in retrieving the Israelite towns that had come under Aram's control. That Israel's King Jehoash is successful against Aram three times reminds us that all this takes place under the watchful eye of the Lord, as spoken through the prophet Elisha before Elisha's death. However, now that Elisha is gone, a question mark hovers over the future of Israel.

Theological and Ethical Analysis

At first glance, the chapter yields little more that the typical notations about wayward kings and their ongoing infidelity. Like previous northern rulers, both Jehoahaz and Jehoash are deemed faithful to the cultic practices established under Jeroboam, son of Nebat, and thus are evaluated as unfaithful to the Yahwism as established in Jerusalem. The accompanying stories and elaborating details fill out the records in fairly standard fashion and initially give the impression that there is "nothing new here under the sun." Led by these kings, Israel continues to move farther and farther away from the Lord toward other attractions and its own demise.

Yet hints across the text suggest that God never abandons Israel. Embedded in the chapter one finds direct and indirect evidence of the overtures God continually makes in an attempt to woo the people back to the divine heart. As soon as Jehoahaz entreats the Lord for relief from Aram's oppression, the Lord responds and rescues Israel from this menace (v. 4). In what follows, God provides a "savior" (v. 5). That the account reports Israel continuing to walk in sinful ways (v. 6), and thus punished by Aram (v. 4), implies rescue by God over and over again. Even at the end of Jehoahaz's reign, though his forces are depleted, Israel's independence of Aram's oppression signals God's repeated response of protection and rescue.

More concretely, God's promise of protective presence is made manifest to Joash, Jehoahaz's son, in his encounter with the Lord's prophet, Elisha. When the king comes to him riddled with fear of powerlessness before Aram's threat, the prophet reasserts the promise of the Lord's protection. With two signs he foretells of God's victory over the enemy on behalf of Israel. Even after the prophet has died, the episode of the dead man whose life is restored signals that the prospects of life over death and blessing over curse still reside in Israel.

Finally, the two closing accounts of these two kings' encounters with Aram offer further evidence and assurance of the Lord's ongoing care of Israel. To Jehoahaz, the Lord is gracious, compassionate, and faithful in a way that stems as far back as the divine covenant with Israel before it became a nation. During Joash's reign, the defeat of Aram and the recovery of captive Israelite territories fulfill the prophet's promise enacted by the Lord's "arrow of victory" (v. 17).

The juxtaposition of the abiding presence and enduring protection of the Lord over Israel and the persistent turning away from God by Israel under the leadership of these kings is staggering. God continually matches human infidelity with divine fidelity and responds to human sinfulness with a parental discipline intended only to entice the sinner home. The repetition of this cycle prompts one to wonder: for how long? How long will God continue to court Israel, or for that matter, pursue us if we continue to turn away? Are there limits to the number of times God will respond to our repeated waywardness? What is the nature of a God who seems endlessly driven to attending those who offer no attention in return?

2 KINGS 14

As this chapter opens, attention is turned initially to Judah and to the reign of King Amaziah. However, that southward gaze is quickly redirected by a rising conflict with Israel in the north and with its king, Joash, and his son Jeroboam. Though the strife with Aram appears to have abated, a new crisis erupts on the horizon—a war between Judah and Israel.

Literary Analysis

The chapter begins with a focus upon Judah's king, Amaziah, son of Joash, and later presents a brief note regarding his son Azariah's reign. Hence, as it opens, the narrative provides the account of two southern kings, which appears to parallel and overlap with the previous chapter's record of two northern rulers. Though the spotlight on Amaziah navigates the first part of the chapter (vv. 1-7), the singularity of its focus is soon compromised. An account of Amaziah's exchanges with Jehoash of Israel intervenes, resulting in the details of a war between the two states

(vv. 8-14). As the north, under the leadership of Jehoash, over-powers Amaziah (vv. 8-14) the direction of the narrative appears to coincide with the outcome. The dominance of Israel over Judah in that battle corresponds to the shift away from an initial exclusive concern for Amaziah. A second narrative interruption again distracts attention from Judah. Verses 15-16 provide a summary of the northern king's reign that parallels the earlier record (2 Kgs 13:10-13). The narrative then returns to Amaziah, offering a report of his death and burial. This is complicated by the account of his murder (vv. 19-20). An addendum relating the reign of his son, Azariah (vv. 21-22), draws closure on these very compromised accounts of the two southern kings.

The final portion of the chapter reverts back to the north and reports on Jehoash's successor and son, Jeroboam II (vv. 23-29). After he is introduced he receives the characteristic negative evaluation, but the account of his accomplishments that follows creates tension with this theological assessment. Even the Deuteronomist remarks that this king fulfills the word spoken by Jonah, son of Amittai, the prophet. When his death and burial are recorded his achievements are reiterated in a regnal summary, thus highlighting their importance.

Across this chapter, what began as a focus upon southern kings is gradually and skillfully renegotiated to fix upon northern kings. In the process, the story of Judah's King Amaziah and the brief summary accorded his son Azariah appear strangely in the service of highlighting and rounding out the details of the reign of Israel's King Jehoash, who was introduced in the previous chapter. To further complete the focus upon the north, the chapter ends by featuring the reign of Israel's King Jeroboam II.

Exegetical Analysis

Reign of Amaziah in Judah (14:1-7)

With attention now shifted to the south, the chapter opens with a summary of Amaziah's reign in Judah. In characteristic fashion, the age at which he assumed kingship is noted, twenty-five years, and the length of his tenure as king is recorded as twenty-nine

years. His father, Joash, and his mother, Jehoaddin, are both identified. As expected, the Deuteronomistic evaluation of the king
follows on the heels of this introductory biography. Though
Amaziah "did what was right in the sight of the LORD" (v. 3), an
air of reserve surrounds the assessment. The record draws a contrast between this king and David, suggesting he never quite
reached the benchmark that was established by his more accomplished ancestor. Moreover, the positive appraisal is further qualified by Amaziah's maintenance of the "high places," where the
people continued to sacrifice and make offerings. In this sense, he
was a lot like his father, Joash, who received a similar assessment
(2 Kgs 12:2). The connection between father and son went much
deeper than mere tolerance for cultic improprieties. Amaziah's
first recorded action, marking the official commencement of his
reign, is to avenge his father's death. Though he kills the servants
who murdered his father, he spares their children. In an unusual
citation of Deuteronomic law, his action is interpreted as fulfillment of the Mosaic proscription, which prohibits putting children
to death for the sins of their parents and vice versa (Deut 24:16).
His deed is not recorded to document his maliciousness or as an
act of unchecked violence. Rather, it is set in the record as a disci-
plinary action allowed by Torah. Ironically though, the very ones
he spared may be those who are later responsible for his death
(vv. 19-20).

The account of Amaziah's actions now moves beyond the
domestic sphere to the international scene. The restraint he
observed at home in punishing the servants responsible for his
father's death has no counterpart when he takes up the campaign
against Edom, Judah's eastern neighbor. He kills ten thousand
Edomites in the Valley of Salt, a location that most likely refers to
the southern Arabah. No explanation for the hostilities is given.
David once fought the Edomites (1 Sam 8:13-14), suggesting
ongoing conflict between the nations. It is possible that Edom may
have been capitalizing on Judah's recent struggles with Hazael and
the threat that he posed. The account of Judah's victory over
Edom is not detailed here. Its brevity crafts the impression of
a quick, efficient takeover of this menacing neighbor. The note

concerning Amaziah's renaming of Sela, Edom's capital and stronghold, as Jokthe-el, confirms that Judah would now govern here. Although the meaning of "Jokthe-el" remains uncertain, the gesture of renaming is clear. Assigning new identity to persons or places is an expression of domination over a people or a site. Moreover, this brief note about Amaziah's victory over Edom may actually serve less to inform about this battle and more as an explanation of Amaziah's curious challenge to the king of Israel that follows.

Battle between Judah and Israel (14:8-14)

An overture by Amaziah to Jehoash of Israel leads to a hostile exchange that precipitates warfare between the two states. The description of the event comprises the majority of this Judahite king's record. Whether foolish or not, Amaziah initiates a one-on-one encounter between himself and Jehoash, the king of Israel. The meaning of the expression "come, let us look one another in the face" (v. 8) remains unclear to scholars and thus need not be understood initially as a hostile overture. Amaziah may have been hoping to establish more equitable relations with the north. Since the time of the Omrides, relations between the two sibling states were uneven and antagonistic, with the north always dominant. However, Jehoash's response makes clear that he does not take kindly to the invitation. If more equitable relations were the goal, he evidently would not even consider a shift in the balance of power. With the most intimidating language, his response to Amaziah is twofold.

First, Jehoash insults the southern king with a parable (v. 9). The story, an ill-fated proposed betrothal of a thornbush and a stately cedar, foreshadows the results of any such exchange between Judah and Israel respectively. When a wild animal passes by, it utterly tramples the thornbush. Thus, Jehoash makes clear that the viability and strength of the two nations are of a completely different degree. Judah is pathetically vulnerable before Israel. The southern nation does not approach the likes of the stately, powerful north. The prospects of approaching more equitable relations are completely unthinkable in Jehoash's view.

Jehoash follows up this cryptic hostility with a more candidly explicit rejection (v. 10). He defines Judah's recent defeat of Edom as creating a dangerously false sense of self-confidence in Amaziah. With patronizing rhetoric, he urges the king to be content with his small victory and not to overestimate his military prowess before Israel lest he and the nation of Judah be demolished.

Although the account explains that Amaziah would not heed Jehoash's threat, what he did to instigate the war is not stated. The battle occurs when Jehoash, king of Israel, marches up to Beth-shemesh in Judah and is completely victorious. King Amaziah is captured, Jerusalem is attacked, and part of its fortifying wall on the west is destroyed. To add insult to injury, the temple so recently restored by Amaziah's father (2 Kgs 12:4-16) is ransacked of all its gold and silver vessels, as is the king's own house. Finally, we are told that Jehoash also takes hostages. Because Amaziah, who was initially noted as captured, remains on the throne in Judah, it may be that the hostages were taken as ransom for the king's life. Hence, despite the somewhat positive appraisal Amaziah receives before the Lord, he is not exempt from the wrath and hostilities of his bordering sibling state. Similarly, despite the negative assessment of virtually all the northern kings, including Jehoash, who have followed in the path of Jeroboam, the prospect of divine punishment for infidelity must have seemed only a dim illusion. Perhaps it was even rejected out of hand as pure fallacy when measured against Israel's military achievements.

Two Regnal Summaries (14:15-22)

What began as an account of the reign of Judah's King Amaziah shifts with the weight of the power manifested by Israel's ruler Jehoash. Instead of the expected follow-up story on Amaziah, another summary documenting Jehoash's reign intrudes and amends the earlier account (2 Kgs 13:10-13) by highlighting again his victorious battle against Amaziah. As is typical, we are reminded that Jehoash's other deeds, like those of his predecessors, are recorded in the Book of the Annals of the Kings of Israel. A death and burial notice, followed by a citation that Jehoash's son,

Jeroboam, succeeds him on the throne, reminds us that the Jehu dynasty continues in all its strength in the north.

Death is thought to render both conqueror and conquered on equal footing. Although this may be true, the narrative distinguishes between the manners of death of these two rulers. When Amaziah's summary follows, we hear that although he survived Jehoash on the throne by fifteen years, his end is not uneventful like that of his Israelite counterpart. After surviving the defeat by the north, Amaziah loses his life at the hands of his own people. Some in Jerusalem conspire against him and though he seeks refuge in Lachish, southwest of the capital, they pursue him there. It remains uncertain whether those he left alive in observance of Deuteronomic law when he avenged his father's death committed the crime (vv. 5-6), or whether some insurgents who were unhappy about his war and subsequent defeat at the hands of Jehoash were responsible. However, it is clear that the emenity directed toward the king by some constituency of his own people was reserved for Amaziah himself and not directed at the house of David. Following his death, the record notes that the people of Judah immediately take Azariah, Amaziah's son, and crown him king at the young age of sixteen. An unexpected sidebar hints at Azariah's upcoming ambitious career. He restored Elath in the south to Judah's control. But the account ends as it should, with a final note on Amaziah. Having been brought back to Jerusalem after his death, he was buried with his ancestors.

Jeroboam II Reigns in Israel (14:23-29)

The file on Jeroboam opens by situating the beginning of his reign in the fifteenth year of King Amaziah of Judah's tenure. Though Jeroboam occupied the throne for forty-one years, the recorded account here is quite abbreviated. This is particularly noteworthy given historical reconstructions that argue for the political and territorial zenith that Israel achieved under Jeroboam II. Like all other northern kings, as well as his namesake, Jeroboam is negatively assessed. He, too, "did what was evil in the sight of the LORD" (v. 24), causing Israel to turn wayward. But this initial assessment is dissonant with the follow-up report on some of the highlights of his reign.

Jeroboam is responsible for restoring the northern border of Israel all the way up to Lebo-hamath, and the southern border all the way to the Sea of Arabah (v. 25). This expansion of Israel's northern boundaries to include the Aramaen territories of Hamath and Damascus, as is noted later, continued the recovery work of his father, who had begun to retrieve Israelite towns taken earlier by Hazael (2 Kgs 13:25). This incorporation of Aram put an end to the persistent threat from the north and, for the first time in Israel's history, reinstated the original borders of the northern territories that were established under Solomon (1 Kgs 8:65).

Moreover, all these accomplishments are according to the word of the Lord as set forth by the prophet Jonah, son of Amittai from Gath-hepher (v. 25). The book of Jonah, a short story that critiques prophecy but is not itself prophetic literature, may have taken the name of its protagonist from this verse. Given the authorization accorded the prophet Jonah's pronouncement in this record, it is noteworthy to observe what is omitted. Though both the prophets Amos and Hosea work in Israel during the career of Jeroboam II, they receive no mention at all.

That the Lord, with Jeroboam as divine instrument, has done all this is given further explanation. Just as God's witness of the distress of Israel in Egypt prompted divine intervention on behalf of the people (Exod 2:23-24), so now the Lord "saw that the distress of Israel was very bitter" (v. 26). The expression "there was no one left, bond or free" (v. 26) is likely a colloquialism narrating the comprehensive hopelessness that there was no one who could possibly act on Israel's behalf against its enemies. Rather, the matter required God's intervention, and Jeroboam becomes God's agent in saving Israel. The concluding note that the Lord "saved them by the hand of Jeroboam son of Joash" (v. 27) is particularly striking when read in tandem with the negative assessment accorded to this king earlier.

The familiar format of the closing summary that follows quickly nullifies all the strangeness surrounding what has just been reported. Like the record on the previous kings, we are alerted to annals where all else that Jeroboam did is recorded. Once again reference is made to recovered territories, namely Hamath and Damascus, as noteworthy achievements of his career. When Jeroboam dies, he too sleeps with his ancestors, presumably in Samaria. His son Zechariah follows in his footsteps and ascends the throne.

Theological and Ethical Analysis

In this chapter, Amaziah's positive evaluation as well as his obedience to the law of Moses attest to his fidelity, but are followed by what appears to be evidence of divine disfavor. First Judah is defeated by Israel and then Amaziah himself is the target of a conspiracy that ends his life. By contrast, Joash and his son Jeroboam are both rated negatively before the Lord, in the fashion typical of most all the northern kings, by the Deuteronomist. Yet, these two kings appear to enjoy the tangible evidence of divine blessing. Joash accomplishes victory in a battle with Judah, and Jeroboam is the instrument of the Lord in saving Israel from its enemies.

Throughout the books of Kings, the Deuteronomistic understanding of divine justice is often portrayed as rigidly formulaic: God rewards good and punishes evil. In this theological equation, divine response depends largely upon human response. A person who obeys the law or follows God's statutes warrants divine blessing in the forms of prosperity, long life, offspring, and protection from adversity. By contrast, disobedience was thought to evoke the divine punishment: loss in battle, threats to the nation, illness, and/or premature death.

Despite its commonalties with accounts of kings that have come before, this chapter jars one's growing confidence about God and how God acts. Indeed, the identification of what is good and how it is rewarded, along with what constitutes evil and what qualifies as punishment, start to appear as largely a matter of human interpretation. In turn, as this human interpretation becomes the basis for theologizing about the divine, we begin to proceed with greater caution before the topsy-turvy events of this chapter. Is God acting out of character here or did we have it wrong up until now?

First, we must recognize that it is easy for theology to become the instrument of religious triumphalism. How God is understood too often coincides with the interests and advancement of the allied political and social parties. That the good fortune of one people is deemed a well-deserved, divine blessing already passes judgment on another people who suffer. The account of a sinful Israel being saved by God through means of sinful Jeroboam disrupts this simplistic and frequently self-serving understanding of how the Lord interacts with humanity. God can save the sinner as well the virtuous—thank God! And God can use the sinner as well as the blessed to do divine work. Moreover, our experience of divine goodness most likely has little to do with us deserving such abundance. Rather, as this chapter illustrates, it is the freely given gift of God bestowed upon sinner and just alike.

Second, this chapter's challenge to reigning theological paradigms sets forth a more serious concern. Thus far, the persistent iniquity for which kings are indicted across the book of Kings is idolatry. Yet all this seems very remote in our Jewish, Christian, or Islamic world where we assume God's oneness. However, the manner in which one conceives of God can itself be idolatrous. Fashioning an image or understanding of the divine that creates a God who is manageable and predictable borders on such practices. Moreover, fashioning a God who favors us over and against our enemies is not only self-serving but also promotes a false god. Today, more than ever, such triumphalistic idols must be abolished. Alternatively, as this chapter illustrates, God enlists both sinner and saint in bringing about the divine plan. God appears to dole out rewards according to what people need and not according to what they deserve. We should take great comfort in having our theology so disrupted.

2 KINGS 15

Whereas this chapter continues the account of the sibling monarchies, the circumstances of the previous record now appear reversed. In chapter 14, Judah appeared naive and vulnerable over against Israel's stamina and power. However, in the upcoming narratives, endurance and stability mark the portrait of Judah in contrast to the calamitous collision course that Israel has embraced.

Such neat and tidy representations are always suspect, however. Concluding notes about Judah hint that it will not be exempt from the foreign enemy that will bring Israel down.

Literary Analysis

The chapter continues the record of the northern and southern monarchies. In lockstep fashion, it sets forth brief individual summaries on seven more kings. Its form and organization coincide with its content. The power imbalance of the previous chapter has shifted. The security and sovereignty of Israel that dictated the outcome in the recent battle between the sibling rivals appear to be unraveling. A succession of five different kings—Zechariah, Shallum, Menahem, Pekahiah, and Pekah—jockey for control over the people of the north, while during this same period only two kings reign in the south. These internal rumblings in Israel destabilize the nation, making it an easy target for the appetites and assaults of an international power. At the same time, the files on these five northern rulers, characterized by persistent murder and intrigue, are enclosed by two accounts of Judahite rulers, Azariah and Jotham (vv. 1-7, 32-38). Both rulers' long, stable careers went uninterrupted by either internal or external strife. The assessment of the two southern rulers as having done what was right before the Lord further contrasts with the repeated evaluation of the northern kings as displeasing and unfaithful before God's sovereignty. Hence, the accounts of the two Judahite kings that begin and conclude the chapter form a sharp contrast to the rapid and tumultuous succession of five Israelite kings that unfold within.

Easily isolated units mark the opening and closing of the individual records (vv. 1-7, 8-12, 13-16, 17-22, 23-26, 27-31, 32-38) that comprise this cavalcade of files. Only scant information distinguishes the individual units. The brevity of details allows no plotline to develop that would set apart any one of the summaries, yet taken together they build a subtle climax. Racked by internal strife, Israel teeters on the verge of total demise, a crisis enhanced by the threat of Assyria. Links with the past and ties to the future also tether together these individual units. The reign of Zechariah that is rapidly overthrown by Shallum's coup severs a connection with a stable past. Here the Jehu dynasty closes. However, when Menahem cuts short Shallum's royal career, the threat of Assyria must be appeased with tribute. Such gestures will soon court Israel's end. Moreover, the brevity and rapidity with which these accounts are filed suggest that the events are moving quickly toward a final showdown. The monotonously repetitive evaluations citing the evil of these northern kings add to this impression, conveying an air of inevitability concerning Israel's end. On the heels of this parade of summaries, the finale in chapter 17 of Israel's destruction will bring no surprises. Though the peaceful reigns of the two southern kings frame and highlight the turmoil in the north, the nation of Judah will not remain immune to strife. At the conclusion of the chapter, the account of Jotham's tenure hints of future threats from Israel and Aram. Hence, Judah's tranquility here is only temporary.

Exegetical Analysis

Azariah Reigns in Judah (15:1-7)

The chapter opens with an account of the reign of one of Judah's great kings, Azariah, also known as Uzziah. In the first of the three parts (vv. 1-2, 3-4, 6-7) structuring the overview of his career, an introduction (vv. 1-2) sets forth the characteristic biographical information. Succeeding his father Amaziah to the throne, Azariah's reign was coterminus with another great ruler, Jeroboam II, in the north. Azariah's mother was Jecoliah and he ascended the throne at the young age of sixteen. In the second segment of this report (vv. 3-4), the familiar theological assessment renders Azariah like many of the southern kings. Though he is not compared to David, he is assessed as doing what was pleasing in the sight of the Lord (2 Kgs 14:3). Still, like other Judahite rulers, he allows shrines in the high places to remain. That the people continued to frequent these sites qualifies his otherwise positive appraisal.

The third and final unit constituting the account on Azariah (vv. 6-7) records what has become a formulaic conclusion for these rulers. Upon his death Azariah was buried in the city of David with other kings. The Book of the Annals of the Kings of Judah is said to have recorded all the rest of his deeds.

Aside from this very characteristic summary of his career, verse 5 affords the only distinguishing bit of information about Azariah. At some point, he was afflicted with leprosy. Moreover, in the brief note here, the affliction is assigned divine origin. In the Deuteronomistic perspective, stating that "the LORD struck the king" (v. 5) suggests some culpability on the king's part. Following the report that the people still worshiped at the high places (v. 4), the notation about his leprosy gives the impression that this affliction was punishment from God because of the failure to tear down the high places and centralize the cult. However, the chronicler's lengthy account of Azariah's career attributes his leprosy to punishment for a different sin (2 Chr 26:1-23). Moreover, the chronicler's account affords a portrait of Azariah that not only matches the positive assessment of this lengthy career, but also explains it. Azariah was a great builder and statesman. He was successful at forming and leading military campaigns. Like Solomon, he was a significant international presence who was even able to exact tribute from Ammonites (2 Chr 26:8). However, his pride became his downfall. Entering into the Holy of Holies, Azariah tried to usurp the duties of the priests and was punished with leprosy, which broke out on his forehead (2 Chr 26:20). As a consequence, he "lived in a separate house" (v. 5) and his son Jotham ruled as regent until Azariah's death. Hence, the chronicler understood Azariah's leprosy as the result of misjudgment regarding cult—misjudgment stemming from pride and overzealousness rather than tolerance of the high places.

Five Kings in Israel (15:8-31)

During the apparently stable reign of Azariah in Judah, files on five northern kings—Zechariah, Shallum, Menahem, Pekahiah, and Pekah—chronicle a most unsettling time. The separate summaries of the five kings of Israel who reign during Azariah's time in Judah constitute the centerpiece of the chapter (vv. 8-12, 13-16, 17-22, 23-26, 27-31). Although each is more or less structured by the characteristic introduction, theological assessment, and summary, the accounts are exceedingly brief, affording scant information about each ruler when considered individually. However, when taken together, a portrait of a nation in rapid decline begins to emerge.

Across the introductions, the number of years each king reigns suggests an ongoing struggle for rulership that not only contrasts with the long and powerful governance of the preceding Jehu dynasty, but understandably destabilizes the nation as well. Zechariah, son of Jeroboam, lasted only six months on the throne. His quick demise brought an end to the Jehu dynasty (v. 12), thus fulfilling the divine word regarding this family's reign (2 Kgs 10:30). Shallum, son of Jabesh, responsible for truncating Zechariah's career, endured as king for only one month. Perhaps because of his tyrannical policies, Menahem, son of Gadi, who disposed of Shallum, lasted ten years, followed by his son, Pekahiah, whose career was much briefer. Pekah, son of Remaliah, removed Pekahiah after only two years. Though Pekah ruled for twenty years, he was not exempt from the same violence to the kingship with which he had gained the crown. Eventually, Hoshea, son of Elah, removed him from power. However, for an account of Hoshea's career that coincides with the final days of Israel as a nation, we must wait until chapter 17.

As we have come to expect, the second part of all but one of these royal summaries offers a theological assessment of the ruler. Perhaps because Shallum was on the throne for only one month, no assessment accompanies his regnal resumé. However, the evaluations of Zechariah, Menahem, Pekahiah, and Pekah each lodge the negative verdict that these kings persisted in doing "what was evil in the sight of the LORD" (vv. 9, 18, 24, 28). Individually, they stand in line with and echo the assessments of Israel's previous kings. Collectively, they suggest a comprehensive waywardness that sets Israel in a downward spiral and dims any hope that the nation's people will return to the Lord.

Finally, the concluding summaries on each of these rulers corroborate in both what they include and what they omit. The Book of the Annals of the Kings of Israel is cited in every instance

(vv. 11, 15, 21, 26, 31) as the familiar reference where the rest of their deeds are recorded. However, only in the instance of Menahem is reference made that he was buried with his ancestors (v. 22). This is a likely consequence of his son Pekahiah's initiative as he takes his father's place on the throne. In the other four summaries, there is no mention of where the rulers are laid to rest. The silence surrounding their burial location, along with the unsettling ways each of them came to their end, conveys the impression of the unrest that now afflicts the whole nation.

Whereas these reports cohere with the three-part format we have become so familiar with across the Deuteronomistic history, what is additionally included in each instance becomes the distinguishing feature of the individual ruler and his legacy. It is said that Shallum struck down Zechariah "in public" (v. 10). This public nature of his demise suggests not only groundswell support for his ousting, but also serves as visible evidence that God's word concerning the Jehu dynasty has been fulfilled. Similarly, the account of Shallum is distinguished not by this king's accomplishments, but by Menahem, who strikes him down and kills him. The distinguishing feature of Menahem's tenure is also a threat to the throne, but this time the terrorizing force comes from the outside. Assyria has to be paid off in huge amounts of silver that Menahem extracts from the people over a long period of time. His son Pekahiah's record includes a threat, but this time from within. His own captain, Pekah, conspires against him and along with fifty Gileadites kills him in his palace (v. 25). Finally, in what has become across these accounts a not infrequent bit of information, Pekah too falls victim to Hoshea's conspiracy and tyranny and is murdered. There is little here upon which to recommend the records of any of these five kings individually. Collectively, there is much to anticipate and fear. The threats fueling the regnal turmoil exist both within and outside Israel. Although each king resorts to violence to curb the threat, violence visits all of them except Menahem and brings about their end. Moreover, the threats have consequences not only for these kings but more importantly for Israel as well. The nation is being hurled to its final moment before the Lord and the Lord's instrument of wrath,

Assyria. While these kings self-servingly struggle for power and the throne, Israel has begun to struggle for its survival before another power.

Jotham's Reign in Judah (15:32-38)

The chapter closes with a return to Judah. The seventh regnal summary fixes upon Azariah's son, Jotham. Mentioned earlier (v. 5), Jotham's rule as a regent was the result of his father's affliction and incapacitation. The record notes his assumption of the role. Like all the previous summaries, three units structure the documentation on his reign (vv. 32-33, 34-35, 36-38). The introduction (vv. 32-33) dates his royal tenure as concurrent with Pekah, son of Remaliah's rule in Israel. It was during this time that Assyria had begun its campaign of terror (v. 29), sending shock waves through the western states. Jotham's reign as king is chronicled as sixteen years, and his mother's name was Jerusha, daughter of Zadok. Hence, whereas the introduction follows the expected protocol, we glean some important and distinguishing information about Jotham. Most significantly, his maternal roots place him in a priestly circle, if not in a priestly family.

When the second unit of this report records the Deuteronomistic evaluation of Jotham, it fits his familial background. Like other kings in the Judahite line, Jotham did what was pleasing in the sight of the Lord, even though the people continued worshiping at the high places. However, of all the deeds he might have done during his sixteen years as king, the only one recorded has to do with the temple. The summary notes that Jotham "built the upper gate of the house of the LORD" (v. 35), which testifies less to his reputation as a builder (2 Chr 27:3-4) than it serves to emphasize his priestly background and his concern for the temple. Even in the face of Assyria's threatened advance, a king with a priestly background and a concern for the temple of the Lord should bode well for Judah.

The concluding unit (vv. 36-38) on Jotham's reign ruptures such confidence and incites unrest. As is expected, the passage notes that Jotham's deeds are recorded in the Annals of the Kings of Judah and that when he died he too was buried with his ancestors in the city of David; then it further discloses that Aram and Israel have begun to exert threatening pressure upon Jotham. Even more unsettling, the text indicates that God instigated that hostility. Hence, as the record brings Jotham's reign to a close, it also discloses that Judah, too, is at risk before both the malevolence of Assyria and the unknowable ways of God. Whether Jotham responded to these affronts from the north remains uncertain. However, as we will see, the fallout from these confrontations is inherited by his son, Ahaz, who is named here as Jotham's successor to Judah's throne.

Theological and Ethical Analysis

The sparse formulaic nature of the summaries of each king and his reign appears less in the service of preserving significant information about the individual ruler and more in the interests of disclosing the story of the nation and its destiny. Taken together, the civil strife, murder in public places, struggles for control, incompetence, and deception work together to write the final saga of the nation's story. Israel is hurling itself in the direction of death. Judah is not far behind. Nonetheless, the format of these chapters, fixing attention, though markedly abbreviated, upon each ruler gives us pause and teaches its own lesson. The brief but nevertheless individual assessment of each ruler contributes to the impending verdict against Israel and then Judah. It also suggests the role and responsibility of each king for the lamentable turn of events that brought the royal history to its end.

The unfolding of history here is not determined by the direction navigated by an illusive persona called nation, institution, government, social group, or even relationship. Individual persons are the operative forces in each of these constructs. The dynamics of action and nonaction, fidelity and infidelity, virtue and vice are at work here in the freedom of each individual human being. The importance of the Deuteronomistic historian's focus of a momentary spotlight on each ruler contributes to an understanding of the larger story of how Israel and then Judah arrive at their end. It also suggests that the fate of a collective impersonal institution is always directly tied to the credit or the culpability of individual players. What is true here about a nation is true about other social institutions in our own lives. Religious bodies can fail or flourish as the result of choices made by individuals within those arenas. Relationships may grow deeper or become dysfunctional because of particular persons and their decisions within those parameters. Societal organizations, even those bent upon admirable causes, can succeed or fail depending in part upon the decisions made by the responsible parties. To some degree, familial, institutional, national, international, and even global ills or achievements stem from the day-in, day-out choices of individuals.

Ignorance about the impact of individual choices on the course of humanity is egregious on its own. The belief that an immoral choice, the satisfaction of a vice, or an orientation toward some infidelity in our individual lives is "our business" and does not matter in the realm of a larger social arena is especially reprehensible. It licenses us to live under the deception that what we do has no consequences for others in the human community. Though we are not kings of a monarchy where the impact of our every word or action is palpable, every choice we make does move the human community closer or farther away from the goal of human existence: kinship with our God. Indeed, as this chapter demonstrates that the destiny of Israel was tied to the decisions and actions of each and every ruler in Israel, it also invites us to an awesome and sobering reflection in our own life. Each of us bears some responsibility for the destiny of our world.

2 KINGS 16

The Assyrian force that threatened several of the Israelite kings in the previous chapter was not fixed solely upon that nation. Under Tiglath-pileser, its ambitious military campaign forging westward posed a danger to every state in its path. Judah, too, would now confront Assyria's impending assault complicated by other threats. In response to these gathering clouds, Ahaz, king of Judah, will have to make a choice regarding Assyria that is different from the path of resistance that Israel is following. Despite their varying courses before the enemy and their ongoing sibling hostilities, both Israel and Judah will be rendered on equal footing. Before Assyria, they will both be assessed as vulnerable, and before God, they will both be found wanting.

Literary Analysis

The chain of abridged reports featuring seven kings that fashioned the previous block of Deuteronomistic account ceases here. Instead, for the entire chapter, the narrative camera zooms in and focuses upon Ahaz, Jotham's son and successor to the Davidic throne in Judah. Characteristic opening and closing summaries (vv. 1-4, 19-20) demarcate this focalization as distinct from what has preceded and what will follow. These regnal summaries introduce and bring to a close the account of Ahaz's reign, while enshrining a three-part narrative record that marks his rule (vv. 5-9, 10-16, 17-18).

The introduction reports biographical information about Ahaz with the conventional format. The three-part record that follows substantiates the legitimacy of a disquieting assessment. In the first unit (vv. 5-9), Judah is besieged by Aram and Israel, prompting Ahaz to make an overture to Assyria for assistance and protection. The second unit (vv. 10-16) fixes our attention upon Ahaz and the way in which his new political affiliation with Assyria achieves its fullest expression through the king's compromise in the area of cult. He orders a replication of an Assyrian altar be built in the temple and that sacrifices regularly be offered upon it.

In the middle of the second unit, Ahaz's cultic machinations assume center stage (vv. 12-14). He inspects the new altar, goes up to it, and offers his own daily sacrifices upon it. Ahaz's cultic activity serves not only as a chiastic center of this second unit, but also as the focal point of the chapter.

The third unit comprising the account on Ahaz (vv. 17-18) returns again to his activity in verse 8, where he sought to please the king of Assyria and buy his favor. Alterations in the temple are conducted to appease the Assyrian ruler. Thus, Ahaz appears to continue down the path of apostasy, trusting in the rule and power of Assyria rather than trusting in the Lord.

Given the turn of events in this chapter, the closing summary on Ahaz is rather unremarkable (vv. 19-20). Moreover, although the chapter appears quite independent in its form and content, references throughout tie it to what has preceded and what follows. Here the threat of Israel and Aram's pressure on Judah, forecasted in the previous chapter (15:37), materializes. At the same time, Ahaz's enlistment of the Assyrian force against the northern states begins the end of Israel that will be related in the upcoming chapter.

Exegetical Analysis

Introduction to Ahaz's Reign (16:1-4)

Ahaz's reign is reportedly simultaneous with the tumultuous tenure of Pekah, son of Remaliah in Israel. Recall that during Pekah's kingship Assyria began its land-grabbing policy, targeting territories in the north of Israel and beyond (2 Kgs 15:29). Ahaz is twenty years old when he comes to the throne. During his twenty-year career, Judah takes a marked detour from its course of fidelity to the Lord. The four previous kings—Joash, Amaziah, Azariah/Uzziah, and Jotham—reputedly had been mindful of the Lord. Their frequent attention to temple matters, along with the positive theological assessment evaluating each reign, set a contrasting precedent to the orientation of northern kings and their antics. Now, with Ahaz's rule, any notion that the southern kingdom was back on track is summarily dashed. That "he did not do what was right in the sight of the Lord his God" (v. 2) summarizes Ahaz's legacy.

Against this negative assessment leveled early in the introduction, two follow-up comparisons further dramatize this uncomely evaluation. First, Ahaz is compared to David with whom he has nothing in common. Then, he is likened to the Israelite kings whose characteristics he shares. Added detail suggests that Ahaz not only resembles the Israelite rulers in their waywardness, but might even surpass their egregious ways.

The text reports that Ahaz made his son pass through fire (v. 3), a practice likely related to the cult of Molech where the appetites of bloodthirsty deities had to be satisfied with child sacrifice. Strictly forbidden by Deuteronomic law (Deut 18:10), this practice is identified with the reprehensible deeds of those whom the Lord drove out when Israel was first established in the land. The resort to this abominable practice is not the only justification for Ahaz's negative theological evaluation; the account continues with further details that anticipate the lamentable course his reign will take.

Ahaz frequents the high places and offers his sacrifices there (v. 4). Since the time of Solomon, only the people continued to visit the local shrines. According to the Deuteronomistic historians, this was not acceptable before the Lord; nonetheless, as long as kings made their offerings and sacrifices in the temple, the people's persistent visitation to the high places was tolerated. However, now the king himself is worshiping at these local sites. Moreover, the phrase "on the high places, on the hills, and under every green tree" (v. 4), used to describe Ahaz's activities, is an emblematic expression of the prophets' denunciation of objectionable religious practices (Isa 9:13-17; 10:5-6; Jer 7:31; 19:5; 32:35; Ezek 33:11). Thus, the introduction of Ahaz's record concludes with a comprehensive indictment of Ahaz's infidelity before the Lord.

Ahaz Turns to Assyria (16:5-9)

The theological judgment against Ahaz in the opening of the chapter anticipates the political fallout that quickly follows. The complex events that rapidly unfold are presented in summary fashion. First, the rising hostility of Aram and Israel toward Judah reported during Jotham's reign (2 Kgs 15:37) now achieves its full force. The northern forces enter Jerusalem and threaten Ahaz, though they do not overpower him. The king's troubles are not limited to this assault. Immediately following, we read that Edom recovers Elath in the south, suggesting that pressure from all sides assails a weakened Judah. In addition, the looming cloud of the Assyrian threat hovers not only over the northern states, but casts its shadow over Judah's fate as well. Israel and Aram's threat to Judah was likely over its unwillingness to join the anti-Assyrian coalition, a resistance movement among the northern states determined to stalemate an Assyrian takeover. Ahaz must decide whether or not to join the threatened states, standing firm and united against the Assyrian giant. The record suggests no delay in his decision. His trust in Assyria during this time of crisis attests to his lack of trust in God. Ahaz offers to become the "servant" and "son" of the Assyrian ruler, rendering Judah a vassal state (v. 7) in exchange for Assyria's rescue from Israel and Aram's threat. The prophet Isaiah had warned Ahaz against the temptation to trust in finite powers that can be seen, but Ahaz paid no attention (Isa 7:1–8:10). Instead, he backed up his promise of fidelity to the new Assyrian suzerain with gifts of tribute, making a present of the gold and silver from the temple and the king's house to the Assyrian ruler. With this tangible exchange, the agreement is sealed.

Assyria immediately responds by marching against Aram at Damascus. The king of Aram is killed and the people are made Assyrian captives. Though the record gives no indication of Assyrian hostility toward Israel in response to Ahaz's request, the prospect that the Assyrian engine will soon roll into Israel is all but certain. Thus, the kinship between Assyria and Judah that Ahaz courts not only assigns vassalage to Judah but also initiates the beginning of the end for Israel.

Ahaz Makes Temple Alterations (16:10-16)

This second and central segment of tradition continues the account of Ahaz's reign. Two units consisting of communications between Ahaz and his religious official Uriah (vv. 10-11, 15-16) frame a narrative description centered upon the king presiding in the temple (vv. 12-14). Given the negative theological evaluation he received in the introduction, a ring of suspicion circumscribes any portrait of Ahaz in the act of worship. The surrounding dialogue between Ahaz and Uriah the priest encourage this skepticism.

The first set of exchanges is prompted by Ahaz's symbolic visit to Damascus where Tiglath-pileser has conquered Judah's nemesis, Aram (vv. 10-11). The narrative reports that upon seeing the altar in Damascus, Ahaz sends a blueprint of it to Uriah back in Jerusalem. Though we do not hear of any explicit order to build the altar, Ahaz evidently commanded the priest to do so. The report notes that Uriah built the altar according to Ahaz's specifications, completing it before he returned from Damascus. The account does not make clear whether the altar Ahaz saw and replicated was Syrian or had been erected by the Assyrian conquerors. It is plausible that Ahaz had the altar built in order to offer sacrifices to the newly victorious Assyrian gods. Building such an altar expressed Ahaz's status as "son" and "servant" to the Assyrian suzerain and the homage he now owes to the Assyrian gods.

In the concluding exchange between Ahaz and Uriah the priest (vv. 15-16), an order is given for the new altar to be the designated site for all offerings. During Solomonic times, the original bronze altar was reportedly inadequate for the size and number of sacrifices performed by the king. Hence, the innovation appears to improve the temple. Ahaz's instructions to Uriah about the various offerings of the priests, the king himself, and the people, which now are to be conducted from the newly erected altar, addresses pragmatic concerns. The new altar serves the large number and size of sacrifices better than the previous one. At the same time, the replication of an altar to honor Assyrian deities' victory in Damascus better accommodates Judah's vassalage to Assyria. Thus, the change serves rising political interests.

Ahaz himself is at the narrative center of these two surrounding exchanges between the king and his priest regarding the construction of the new altar and its use. When he returns from Damascus and his encounter with Tiglath-pileser, he immediately visits the temple. The narrative slows down and focalizes upon this ruler as he first inspects and then presides at the new installation in Jerusalem's cultic center. Though the altar and the worship he conducts upon it here are matters of high importance, the report spotlights Ahaz. The king, as the cultic official before the newly constituted altar, is subject of a parade of verbs: he "viewed," he "drew near," he "went up," he "offered," he "poured," he "removed," he "put," he "commanded." Officiating in the temple of the Lord, the king fosters the religious identity of Judah and its affiliation with Yahweh. Sacrificing on a replica of an altar upon which Assyrian deities were likely honored, the king serves the immediate political interests, identification, and the presumed obligations of vassalage. Worship of the Lord is at odds with political fidelities associated with the new altar. Whether such contradictions, bordering on hypocrisy, can be accommodated in the tradition of covenant remains to be seen.

Ahaz's Tribute to Assyria (16:17-18)

At first glance, this third and final segment reporting on the reign of Ahaz suggests that he, too, attends to the temple and its restoration, as did the immediately preceding rulers. As the brief description unfolds, however, what appears as Ahaz's temple renovation shows itself to be a plundering of the temple to pay the tribute Assyria demanded. Ahaz cuts off the frames of the stands and removes the lavers that served the libations of the priests in the temple, bronze vessels that have stood in the house of the Lord since the time of Solomon (1 Kgs 7:27, 38). He also retrieves the bronze oxen by removing the sea and setting it on a makeshift stone foundation. The text says Ahaz collected the bronze "because of the king of Assyria" (v. 18), suggesting that the tribute in gold and silver gathered earlier from the temple (v. 8) is now to be followed by payments in bronze. Hence, whereas his vassalage appears to have saved Judah and Ahaz from any further assault by Aram and Israel, it also appears to be particularly costly. Indeed, his fidelity to Assyria may cost Judah salvation itself, salvation by the Lord.

The Conclusion to Ahaz's Reign (16:19-20)

Ahaz's actions reap long-term effects for Judah and more immediately devastating consequences for Israel. His turning away from the Lord both in the cult and in politics is blatant and comprehensive. As the report of his unprecedented reign comes to a close, the return to the stereotypic style and format of its regnal conclusion seems especially abrupt. The story of Ahaz's reign breaks off and as usual we are referred to the Book of the Annals of the Kings of Judah for the account of the rest of his deeds. Given all his antics and his grave covenant violations, it seems a bit odd that this king is still laid to rest in the city of David and buried with his ancestors. As the Deuteronomist comes to terms with the traditions about Ahaz, perhaps the most hopeful note sounded is that Ahaz's reign finally ends and he will be replaced. Hezekiah, his son, succeeds him.

Theological and Ethical Analysis

A tone of desperation permeates the account of Ahaz's reign. Though the literary arrangement centers our attention upon the king engaged in worship in the temple of the Lord (v. 13), the flurry of surrounding activities stands at odds with this traditionally commanding image. The confidence that kingship should conjure is gone. The appearances of faithful rule cannot compel a sense of hope and trust. The dysfunctional character of the ruler and his policies are no longer a matter of debate. Politically, the nation is in danger from every direction. Israel and Aram level their assault from the north. Assyria's forces stand like ready arrows aimed from the east, and Edom exercises its strength in the south. Ahaz inherits a very difficult and dangerous situation, but Ahaz's own lack of fidelity to the Lord occasions the gravest endangerment of all to the nation.

Still, the text of the prophet Isaiah suggests that God remains deeply present during this time of crisis (Isa 7:3–8:10). Isaiah offers Ahaz divine counsel and extends again the invitation to trust in the Lord. The prophet even urges the king to ask God for a sign confirming that, indeed, God will act to save this nation. Reception of an offer to trust solely in the Lord has its own requirements, however. It demands the kind of belief that has been nurtured over time that grows out of a lifelong discipline of attention fixed upon the Lord. It is seeded by a past where words and actions cooperate together as an expression of one's faith.

Unfortunately, evidence of that kind of persistent lifelong orientation toward the Lord is nowhere present in the account of Ahaz's reign. Instead, hypocrisy, contradictions, and incautious decision making predominate. Threatened by hostile Israelite and

Aramaic forces, Ahaz shortsightedly enlists Assyria's military prowess rather than the Lord's help for assistance. The consequences of his decision are many and catastrophic. Though he continues to offer sacrifice to his Lord, Ahaz must now offer gold, silver, and bronze to another lord. Though he continues to worship in the temple, he must also rob the temple. Though he continues to set forth sacrifices of grain, drink, and blood offerings before Yahweh, he does so on an altar designed for other gods. Fearing subjugation by the forces of the north, he ends up becoming subject and servant of another more dangerous force.

2 KINGS 17

A curious shift takes place in this chapter. The long reportorial fixation on the rulers of Israel and Judah that has governed the framework of the second book of Kings ceases here. In place of another detailed report on the deeds of one or more kings, introduced by an opening biographical summary, the bulk of the narrative shifts its focus to the people. As it records the anticipated fall of Samaria to Assyria, the most significant turning point in Israel's history, the narrative moves its attention to the people's responsibility for the event and its impact on them.

Literary Analysis

Across the books of Kings, Israel and Judah's rulers have not only monopolized the spotlight of the accounts recorded here; the theological evaluation has assigned them the bulk of credit or blame for the course and condition of the people's lives. The form and content of the opening of this chapter urges us to expect the same. Employing the characteristic regnal summary, the chapter begins by introducing Hoshea's reign in Samaria (vv. 1- 6). The negative theological evaluation prepares us for the report that antagonistic relations with Assyria eventually lead to his imprisonment, the people's captivity, and the fall of Israel. However, the two-part narrative elaboration that follows this opening account is quite unexpected (vv. 7-23, 24-41).

In part one (vv. 7-23), the people of Israel, not the kings, are pointedly implicated by this calamitous turn of events. First, their actions are specifically identified as the cause of their own exile and captivity by Assyria (vv. 7b-8). Next, a lengthy narrative amasses the evidence upon which judgment has been made (vv. 8-17). Despite the variety represented in this catalog of their misdeeds, the sinfulness of the people coheres under a common umbrella—apostasy. Hence, God's punishment renders them exiled from the land. As if to match the breadth of this condemnation with the scope of the misdeeds, the indictment is repeated (v. 7). However, this time its horizons extend to include Judah. Although the two kingdoms remain hostile opponents, the account of Judah's sins renders them on equal footing (vv. 19-20). Judah participated in the ways of apostasy and hence, it too will be exiled like Israel. This first half closes in the same way it opened, with a reference to a king (vv. 21-22).

Part two presents another kind of unexpected account (vv. 24-41). Now the narrative description turns to Assyria's resettlement of foreign populations in the land of Israel. Following an introductory verse (v. 24), two sections narrate in different ways the apostasy of these new inhabitants in the area of Samaria (vv. 25-33, 34-40). In the first section, a storylike account discloses that this resettlement of new peoples in the land quickly leads to widespread religious syncretism. The second section sets forth a theological commentary on these circumstances in the land and brings the chapter to a close (vv. 34-41). Hence, the two parts of the chapter are bound together by the repeated motif of the infidelity to the Lord, first on the part of Israel and then on the part of the new occupants of the land under Assyrian rule.

Exegetical Analysis

Hoshea's Reign in Israel (17:1-6)

The similarities between the opening of this chapter and the beginning of past chapters gives no indication that what follows differs radically from what has come before. The introduction to Hoshea's kingship gives no hint that with his kingship both the course of Israelite history and the manner in which it is recorded changes forever. Instead, the familiar regnal summary takes up the reign of Hoshea in Israel that was introduced earlier in 2 Kgs 15:30. Like many of the rulers before him in the north, he came to the throne by violence. He rules during the same era as Ahaz in Judah and his reign lasts nine years. The account then offers a theological assessment that again does not prepare us for what is to follow. That Hoshea is evaluated negatively but not quite as badly as preceding Israelite kings certainly does not fuel anticipations of Israel's end under his leadership. Indeed, he did pay tribute to Assyria, making Israel a vassal state, but the narrative records that Hoshea did his best to court an alliance with Egypt's pharaoh in order to cast off subjugation and free the nation of this economic burden. Still, sympathy for Hoshea's inherited circumstances ends here. This king who came to the throne by conspiracy (2 Kgs 15:30) is now accused of the same act by the new Assyrian king, Shalmaneser. Although the rulers of this eastern giant have changed, its international ambition remains the same. Assyria is set on controlling all the land west to the Mediterranean.

The last we hear of Hoshea, he is taken captive and imprisoned by the Assyrian forces that have invaded Israel. Instead of offering a conclusion to this biographical summary, the narrative shifts attention from the imprisoned king to the national situation in Israel. Though the account is brief and recorded in summary fashion, it conveys a comprehensive nature of the end. All the land is invaded. The capital city, Samaria, is besieged, and Assyrian forces occupy the surrounding territory. Most devastating of all, Assyrian military tactics involved exchanging populations between conquered territories. Thus, Israelite leaders are taken captive and resettled in lands far away. Here Assyrian territories are named as the relocation sites, making the description of the deportation ever more alarmingly real and vivid.

An Exile Grounded in Apostasy (17:7-23)

The narrative opens and closes by tying the comprehensive waywardness of Israel to the past. In the opening, the people are accused of turning away from the God who liberated them from the bondage of Egyptian slavery (v. 7). In the conclusion, their sinfulness is tied to the era of Jeroboam's kingship when God first tore Israel away (vv. 21-23). Hence, the beginning and ending of this narrative spotlight key moments in the chronicle of Israel's persistent waywardness, creating a feeling of on-the-spot reporting of the indictment.

The intervening recitation of the people's misdeeds is extensive and verbose (vv. 8-20). In general, Israel is charged with a comprehensive failure to obey the laws and the statutes of the covenant. However, when their sinfulness is elaborated, virtually all the deeds with which they are indicted speak specifically to their failure to observe the first commandment. They chase after other gods and follow customs of foreign people. Their secretive misdeeds conjure deception before the Lord. They build high places for their offerings and erect abominable sacred pillars and poles. They fashion false images and worship false idols; specifically, they worship the two cast images of calves dating back to Jeroboam's time (1 Kgs 12:28). They serve the host of heaven and Baal, and perhaps even honor Molech by passing their children through the fire. Uncertainty prevails regarding the meaning of this expression or the practice it refers to. Relevant comparative Near Eastern data citing ritual human sacrifice in honor of Molech attempts to draw lines of connection between this text and the rituals required by that Canaanite deity (Smith, 132-33). Israel has chosen such practices along with divination and augury over and against the observation of the statutes and laws of the covenant. The citation of many of the same sins over and over throughout this extended elaboration conveys a sense of the repetition and longevity that characterize this waywardness. The preponderance of Israel's misdeeds overrides and obliterates all that God has done. Hence, the record serves to justify God's punishment.

Interspersed across the account are references to God's rebuffed overtures. God sent warnings (vv. 13, 15). Divinely appointed seers visited the people (v. 13). References to the prophets God set among the people recall the work of Elijah and Elisha. Finally, the narrative repeatedly refers to God's anger and wrath, the reason for the punishment (vv. 11, 17). This interspersing of divine warning and overtures with the exhaustive listing of the people's iniquities further emphasizes that the punishment is justified.

As if to dash all hopes for reinstatement, not only will Israel be cast out from the Lord's sight, Judah too has been earmarked for punishment (vv. 19-20). It receives its own condemnation; like Israel, its punishment will take the form of exile. Infidelity before the Lord has reached a fatal limit. All has come to an end and the responsibility for this fateful finale is laid at the feet of the people themselves. The exile will not be temporary. As if to witness to that fact, as the narrative description closes, exile is described as a permanent condition continuing "until this day" (v. 23).

The Resettlement of Samaria (17:24-41)

If the focus upon the people of Israel and their sinfulness in the previous section was unprecedented in this chronicle of kings, the account that follows is even more unusual. Now the narrative turns to the resettlement of Samaria by Assyria with captives from other nations. Made up of two distinct parts (vv. 25-33, 34-41), the section opens with a tally of the places from which the new exiles were settled into Israel's former capital and its surrounding cities (v. 24). A storylike report frames the first section. These captive newcomers continue to worship their own gods and give no attention to the Lord. In characteristic Deuteronomistic fashion, the account notes that they are punished for their apostasy. The Lord sends lions to attack them (v. 25). The problem is set before the king of Assyria and framed as if a lack of knowledge concerning the "god of the land" has brought about the punishment (v. 26). As if assenting to the explanation, this unnamed Assyrian king quickly formulates a solution. He orders an Israelite priest be brought back to the land in order to teach the new inhabitants concerning the "god of the land" (v. 27). At the heart of this story lies a basic theological misunderstanding. Yahweh is not a god of the land who can be worshiped alongside the gods of other lands.

Whether the people are recalcitrant in their ways or this priest is just a poor teacher remains unclear, but each group of foreigners continues its own cultic practices and the worship of its own lords alongside Israel's God. The fullness with which the narrative elaborates the newcomers' idolatry suggests the magnitude of the priest's failed attempt. The gods that these people continue to worship in Samaria are named (vv. 30-31). It is also noted that they make shrines and offerings to their gods in the high places once erected by Israel. Moreover, they do this while also worshiping the Lord with their variously appointed priests and their own cultural customs. Thus, the objectionable practice of apostasy now becomes intensified.

Verse 34 acts as a transition, which summarizes that this sinful activity continued even to the time of the writing of this report (v. 34a), but also introduces the next section (v. 34b). It specifically connects the foreigners' iniquity with the deeds forbidden by the law and statutes of the Lord that Israel was called to obey. That these outsiders now living in the land are bound by the same commandments suggests that they too are invited into the covenant. Again, the theological assertion that the Lord is not tied to the land but is God of all peoples reverberates at the heart of this account. Extending the option of covenantal relationship with this God to these foreign populations manifests theological radicality.

A theological commentary confirming this invitation follows (vv. 34-40). Addressing these people in the second person, "you," it reminds them that the Lord's covenantal relationship with Israel now extends to them and they are specifically forbidden to worship any gods but Yahweh. It rehearses the observances of worship and practice that must characterize exclusive fidelity to the Lord. With language that is deeply Deuteronomistic it invites these people to the same liberation from bondage that Israel encountered in Egypt. Finally, having set before them the covenantal option, the prospects of salvation, and the requirements therein, it also pronounces judgment for their sinfulness. They have not listened but have continued in their idolatrous practices. Again, the writer's statement that this has lasted "to this day" describes the continuation of their apostasy and lends the authenticity of a witness to these events (v. 41).

Theological and Ethical Analysis

Chapter 17 offers an overview of the regrettable fall of Israel. Here the people stand alongside the kings in culpability. More notably, they seem to bear the brunt of the judgment on this long-term infidelity. The account drives home a daunting lesson about the consequences of decisions made by those in authority. As sovereigns lead people down the path of iniquity, sinfulness multiplies exponentially. But this account not only testifies to all that Israel has lost in the course of these unfortunate events; it also discloses that God has lost too.

Throughout a long and extensive salvation history stemming back to the ancestors, God has remained present and self-revelatory to Israel. Yet, in this account of Israel's final hours, a profound confusion about who God is predominates. At least on the surface, the litany of their misdeeds coheres to indict the people of widespread apostasy. Their crimes of infidelity, however, also indicate a rampant misunderstanding about who this God is and where this God is to be found. Misguided theology has led them to look for God in places where the Lord does not reside.

The construction of sacred poles and pillars related to fertility cults indicates confusion about God's relation to the forces of nature, identifying God with these natural elements rather than as the creator of them. Sacrificing on high places and passing children through the fire indicates that Israel was profoundly out of touch with all that God wants or desires. The Assyrian king addresses the calamities befalling the newly resettled population in a way that makes clear idolatry is the root of the problem. In so doing, he presents another theological fallacy. He mistakenly identifies the Lord of Israel as the "god of the land" (vv. 26, 27).

Covenant, the construct shaping the relationship between God and Israel, bespeaks a God who is relational and personal. In the Deuteronomistic scheme, covenant not only extended an invitation of life over death and blessing over curse to the people; it offered an unfathomable disclosure about the nature of God. This is a God who wanted the people to live prosperously. Moreover, this God is not some illusive divine force. This God promised to be present and entered into a covenant of fidelity. "I will walk among you, and will be your God, and you shall be my people" (Lev 26:12). God longs for relationship—a relationship that not only binds the people together, but also binds God to them. This is a God deeply caught up in every aspect of the people's lives. How they treat themselves and their neighbors, the members of their family, and the blessings of life all work to foster or destroy their incredible bond with the Holy One. From the time of Abraham and Sarah, Israel was called to be a means whereby God could draw all unto the divine self. This people would be a blessing by which all might be blessed (Gen 12:2-3). Later, prophets such as Isaiah would make the universality of God even more explicit (Isa 2:2-4, 11-18, 20). Zion would be earmarked as the place where all would be drawn to God, where all nations might stream, beat their spears into plowshares, give up enmity, surrender hostility, and choose life together, offered by this incredible God.

The travesty of Israel's confusion leading to its demise is lamentable. Even more devastating is the fact that it is not an isolated event in the chronicle of human history. It finds company over and over in the course of human events. Most notably, it echoes again in the events of our time, grounded in the endurance of the same profound theological misunderstanding. God is still associated with land and claimed to be Lord of some people but not of others. The God of organized religions often evolves into religious power *over* others rather than for others. Religion grounded in such theology breeds antagonistic relations between groups rather than building up the human community. Such rampant hostilities and aggressions in the name of the Lord actually end up obscuring the Godhead and what this God desires. At the same time, other graven idols fashioned by imperialistic politics and economic systems that exploit those in need court our attention and prescribe what should be the objects of human questing. These, rather than a longing for the Lord, drive human desire and motivate the course of people's lives. Theological misconceptions and false idols of the modern world obscure what is still being offered. Yet, the Lord persists in extending the invitation to covenantal relationship, to be our God and for us to be God's people. How unthinkable is that?

2 KINGS 18 AND 19

Chapters 18–19 concern the threat that Sennacherib, king of Assyria, poses to Judah. Together with chapter 20, they set forth a prolonged account centering on the reign of Hezekiah. Perhaps the extended attention on this king can be explained as a result of his exceedingly positive evaluation, or perhaps now that the north has been destroyed and the people of Israel exiled, all hope rests in the course that Judahite kings travel. Perhaps the description of Hezekiah's rule is extensive because even though Hezekiah stands as an exemplary model of covenantal fidelity, his reign unfortunately marks the beginning of Judah's end.

Literary Analysis

The biographical resumé of Judah's new King Hezekiah (vv. 1-8) introduces chapters 18–19. It is followed by an unprecedented theological assessment. Hezekiah surpassed all other kings in his fidelity to the Lord. The lengthy, detailed form of this regnal summary eclipses the abbreviated format employed for kings' biographical introductions thus far.

Following, an abrupt pause momentarily halts the attention on the glorious reign of Hezekiah. A report interrupts, offering a brief rehearsal of the already reported capture of Samaria and the exile of the Israelites (vv. 9-12). The juxtaposition of this summary and Hezekiah's account serves to suggest the chronological simultaneity of events. Moreover, this repeated summary of the fall of Israel may also function as a contrastive warning to Judah, no matter how faithful this new king may be.

Next, three cycles of threats by Sennacherib, king of Assyria, accompanied in each case with responses by King Hezekiah, follow and structure the account (vv. 13-16; 18:17–19:7; 19:8-19). In the first round, Sennacherib actually comes to the cities of Judah, attacks them, and demands that Hezekiah pay a steep tribute before he will retreat (vv. 13-14). Hezekiah concedes and further divests the temple of gold and silver in order to quell the attack and the economic appetite of this Assyrian sovereign (vv. 15-16). In the second cycle, Sennacherib sends his messengers to Hezekiah. Hezekiah's emissaries meet them (vv. 17-37). Two exchanges take place wherein once again the Assyrian threat is imposed upon the king and the people. This time, Hezekiah responds by turning to the Lord and consulting the prophet Isaiah (19:1-7). Finally, a third and final round of interactions takes place between the two kings. This time Sennacherib sends his messengers with a threatening letter to Hezekiah (19:8-13). In response, Hezekiah turns directly to the Lord, and in a lengthy prayer, rich with persuasive rhetoric, he places his trust completely in God (19:15-19).

In the course of these three exchanges, interesting shifts take place, manifesting a theological lesson. Sennacherib's hostile overtures to Hezekiah become increasing indirect. First, Sennacherib threatens the king and his territories. Next, he sends his representatives and an army to deliver a verbal ultimatum. Finally, he makes a last threat of hostility in writing by means of a messenger. Hezekiah also undergoes a change across the three encounters. To the first threat, he caves in completely and pays Sennachrib tribute. In the second confrontation, he responds by turning to the Lord and seeking advice from the prophet Isaiah. In the third and final exchange, Hezekiah responds to the written hostility by expressing his complete and total confidence in God. Thus, the account here sketches an image of a king who trusts in the Lord. This trust is not instantaneous, however. It grows over the course of three exchanges and as the threat mounts. At the same time, Hezekiah's faithful response appears to coincide with the retreat of the Assyrian king. Hence, the testimony to Hezekiah's unparalleled trust in the Lord, echoed in the biographical introduction (vv. 1-8), must be heard as the summary of his faith that grew over a lifetime.

A response and intervention by the Lord on Hezekiah's behalf closes the chapter (vv. 20-37). First, divine response comes in the form of a three-part proclamation of the word of the Lord by Isaiah. The prophet promises the king divine rescue (vv. 20-28, 29-31, 32-34). Then, a report of God's direct action against Assyria on Judah's behalf follows (vv. 35-37). The angel of the Lord defeats Sennacherib's army and the Assyrian ruler's own sons successfully conspire to murder him. Hence, the organization of the account along with the shift that takes place across characters dramatizes the urgent message of the Deuteronomist. Obedience and trust in the Lord bring divine protection and prosperity.

Exegetical Analysis

Introduction to Hezekiah's Reign (18:1-8)

Though the exact chronology of Hezekiah's reign poses problems for scholars, the introductory summary here records that he came to the throne during the third year of Hoshea's rule in Israel. Hezekiah was twenty-five years old when he ascended the throne. Son of Ahaz and Abi, the daughter of Zachariah, Hezekiah's reign lasted a long twenty-nine years. The verdict surrounding his royal tenure evaluates him in an exceedingly positive light. Indeed, he surpasses all kings before him and those who come after him. He is described as David's counterpart but without any of the qualifications to modify the high praise. When his great ancestor Moses is mentioned, the account even indirectly implies Hezekiah's equal status. As one of his many cultic reforms, he destroys the bronze serpent dating back to the time of Moses in the wilderness, which the people had evidently come to worship over the years (v. 4b). In somewhat uncharacteristic fashion, the evaluation goes on to enumerate the first activities of this king, all of which only serve to confirm the high theological evaluation he receives.

Hezekiah is depicted as an aggressive reformer. He centralized the cult by abolishing the many local sites and objects that distracted the people's attention away from the temple. The language describing his campaign narrates his deliberate, uncompromising stance toward Yahwistic worship. He "removed," "broke down," "cut down," and "broke in pieces" (v. 4) all the cultic objects and shrines that detoured the people away from worship of the Lord alone. Moreover, his actions were matched by a heart set upon the Lord. His trust in the Lord was unsurpassed (v. 5). That he "kept the commandments that the LORD commanded Moses" (v. 6) made him a model of Torah faithfulness for all time. That "he held fast to the LORD" testifies to the tenacity of his relationship with

God (v. 6). Finally, that "he did not depart from following him [the Lord]" witnesses to his attention to God in all things (v. 6).

The result of such unmatched fidelity is a triumph for the Deuteronomist to report. The record indicates that as a result "the LORD was with him; wherever he went" (v. 7). Thus the covenantal promise of divine presence manifests its fullness here, backed up by concrete evidence. Hezekiah rebelled successfully against Assyria and refused to serve the foreign sovereign. In addition, he was victorious in his military struggles with the Philistines over boundary lines, a group that previously only David could defeat.

Israel's Capture and Exile (18:9-12)

With no segue, the record seems to turn abruptly away from Hezekiah's introduction to a rehearsal of the fall of Israel to Assyria. In the seventh year of Hoshea, king of Israel, Shalmanesser, who was then king of that much-feared foreign power, marched into Samaria. The earlier account of the assault on Israel's capital city and the exile of the Israelite population are replayed here. However, several features skillfully yoke this seemingly extraneous account to the opening introduction of Hezekiah's reign. Twice Hezekiah is made the point of chronological reference for the recap of these events. It was during Hezekiah's fourth year that Shalmanesser first marched against the north. Next, a reference to Hezekiah's sixth year on the throne marks the end of Samaria and the beginning of exile for the Israelites. However, other parallel references suggest that the writer intended to convey more than the chronological simultaneity of events between Hezekiah's time as king and the fall of Israel. The reference to the people's failure, "they did not obey the voice of the LORD their God" (v. 12), contrasts sharply with the accolades previously paid to Hezekiah. Moreover, the closing reference to Moses and the law he commanded hearkens back to the praise afforded Hezekiah for keeping "the commandments that the LORD commanded Moses" (v. 6). Implicitly, the narrative suggests that Judah's preservation from the Assyrian assault has a lot to do with Hezekiah's fidelity to the Lord. Moreover, it also subtly suggests a warning. In the absence of Hezekiah-like faith, Judah's fate could easily duplicate that of its sibling Israel.

First Threat to Hezekiah by Sennacherib (18:13-16)

During the reign of Ahaz and Hezekiah in Judah, Assyria has become a superpower. No one had been able to challenge its military escapades. Once again, it threatens Judah. This first encounter between Sennacherib and Hezekiah takes the form of a series of exchanges. First, the Assyrian leader sends shock waves through the nation by attacking and taking control of the "fortified cities of Judah" (v. 13). The threat of the Assyrian forces here is very imposing. These are Judah's urban centers, prepared to defend themselves against an enemy assault. Though the narrative gives no indication of the nature of the struggle or the degree of their resistance, their utter incapacity to ward off the Assyrians attests to the military upper hand that Assyria has gained over the past years.

Immediately, Hezekiah responds with a proclamation of subservience (v. 14). His admission that he has wronged the Assyrian king suggests that he must have withheld tribute, a perpetual burden that his father had obligated Judah to pay (2 Kgs 16:8). So grave was the Assyrian response to Hezekiah's act of defiance that now Judah's king must pledge to pay whatever obligation Assyria's lord decides in exchange for Assyria's withdrawal.

The Assyrian ruler takes full advantage of Hezekiah's submissive posture and makes exorbitant demands of gold and silver. It seems that Hezekiah can only respond obediently to this power-wielding despot, so he strips the temple of the Lord and his own palace of gold and silver. However, the thought that any gesture can buy this military monster's retreat is pure fantasy. Memories of his father, Ahaz, stripping the temple of bronze to pay off another Assyrian sovereign echo in the narrative (2 Kgs 16:17-18). Hezekiah's submission to this insatiable Assyrian lord will always be costly and will never bring peace. Moreover, it will continually press him to compromise his behavior and his trust in his true Lord. Hezekiah must choose which sovereign will claim his homage in the future.

Second Threat of Assyria to Hezekiah (18:17–19:7)

The second encounter unfolds under hostile exchanges between representatives of both nations. The narrative opens by introducing three appointees that Sennercharib has sent to conduct a verbal battle with Hezekiah (v. 17). The approach of the Tartan, the Rabsaris, and the Rabshakeh, along with a great Assyrian army, to Jerusalem is clearly aimed at intimidating the city and its officials. The forces position themselves at the unprotected water source, the upper pool, outside the city, further emphasizing Jerusalem's vulnerability. Instead of appearing himself, Hezekiah sends his representatives—Eliakim, Shebnah, and Joah—to meet with them (v. 18).

Rabshakeh speaks first. His might is evident in his speech. He is a skilled rhetorician sent to propagandize by undermining Hezekiah and winning popular support for Assyria's occupation of Jerusalem without military invasion. Hence, he conducts a fiery battle with words. He seeds fear, suspicion, and self-doubt among those in earshot (vv. 19-25).

Rabshakeh begins by characterizing Hezekiah's trust in Egypt as being foolhardy. Instead, he calls Egypt a "broken reed of a staff" (v. 21). He discounts Hezekiah's own resistance of Assyrian rule as gambling with the people's destiny. Finally, Rabshakeh dismisses Hezekiah's trust in the Lord for protection against Assyria as spurious. Such trust is not even supported by this Judahite king's own actions. After all, Hezekiah himself ordered the dismantling of local shrines to the Lord. With this allegation, he seeks to ally himself with the locals who support these shrines. Finally, he pulls out all the stops, claiming that Assyria, not Hezekiah, is the instrument of the Lord. Using Judah's theology against itself, he professes Sennacherib's success as a sign that Assyria is indeed the agent of Judah's God.

When Hezekiah's emissaries respond to Rabshakeh, they object, but not to what he says (v. 26). Instead, they urge him to speak in Aramaic, not in the language of Judah, so the people gathered will not understand. Rabshakeh scoffs at their request (v. 27). Persuasion of the people is precisely what he has come to do. Seizing the moment, he directs his second oration to the people

(vv. 28-35). He devotes the rest of his discourse to discounting both Hezekiah's faith and Hezekiah's God, as well as undermining the promises that the king holds out to the people if they too trust in the Lord. With logic and eloquence, the Assyrian official tries to discredit Hezekiah's faith and to build up suspicion regarding his relationship with God. The repetition and adamance of his speech discloses something further. It actually confirms that the Lord is the greatest threat against Assyria that Hezekiah has at his disposal. Indeed, before the Lord, Assyria is questioning its attack on Jerusalem. The people respond with silence. The account discloses that their lack of response puts them in compliance with Hezekiah's order (v. 36).

They are evidently still more grounded in their allegiance to Hezekiah and persuaded by his faith in the Lord than by this Assyrian's rhetoric. However, when Hezekiah's officers hurry to relay the message of Rabshakeh to the king, they betray their distress, tearing their robes as a sign of their desperate repentance (v. 37). This time Hezekiah does not fold under the Assyrian pressure. Instead, he directs all of his actions toward the more difficult path of turning toward and trusting in the Lord in a time of crisis. He, too, tears his garment and puts on sackcloth as a sign of repentance. Then he goes into the house of the Lord (2 Kgs 19:1). Finally, he sends his officers to seek the counsel of the prophet Isaiah. With an oracle, the prophet urges Hezekiah not to fear. God will plant a rumor that will drive Sennacherib back to his own land where he will meet his death. Upon hearing the word of the Lord, Hezekiah must choose whether to heed the advice of Isaiah even though the resolution of the crisis that the prophet foretells is vague. That the final cycle of exchanges opens with a further threat from the Assyrian sovereign indicates that unlike his father Ahaz, Hezekiah stood firm in his trust in the Lord by not surrendering Jerusalem.

Third Threat of Assyria against Hezekiah (19:8-19)

The opening account of Rabshakeh's departure from Jerusalem and his return to Lachish is followed by a report of the Assyrian king's departure from Lachish and presumably his retreat to

Assyria (v. 8). Although the narrative gives no reason for the sovereign's exit, the word of the Lord promised by the prophet provides an explanation. Something the king heard made him leave. King Tirhakah of Ethiopia's intention to conduct a military assault against the Assyrian forces may have caused his abrupt departure (v. 9). Word of the Ethiopian threat may have been the very rumor promised by the prophet to Hezekiah concerning Sennacherib. Still, though the Assyrian king has retreated, the Assyrian intimidation of Hezekiah has not abated. For the third time, a threat comes, this time in the form of a letter delivered by one of Sennacherib's footmen. Though the hostile correspondence is addressed to Hezekiah, it is not directed toward him (v. 14). Instead, the written message directly challenges the Lord. God is accused as being the great deceiver courting Hezekiah and the rest of Jerusalem's fidelity. God is the great pretender, convincing them that somehow the Lord is different than all the other gods that Assyria has so successfully defeated. The audacity of the Assyrian leader is enough to make the believer shudder in the presence of such recklessness before the Lord. Nevertheless, the gravity of the threat lodged in the writing is dwarfed by the magnitude of faith and confidence in the Lord, expressed in Hezekiah's response.

This time Hezekiah turns to God with a prolonged prayer. In the face of this third Assyrian malediction, the opening and closing of Hezekiah's lament witness to his own acknowledgment of the Lord and only the Lord (vv. 15, 19). In the first part of the prayer, he acknowledges that the Lord is God over all. Before all kingdoms in heaven and on earth, God stands as the creator (v. 15). Next, Hezekiah humbly sets his petition before God. He beseeches God to hear and see what has transpired and asks God to act against Assyria. Indeed, he relates all that the foreign oppressor has done to insult the Lord. However, he makes clear his own certainty that the Assyrians' power has not come by gods of their own fashioning. Finally, Hezekiah asks for salvation for the people not only for themselves but also for the whole of humanity. He requests that God save them "so that all the kingdoms of the earth may know that you, O Lord, are God alone"

(v. 19). His prayer is effusive and the pinnacle of his recorded career. Up until this point we have heard about Hezekiah. Finally, the narrator depicts some of Hezekiah's deepest, most plaintive whisperings to the Lord.

Divine Response and Intervention (19:20-37)

Immediately after Hezekiah's prayer, a two-part report of God's response in word and deed follow (vv. 20-34, 35-37). In contrast to the second threat, when Hezekiah commissioned his officers to seek the word of the Lord from the prophet Isaiah, the prophet himself now seeks out King Hezekiah to deliver the Lord's word to him. The prophet's pronouncement is comprised of three oracles (vv. 21-28, 29-31, 32-34). The first oracle is a lengthy poem in which Yahweh addresses not Jerusalem's fate or even Hezekiah's destiny, but Assyria's future (vv. 21-28). Jerusalem, "virgin daughter Zion," is only mentioned as a humble sufferer that Assyria has taunted, shamed, and reviled. Assyria is the one spoken to here. Its exercise of formidable power over Zion is tossed before its face. Moreover, in Assyria's arrogance, it claims to have ventured as far as the fortified regions of Lebanon and Egypt with its chariots. Parading before Assyria its own self-aggrandizing claims—"I have gone up the heights of the mountains"; "I felled its tallest cedars"; "I entered its farthest retreat"; "I dug wells"; "I dried up with the sole of my foot" (vv. 23-24)— the Lord mocks the empire's self-delusion and miscalculated sense of power. Assyria has promoted the belief that it is responsible for its own accomplishments. It acts on the illusion that it determines its own future. Indeed, it functions under the dangerous misunderstanding that it charts and governs the future of the Fertile Crescent.

Now the Lord confronts Assyria's boasts with an ominous theological lesson. From the beginning of time, the Lord has been the earth's determining force. Before Assyria even existed, the Lord knew of it, both its comings and goings. God even knows about its ludicrous ranting against the Lord right now. Because of the Lord's place in the universe, the tables are about to turn for Assyria. The hook with which this oppressive nation has been leading off exiles from their lands is about to pierce its own nose, and with it, they themselves will be led off by the Lord.

In the second part of the word of the Lord addressed to Hezekiah, the king is promised an unsolicited sign of deliverance (vv. 29-31). The Lord pledges the provision of food from the earth over the next three years, making the divine intervention tangible and visible. The God who reigns over the kingdoms of the earth also controls the soil. The people will be nourished even when they do not sow. "This year you shall eat what grows of itself, and in the second year what springs from that" (v. 29). The third year signals the reinstatement of self-rule and control over their destiny. At that time, they can "sow, reap, plant vineyards, and eat their fruit" (v. 29). As the earth's bounty allows for their survival, so too does the remnant from Jerusalem enkindle the reestablishment of Judah. This section ends by reminding the king that God's zeal constitutes the divine motive behind this restoration. God's unconditional passion for this people drives the outcome.

Now, in the third and final part of the prophet's word to the king, the Lord's deliverance becomes even more concrete. All the images of Sennacherib's control over Jerusalem are dashed. The Lord promises, "He shall not come into the city, shoot an arrow there, come before it with a shield, or cast up a siege ramp against it" (v. 32). Jerusalem will indeed be saved because the Lord will defend the city. The oracle here offers comfort and assurance in the form of a promise. Sennacherib will return and not come into this city. Moreover, the Lord does all this for the sake of David and for God's own sake. This is the God who long ago entered into covenant with the people and who continues to keep those promises. Words and promises are quickly followed and fulfilled by the Lord's deeds. Sennacherib's fate is just as the Lord promised (v. 35). In a brief but dramatic report, images of divine deliverance unfold. The angel of the Lord strikes the Assyrian encampment at night. With a scene reminiscent of the exodus drama (Exod 14:30), the morning light witnesses to the vast number of Assyrians who lie dead in the camp (v. 35). The Assyrian king flees and returns to what he expects remains his safe haven, Nineveh, the capital of Assyria. However, unbeknownst to him, a conspiracy among his own sons plots his end. Thus, Sennacherib, worshiper of the idol Nisroch, the king who has wielded an unbridled violence, now meets his death by the same violence he has foisted upon others (v. 37).

Theological and Ethical Analysis

Chapters 18–19 offer readers an unparalleled reflection on the dynamics of faith. Though Hezekiah stands as a towering model of steadfast dependence upon the Lord, it was not always so. Initially, when faced with the Assyrian threat, he was willing to kowtow to the demands of this finite imperialist in exchange for a temporary security. However, before Sennacherib whose violence knew no limits, Hezekiah's servitude would never be enough. The Assyrian despot's unquenchable hunger for power would never be satisfied with what the Judean king could supply. Quick-fix, shortsighted efforts do not put an end to fears, intimidations, questions, or danger. The journey of faith frequently begins in just such crises. Amid threats to our very existence, when there seems no escape, we are often put in touch with our need for God. The spirit of God roams in the spaces of disbelief or wavering faith. It moves about attempting to enkindle an interest and a response, a glance in God's direction. Gradually and compassionately it woos us to bank our life and its meaning on a more infinite investment.

When faith ignites, its manifestation flies in the face of common sense. Indeed, Hezekiah's circumstance as well as his eventual decision to seek out and follow God's word was indefensible by human standards. It lacked political savvy; some might even charge that it lacked a level of public responsibility. This king decided to set his heart upon a God who cannot be seen or heard, rather than upon a tyrant whose violence and vengeance had been made audible, visible, and palpable throughout the land.

The evidence of Hezekiah's awakening faith manifested itself as trust in an extreme sense. This same radicality characterizes faith today, beckoning us to abandon logic when rational outcomes would often leave us imprisoned in crisis. It summons us to admit human limitations before an absolute Lord, who from the beginning of time is creator and maintainer of the universe. It invites us to let go of our fears in exchange for the secure knowledge of the divine eternal presence abiding in our lives. Finally, it urges us to surrender our finite questions about how we will endure or be saved for a faith in an infinite God whose "ways [are] higher than [our] ways and [whose] thoughts higher than [our] thoughts" (Isa 55:9). This faith calls for the drama of choice, requiring us to forsake one path and begin following another wholeheartedly. It summons us to decide against falling deeper into the whirl of self-absorption in the midst of crisis, pretending to cope, or believing that others will save us. Instead, we are invited to trust and free-fall into the arms of our awaiting God.

On God's part, a response is never delayed. It is immediate, multiple, and concrete. God responds through others sent to us. Twice Isaiah delivers the word of the Lord to Hezekiah. Each time, the word carries greater clarity and assurance as to how God will address the Assyrian threat. God promises a trustworthy presence and offers a response to the mundane concerns of human existence. God supplied the people with food from the unplanted soil. The Holy One also addresses our concerns about the unknown or about the future. According to the prophet, God promised to become the guarantor of agricultural productivity in the years to come. The unfolding of the divine response is not confined to the witness of the day-in, day-out manifestations of individual lives, however, but is also perceived in the turn of world events. Sennacharib returns to Nineveh only to have his worldwide escapades brought to an end by his own sons.

From the turn of events marking the end of Assyrian rule to the germination of unplanted seed from previous years' sowing in Judah, the Lord does not insult human trust. In this cycle of faith, each encounter or glimpse of God pushes the human being into deeper and fuller belief. As this cycle repeats, it eventually culminates in an unimaginable willingness to surrender one's whole life to God. Such relinquishing of one's self before the Lord is not grounded solely in an individual's faith maturation. Eventually, it erupts out of the staggering awareness that this is precisely what God has done for us.

2 KINGS 20

In this chapter, the course that divine providence has mapped out for Judah's final days matches Hezekiah's fate. Threatened by illness, Hezekiah is restored to health for fifteen more years before his eventual death. Similarly, the Lord promises Judah's deliverance from the current menace, Assyria. Sadly, the divine word also foretells Judah's own end by Babylon. Hence, this brief account witnesses to the enduring conviction that deliverance and destruction are God's prerogative.

Literary Analysis

Two episodes and a death notice concerning Hezekiah follow up and join with the preceding chapters to complete the king's story. The opening, "in those days," loosely joins what follows here with the events of the preceding record (v. 1). Accounts of two distinct incidents in Hezekiah's reign structure the chapter (vv. 1-11, 12-19). Each of these episodes in turn divides easily into two parts.

In the first incident, Hezekiah's illness and subsequent cure craft a thinly composed plot (vv. 1-3, 4-7). With the greatest economy of words, part one narrates the king's grave illness, an unsolicited death notice according to the word of the Lord spoken by the prophet, and Hezekiah's anguished, prayerful response (vv. 1-3). The second half of the tale turns on God's answer to Hezekiah's outpouring of sorrow and entreaty (vv. 4-7). The prophet's disclosure of the word of the Lord governs the account. Hezekiah will go up to the temple of the Lord in three days. Not only will his health be restored, but also fifteen years will be added to his life. Finally, Jerusalem will be delivered from the Assyrian threat. Here, the restoration of the king's health is juxtaposed with the restoration of tranquility and security in the capital, as if the two were related. The scene closes with the fulfillment of the prophetic word. The account concludes with a sign given to the king to confirm the prophet's word.

The second episode (vv. 12-19), though distinct from the preceding incident, is loosely linked to what comes before by the introductory phrase "at that time" (v. 12). Also divided into two parts (vv. 12-13, 14-19), the scene opens with Hezekiah receiving visitors from Babylon to whom he displays all the treasures of his house, storehouses, and the entire kingdom. It is precisely on the heels of this seemingly innocuous visit that the second part of this episode unfolds. A series of exchanges between Isaiah, the prophet, and Hezekiah address the present visit and its future ramifications. The prophet then sets forth an oracle that portends the end of Jerusalem and the house of David at the hands of Babylon. However, the oracle must have been too cryptic for the king. Hezekiah replies that the word of the prophet proclaims security and peace for the future.

The chapter closes by summarizing Hezekiah's reign (vv. 20-21). Reference is made to his great power, some of his projects, the characteristic burial notice and the name of his successor, his son Manasseh.

Exegetical Analysis

Hezekiah's Illness and Cure (20:1-11)

The first part of this brief narrative establishes the problem (vv. 1-3). King Hezekiah, recipient of God's promise that Jerusalem will be preserved, is himself ill unto death. The report is exacerbated by the prophet's following proclamation that indeed Hezekiah is in his final hours. The king's desperate entreaty to the Lord offers the only prospect that what seems ordained as the king's destiny here might be reversed. Hezekiah never really prays for restoration of health, only that God would look upon him because of his fidelity. Despite the gravity of the royal predicament, the brevity with which the crisis is related suggests this opening is less important than what follows. The report of the king's terminal condition, the prophet's verification that death is near, and the king's response of grief and prayer are mere background information for the pronouncement of the word of the Lord that will be featured in the second part.

Just as the Lord heard the king's prayer concerning the fate of Jerusalem (2 Kgs 19:15-19), the Lord responds to Hezekiah's plea here. The prophet Isaiah is commissioned once again to deliver an oracle, announcing the reversal of the king's fate. The announcement reminds us that God's action in the present is consistent with how the Lord has been present with Israel from the very beginning. Just as the Lord responded to save Jerusalem in answer to the king's prayer, so too does the Lord respond to Hezekiah's petition and free him from his illness. Consistent with the God who from a time long ago heard, saw, and answered, liberating the Israelites of their affliction under Egyptian rule (Exod 2:24-25), God now has seen Hezekiah's tears and heard his prayer (v. 5).

The oracle sets forth a threefold promise whereby the fate of the city is tied to the fate of the king. Hezekiah will be healed and will go up to the temple of the Lord in three days. The addition of fifteen years to his life provides stability to the nation in its staunch resistance to foreign threat. Hence, with the king's deliverance comes Jerusalem's deliverance. Assyria will not overpower the capital. The holy city so dear to the heart of the Lord will be rescued once and for all from the Assyrian invasion.

Finally, the divine motive prompting this intervention parallels a similar impetus behind the promised salvation of Jerusalem in 2 Kgs 19:34. God's election of the house of David propels the rescue of Hezekiah from death. Moreover, God's own integrity is at stake. Fidelity to the promises from the ancestral traditions underwrites the Lord's actions on Judah's behalf.

A poultice of figs ordered by the prophet mediates the divine promise of healing. Prayer and action work together to bring about a word regarding the divine intent. The crisis of Hezekiah's life-threatening illness is on the way to resolution and thus the plot can conclude. But a follow-up conversation between the prophet and the king extends the lesson on faith. Hezekiah asks the prophet for a sign that the promise of his healing will be fulfilled. At first, the request could be read as a cloud of doubt rising over the narrative, diminishing Hezekiah and the great faith he has manifested thus far. However, it can also be viewed as an honest admission on the part of one who needs to grow in his faith. The contrast to his father, Ahaz, in this regard is ironic. Isaiah urged Ahaz to ask for a sign that trusting in God's protection against both the threat from the northern states and from Assyria would reap deliverance, but Ahaz chastised the prophet, saying he will not put "the LORD to the test" (Isa 7:12). Never acknowledging his own waning faith, he then refused to trust in God and instead became the vassal of Assyria. By contrast here, Hezekiah admits his need for a sign, even asking outright for some tangible evidence that God's promise will materialize. His fate and the stability of Jerusalem rest upon the divine word. That the prophet never hesitates or questions the king's request further endorses the legitimacy of his appeal. The sign is given and confirms the promise of a healing that will reverse the death sentence. As God adjudicates over the minutes, hours, days, and seasons in the earth's temporal realm, God turns back time for Hezekiah. He will be granted fifteen more years to rule.

Envoys from Babylon (20:12-19)

Though distinct in subject matter, the opening expression, "at that time," and a subsequent reference to Hezekiah's illness joins this account with what precedes. Two encounters comprise the brief, uncomplicated story line (vv. 12-13, 14-19). First, a delegation from Merodach-baladan, king of Babylon, pays the ailing Hezekiah a call. Although we have no record of the verbal exchanges that occur, the report indicates that something happens. The Babylonian envoys bring letters and gifts to the Judahite king. He in turn not only welcomes them but shows them all the treasures of his house, storehouses, and "all his realm" (v. 13). Such a display indicates more than a host who excels in hospitality. Hezekiah might well be demonstrating that he is in a position to be an equal ally with Babylon, or even that he has the economic means to strike a bargain. Babylon just might be the means finally to be rid of the persistent Assyrian menace that is hovering over Jerusalem.

Immediately after this visit, a second encounter takes place between the prophet Isaiah and Hezekiah (vv. 14-19). Isaiah interrogates the king regarding the men, asking what they said and where they came from. Though he identifies Babylon as their place of origin, Hezekiah does not answer the prophet's inquiry as to what was discussed. Next, to the prophet's question about what they saw in the king's residence, Hezekiah answers straightaway. He relates to the prophet that there was nothing he did not show them.

Joining this account to the previous one, the prophet pronounces an oracle. However, in contrast to the oracle of deliverance regarding the king, this one promises that Jerusalem's fate will be destruction. Though Hezekiah is not blamed for the end forecast for the holy city, the oracular language plays upon the king's earlier report concerning his visitors. "All that is in [his] house," which he showed to these envoys, will eventually be carried off to Babylon (v. 15). In a reversal to the king's disclosure that there was "nothing in my storehouses that I did not show them" (v. 15), the prophet proclaims, "Nothing shall be left" (v. 17). Moreover, even Hezekiah's own sons will be exiled and made eunuchs in the service of the Babylonian sovereign. Whether this refers to their status as castrated males or to their servitude, which removes them from their previous royal status, is unclear. Nonetheless, with the severing of Hezekiah's line, David's house will clearly end.

Hezekiah's response to the prophet is curious. Whether naive or foolish, the king takes comfort in the prophet's word. It seems that Hezekiah is willing to exchange whatever it takes to acquire peace and security in his time. However, his willingness to engage Babylon indicates his utter lack of understanding regarding the long-term cost of this new courtship.

The End of Hezekiah's Reign (20:20-21)

The concluding summary on Hezekiah's reign turns attention away from this judgment against Jerusalem and fixes upon the regnal record. Another reference to the water system built at Hezekiah's initiative emphasizes the significance of this success. The threat of a siege is greatly diminished by Hezekiah's innovative aqueducts that bring water underground directly into the city. Ironically, though this persistent threat to Jerusalem's well-being has finally been averted, another imposing cloud looms on the horizon. The malice of Manasseh, Hezekiah's son, named here to ascend the throne, will quickly cultivate and legitimize the destruction of the city foretold by the prophet.

Theological and Ethical Analysis

Though the crisis surrounding the king's life is resolved, another erupts out of Hezekiah's continued rule. Moreover, as the drama concerning Jerusalem unfolds, so too does God's self-revelation. In the first brief account of Hezekiah's illness, the record witnesses to God's uncompromising willingness to be involved in human life. This is a God who not only acts on behalf of an individual and his plight, but is moved to do so in the wake of human need, grief, and suffering. The Lord, promising to restore Hezekiah's health, provides more than what the king requests. God acts to bring an end to the Assyrian threat to the city. Here, the God who intervenes in the life of an individual during a time of crisis also proves instrumental in the national and international sphere when hostilities and threats arise. Indeed, the threat of Assyria did abate. With health comes peace.

What is more, Hezekiah asks for a sign confirming the divine promise. When this occurs, God not only responds again, but also manifests divine control over the cosmic forces. Time itself is turned back. Hence, this great God who acts on behalf of an individual in need, and over the powers by which states exert international control, now reveals control over the created universe. This is the Unimaginable One who, while creator and maintainer of all the elements of the cosmos, is also caught up in individual lives.

The second half of this story interjects a more sobering note. Though God determines the courses of the universe, this great Holy One has also entered into covenant relationship with humanity—a relationship founded upon fidelity. As this story shows, whether out of a sense of justice or a limit to divine patience, God will not be ignored or rebuffed eternally. If God is God, the scope of the divine power that creates is also accompanied by the invincible capacity to destroy. The fear and trembling cultivated by a God who creates must also be tempered by an appropriate fear and trembling stirred before God's capacity to overturn creation. In this story, a people have tested divine patience over time that now necessitates a just judgment. Such a glance at the boundless ways of God should stir an urgent inquisition concerning our own life. Does God still wait for us? If divine patience with us grew thin today, what might constitute God's predilection in regard to our own destiny?

2 KINGS 21

The peace and tranquility that the Lord's intervention brought about on behalf of Hezekiah is summarily dismantled in this chapter. Like a rebellious son railing against his father, Manasseh reverses the path of fidelity that Hezekiah had begun to forge. In the process, Manasseh produces more than enough reason to justify the upcoming end of Judah and Jerusalem. He makes his name synonymous with unsurpassed malevolence. When Amon succeeds him, he follows his father's footsteps, dashing all hope for averting divine punishment.

Literary Analysis

The records of two kings, Manasseh and his son Amon, make up this chapter. However, the first part of the record, which concerns Manasseh, the very worst of the Judean kings, constitutes the majority of the report (vv. 1-18). The follow-up summary of Amon's tenure is brief, indicating that he merely replicated his father's ungodly ways. Thus, the record on Amon serves primarily to reinforce an already abominable situation. Reportorial form governs both accounts. The account of these lamentable reigns includes no character development, no direct discourse, and no plotline punctuated with conflict. However, its placement on the heels of the record narrating Hezekiah's fidelity does build tension. The deeds of Manasseh overturn all that his father, Hezekiah, had done to fix Judah's heart on God. Given this prelude to the upcoming narrative of Josiah's reign, one can only wonder if Josiah's efforts at religious reform will not be in vain (v. 24). After the comprehensive evil promoted by Manasseh, can there be any more chances for salvation of Judah left in the divine heart?

An introduction and conclusion (vv. 1-9, 16-18) to Manasseh's reign enclose the central proclamation of the word of the Lord by the prophets against this king. The repeated accounts of Manasseh's evil "in the sight of the LORD" (vv. 2, 6), and by consequence, the evil that the people did (vv. 9, 16), infuse a negative tone throughout the record. After the characteristic introduction to Manasseh's biography and the immediate negative theological evaluation, a litany of evidence justifies the assessment.

Reiteration of this same assessment in regard to the people's iniquity begins the concluding remarks on this king's career (vv. 16-18). We are reminded not only of Judah's falling away from the Lord (v. 16), but also of Manasseh's shedding of innocent blood. In this regnal conclusion, the familiar reference to the Book of the Annals of the Kings for further accounts of Manasseh's deeds is disquieting. That Manasseh's activity exceeds what is already recorded here conjures a sense of hopelessness at the prospects of deliverance from divine punishment.

The follow-up account of Amon's reign can only reinforce the legitimacy of this assessment. With the exactingness of an obedient son, he follows in his father Manasseh's path of disobedience before the Lord. The conspiracy that ends Amon's life matches the pattern of his own vexed ways. At best, the summary of his reign functions to urge acceptance of the doom about to befall the nation.

Exegetical Analysis

The Reign of Manasseh (21:1-9)

The familiar order with which this regnal report on the kingship of Manasseh begins contrasts sharply with the disarray that develops during his lengthy tenure. Immediately after identifying Manasseh in relation to his mother, Hephzibah, the theological evaluation forms a prelude to the upcoming lengthy exposition. Manasseh "did what was evil in the sight of the LORD" (v. 2). The ensuing description crafts a portrait of a completely reprehensible ruler. The scope of his apostasy knows no limits. His rebuilding of the high places hearkens back to some of the oldest sins associated with the monarchy (2 Kgs 17:7-18). His installation of more altars in the temple to other gods duplicates the practices of some of the most recent rulers (2 Kgs 16:11). When he passes his son through the fire, he appears like his grandfather, Ahaz (2 Kgs 16:3). When he erects altars for Baal and makes a sacred pole he is compared to Ahaz of Israel, whose reputation for iniquity surpassed even that of Jeroboam. Finally, Manasseh's penchant for waywardness in the end rises above all of these. He practices sorcery, consults mediums, and even installs altars for worshiping all the host of heaven. Setting the carved image of Asherah up in the temple, he makes the Lord a God among gods (v. 7).

What is worse, all indications suggest that Manasseh's introduction of all these abominations is completely of his own accord. No hints in the record indicate that political threats prompt his extremism. Nothing indicates that outside forces insist on the nation's homage to foreign deities. Under Manasseh's watch, religion is reduced to a cultic hodgepodge. These are the antics of one who lacks all faith in God, who believes that his religious machinations and excesses in worship before so many deities carry no risk. Alas, the people and the nation are, indeed, in acute danger. Leading them astray by his sinful ways, Manasseh has gambled away the destiny of the people and the nation, which are pronounced lost by the Lord. So despicable and errant is Manasseh's influence that he "misled them to do more evil than the nations had done that the LORD destroyed before the people of Israel" (v. 9).

The Oracle of the Lord (21:10-15)

The record wastes no time reporting the divine judgment on Manasseh's reign. The Lord speaks not through only one prophet but with a chorus of prophets, as if there is widespread consensus concerning Manasseh's standing before God. Indictment and punishment organize the pronouncement. First, a threefold indictment summarizes the king's numerous offenses (v. 11). He has committed abominations, he has exceeded the wickedness of the Amorites, and he has led Judah down this sinful path. Next comes the elaboration of judgment with its consequences for Judah and Jerusalem. The description suggests that the punishment coming their way is difficult to behold. Indeed, "the ears of everyone who hears of it will tingle" (v. 12). Like an urban appraiser examining and deciding which building should be demolished, the Lord will use the measuring line with which Samaria was found wanting and render the same verdict concerning the remnant, Judah. Metaphors of the "measuring line for Samaria," "the plummet for the house of Ahab," "as one wipes a dish," and "a prey and a spoil to all their enemies" preside here as if no direct description can capture what is about to take place in the precincts of the capital. As this people's sinfulness has a history dating all the way back to Egypt, so too does God's anger (v. 15). So severe are the offences they have amassed that the Lord who has been endlessly compassionate and forgiving is now ready to hand them over to their enemies. Though Judah constitutes the remnant, it will not be spared. All that is left of the divine inheritance will be dashed.

Concluding Summary on Manasseh (21:16-18)

As the report on his reign closes, we are reminded once again of the incredible wickedness of this ruler. As if his excessive apostasy were not enough, the account notes he has shed rivers of innocent blood (v. 16). The references may be to human sacrifices. In addition, we are reminded again of the far greater consequence of Manasseh's wrongdoing. With his sin he has led others to sin! All of Judah has been rendered evil in the sight of the Lord. When the characteristic citation is made to the Book of the Annals of Kings, Manasseh's entry is said to record all the "sin that he committed" (v. 17). Finally, Uzza's garden is noted as Manasseh's burial place. That a son of this religiously reckless ruler succeeds him cultivates only numbness and apprehension. The summary on Amon, Manasseh's son, which follows, argues that such a response is legitimate.

The Reign of Amon (21:19-26)

In the shadow of his father's unsurpassed sinfulness that will bring about the fall of Judah, the record on the short career of Amon appears as an insignificant appendix. Son of Meshullemeth, daughter of Haruz of Jotbah, Amon reigns in Jerusalem only two years. His negative theological assessment affords him his only notoriety. He did the evil his father did (v. 20), walking his father's ways and serving the idols his father served (v. 21). The inclusion of this account of Amon's reign seems more in the interest of serving continuity in the regnal chronicle than in any real interest in this ruler. He is a pathetic duplicate of his father.

Perhaps the only noteworthy detail here has to do with the circumstances surrounding his death. His own servants conspire to kill him, a plot that they successfully hatch. However, after his death, "the people of the land killed all those who had conspired against King Amon" (v. 24). This brief note on the king's death hints that there is disorder in the capital. As the kingship weakens, Jerusalem becomes a hotbed of conflicting allegiances. Amid this unrest, the people of the land name the son of Amon, Josiah, king.

Theological and Ethical Analysis

Sin. In many religious traditions, discussion surrounding the matter of sin has receded into the background. In an effort to emphasize the positive dimensions of one's faith life, the topic is frequently avoided. Even in homilies dedicated to opening the meaning of Scripture in worship, the word *sin* seems to have fallen out of most preachers' vocabulary.

But sin does exist. It manifests itself not so much as an individual act, but as a whole life orientation. It is less a misdeed, one thoughtless act of cruelty, or a single action contrary to a code of morality than it is a habit of repeated violations against humanity and God that develops over time. The effects of such persistent behavior or choices alienate us from our own humanity and from others. As it becomes a habit, sin charts a way of life to whose negative consequences one becomes numb. Gradually sin defines itself as an orientation navigating one's life away from relationship with God and others, eventually landing one in a personal space where prospects for that kinship are no longer even possible.

Unchecked, sin does not remain personal or private in its manifestation. As it gains definition and momentum, it involves others. It can give rise to scandal. It can generate direct or indirect harm.

Most glaringly of all, one's sin can even cause others to be captivated by its deceptive attractiveness. Thus, it can enjoin others to participate in its deadly labyrinth. As the narrative enumerates Manasseh's apostatic choices, it frequently recites how what he did was sinful or evil in the eyes of the Lord. Toward the end of the opening summary we read that the report of his infidelity toward God in the form of elaborate idolatry now has caused the people to sin as well. Even in the summary marking the end of his record, his shedding of innocent blood throughout Jerusalem is accompanied by the testimony to all those in Judah that he also has caused to follow this evil path. Hence, not only did his sinful path harm others, but many joined with him.

Over the course of time, evil that remains unbridled and unrepented alters who one is. It changes our own self-understanding, redefining us in relation to our past and to others. Israel, who in its past was identified as "the liberated," is now the people who have been unfaithful, "since the day their ancestors came out of Egypt" (v. 15). Judah, the remnant constituting the Lord's inheritance, is now ready to be surrendered as prey to its enemies. The exile that Israel has incurred and to which Judah is about to surrender, dismantles their very identity.

So simple is the lesson that its import may be missed. As sin orients one's life, it not only cuts one off from others, but also from the very presence of God. In the biblical story, the moment of this severing—this experience of being cast out by God—is so unimaginable that only metaphoric imagery can point to its coming. "The ears of every one who hears of it will tingle" (v. 12).

As this turning away takes hold of us, it enlists our whole attention. It governs energies, directs decision, defines hopes, and steals the heart. Only when it is too late does one grasp what is lost. In the instance of Manasseh and the people, it will bring about their complete and total end. Like "a prey and a spoil" they will be delivered to their enemies (v. 14).

In his commentary, Richard Nelson (pp. 251-52) calls our attention to the surprising account in 2 Chronicles at the end of its record on this king. There, a tradition is preserved that Manasseh offers a prayer of repentance toward the end of his life. Such an

inclusion seems completely out of place here with all that has transpired. Though he might have repented, it evidently was too late.
Judah and Jerusalem soon fall to Babylon. However, perhaps it
does reinforce the lesson of this chapter. As the account here calls
those who read and reflect upon this difficult story of Manasseh's
turning away from God, it may also summon us to reflect upon
our own need for repentance.

2 KINGS 22 AND 23

The reign of Josiah narrated across these two chapters forms the
pinnacle of the Deuteronomistic account of the royal history. In
contrast to Manasseh's reign, the kingship related here serves as a
template of fidelity and submission to the divine word. Josiah is
unsurpassed in his repentance and his cultic reform both in
Jerusalem and the surrounding regions. Though the account of his
lengthy tenure offers a completely congruous portrait of one who
is uncompromising in his attention to the divine covenant, a narrative tension erupts at the end of the story that never reaches resolution. Despite Josiah's incomparable faithfulness, God will still
bring an end to the nation. Such a conclusion disquiets the reader
and ruptures theological assumptions embedded across the
Deuteronomistic narrative.

Literary Analysis

The reign of Josiah spans and structures the bulk of chapters
22–23 (2 Kgs 22–23:30). Only two brief concluding records
(2 Kgs 23:31-35, 36-37) concerning the kingship of his two sons,
Jehoahaz and Jehoiakim, who rule in succession after his death,
turn momentary attention away from the narrative's preoccupation with Josiah. Both in form and content, the narrative framework attests to the author's unqualified regard for Josiah. Model
of righteousness and fidelity, his commands shape the story line
across the unfolding account. As a key reason for Josiah's reputation as cultic reformer, a covenant renewal ceremony constitutes
the narrative centerpiece around which the record is structured

(2 Kgs 23:1-3). As Josiah gathers all the elders and the people, he reads them the laws and statutes of the covenant. His own professed faith enjoins them to participate in this renewal. In paired chiasmic fashion, everything reported in the record processes toward and away from this central celebrated moment.

An introduction (2 Kgs 22:1) and conclusion (2 Kgs 23:28-30) to the account of Josiah's reign frame the outermost limits surrounding this famous moment of covenant renewal. The introduction is notably brief. As if with haste, it notes without amplifying detail the age of Josiah at the time of his ascension to the throne, the number of years he reigned, and his mother's name. The concluding account follows a more characteristic format. It references the Book of the Annals of the Kings for further details about Josiah and his deeds, and briefly sets forth details of his death at the hands of Pharaoh Neco of Egypt. Finally, it ends with a burial note and record of his son Jehoahaz's ascent to the throne.

As we move inward toward the narrative focal point, the covenant renewal, a second pair of parallel texts surrounds and reports on this king (2 Kgs 22:2; 23:25-27). Following the introduction, a theological evaluation of Josiah ranks him as equal to the likes of David (2 Kgs 22:2). Indeed, the narrative description may suggest that he even surpasses David in his fulfillment of the Deuteronomic expectations of steadfast faithfulness. The same evaluation elevating Josiah above all other kings repeats just before the conclusion to his record (2 Kgs 23:25-27). The verses make clear this ruler's unsurpassed status before the Lord. Elaborating detail highlights the favor God shows him because of his fidelity to the covenant statutes.

Finally, two accounts of commands by Josiah concerning the temple and its surroundings and reports of their fulfillment (2 Kgs 22:3-20; 23:4-24) immediately frame the scene of Josiah presiding over the covenant renewal. In the first account, Josiah's orders yield the discovery of a law book and the interpretation of its contents. In the second, Josiah's commands stem from the finding and interpretation of the law book.

The sets of accounts—the introduction and conclusion (2 Kgs 22:1; 23:28-30), two theological evaluations (2 Kgs 22:2; 23:25-

27), and two narratives about the temple and law book (2 Kgs 22:3-20; 23:4-24)—work to emphasize Josiah's greatness and his submissiveness to the Lord. Structurally, they also function to enshrine and fix attention upon Josiah's covenant renewal (2 Kgs 23:1-3). Not only is the focus of the gathered people and priests upon the king; the chiasm also centers narrative gaze upon Josiah as he responds so publicly with "all his heart and all his soul" to the Lord (2 Kgs 23:3). In addition, by his act of great fidelity to ancient sacral covenant tradition, he resembles the great law-maker Moses. His faithfulness prompts the people to promise their fidelity to God. Indeed, as the later evaluation recounts, "Before him there was no king like him . . . nor did any like him arise after him" (2 Kgs 23:25).

Exegetical Analysis

Josiah's Introduction and Theological Assessment (22:1-2)

In a real sense, the opening summary and theological evaluation of Josiah's monumental reign is quite modest. With the greatest economy of words, it sets forth his biographical background. Josiah came to the throne at eight years of age, and he ruled for thirty-one years. His mother, Jedidah, was the daughter of Adaiah of Bozkath. As is typical, the theological assessment immediately follows. However, the three characterizations that make up this evaluation progressively signal someone quite uncharacteristic. First, the appraisal of Josiah declares, "He did what was right in the sight of the LORD" (v. 2a). The affirmation already distinguishes him from his predecessors. Only a few Judean kings ever received such unqualified assessment (1 Kgs 15:11; 2 Kgs 18:3). The next evaluation advances his status further by allying him with the paradigmatic king. He "walked in all the way of his father David" (v. 2b). The third and final appellation, "he did not turn aside to the right or to the left," sets Josiah above all previous rulers (v. 2c).

The record draws upon a Deuteronomic text in praising Josiah's righteousness. The phrase, "not turning to the right or to the left" is used to describe the ideal Israelite king who is guided in all

things by Torah (Deut 17:14-20). The language thus associates
Josiah's fidelity to the law with Moses. By linking him with the
Mosaic Torah, the evaluation implicitly links Josiah to Moses
himself. For all its brevity, this threefold assessment elevates Josiah
above all other kings, associates him both with David and Moses,
and makes him the quintessential custodian of the Torah. The lack
of elaboration with which this introduction of such a towering figure is set forth suggests an eagerness to get to the extended
account that follows, certifying Josiah's greatness.

The Temple and the Law Book (22:3-20)

Two different commands by Josiah demarcate the two parts of
this account (vv. 3-10, 11-20). In the first section (vv. 3-10), Josiah
sends for and commissions his secretary, Shaphan, with directions
concerning the payment of workers at the temple. His directives
indicate that repairs and renovations are underway during his
eighteenth year on the throne. Shaphan is to retrieve the money
kept in the temple treasury that has been collected from the people and hand it over to those in charge of the building's repairs.
The money is for payment of the laborers and for the purchasing
of supplies. Josiah's confidence in the temple workers is indicated
by his instruction to Shaphan that no accounting of expenditures
be required of them. This level of trust suggests the caliber of amicable relations between the king and his people.

Shaphan evidently fulfills the directives of his king (v. 9).
However, in the process of his carrying out the king's orders, an
exchange takes place between the king's secretary and the temple
high priest, Hilkiah, which turns the story in another direction.
Hilkiah informs Shaphan that a law book has been found in the
temple precincts. Deuteronomy 31:26 indicates that the place for
the law book is alongside the ark. By depicting the discovery of
the law book during the temple repairs, the narrative suggests
that it was not where it was supposed to be and perhaps had been
lost for a number of years. Questions surface regarding the exact
content of the law book. An extensive cultic reform by Josiah
immediately following its discovery (2 Kgs 23:4-24) gives the
impression that its contents legislated the cult and proper worship

before the Lord. This has led many to surmise that perhaps the discovered law book was some early tradition of what later became the book of Deuteronomy.

When Shaphan returns and gives a report concerning the fulfillment of the king's initial orders, he also informs the king regarding the discovery in the temple. Upon hearing the contents of the book, Josiah tears his robe in a gesture of grief and despair (v. 11). What he hears evidently signals how far removed he and the people are from the covenantal commitments made in their name.

Josiah's second order signals the beginning of the second part of the narrative (v. 12). His next set of directives is so important that he commissions a whole cohort of officers—Hilkiah, the priest; Ahikam, son of Shaphan; Achbor, son of Micaiah; Shaphan, the secretary; and his own servant, Asaiah—with the responsibility to inquire about the authenticity of the scroll. Aware that the people and all of Judah are in danger, Josiah acts to intercede before the Lord. The company of royal officers consults Huldah, the woman prophet, who is identified both in relation to her husband, Shallum, son of Tikvah, and in conjunction with her occupation in the temple. She is a prophet. No special comment accompanies her identification as a prophet, as if it was common for a woman to play such a role. Moreover, the importance of the inquiry being directed to her suggests the prominence with which her word was regarded during that time.

With a two-part oracle, Huldah delivers God's response to the king's inquiry. First, the word of the Lord addresses the fate of the nation. The divine verdict is that because of its enduring apostasy, God will bring disaster upon Judah. Their persistent worship of other gods, deities crafted by their own hands, leaves no hope for a reduced sentence. God's wrath has been kindled against them for the last time. Never before has the promise of punishment been quite so unrelenting and unconditional. This is the tension underlying Josiah's reign. As the second part of the oracle indicates, he can save himself, but he cannot reverse the divine judgment in regard to the people.

In the second part of the word of the Lord, Josiah is exempted from this disastrous ruin because his "heart was penitent" and he humbled himself before God (v. 19). His weeping, tearing his clothes, and turning with his whole heart have merited God's mercy, and Josiah will not live to see his people's fate. Hence, his reaction before the Lord was sincere and therefore counted, but only for himself. His recompense cannot make amends for the nation. There is a moral problem here. Though over the years individual kings led the people astray and caused them to sin, one ruler's penitent and humble heart cannot make recompense on their behalf. However, as we will see in the accounts that follow, Josiah seems unaware of this limitation. All his actions suggest that he is determined to try.

The Covenant Is Renewed (23:1-3)

Following the report of Huldah's exegesis of the newly discovered book and its contents, the narrative depicts Josiah's response. As Shaphan read the contents of the book to the king, the king now reads it to the people in a public ceremony. The language and sequence that unfolds here parallels the account of the covenant-making ceremony in Deut 29:1-27, affirming the identification of Deuteronomy as "the book of the covenant."

The literary centrality of this account suggests its importance; the Deuteronomistic writers assess Josiah as the ideal king. Though no direct speech is heard, the narrative description trains our complete attention upon Josiah. As grammatical subject of the report and center of the ceremony, he directs, goes up, reads, stands, and makes a covenant. The language of the account continuously conveys the comprehensive nature of what takes place. The narrative leaves no doubt that everyone attended. In addition to listing the elders of Judah and Jerusalem, and the people of Judah, the passage also cites the inhabitants of Jerusalem, the priests, the prophets, and the people both great and small. The word *all* is used five times to make clear the scope of these various groups present for the cultic event. No one was absent.

The sense of completeness also extends to the scope of that to which the king now binds himself. He pledges to obey the commandments, the statutes, the decrees, and "the words of this covenant that were written in this book" (v. 3). Finally, the fullness with which he makes this covenant coincides with the completeness of what he pledges in the presence of all the people. Josiah makes his commitment with "all his heart and with all his soul" (v. 3). The fullness and totality of Josiah's pledge of fidelity to God evoke a comprehensive response on the part of the people. The narrative reports that "all the people" join the king in renewal of covenant as if with one unanimous response (v. 3). Once again, the gravity and import of the king's role makes itself clear. In the past, kings' practices of apostasy lead the people astray. Here Josiah's covenantal faithfulness evokes the people's complete and total commitment to God as well. Whether this commitment will last and be actualized in how they live their lives, or be sufficient to reverse the promise of divine punishment upon them, remains to be seen.

Josiah's Cultic Reform (23:4-24)

The preceding list of actions emphasizing Josiah as an ideal king in the process of renewing covenant is followed here by another parade of his actions confirming his commitment to the Lord. However, this time his commands and activities fix upon removing all the abominations and semblances of apostasy that have accumulated in the capital, across the nation, and beyond. The lengthy account of this massive cultic cleansing witnesses to Josiah's determination to act upon the renewed covenant. He not only instigates, but also is directly involved throughout the cultic purge. Moreover, the account discloses just how vast and varied apostate practices had become.

As he sets out to reform Judah's worship and center it upon the Lord, Josiah disposes of people, places, and things. He abolishes the cultic priests in and around the temple who serve Baal and conduct worship to the sun, moon, and the constellations. He closes down the houses of women who weave clothes for Asherah. Functionaries at the high places from Geba to Beer-sheba are also targeted and put out of work. He purges from the region all the cultic objects associated with apostasy. Josiah rids the temple of images of Asherah and Baal, and he burns the chariot of the sun (v. 11). Altars to foreign deities—to Astarte, the abomination of the Sidonians; Milcom, the abomination of the Ammonites; and Chemosh, the abomination of Moab—he orders destroyed. He smashes and burns pillars and sacred poles tied to worship of false deities. As Josiah earmarks places for cleansing and destruction, the geographic pattern moves outward from the temple in Jerusalem to the surrounding regions of Judah and beyond, up to Bethel in the north. After first cleansing the temple, Josiah defiles the places in the valley of Ben-hinnom associated with child sacrifices (v. 10). Topheth, one of the sites in the valley of Ben-hinnom, had long been associated with the worship of Baal and the sacrifice of children to the god Molech during the reigns of Solomon, Ahaz, and Manasseh (2 Kgs 23:10; 2 Chr 28:3; 33:6; Jer 32:35). Josiah's defilement of the valley makes it impossible to continue such practices. From Beer-sheba to Geba he dismantles altars and cultic high places. Finally, he heads to Bethel where he pulls down the altar associated with Jeroboam's sin and then proceeds to do the same to all the high places of Samaria (v. 19).

Despite how widespread and vast Josiah intends the reform to be, his actions remain judicious. When he encounters a monument indicating the burial place of a reputed man of God in the north, he gives orders for the bones to remain undisturbed and at rest (v. 18). Moreover, Josiah's efforts to bring the cult in line with fidelity to the covenant are not all negative. He also orders the reinstatement of the observance of Passover, the first time the feast has been observed since the time of the judges (v. 21). Finally, as the account of this far-reaching campaign comes to a close, remnants of anything or anyone that could lead the people astray—mediums, wizards, terephim, idols, and all the abominations—are ordered removed. The concluding summary once again makes clear the motive behind Josiah's extensive effort. All that he does, he enacts in order to bring the nation in line with the laws and statutes as written in the book found by Hilkiah (v. 24).

Theological Evaluation of Josiah (23:25-27)

The preceding section's observation that the law book governed and guided Josiah in his every reform, anticipates the praise reiterated here. The concluding theological evaluation parallels as

well as elaborates the opening theological assessment (v. 2). Now
with all the evidence to support such praise, the account heralds
Josiah as above all other kings. No one before or after him comes
close to his consummate repentance and steadfast fidelity. He is
the quintessential Torah keeper. Moreover, the introductory evaluation likened him to David; here the utterance of Moses' name
extends the scope of Josiah's alliances across sacred tradition.
Further, the reported seriousness and adamancy with which he
entered into and followed the covenant "with all his heart and all
his soul" (v. 3) is extended here to include "all his might" (v. 25).
The theological assessment at the opening of his reign, reiterated
and elaborated here, frames Josiah's career and life in a positive
light, as if to wall him off from the fate still hovering over Judah.
The uncompromisingly positive portrait intensifies the theological
problem lurking in this narrative. Despite Josiah's unmatched
fidelity, not even this emblematic kingship grounded in the renewal
of covenant can derail the horrific threat to the people (2 Kgs
21:10-15).

A follow-up reminder asserts that the sentence pronounced
against Judah is still in place. The identification of Manasseh as
justification for the persistent judgment symbolizes all the accumulated abominations and infidelities that cannot be remedied
(v. 26). Manasseh stands as the antitype to Josiah. He represents
the travesties and malevolence that have amassed across this line
of kings and that outweigh even Josiah's virtue. God's judgment
stands firm. Judah will go the way of Israel. Neither Jerusalem nor
the temple, the site for the divine name, will be preserved. Though
Josiah's career encouraged hope that God's anger might abate, his
fidelity was not enough. All will be dashed.

Regnal Summary on Josiah's Reign (23:28-30)

Notice of Josiah's death signals the beginning of the end for
Judah. The opening of the final summary is standard, giving no
indication of the unexpected events that will bring down this
pious king. Assyria has continued to suffer a loss of power and has
thus courted relations with Egypt in an effort to stand firm against
the rising power—Babylon. The summation of Josiah's reign

reports that when Pharaoh went to the river Euphrates to assist the Assyrian king, Josiah went up to meet him. The expectation of battle is nowhere indicated. Nonetheless, at Megiddo, Josiah dies a violent death at the hands of Pharaoh Neco. All Josiah's devoted and faithful rule could not preserve him from an apparently dreadful end in the midst of a military confrontation. This is the first indication that the upcoming events hurling Judah to its promised demise are about to commence. Indeed, there is evidence in the report that the destruction has already begun. After his servant brings Josiah's body back for proper burial in his own tomb, the people decide who the next king will be. They pass over Jehoiakim, Josiah's rightful heir, and anoint the younger son, Jehoahaz, as his father's successor. The action indicates that trouble is brewing and factions exist within the royal class. Such internal divisions weaken the state, leaving it susceptible to international controls.

Captivity of Jehoahaz (23:31-35)

The two narrative summaries following the account of the death of Josiah in this chapter not only report upon the reign of the two subsequent kings; they make up two of the four regnal reports that describe the decline and end of Judah. As the chapter closes, we hear of the tumultuous reigns of Jehoahaz and Jehoiakim. In the last chapters (24–25), the report of the two final kings brings the history to its close.

Jehoahaz ascends the throne replacing his father Josiah at the age of twenty-three. Although he is neither the oldest nor the next in line, Jehoahaz is the choice of the people of Judah. Characteristic of regnal introductions, we first learn of his parentage. He is the son of Hamutal, daughter of Jeremiah of Libnah. The theological assessment that follows places him among the disobedient kings who make up the majority of the nation's history. Like most of his predecessors, Jehoahaz "did what was evil in the sight of the LORD" (v. 32). That his reign lasts but three months seems to confirm this assessment. Pharaoh Neco, who ended the life of Josiah, continues to assert his control over the throne of Judah. He confines the new ruler to Riblah in the land of Hamath and thus prevents him exercising his leadership. In this way, the Egyptian ruler displays his power over Judah and curtails any notion that the people and their choice will be honored. Indeed, this is the start of a new regime.

In place of Jehoahaz, Egypt appoints Eliakim, another son of Josiah, to the throne. Though the record notes his reign lasted eleven years, Eliakim is hardly a king. With Judah as vassal of Egypt, he is but a puppet. Pharaoh changes his name to Jehoiakim and forces him to pay expensive tribute of gold and silver. Three times the narrative highlights this obligation—"Jehoiakim gave the silver and gold to Pharaoh"; "to meet Pharaoh's demand for money"; "to give it to Pharaoh" (v. 35). The repetitive rhetoric underlines the shift in Judah's status. It has become a vassal state under Egyptian suzerainty. Moreover, the citizens bear the weight of the burden of tribute. Jehoiakim exacts "the silver and the gold from the people" (v. 35). As the account hurls toward the finish line, it is laced with irony. This move toward the end of Judah's existence is not just the conclusion of its status as a nation-state. It is the beginning of the end, where salvation history itself will seem to be reversed. Egypt, the place where according to tradition Israel was once liberated, asserts its power and imposes its burden upon the people again.

Jehoiakim's Reign (23:36-37)

The disruption that rapidly unfolds across the tenure of these final kings is mirrored in the disruption of the characteristic format of regnal accounts. In the previous file on Jehoahaz, we learned about Jehoiakim's ascent to the throne and his vassalship to Egypt even before encountering his regnal introduction. Now, a typical regnal summary supplies that initial information. Jehoiakim comes to the throne at age twenty-five and is the son of Zebidah, daughter of Pedaiah of Rumah. Though he rules eleven years, we already know that Judah will be Egypt's vassal. A kingship compromised by subservience to a foreign power receives the expected theological assessment. Jehoiakim, like so many of his ancestors "did what was evil in the sight of the LORD" (v. 37). The evaluation has become frequent for these kings, as if to diminish any optimism about a divine rescue. The persistent compromise of religious commitment manifested here in yet another king yields the anticipated outcome. Judah will be destroyed. In the next chapter, another foreign power will assert itself from the east as a consequence of this turning from the Lord. The account of Jehoiakim's reign introduced here will be brought to its close in the wake of the new assault. Concrete manifestations of the consequences of Judah's waywardness will surround it from both east and west.

Theological and Ethical Analysis

Despite Josiah's unsurpassed fidelity and immense effort to bring cult into conformity with covenant, the narrative ends with a hauntingly unresolved problem. The divine sentence that promised Judah the same fate as Israel still stands. They, too, will be driven from the land. Given Josiah's massive cultic reform, the persistence of the negative judgment against the nation would seem to fly in the face of the Deuteronomistic theology. Does not repentance yield divine compassion? Does not turning again toward the Lord reap forgiveness? The assurance of destruction for Judah here amid covenant renewal and comprehensive expunging of all forms of apostasy puts the reader on edge. At the end of these chapters we are left to grapple with an enduring theological problem.

Perhaps the conundrum points less to any kind of theological difficulty suggesting divine recalcitrance and more to a blind spot in our understanding of conversion. Indeed, the people did participate in the cultic renewal. Many of them carried out orders to dismantle shrines and close down houses of cultic prostitution. The narrator makes it very clear that "all" the various constituencies that made up Judah were present for the covenant renewal. The account is silent about their conversion and their recommitment to God, however. Indeed, only Josiah is described as turning to the Lord "with all his heart and all his soul" (v. 23:3). Whereas the narrative reports that "all the people joined in the covenant" (v. 23:3), whether they did so with all their heart and soul or only as a rote cultic action remains in question.

Moreover, at the end of the account of Josiah's life, we hear that the people choose their own successor to the throne. Instead of Eliakim, Josiah's legitimate heir to the throne, they anoint Jehoahaz. Was there growing dissatisfaction as a result of Josiah's reign? It is not difficult to imagine that Josiah's grand innovation created tremendous new burdens for the people. His cultic program enjoined economic shifts that changed village life. The dismantling of local shrines and high places altered the local economies. People employed at those sites lost their livelihood. Women weaving clothes for deities were also suddenly without jobs. Villagers all around Judah now had to travel to Jerusalem to satisfy their religious obligations. Revenues related to the cult necessarily shifted from providing economic support of the village to fortifying the economy of the capital.

Jeremiah, who prophesied during this time, acknowledged that the people did come up to the temple (Jer 7). However, though they came to worship, they brought with them unconverted lives. In his temple sermon, the prophet juxtaposes their cultic practices associated with the temple with their moral improprieties. Elsewhere, he indicates that as a result, their spiritual emptiness had become more acute. The people are in a place where they can no longer return to the Lord. Though they practice abominable deeds, they feel no shame. "They did not know how to blush" (Jer 8:12). They have lost their conscience; their incapacity to know right from wrong makes life in covenant with the Lord impossible.

The account gives the reader pause. Indeed, conversion, a turning of one's heart to the Lord, does yield divine forgiveness, but is there a point where people can become so estranged, so far removed from the divine summons that they can no longer even recognize God's call? Are there human choices that put us outside the prospects of return, at least for a time? In such a case, disruption in life leading to a kind of exile may actually be the only avenue for return. That God allows the forces of evil and their consequences to hold sway in life may actually be an expression of divine compassion. It may be the only way to rupture this spiritual impasse, this shortsightedness. Judgment may save us from ourselves. Exile may be not only punishment for a wayward path

in life, but an awakening to the prospect of return. It may be the
only intervention left to the Lord to put us in touch once again
with our need for God. If this is the cost, God may not be bent
upon destroying a people or an individual, but rather uncompromisingly determined to win back human hearts.

2 KINGS 24 AND 25

The reign of Jehoiakim that began under Egyptian imposition
closes under bondage to a new suzerain: Babylon. Here, the
account of the reigns of the two upcoming rulers describes Judah's
siege by this new hostile force. The Babylonian assault on Judah
and two deportations of its inhabitants constitute the conclusion
to the nation's story as well as the end to the books of Kings.
These lamentable events appear to fulfill the Lord's promised
word of judgment and punishment.

Literary Analysis

As the account of Judah heads to the finish line, its dominant
role in the story line and that of its rulers diminishes. Four initiatives on the part of Babylon begin to overshadow and replace the
centrality of the nation and its kings. As these hostile overtures
override the stories therein, they divide the final chapters into four
parts (2 Kgs 24:1-7; 24:8-17; 24:18–25:26; 25:27-30). Each is
marked by a focus on Babylon.

The first manifestation of Babylon's presence in the story serves
as an introduction to chapter 24 and brings closure to the account
of Jehoiakim's reign (2 Kgs 24:1-7). The sovereignty exercised by
Egypt over Judah during Jehoiakim's eleven-year watch is about
to be transferred to Babylon. After three years as its vassal state,
Judah succumbs to the consequences of Jehoiakim's lamentable
decisions. He attempts to resist the Babylonian king,
Nebuchadnezzar's, lordship over the nation. The ill-fated rebellion
unleashes a horrible attack. Judah is overrun not only by the
Babylonian forces but also by other neighboring nations that are
most likely under Babylonian rule. Despite this dramatic turn of

events, the closing comments on Jehoiakim's rule are quite formulaic and characteristically neutral. The only indication that something is awry stems from a follow-up notation to this ruler's regnal summary. Instead of concluding on the note that his son, Jehoiachin, succeeds him, the narrative continues informing us that Egyptian domination has been supplanted by Babylonian rule. Moreover, this new suzerain imposes its power not simply in Judah, but across most of the Fertile Crescent.

The second division of the chapters attempts to restore a sense of calm to the story line (2 Kgs 24:8-17). It begins with the reign of Jehoiakim's successor son, Jehoiachin, but after a brief introduction containing the usual biographical information and a negative theological evaluation, the account of Babylon's campaign against Judah continues (2 Kgs 24:10). The record now fixes upon the ransacking activities of this intruder and his policy regarding colonized people. The most skilled of the Judean inhabitants, along with the members of the royal household and Jehoiachin himself, are deported to Nebuchadnezzar's own country. Nebuchadnezzar's departure from ravaged Judah signals the close of this section. As he leaves, Nebuchadnessar appoints Mattaniah, Jehoiachin's uncle, as ruler and changes his name to Zedekiah.

As if to maintain a sense of normalcy amid the most catastrophic of events, the third division of these chapters begins by reporting characteristic biographic information about Zedekiah, the newly appointed king (2 Kgs 24:18–25:26). Immediately following the negative theological assessment that has become so typical it hardly attracts attention, we hear that Babylon has seized Judah once again.

Zedekiah's rebellion against the Mesopotamian giant occasions this new onslaught. Grossly miscalculating the odds against him, Zedekiah's attempt at freedom prompts Babylon's final blow against the nation. The rest of the account focuses upon the details leading up to the capture of Zedekiah himself, the total devastation of Judah's countryside, and finally the looting and razing of the temple of the Lord by the Babylonian armies under Nebuchadnezzar's command. Once again, as he exits, the remains of Judah lie in shambles and Nebuchadnezzar appoints another ruler, Gedaliah, to oversee what is left of the ravaged region. The disrupted conditions quickly lead to revolt. The new governor, Gedaliah, is killed and those responsible flee to Egypt.

The fourth and final section of these chapters is situated in Babylon (2 Kgs 25:27-30). Jehoiachin is reportedly in exile in Babylon with the other deportees. Under the order of King Evil-merodach, the new Babylonian ruler, Judah's king Jehoiachin is released from prison. Provisions are afforded him and he is welcomed at the Babylon king's table for meals. As if to end on a note of hope, the books of Kings conclude by spotlighting the well-being of the existing legitimate descendant of the Davidic line.

Exegetical Analysis

The End of Jehoiakim's Reign (24:1-7)

The ominous opening verses here define the new crisis that erupts during the later part of Jehoiakim's kingship. Nebuchadnezzar, king of Babylon, on the move, "came up" toward Jerusalem (v. 1). Any worry that his "coming up" might be an unfriendly gesture is immediately confirmed. King Jehoiakim becomes his servant for three years. Subjugation under Egypt is now supplanted by vassalship to Babylon. The first crisis in the report is quickly compounded by a second crisis. After three years of paying tribute to this new overlord, Jehoiakim rebels. The military odds are against him. Most importantly, because of the theological case against the whole nation of Judah, this rebellion not only initiates a fierce invasion by the Chaldeans, Arameans, Moabites, and Ammonites; it also occasions the swift implementation of the impending divine judgment. Following the opening narration of these events, a theological exposition makes clear that these calamities confirm and fulfill the divine pronouncement against the nation. Once again Manasseh's unsurpassed sinfulness is rehearsed as a sign of how far removed from the Lord the line of Judahite kings has strayed, along with the people whom they governed.

Despite the catastrophic events toward the end of his reign, the death and burial notices on Jehoiakim are quite ordinary, even unremarkable. There is no indication that he dies a violent death. The usual citation of the Annals of the Kings of Judah is referenced for further accounts concerning his deeds. Along with the typical note that he is buried with his ancestors, his son, Jehoiachin, is named to succeed him. However, a follow-up note to his record indicates a complex situation of international shifts taking place at this time. Concerning these shifts, our narrative offers only the briefest of summaries. Babylon now exercises control over most of what was once the nation of Israel during Solomon's time. Much of the vast expanse of the Fertile Crescent, from "the Wadi of Egypt to the River Euphrates" (v. 7) now resides under Babylonian jurisdiction.

The Reign of Jehoiachin (24:8-17)

The introduction to Jehoiachin's reign could cultivate the incorrect impression that things are returning to normal. In familiar reportorial style, the narrative registers the typical details. He was eighteen years old when he ascended the throne. His mother Nehushta, the daughter of Elnathan of Jerusalem, is named. However, that he was on the throne but three short months signals a continuation of the crisis that had begun during his father's time. The theological assessment concurs. Jehoiachin's assessment not only matches that of his father, but also specifically draws attention to their parallel infidelity. The continuity in theological evaluation between father and son diminishes all hope for a change in the course of events.

In the verses that follow, the account of Babylon's campaign against Judah and its catastrophic consequences continues. King Nebuchadnezzar comes up to Jerusalem (v. 11). Unlike his father, Jehoiachin does not rebel, and unlike his great-grandfather, Hezekiah, Jehoiachin does not resist. Instead, he surrenders himself and all those of his household to the Babylonian despot. This surrender evidently licenses the Babylonian forces to loot and desecrate the temple and the king's palace. Treasures stemming from the time of Solomon are broken or confiscated. In addition, members of various classes of Judahite society are gathered and marched off to exile. The roster of captives includes officials, warriors, artisans, smiths, all the elite, the royal household, and all those strong enough for warfare in the Babylonian army. This first deportation robbed the region of its talented workers, its skilled leaders, and those able to defend the people left behind. The record makes clear that only the "poorest people of the land" were left in Judah (v. 14). Despite the ruinous events narrated here, no emotion punctuates the reporting. A tone of inevitability permeates the narration of the nation's collapse.

This section does not conclude with the account of Jehoiachin's capture. Though his reign has ended, he has not. Jehoiachin is exiled. In his place, Babylon's king appoints Jehoiachin's uncle, Mattaniah, as king. In a gesture signaling his control over this newly appointed regent of the conquered land, Nebuchadnezzar changes Mattaniah's name to Zedekiah. As this record draws to a close, the legitimate heir to David's throne is not deceased but imprisoned. A significant constituency of Judah's people is now in exile. Hope that this crisis will be resolved in Judah's favor grows dim.

Zedekiah's Reign in Judah (24:18–25:26)

Zedekiah ascends the throne at twenty-one years old. Like Jehoiakim, he reigns for eleven years in Judah. Once again, the record supplies the expected biographical information. He is the son of Hamutal, daughter of Jeremiah of Libnah. At this stage in the theological history, the theological assessment of his reign is of no surprise. That he did what was evil before the Lord only reinforces the account of the events unfolding around him. A follow-up note comments that Judah and Jerusalem so incited the Lord's wrath that they were cast out from the divine presence. The promise of covenant that God will be with them cannot be manifest now. They have been expelled from the Holy One's presence.

The account of Zedekiah quickly becomes a record of still another attack on the nation by Babylon. Instigated by Zedekiah's rebellion, a siege led by Nebuchadnezzar seals off the capital and stops any supplies entering or leaving it (v. 1). Conditions continue for so long that famine threatens the inhabitants of the holy city. Zedekiah himself, in an effort to flee the siege, escapes at night through a breach in the wall with his bodyguards and soldiers. However, his status as a fugitive is short-lived. The Chaldeans pursue him to the plains of Jericho where he and his army are overtaken. Transported to Riblah, Zedekiah is made to watch his sons' execution and then he himself is escorted away to prison in chains.

Back in Jerusalem, the Babylonian king's officer, Nebuzaradan puts an end to all hopes for restoration and destroys any symbol that might conjure allegiance to the previous establishment. The house of the Lord, the palace, and the dwellings of Jerusalem are burned to the ground. Walls surrounding Jerusalem that could fortify any resistance movement are destroyed. A further round of deportees is gathered up. Anyone that might emerge as a potential leader amid these ruins, or any able-bodied person who could be of service in Babylon, is escorted into exile. The poor are left to till the land and to tend whatever vineyards remain. In addition, treasures and valuables from the rubble are gathered up for deportation to Babylon. Mention of such artifacts as the bronze sea, pots, basin stands, and snuffers recall the careful work during the Solomonic time to equip the temple with the necessary accoutrements. All gold and silver artifacts are gathered and carried off. What remains of the temple of the Lord becomes loot for ravagers of the city. Now, all is viewed only for its economic value, confiscated and taken to a foreign land.

The officials associated with the temple—priests, guardians of the threshold, and others, along with the remaining city officials— are rounded up and deported to Riblah. There they meet their death at the hands of Nebuchadnezzar himself. A follow-up note concerning this second deportation offers an all-too-obvious summary of these events. "So Judah went into exile out of its land" (v. 21).

As the Babylonian officials head back to their national posts, once again they appoint an official, Gedaliah, to govern over the poor left behind in the land. Though Gedaliah serves as governor, it is not long before the chaos afflicting the land ignites new conflict. Confronting a resistance movement, Gedaliah calls upon this assembly of captains and their forces to serve the king of Babylon in exchange for a promise that "it shall be well with you" (v. 24). Months later, another constituency of the royal family hunts down Gedaliah and kills him, along with his Judean and Chaldean supporters. Finally, what people remain in the land, along with the army officials who overthrew Gedaliah, seek refuge in Egypt. Fear of Babylon drives them back to the very place where in the course of salvation history they were once oppressed as slaves.

Jehoiachin's Release in Babylon (25:27-30)

Fittingly, as the narrative tells the story of these people it must end where they end—in exile. Jerusalem has been destroyed. The countryside stands in ruins. All that symbolized identity for these people has been stripped away. King Jehoiachin, who is imprisoned with them in Babylon, remains perhaps the only thread connecting them with a past, but even the link that kingship might provide with the former times has been altered forever. Thus, the narrator dates this final brief note not according to the reign of this king, but according to the event that has rewritten salvation history—his exile.

The reader as well as the exiles are on watch. A new king ascends the throne in Babylon, and with this new establishment Jehoiachin is released from prison. Moreover, the narrative account continues to refer to him as king of Judah. This remaining Davidic descendant is elevated to a position at the king's table and granted provisions for the rest of his days. But what of the people exiled with him? Does hope spring anew from Jehoiachin's elevated status? Does this turn of events stir false hope that delays the kind of soul-searching and confession before the Lord that will ready the people for return?

Theological and Ethical Analysis

As the books of Kings draw to a close, a perplexing cloud of ambiguity hovers over the conclusion. The nation has been destroyed. Most of the people are exiled to Babylon. A few remaining in Judah eventually seek refuge in Egypt. Moreover, the ramification of these devastating events is not confined to Judah's demise. The impact of their rumblings reaches far beyond the history of Israel and Judah as nations now destroyed. The gravity of these events echoes across the whole of salvation history. To Ur, the very region in the Biblical tradition out of which God called Abraham and Sarah, the people have returned (Gen 15:7); but now they take up a new identity, that of encumbered exiles in Babylon. Moreover, Judahite refugees have fled for safety to Egypt, the very place out of which God liberated the ancestors from the bondage of slavery (Exod 13:3). As these books come to a close, salvation history itself seems to have become twisted, if not reversed. The divine interventions that brought the ancestors out of Mesopotamia and later granted freedom to these same people suffering under Pharaoh's oppressive rod, appear now to have been overturned. They have gone back to Babylon and returned to Egypt. In the process, the people have forfeited their land, their status as a nation, and their temple. More importantly, what it means to be Israel is in danger of being lost.

The image of Jehoiachin in captivity occasions further ambiguity in these closing verses. Though their king is with them in exile, his presence seems hardly a positive reliable sign regarding prospects for the future. Jehoiachin's release from prison and the promised provisions for his remaining days offer only a frayed thread of hope with which to weave a broken community's confidence about any positive outcome to the present tragedy. Even after he has set aside his prison garment and he dines regularly at the king's table, Jehoiachin's image conjures only the slightest bit of optimism. Though clothed in his royal garments again, he is a king without a kingdom. Though seated at a royal table, he is a ruler without a throne. Though provided for in life, he is no king among this foreign people.

The lament of the deportees lodged in other books of the canon echoes in the margins of this final account—"By the rivers of Babylon—there we sat down and there we wept when we remembered Zion" (Ps 137:1). Most profound perhaps is the stark absence of God in these final recordings. We are left to wrestle with our own conclusions. Josiah's cultic reform was ineffective in turning back the Lord's anger. The sins of the generations accumulate to grievous effect. Any objection that some of those now exiled might not have deserved their destiny is beside the point. All are being punished and all seems lost. The absence of the divine voice suggests that this time there is no return. Even the Deuteronomist theologians whose confident understanding of God as rewarding good and punishing evil must have been shaken. The emotionless finality of these events hosts haunting spiritual listlessness and summons deep soul-searching.

Yet, in the darkness of these meditations, the oddness of the account of Jehoiachin's release from prison as the conclusion to these books beckons our attention and dares us to hope. Though exiled, the portrait of Jehoiachin alive and among the people amid these catastrophic events returns to an earlier tradition, God's covenant with David (2 Sam 7:14-16). God's promise of the enduring line resounds in the account of Jehoiachin living among the exiles. However, the accompanying guarantee to David of a kingdom that would endure confounds us as we entertain images of exiled people in Babylon. The dynastic promises of covenant crafted a vision of an enduring reality, but perhaps they had gotten it wrong. The notion of an unconquerable political entity reigning over all other nations defined our limited vision, but not God's. The enduring kingdom promised by God is of a different kind and remains yet to be fully realized. Despite the destruction of the nation, salvation history on the way to realizing this kingdom will continue.

The future of God's saving deeds has already been envisioned in the prophetic words of the past. "Therefore, I will now allure her, and bring her into the wilderness, and speak tenderly to her" (Hos 2:14). Israel will be liberated from this foreign place and brought through the desert again on the way to becoming "God's people." Like the salvific events of the tradition, this people will be led out of their present physical and spiritual bondage and back into the presence of God. The Lord has not deserted them, but is readying them for return.

Indeed, the image of exiled Jehoiachin at the end of these books endures as a sign not only of what is lost, but also of what is yet to come. It heralds the end of the nation and of an era of infidelity to a call. It coaxes tears and regret, prompted by hindsight. However, the image of Jehoiachin preserved among them in Babylon also lifts the exile out of spiritual despair. It affirms God's fidelity to the covenantal promise made to David. It anticipates that God will call their name again, bring them out of bondage, and continue to dwell among them. The immensity of the divine patience and care for God's people reverberating beyond these chapters enkindles new confidence in exiled hearts stricken with hopelessness. For the believer reading these closing verses, it sows seeds of hope even for the darkness of our own days.

SELECT BIBLIOGRAPHY

Auld, A. Graeme. *I & II Kings*. The Daily Study Bible Series. Louisville: Westminster John Knox Press, 1986.

Brueggemann, Walter. *1 & 2 Kings*. Smyth & Helwys Bible Commentary. Macon, Ga.: Smyth & Helwys, 2000.

Camp, Claudia. "1 and 2 Kings." In *The Women's Bible Commentary*. Edited by Carol A. Newson and Sharon H. Ringe. London: SPCK; Lousiville: Westminster John Knox Press, 1992.

Cogan, Mordechai, and Hayim Tadmor. *II Kings*. Anchor Bible Commentary 11. Garden City, N.J.: Doubleday, 1988.

Cohn, Robert. "Literary Technique in the Jeroboam Narrative." *Zeitschrift fur die Alttestamentliche Wissenschaft* 97 (1985): 23-35.

———. *2 Kings*. Berit Olam: Studies in Hebrew Narrative and Poetry. Edited by David W. Cotter. Collegeville, Minn.: Liturgical Press, 2000.

Coote, Robert, ed. *Elijah and Elisha in Socioliterary Perspective*. Atlanta: Scholars Press, 1992.

Fewell, Danna N. "Sennacherib's Defeat: Words at War in 2 Kings 18:13–19:37." *Journal for the Study of the Old Testament* 34 (1986): 79-90.

Fretheim, Terence E. *First and Second Kings*. Louisville: Westminster John Knox Press, 1999.

Fry, Peter. *Spirits of Protest*. Cambridge: Cambridge University Press, 1976.

Garcia-Treto, Francisco O. "The Fall of the House: A Carnivalesque Reading of 2 Kings 9 and 10." *Journal for the Study of the Old Testament* 46 (1990): 47-65.

Gray, John. *I & II Kings: A Commentary*. 2nd ed. Philadelphia: Westminster Press, 1970.

Hauser, Alan J., and Russell Gregory. *From Carmel to Horeb: Elijah in Crisis*. Journal for the Study of the Old Testament Supplement 85; Bible and Literature 19. Sheffield: Almond, 1990.

Hens-Piazza, Gina. *Nameless, Blameless, and Without Shame: Two Cannibal Mothers Before a King*. Edited by Barbara Green. Collegeville, Minn.: Liturgical Press, 2003.

Hobbs, T. R. *2 Kings*. Word Biblical Commentary. Waco: Word Books, 1985.

Jones, Gwilym H. *1 and 2 Kings*. New Century Bible Commentary. 2 vols. Grand Rapids: Eerdmans, 1984.

Knoppers, Gary N. *Two Nations Under God: The Deuteronomistic History of Solomon and the Dual Monarchies*. Vol. 2: *The Reign of Jeroboam, the Fall of Israel, and the Reign of Josiah*. Harvard Semitic Monographs 53. Atlanta: Scholars Press, 1994.

Lasine, Stuart. "Reading Jeroboam's Intentions: Intertextuality, Rhetoric, and History in 1 Kings 12." In *Reading Between Texts: Intertextuality and the Hebrew Bible*. Edited by Danna Nolan Fewell, 133-52. Louisville: Westminster John Knox Press, 1992.

———. "The Riddle of Solomon's Judgment and the Riddle of Human Nature in the Hebrew Bible." *Journal for the Study of the Old Testament* 45 (1989): 61-86.

Long, Burke O. "A Darkness Between Brothers: Solomon and Adonijah." *Journal for the Study of the Old Testament* 19 (1981): 79-94.

———. *1 Kings with an Introduction to Historical Literature*. The Forms of the Old Testament Literature 9. Grand Rapids: Eerdmans, 1984.

———. *2 Kings*. The Forms of the Old Testament Literature 10. Edited by Rolf P. Knierim and Gene M. Tucker. Grand Rapids: Eerdmans, 1991.

Montgomery, James A. *A Critical and Exegetical Commentary on the Books of Kings*. Edited by Henry Snyder Gehman. International Critical Commentary. Edinburgh: T & T Clark, 1951.

Nelson, Richard. *First and Second Kings*. Interpretation. Atlanta: John Knox Press, 1987.

Provan, Iain. *1 and 2 Kings*. New International Biblical Commentary. Peabody, Mass.: Hendrickson, 1995.

Rofé, Alexander. *The Prophetical Stories*. Jerusalem: Magnes Press, 1988.

Savran, George. "1 and 2 Kings." In *The Literary Guide to the Bible*. Edited by Robert Alter and Frank Kermode, 146-64. Cambridge: Harvard University Press, 1987.

Seow, Choon Leong. "First and Second Books of Kings." In *The New Interpreter's Bible Commentary*. Vol. 3. Edited by Leander E. Keck. Nashville: Abingdon Press, 1999.

Simon, Uriel. "I Kings 13: A Prophetic Sign—Denial and Persistence." *Hebrew Union College Annual* 47 (1976): 81-117.

Smith, Mark S. *The Early History of God.* San Francisco: Harper & Row, 1990.

Sternberg, Meir. "Time and Space in Biblical (Hi)story Telling: The Grand Chronology." *The Book and the Text: The Bible and Literary Theory.* Edited by Regina Schwartz, 81-145. London: Blackwell, 1990.

Viviano, Pauline A. "2 Kings 17: A Rhetorical and Form-Critical Analysis." *Catholic Biblical Quarterly* 49 (1987): 548-59.

Walsh, Jerome T. *1 Kings.* Berit Olam: Studies in Hebrew Narrative and Poetry. Edited by David W. Cotter. Collegeville, Minn.: Liturgical Press, 1996.